MILTON STUDIES
52

❧ MILTON STUDIES ❧

Volume 52

Edited by Laura L. Knoppers

DUQUESNE UNIVERSITY PRESS
Pittsburgh, Pennsylvania

Milton Studies is published annually by Duquesne University Press as a forum for Milton scholarship and criticism. Essays submitted for publication may focus on any aspect of John Milton's life and writing, including biography; literary history; Milton's work in its literary, intellectual, political, or cultural contexts; Milton's influence on or relationship to other writers; or the history of critical response to his work.

Manuscripts should conform to *The Chicago Manual of Style* and be approximately 8,000–12,000 words in length. Authors should include a written statement that the manuscript is being submitted exclusively to *Milton Studies*. We encourage electronic submissions in Microsoft Word format, sent to llk6@psu.edu, followed by one hard copy (printout) of the essay sent by regular mail to Laura L. Knoppers, Editor, *Milton Studies*, Department of English, Burrowes Building, Penn State University, University Park, Pa. 16802.

Milton Studies does not review books.

Within the United States, *Milton Studies* may be ordered from the Duquesne University Press, c/o CUP Services, 750 Cascadilla Street, Box 6525, Ithaca, N.Y., 14851-6525. Toll free (800) 666–2211.

Copyright © 2011 Duquesne University Press

Published in the United States of America by
DUQUESNE UNIVERSITY PRESS
600 Forbes Avenue
Pittsburgh, Pennsylvania 15282

ISSN 0076-8820
ISBN 978-0-8207-0451-7

∞ Printed on acid-free paper

CONTENTS

Milton Reading

PREFACE

While Samuel Johnson notoriously denigrated Milton as an "acrimonious and surly republican," it is precisely the heterodoxies of Milton's political, philosophical, and theological thought that have garnered much recent critical interest. Engaging this current scholarly conversation, the first two sections of this volume examine Milton's politics and theology, while the third and fourth sections point to distinctive (and often unorthodox) ways in which Milton shaped his readers or carried out his own practices of reading and writing.

Opening the first section, "Politics and Geopolitics," Nicholas McDowell reconsiders the ascription of a Laudian idiom to Milton in the 1630s, (part of an ongoing debate over how radical the young Milton might have been), by situating Milton's early devotional lyrics alongside those of other Cambridge poets, including future New Model Army chaplain John Saltmarsh and future Catholic Richard Crashaw. In the essay that follows, William Walker examines Milton's late prose work, *The Readie and Easie Way,* in light of an early modern vocabulary of republicanism, marking Milton's differences from such contemporaries as Marchamont Nedham and James Harrington. Third in this section, Su Fang Ng calls for attention to the new seventeenth century commercial rivalry between the United Provinces and England, especially in the Dutch Indies, as an important context for understanding the dual characterization of Satan as emperor and merchant in *Paradise Lost.*

In the second part, "Theology," two essays offer a new understanding of theological satire in *Paradise Lost.* Christopher Baker reads the striking vocabulary of engorging in Eve's eating of the fruit as a satanic Eucharist, drawn from the language of the Gospel of John and parodying Catholic transubstantiation. Neil Graves argues that Milton depicts an orthodox Trinity in *Paradise Lost,* not in heaven but in hell, deliberately constituting Satan, Sin, and Death as a black parody of both Eastern and Western Trinitarian doctrine.

Our volume then moves to essays that bring new lenses, theoretical and philosophical, to reading Milton's epic, before turning to Milton himself as a reader in close historical and intellectual context. In the volume's third section, "Reading Milton," Stephen Hequembourg traces a "monist" hermeneutic in *Paradise Lost,* arguing that the success or failure of Milton's animist materialism depends on the reader's ability to distinguish between the literal and the figurative, to resist reading metaphorically what for Milton is literally and physically true. In the essay that follows, Ayelet Langer brings the concept of time in the metaphysical system of the twentieth century philosopher J. M. E. McTaggart to bear on a reading of two distinct time structures, fallen and unfallen, in *Paradise Lost.*

In the final section, "Milton Reading," Jeffrey Miller examines Milton's lost *Index theologicus* in relation to extant commonplace books, structured in refutation of the notorious Jesuit theologian and cardinal Robert Bellarmine, to shed new light on the significance and use of the *Index* and on Milton's reading and writing practices. Finally, Russ Leo examines *Samson Agonistes* in light of Milton's reading of and engagement with other seventeenth century theorists of tragedy who translated and glossed Aristotle's *Poetics,* showing Milton's important departures, particularly in his radical revision of the concept of *lustratio.*

The Milton who appears in this issue debates and parodies, reads and writes, responds and reconfigures. This Milton puts his own distinctive imprint on theology, politics, geopolitics, natural philosophy, philosophy, and literary genre. His writings, both in prose and poetry, evince not orthodoxy but animist materialism, revision of Aristotelian tragedy, parodies of the Catholic Eucharist and orthodox Trinitarianism, refutations of the Catholic Bellarmine and of his own erring fellow Protestants, and mockery of England's mercantile rivals, the Dutch. Such concerns do not detract from but generate and inspire his literary art, his deft use of metaphor and simile, his complex characterization and powerfully imagined narrative. This may not be Samuel Johnson's Milton. But the essays in this volume engage some of the most exciting debates about Milton and his works in current scholarship. To this debate, this issue welcomes new voices, as well as more established scholars.

At the same time, we say good-bye to a good friend and long-time colleague, Marshall Grossman, who passed away in late March 2011 after a brief battle with cancer. Marshall's service on the board of *Milton Studies* was one of many ways in which he encouraged and supported younger scholars in the field. His work on Renaissance ethics, distinctive concepts of the self, narrative form, and authorship culminated in 2011 in a magisterial history of seventeenth century literature. Marshall's brilliant philosophical thought, his humor, and his generosity will be much missed.

Laura L. Knoppers

Politics and Geopolitics

How Laudian Was the Young Milton?

Nicholas McDowell

My title alludes to Barbara Lewalski's 1998 essay, "How Radical Was the Young Milton?" in which she reads the early poems as evidence that "at every stage [of his life Milton] took up a reformist and oppositional stance which prepared him for the choice he would ultimately make: to defend the regicide and undertake to model anew the English church and state."[1] Lewalski's statement may be unusually totalizing—note she writes "at *every* stage"—but it reflects the dominant approach of historically oriented studies of Milton since Christopher Hill's *Milton and the English Revolution* in 1977. The chapter on Milton's early poetry in David Norbrook's *Poetry and Politics in the English Renaissance* (1984) has probably been the most influential argument for seeing the emergence of the revolutionary Milton in the prewar verse.[2] Consequently, even a few years ago my question—"How Laudian was the young Milton?"—would have been regarded as at best facetious, at worst ignorant. But in the wake of the publication of the quatercentenary biography by Gordon Campbell and Tom Corns, we can and should take this question seriously.[3]

William Poole conveniently sums up the most innovative aspect of the Campbell and Corns biography in a letter to the *Times Literary Supplement,*

3

in which he responds to Jonathan Bate's conclusion that the biography gives us no "paradigm-shifting discoveries or reinterpretations." Poole rightly observes that Bate failed to engage with an argument that goes "against the grain of all Miltonic biography since that genre commenced in the early 1680s." Campbell and Corns give us "an initially conservative Milton, the son of a churchwarden in a Laudian chapel-at-ease, writer of a Laudian elegy on a Laudian bishop, educated by Laudians and then Arminians, and commissioned to write an aristocratic masque, [described by Campbell and Corns as] 'the most complex and thorough expression of Laudian Arminianism and Laudian style within the Milton oeuvre.'"[4] This is indeed, as Poole puts it, a "major claim about a major author," and I want to address aspects of it in this essay.

As Poole's précis indicates, the Campbell and Corns argument rests both on archival evidence about Milton's family and contextualized interpretations of the early works, in particular the Latin funeral elegies, the devotional poetry, and the *Mask Presented at Ludlow Castle* (1634). As regards the archival evidence, documents discovered in 1996 show that the Milton family was living in Hammersmith by April 30, 1631, where Milton joined them after leaving Cambridge in 1632. Since Milton's father signed the audit of the parish account books for 1632, he may have served as a church warden at the Hammersmith chapel-at-ease, consecrated by Laud on June 7, 1631.[5] "The timing of the move" to Hammersmith, Campbell and Corns write, "implies that the attraction of Hammersmith for Milton's father was the opening of a Laudian chapel that accorded with his ecclesiastical preferences."[6]

Milton's father had chosen the prominent sacramental Arminian William Chappell to be his son's tutor at Christ's College; the most illustrious scholar at Christ's, Joseph Mede, was a supporter of Laud and a protégé of the Laudians' intellectual father figure, Lancelot Andrewes, for whom Milton wrote his Latin Elegy 3 in 1626. Even though Milton famously seems to have had some sort of falling out with Chappell in 1627, which may or may not have led to his rustication, Milton's new tutor, Nathaniel Tovey, was to be deprived as a Laudian in the 1640s, and so, write Campbell and Corns, "the change of tutor nevertheless ensured a continuity of Arminian and ceremonialist influence, which presumably satisfied a significant criterion as John Milton senior made his choice."[7]

As regards contextualized interpretation of the poetry, the Campbell and Corns position accords with that of Graham Parry's 2006 study of the Laudian aesthetic, in which he highlights the baroque, Counter-Reformation qualities of the Latin funeral elegies on Andrewes and Nicholas Felton, particularly the fascination with apotheosis, and argues that in the devotional verse composed while Milton was at Cambridge, especially "The Passion" and "Upon the Circumcision" but even the Nativity ode, we encounter "a formal, ritualistic expression of devotion, in harmony with new [that is, Laudian] modes of worship that were becoming dominant in the Church." Parry concludes, quietly but sensationally, that the young Milton was "an improbable supporter of Laudian values in poetry."[8]

I want to explore the validity of this ascription of a Laudian idiom to the young Milton in devotional lyric mode through comparison with other Cambridge poets and the kind of devotional verse, particularly Passion poems, that they were writing, both in Latin and in the vernacular, in the early 1630s. I focus particularly on two of Milton's Cambridge contemporaries who would go on to represent two extremes of the religious spectrum in the 1640s. One is well known: the Laudian and eventually Catholic Richard Crashaw (1612/13–47); the other less so: the future New Model Army chaplain and alleged Antinomian John Saltmarsh (d. 1647). Crashaw and Saltmarsh both received the rare honor of having individual collections of verse published as students by Cambridge University Press. In consideration of the devotional modes that won Crashaw and Saltmarsh such acclaim in Cambridge in the early 1630s and how those modes might relate to their divergent theological and ideological directions in the 1640s, I will return to the question of the Laudianism of Milton's early verse, now able to place it in appropriate formal and historical contexts. This comparison may in passing tell us something about the complexities of the relationship between the development of Milton's theological heterodoxies and his attitude toward the Crucifixion. I will conclude with a brief consideration of the relationship of *Lycidas* (1637) to the devotional styles of Caroline Cambridge, for one of the consequences of the Campbell and Corns reinterpretation is to put even greater pressure on the publication of *Lycidas* as the moment when Milton's growing radicalization is registered in his verse.

It is usually assumed that it was in 1630, when he was in the fifth of his seven years at Christ's College, that Milton wrote the little-discussed devotional poem, "The Passion," described by Campbell and Corns as an "attempt to compose a vernacular poem in the baroque idiom he had used in some of his [Latin] funeral elegies."[9] Milton probably composed "The Passion" in March 1630 as part of a series of poems on church festivals, the others being the better known "Ode on the Morning of Christ's Nativity" (1629) and the barely known "Upon the Circumcision" (1631–33?). Certainly the meter and rhyme scheme of "The Passion" are those of the introductory stanzas of the Nativity ode, and Milton refers to the earlier poem in the first stanza:

> Ere-while of Musick, and Ethereal mirth,
> Wherwith the stage of Ayr and Earth did ring,
> And joyous news of heaven'ly Infants birth,
> My muse with Angels did divide to sing.[10]   (1–4)

The composition of poems celebrating the festivals of the liturgical year was characteristic of what Peter Lake calls "the Laudian style" in the 1630s.[11] Milton notably chose to include all three poems in both the 1645 and 1673 *Poems*, but after eight stanzas of "The Passion" a note was added, presumably but not certainly, by the poet: "This Subject the Author finding to be above his yeers he had when he wrote it, and nothing satisfi'd with what was begun, left it unfinisht." This note has been of more critical interest than the poem that it pronounces inadequate. Why does Milton bother to include the poem if he did not even think it worth finishing?

One answer to this is that it is part of his more general design in the 1645 *Poems* to represent himself in terms of a Virgilian "rising poet," experimenting and mastering lyric genres in preparation for the career as the national poet of epic.[12] Except, of course, "The Passion" does not, by the poet's own admission, display mastery of its chosen "baroque idiom." Here is the third stanza, in which Milton comes closest to focusing on the bloody body of the crucified Christ:

> He sov'ran Priest stooping his regall head
> That dropt with odorous oil down his fair eyes,
> Poor fleshly Tabernacle entered,

His starry front low-rooft beneath the skies;
O what a Mask was there, what a disguise!
    Yet more; the stroke of death he must abide,
    Then lies more meekly down fast by his Brethrens side.

                        (15–21)

Campbell and Corns, like most commentators, compare this unfavorably with the poetry of Richard Crashaw, who converted to Catholicism just before his early death in exile in 1647: "with a Catholic sensibility," they write, "[Crashaw] shows what could be achieved in the baroque idiom Milton had attempted"; and they quote the first four lines of "Upon the body of Our Bl. Lord, Naked and bloody," first published in the 1646 collection *Steps to the Temple*:

They have left thee naked LORD, O that they had
This garment too I would they had deny'd.
Thee with thyself they have too richly clad,
Opening the purple wardrobe in thy side.[13]

We might also compare "Upon the Circumcision" with Crashaw's "Himme for the Circumcision day of our Lord." Circumcision verse takes the circumcision as the first letting of Jesus' blood and so as a fore-shadowing of the Crucifixion, and celebrates the transcendence of the legalisms of the Mosaic law by the Christian covenant of faith and love. Milton is conventional in theme and tone if rather linguistically wan and colorless in comparison with the vivid, challenging Crashaw:

O more exceeding love or law more just?
Just law indeed, but more exceeding love!
      . . . .
And that great Cov'nant which we still transgress
Intirely satisf'd,
And the full wrath beside
Of vengeful Justice bore for our excess,
And deals obedience first with wounding smart
This day, but O ere long
Huge pangs and strong
    Will pierce more neer his heart.

        ("Upon the Circumcision," 15–16, 21–28)

All the purple pride of Laces,
The crimson curtaines of thy bed;
Guild thee not with so sweet graces;
Nor sets thee in so rich a red.
. . . .
Bid the golden god the Sunne,
Burnisht in his glorious beames:
Put all his red eyed rubies on,
These Rubies shall put out his eyes.
(Crashaw, "Himme for the Circumcision day of our Lord," 5–8, 13–16)

In such phrases as "the purple wardrobe in thy side" and the "crimson curtaines of thy bed," Crashaw displays an intense bodily engagement with the physical suffering of Christ, which is, Corns argues, "utterly alien to Milton's religious sensibility, and that of his Anglican contemporaries.... The English Protestant tradition is reluctant to look so closely or think and feel so deeply about the physical suffering of Christ."[14] The problem with this distinction between Anglican and Catholic poetic sensibilities is that the great majority of Crashaw's vernacular poems are renderings and expansions of the Latin devotional epigrams that were published in Cambridge in 1634, when Crashaw was unquestionably an Anglican, if progressively of the Laudian variety: having come up to Pembroke in 1631, he was elected in 1635 to a fellowship at Peterhouse, the college then at the heart of the Laudian movement.[15]

Whatever the reason Milton chose to include "The Passion" in 1645, does the unfinished and by common consent unsuccessful nature of the poem then display his Puritan discomfort with baroque poetics, and more narrowly with their popularity among Cambridge Laudians like Crashaw? And if he feels such discomfort, why was he trying to write poems in this mode in the first place? A common interpretation of "The Passion" is that it reveals, in the words of John Carey, "Milton's difficulties with the crucifixion as a subject." Campbell and Corns comment, "Milton never did find a way of representing that scene. In *Paradise Lost* the death of the Son receives briefer treatment than Nimrod, while in *Paradise Regained* he averts the reader's gaze from the grisly phase of the Atonement to its more serene precursor."[16] We might read backwards from the Antitrinitarianism of the mature Milton's *De doctrina Christiana* to find a naturally heterodox thinker already uncomfortable with orthodox

Protestant Christology.[17] Yet Campbell and Corns present the poems on church festivals as signs not of incipient *heterodoxy* but of the *orthodoxy* of the young Milton, indeed of his tendency toward Laudian ritualism—although one might argue that Laudianism should itself be seen as a heterodox, minority movement in relation to the Calvinist orthodoxy of early Stuart England.[18]

As we shall see, the "baroque," Counter-Reformation mode in which Crashaw excelled and Milton stuttered was in fact a conventional idiom of devotional poetics in Caroline Cambridge and was respected and practiced even by figures like John Saltmarsh, whom we now categorize confidently as radical Puritans. The practice of baroque devotional poetics in the earlier 1630s, in other words, cannot be said with certainty to have any intrinsic relation to a later attachment to Laudian doctrine or discipline. The fashionable nature of the devotional mode in which Milton was trying to write in "The Passion" and "Upon the Circumcision" is illuminated by two comparative case studies of Cambridge devotional poets in Crashaw and Saltmarsh who were more applauded for their poetic skill in Cambridge in the early and mid-1630s than Milton. If in Crashaw we have a poet whose early devotional verse seems to indicate and anticipate his Laudian and eventually Catholic allegiances, in Saltmarsh we have a figure who was radical more quickly than Milton in the 1640s in terms of both his theology and politics.

Crashaw's verse is best known, as the examples already quoted exemplify, for its use of sensuous, erotic, and unsettling—some have said grotesque—imagery to convey the loving relationship between Christ and human beings.[19] The physicality of the descriptions of Christ's Crucifixion is conventionally associated with theories of sacred poetics that Crashaw derived from his reading of Jesuit and Counter-Reformation writers. This interpretation fits neatly—perhaps too neatly, as we shall see—with Crashaw's later conversion to Catholicism after he left for the Continent when Cambridge was occupied by the parliamentary army in 1643.[20] A fine example of Crashaw's extravagant play with the spiritual significance of the physical ravages suffered by Christ's body is "On the Wounds of Our Crucified Christ," which is a vernacular rendering of one of the neo-Latin epigrams, "In vulnera pendentis Domini," which appeared in Crashaw's first collection, the university volume of 1634, *Epigrammata sacrorum liber:*

O these wakeful wounds of thine!
>Are they Mouthes? Or are they eyes?
Be they Mouthes, or be they eyne,
>Each bleeding part some one supplies.

Lo! A mouth, whose full-bloom'd lips
>At too deare a rate are roses.
Lo! A blood-shot! that weepes
>And many a cruel teare discloses.

O thou that on this foot hast laid
>Many a kisse, and many a Teare,
Now thou shal't have all repaid,
>Whatso'ere thy charges were.

This foot hath got a Mouth and lippes,
>To pay the sweet summe of thy kisses:
To pay thy Teares, an Eye that weeps
>In stead of Teares such Gems as this is.

The difference onely this appears,
>(Nor can the change offend)
The debt is paid in *Ruby*-Teares,
>Which thou in Pearles did'st lend.

The constantly shifting images of blood and water, kisses and tears, rubies and pearls, invoke transubstantiation and sacramental ceremony. Such imagery is difficult to comprehend on a visual, as opposed to an emotional, level, just as the Incarnation and Passion, and their repetition in eucharistic ritual, defy rational comprehension. The use of paradox and antithesis conveys the resolution of the seeming opposites of law and mercy, the "type" of the Old Testament and the "antitype" of the Gospel, through the saving grace of Christ's blood. We saw Milton attempting a similar technique in "Upon the Circumcision" with "O more exceeding love or law more just? / Just law indeed, but more exceeding love!" There is, however, a notable lack of blood in Milton's efforts at ritualistic devotional lyricism.

As Thomas Healy observes in his fine little book on Crashaw's poetic evolution, the vernacular expansions of the neo-Latin epigrams in *Steps to the Temple* tend to increase the physicality of the imagery, consistent with "Laudian ideas on the use of physically exaggerated and explicit imagery in describing sacred events."[21] But if "physically exaggerated and explicit" imagery of the suffering body of Christ became associated with Laudian aesthetics in the later 1630s and 1640s, in the earlier 1630s Crashaw's neo-Latin epigrams served as a study in eloquence even for those who were unquestionably of Puritan sympathies, as is evident from the diary of Thomas Dugard (d. 1683), the headmaster of Warwick School in the 1630s. Dugard's star pupil was none other than Abiezer Coppe, who was to become in 1649 the most notorious of the so-called Ranters, alleged to subvert the divine economy of sin, heaven, and hell through the committing of acts commonly thought to be sinful to demonstrate their release from moral and religious law. In his entries for 1634 Dugard records the 15-year-old Coppe coming round to his house after dinner for extra lessons in Latin and Greek—a salutary reminder that the stereotypical image in the civil wars of the enthusiast as ignorant "tub preacher" often has little basis in reality. Among the texts that Coppe read to Dugard was Crashaw's *Epigrammata*.[22]

Dugard's diary for the period 1632–42 leaves an account of the Puritan circle in which Dugard mixed, revolving around Lord Brooke's hospitality at Warwick Castle. As Ann Hughes demonstrates, Dugard's diary reveals him to have been part of a "'Parliamentary-Puritan connection,' a broad circle of the godly that comprised minor provincial figures and prominent national politicians, and which helped to create the challenge to Charles I's personal rule."[23] However, Dugard's zealous anti-Laudianism evidently did not stop him from enjoying Crashaw's epigrams and using them as a study in neo-Latin eloquence despite the intense and sensuous liturgical imagery that characterizes many of the poems and despite Crashaw's praise, in the prose address to the reader that prefaces the *Epigrammata*, of the Jesuit writers who have provided him with a model of sacred eloquence.

The revelation that the future Ranter Coppe was an avid reader of Crashaw when he was a Puritan youth in Warwick may be a surprise to us, but the news would have been grist to the polemical mill of Samuel Rutherford (1600–61), the Presbyterian professor of divinity at St. Andrew's University. In 1647 Rutherford had responded in some detail to the theological arguments of *Free-Grace; or, The Flowings of Christ's Blood Freely to Sinners* (1645) by the New Model Army chaplain John Saltmarsh, citing Saltmarsh as the leading English "Antinomian"—by which Rutherford meant someone who believes "the Saints are perfect, and their works perfect" in this life and consequently have no need of obedience and repentance. Rutherford warned that the "*Antinomians and Anabaptists* now in England joyne hands with *Pelagians, Jesuits,* and *Arminians*" for they are all "enemies to the grace of God."[24] For Rutherford, Antinomian and Arminian theologies were two sides of the same coin and both heretical inversions of true Calvinist doctrine. In 1648 Rutherford stepped up his attack on Saltmarsh in the vitriolic *A Survey of the Spiritual Antichrist opening the secrets of Familisme and Antinomianisme, in the Antichristian Doctrine of John Saltmarsh, and William Dell, the present Preachers of the Army now in England.* In fact, by 1648 Saltmarsh was no longer a "present preacher in the Army": he had died a memorable death in December 1647 after traveling, though seriously ill, to tell Fairfax and Cromwell that God was angry with them for imprisoning the Levellers.[25]

We should hesitate before dismissing Rutherford's collapsing of Saltmarsh's Antinomianism with Arminianism as purely a polemical convenience. There are both linguistic and theological similarities between Saltmarsh's prose and Crashaw's poetry. In terms of theology there is a shared emphasis on Christ crucified and the assurance of salvation in the writings of the Antinomian Saltmarsh and the Laudian, Catholic-leaning Crashaw. The celebration of the physicality of Christ crucified is also to be found in Saltmarsh's *Free-Grace,* for both Antinomian and Laudian oppose a bleeding, loving Christ—whose blood is a testament to his love—to a Calvinist God of fear who, as Saltmarsh puts it, "commands as a *Lawgiver,* and *Tutor,* or *Minister.*"[26]

In *Free-Grace,* Saltmarsh maintains that those who experience the revelation of the free grace purchased by Christ's death are released absolutely from the bondage of external laws and are perfected on earth, regardless of works: "The Spirit of Christ sets a believer as free from hell, the law and bondage, here on earth, as if he were in heaven; nor wants he anything to make him so, but to make him beleeve that he is so" (140). It is important to note that this is not a proclamation of universal salvation or even of the potential for all to obtain salvation.[27] In the opening page of the tract, Saltmarsh declares his intention is to separate grace from works, "for else it is but a Popish, an Arminian free-grace." And while the Presbyterian heresiographers represented Antinomianism as a belief in universal redemption and thus as a subversion of the Calvinist doctrine of election, the conception of free grace held by Saltmarsh and his fellow army chaplain William Dell really extended Calvinist theology to its logical conclusions.

For Saltmarsh and Dell, if works are irrelevant to salvation and some have been predestined to be saved whether they are sinners in this life or not, then anyone, no matter their status in society or their level of education, could be one of God's saints. They consequently rejected the spiritual authority of education and ordination in favor of the truths vouchsafed by the experience of free grace. Nonetheless, what is striking and provocative about Saltmarsh's formulation is the claim that the revelation of free grace perfects the individual on earth, "as if he were in heaven." The realization of earthly perfection through the grace freely obtained from the "Covenant of the Gospel," which has abrogated the "Covenant of the Law," issues in ecstatic celebration of the Incarnation and of Christ's physical suffering. He writes of Christ's "bloody sweating...his piercing, his nayling, his drinking Vinagar and Gall...his blood flowing out from his feet, hands and side" (*Free-Grace*, 195). This celebration of violence and suffering also involves an erotic aestheticizing of Christ's wounded body: he was "red in his apparel, as he that treadeth the wine-press," but the blood is also "the sweet oyntments or pourings out of spirit" which make "the Virgins follow him" (131, 136). Saltmarsh incorporates the erotic language of Canticles as Christ becomes the Bridegroom who wounds the saved soul as he was wounded, but these are "the woundings and meltings of love"; paradoxically the wound inflicted by Christ on the soul is also a balm, a "Gospel-application" (47, 37–38). The similarities of thought and expression between Laudian poet Crashaw and radical Puritan controversialist Saltmarsh are evident as both dwell on the glories of Christ crucified and the resolution of contraries in divine love.

The similarities become even more striking if we consider "A Divine Rapture upon the Covenant," the verses with which Saltmarsh concluded a 1643 pamphlet:

> See here a chain of Pearls and watery dew
> Wept from the side of God for you,
> See here a chain of Rubies from each wound,
> Let down in Purple to the ground:

> Come tye your Pearls with ours, to make one Ring,
> And thread them on our golden string.[28]

The imagery here is virtually identical to that of Crashaw's "On the Wounds of Our Crucified Christ": incongruous, paradoxical images of tears and pearls, rubies and bloody wounds, beauty and pain strung together in an elaborate, baroque style. It is less surprising that Saltmarsh writes about Christ and grace like Crashaw when we consider Saltmarsh's career in Cambridge in the 1630s. The rhetorical resources Saltmarsh harnessed to express this assurance of salvation also originated in the devotional poetics practiced in Caroline Cambridge, where Saltmarsh had been a neo-Latin poet of some standing. He matriculated in 1627, two years after Milton; in 1636, to mark his graduation as master of arts from Magdalene College, the Cambridge University Press published Saltmarsh's *Poemata sacra latine et anglice scripti*, a collection of sacred epigrams in both Latin and the vernacular dedicated to, among others, the master of Magdalene and Sir Thomas and Lady Metham, recusant gentry in Saltmarsh's native Yorkshire. The language and imagery of Saltmarsh's "A Divine Rapture upon the Covenant" is evidently indebted to that of his neo-Latin epigrams, such as "Aquas mutatis in sanguinem," which are characterized by the same dizzyingly metamorphosing imagery of water, wine, tears, and blood:

> No caede erubit (memorat at miracula Memphis)
> Murice nec ripis it granis unda Suis.
> Unde cruor fluxit? Nunquid nova vulnera sensit
> Neptunis? Venae purpura tanta suae?
> Mirac'lum hoc Mosis minac'lo concolor extat
> Christi: in enima vino, hic sanguine mutat aquas.[29]

Roger Pooley's entry on Saltmarsh in the *Oxford Dictionary of National Biography* declares, "there is nothing in [the *Poemata sacra*] which suggests the political and religious radicalism for which Saltmarsh later became known."[30] But the erotic and aestheticized images of Christ's flowing blood and of drinking and feasting on Christ's wounds that we find in *Free-Grace* are also a recurring feature of the Cambridge epigrams:

> Yet while thou bind'st my wounds up, oh I see
> Thine fresh and bleeding, yawning more than mine.

Lord let thy wounds lie open to me:
To heal my wounds I'le lay them close to me.[31]

The imagery of blood and wine, water and tears in Crashaw's verse is a linguistic representation of sacramental ceremony and so of the "legal" religion that Saltmarsh came to regard by the 1640s, if not before, as a form of carnal bondage over the perfected believer, freed from sin. Nonetheless, his academic training in the composition of neo-Latin devotional verse provided Saltmarsh with a suitably rich, sensuous, and indeed erotic language in which to express the rapturous experience of free grace. The linguistic patterns in both the Laudian poetry of Crashaw and the radical prose of Saltmarsh originated in the academic traditions of prewar Cambridge. It is clear, though, that while Crashaw and Saltmarsh were regarded as heterodox writers by Calvinists in the 1640s, in Caroline Cambridge in the 1630s the poetic style that was to shape the expression of their heterodoxy was uncontroversial—indeed, their verse was honored by publication through the university press.

In fact, the sensuous devotional poetics practiced by Crashaw and Saltmarsh in their neo-Latin verse derives in part from Counter-Reformation texts on sacred eloquence that were apparently recommended reading for Cambridge undergraduates. One of the fullest surviving accounts of the curriculum, "Directions for a Student in the Universitie," probably dating from the 1620s or early 1630s and attributed to Richard Holdsworth (1590–1649), recommends rhetorical textbooks by Jesuits, specifically Nicolas Caussin's *De eloquentia sacrae et humanae* (1619) and Famianus Strada's *Prolusiones academicae, oratoriae, historicae, poeticae* (1617).[32] In the university context, Holdsworth was certainly not, like Crashaw, a Laudian outrider; from 1637 he was master of Emmanuel, where the chapel was never formally consecrated and which was a generally Puritan institution in the first half of the seventeenth century. Although he was to support the royalist cause, in the 1630s he refused to read the Book of Sports.[33] His recommendation of Jesuit books on sacred eloquence reveals that the study of Counter-Reformation texts in Cambridge was certainly not confined to Laudian circles. Counter-Reformation eloquence was part, then, of orthodox academic culture, and even, it seems, orthodox Puritan culture, in early Stuart England; at the same time it provided the linguistic resources not only for an anti-Calvinist Laudian poetics, as might be expected, but for the expression of an Antinomian theology that extended Calvinist doctrine to its logical, if heretical, conclusions.

We cannot explain away Saltmarsh's exercises in neo-Latin baroque as a Laudian phase through which he passed. His first published poem of 1634 was a prefatory poem for *The two famous pitcht battels of Lypsich, and Lutzen wherein the ever-renowned Prince Gustavus the Great lived and died a conquerour: with an elegie upon his untimely death, composed in heroick verse by John Russell, Master of Arts, of Magdalene Coll. in Cambridge.* While it remains unclear to what extent we should identify praise of Gustavus Adolphus in the early 1630s with coherent opposition to Stuart pacifism during the Thirty Years' War, Gerald Maclean has discussed these prefatory poems as an illustration of what he calls "oppositional poetics" under the personal rule, and the opening of Saltmarsh's poem is quoted by David Norbrook as "elaborating a vigorously martial poetics" against the courtly, Cavalier mode of poets like Thomas Carew:

> Let those soft *Poets*, who have dipt their brains
> In am'rous humours, thaw to looser strains.
> Let *Cupid* be their theme, and let them pay
> Service to *Venus* in a wanton lay:
> And let these *Rhymers* of our silken Age
> Unlade their Fancies on an emptie page.
> Mars is thy theme; thy *Muse* hath learn'd to talk
> The *Cannon-Language* of the Warre, and walk
> A loftie March.[34]

Although neither Maclean nor Norbrook make the point, in this poem Saltmarsh does seem to allude to the possibility of state censorship at a time when news reports about Gustavus Adolphus and the progress of the religious wars in Europe had been banned by the Star Chamber:

> And if those eyes, with poison'd flame that shine
> Like Basilisk's, shed poison on a line,
> To blot a syllable that sounds the least
> GUSTAVUS Warre, *Jove* turn them to that Beast.[35]

Saltmarsh was apparently the first person to suggest publicly, in sermon and in print in 1643, that it would be in the nation's interest to depose Charles I: he implied that the death of one family, the Stuarts, would be preferable to the deaths of tens of thousands on the battlefield. The future regicide Henry Marten was ejected from the House of Commons and imprisoned for defending Saltmarsh's sentiments.[36] If we can see in Saltmarsh's 1634 poem on Adolphus some evidence of Puritan militancy while at Cambridge, then Saltmarsh nonetheless continued to write and publish in 1636 in the Crashavian devotional mode that has habitually been characterized as evidence of a Laudian, proto-Catholic sensibility.

Where does this leave Milton, the poet who felt "nothing satisfied with what he had begun" in "The Passion" in 1630? Milton's composition of the poems on the Passion and the Circumcision cannot be said confidently to show either his taste or distaste for Laudian values in the early 1630s; rather, the lyrics reflect his efforts to compose in the devotional mode fashionable in his university at the time. It is agreed that Milton's most successful experiments with the "baroque idiom" are his Latin funeral elegies of 1626 for the bishops Nicholas Felton and Lancelot Andrewes. Milton wrote these elegies in a neo-Latin baroque mode because that is what his peers at Cambridge expected and applauded at the time. Who is to say that Milton did not also compose devotional poems in Latin, in the Counter-Reformation style in which Crashaw and Saltmarsh excelled, but which he chose not to preserve, perhaps because he perceived their even greater inadequacy than his vernacular efforts?

There is nothing inadequate, of course, about the Nativity ode: Corns calls it a "decidedly competitive poem," showing how Milton's poem shares "a familiar repertoire of motifs and conceits" with the Nativity poetry of his contemporaries, including William Drummond, George Herbert, Robert Herrick, and Crashaw. However, "Milton's poem asserts his own self-worth and his own individualism. Though he shares so much of the poetic idiom of his contemporaries, he has nothing of their self-effacement, nothing of their priestliness"; and, though "this is not a radical or puritan or oppositional poem...it reflects a religious sensibility which, as we know, will become radicalized as the crises of the late 1630s develop."[37] But if the Nativity ode successfully shows Milton writing devotional poetry in the style of his contemporaries and trumping them, "The Passion" shows him trying to repeat the trick and failing: there is no sense of the poet finding an individual voice as he does in the ode. Indeed, where the Nativity ode celebrates the violent power of the Christ-child, particularly in the spectacular expulsion and punish-ment of the pagan gods, "The Passion" sees Milton uncharacteristically renouncing epic pretensions, distinguishing his own quiet, "soft" lines from the heroic 1535 *Christiad* of Marco Vida of Cremona: "Loud o're the rest *Cremona's* Trump doth sound; / Me softer airs befit, and softer strings / Of Lute or Viol still, more apt for mournful things" ("The Passion," 26–28).

Of course, Milton's failure to write convincing Passion poetry in the style fashionable when he was a student does not rule out the possibil-ity of the young Milton already feeling emotionally and theologically uncomfortable with images of the bodily pain of the crucified Christ. Glenn Burgess argues that early modern radicalism should not be approached as a "phenomenon with a continuous existence" but as one "forged, and forged repeatedly, from the discursive and cultural materi-als—e.g. the languages—that lay to hand." These languages may be as likely to reinforce as subvert prewar orthodoxies and to be found in the mainstream political, religious, and intellectual culture as in its margins.[38] The language of neo-Latin devotional poetics, which was part of the orthodox education of both Crashaw and Saltmarsh in Caroline Cambridge, was also part of the "cultural and discursive material" from which Saltmarsh forged his radical theology amid the unprecedented religious innovation of the civil wars. It was not, however, among the rhetorical resources on which Milton chose to call in forging his het-erodox theology and tolerationist ideas, and in this we may be able to measure Milton's distance in the 1640s from Antinomian varieties of religious radicalism as much as Laudian ceremonialism, and perhaps see something of the later attraction to Antitrinitarianism.

The comparative examples of Crashaw and Saltmarsh thus warn against any confident reading of the Cambridge Milton as either an opponent or a supporter of Laudian values in poetry. In the Nativity ode, "The Passion," and "Upon the Circumcision," Milton was, rather, trying to write à la mode—though his success with the Nativity ode and failure with "The Passion" may indeed give us some indication of the future development of his religious sensibility and theological prefer-ences. Of course, by the early 1640s Milton was unquestionably opposed to Laudianism in terms of its ceremonial discipline, if not necessarily the

Arminian theological doctrine to which, following his father, he may well have long subscribed.[39]

The question of Milton's attitude to custom and formalism in poetics as in institutional religion is worth pursuing. The sense of a form-bound inauthenticity that we find in "The Passion," and that Milton also seemingly found in his failed lyric, is most strangely conveyed in the final lines before Milton abandons his effort:

> Or should I thence hurried on viewles wing,
> Take up a weeping on the Mountains wilde,
> The gentle neighbourhood of grove and spring
> Would soon unboosom all thir Echoes milde,
> And I (for grief is easily beguild)
> Might think th'infection of my sorrows loud,
> Had got a race of mourners on som pregnant cloud.   (50–56)

The image alludes to the story of Ixion in Pindar's second of his *Pythian Odes:* Ixion thought he was ravishing Hera, but Zeus put a raincloud in her place; Ixion thus begot a race of centaurs. The references to Echo and Ixion's cloud are recalled in strikingly negative images in the *Doctrine and Discipline of Divorce.* In the opening lines of the address to Parliament and the Westminster Assembly in the 1644 second edition, Milton writes of "Custome being but a meer face, as Eccho is a meere voice, rests not in her unaccomplishment, until by secret inclination, shee accorporat her selfe with error....Hence it is, that Error supports Custome, Custome count'nances Error." "Unaccomplishment" is an apt summation of Milton's own description of "The Passion" in the note in the 1645 and 1673 *Poems.* Later in the second edition of the tract, Milton writes of how Jupiter gave to Ixion "a cloud instead of Juno, giving him a monstrous issue by her, the breed of Centaures a neglected and unlov'd race, the fruits of a delusive marriage."[40] The odd choice of image at the end of "The Passion," when read in the light of these later metaphors of insubstantiality in the divorce tracts, perhaps reveals Milton's realization that he is merely trying to write according to the fashionable or customary mode and so failing to attain an original and genuine voice: he becomes aware that he is deluding himself if he thinks the lyric to be the substantial issue of poetic genius.[41] And empty custom will always finally be filled by, or "accorporate" with, error.

Lycidas is the preeminent poem in which the young Milton finds an original voice out of a multiplicity of poetic convention. One of the effects of the Campbell and Corns argument for a conservative and even Laudian Milton in the 1630s is to place even more pressure on the eruption of anticlerical polemic in *Lycidas* as a key moment in the development of the man who takes to controversial prose in 1641. What is the cause of that eruption, or moment of "radicalization"? John Leonard has argued well for allusions in *Lycidas* to the public mutilation of William Prynne and other leading Puritan activists in 1637; Edward Jones has found among the archives some intriguing evidence that Milton's father was cited in a Laudian visitation of Horton in 1637 for violation of a policy regarding his church seat.[42] No doubt there is more archival evidence out there, but I want to offer what I believe might be a new perspective on the jolting language of St. Peter's violent condemnation in *Lycidas* of the state of the English church.

Lycidas first appeared as the final poem in a Cambridge anthology, *Justa Edouardo King Naufrago*, and several of the contributors to the collection apply the baroque techniques of the Passion poetry that had been fashionable in Cambridge to their elegies—most notably John Cleveland (1613–58), a contemporary of Milton's at Christ's College from 1627 to 1632, at which point he moved to a fellowship at St. John's. Cleveland would go on to become one of the most effective and stylistically interesting of the royalist polemicists of the 1640s. His elegy for King begins:

> I like not tears in tune, nor do I prize
> His artificial grief that scans his eyes;
> Mine weep down pious beads, but why should I
> Confine them to the Muses' rosary?
> I am no poet here; my pen's the spout
> Where the rain-water of my eyes runs out,
> In pity of that name, whose fate we see
> Thus copied out in grief's hydrography.[43]

The imagery here is stretched to the point that it can look comically bathetic to modern eyes. We can compare, however, Milton's own rather hyperbolic images of tears as script in "The Passion":

> My sorrows are too dark for day to know:
>   The leaves should all be black wheron I write,
> And letters where my tears have washt a wannish white.
>
>   . . . .
>   For sure so well instructed are my tears,
>   That they would fitly fall in order'd Characters.   (33–35, 48–49)

Cleveland drives to the verge of parody the idiom of the baroque Passion poetry at which Milton had tried his hand at Cambridge and found not to his talent and perhaps not to his taste.

In the final section of *Lycidas*, at least before the third-person coda, we are roused from our mourning by "Weep no more, woful Shepherds weep no more, / For *Lycidas* your sorrow is not dead" (165–66). This clarion call feels like a response to all the elegies that have gone before, which dwell on the grief and tears of King's friends and colleagues: as Lewalski notes, the other elegists are "chiefly clerics and other college fellows [who] associate King closely with the church and university he served."[44] Finally, the Miltonic poet will not cry for the lost watery corpse of Lycidas but celebrate his eternal life in heaven: "With *Nectar* pure his oozy Lock's he laves" (175). *Red* nectar is used specifically in the *Aeneid*, 9.38, to keep the corpse of Patrocles from decaying; the red nectar in the hair of Lycidas perhaps replaces the bloody locks of Christ familiar from the baroque "poetry of tears" tradition.

But Milton also raises pastoral directness and plainness over the "poetry of tears" and its elaborate baroque contortions as we find them in the epigrams of Crashaw and Saltmarsh on the dying Christ and in Cleveland's elegy for Edward King. In "The Passion," that refusal, I have argued, is made essentially on technical poetic grounds; but when we get to *Lycidas* it is driven by something more — by a rejection not only of the Laudian clerical discipline but also of its style, including its by now characteristic poetics of catachresis. The famous exclamation of Saint Peter in *Lycidas*, "Blind mouthes!" (119), was given its definitive explication by John Ruskin: the "blind mouths" are the antithesis of "bishop," one who sees, and "pastor," one who feeds.[45] But Ruskin's account of etymological irony does not quite account for the disorientating effect that the phrase has on readers, who are struck by a surreal image rather than a linguistic pun. For images of "blind mouths" in the "poetry of tears" tradition we could look back to Crashaw's uncomfortable images in the opening stanza of "On the Wounds of Our Crucified Christ" of Christ's bleeding wounds as at once eyes and mouths:

> O these wakeful wounds of thine!
>   Are they Mouthes? Or are they eyes?
> Be they Mouthes, or be they eyne,
>   Each bleeding part some one supplies.

Milton could not have read Crashaw's vernacular rendering of this poem in 1637, but he could have read its Latin original in the 1634 *Epigrammata*. Might the "blind mouths" of *Lycida* convey with shocking force how by 1637 Milton had come to associate a corrupt Laudian clergy with the baroque poetics that made a poet's name in Caroline Cambridge?

University of Exeter

Rhetoric, Passion, and Belief in *The Readie and Easie Way*

William Walker

For all your Politiques are derived from the works of Declamers, with which sort of Writers, the Ancient Common-wealths had the fortune to abound, who left many things behind them in favour, or flattery of the Governments they liv'd under, and disparagement of others, to whom they were in opposition, of whom we can affirm nothing certain, but that they were partiall, and never meant to give a true account of things, but to make them finer or worse then they really are.

—*The Censure of the Rota Upon Mr. Miltons Book,*
Entituled, The Ready and Easie way to Establish
A Free Common-wealth

While observing Milton's ambivalence on the issue of constitutional forms in his major prose of the Commonwealth and Protectorate, many scholars who study Milton's political writings see more decisiveness in *The Readie and Easie Way*. Here, it seems, Milton clearly repudiates monarchy and endorses constitutions that make no place for a king. Here the gloves are off and, no longer constrained to show some respect for the continental monarchies as he was in the *Defences*, Milton at last unequivocally expresses his republicanism (which was always really there), where *republicanism* is defined in terms of the repudiation of monarchy in principle.[1] This view is fortified and affirmed by Eric Nelson, who addresses "the development of republican political theory in the West." Nelson observes that whereas many in late medieval and Renaissance Europe asserted that "republics are *better* than monarchies," no one espoused "republican exclusivism," the doctrine that "republics are the only legitimate regimes." This position, one "that is responsible for the shape of political life and thought in the modern world," had to wait for Milton, for he is "the first European political writer to make a straightforwardly exclusivist argument for republican government." Acknowledging those critics who have noted Milton's ambivalence on constitutional issues in his writings of the 1650s, Nelson claims that the exclusivist argument "develops" in his writings during this decade and is "amplified" in *The Readie and Easie Way* with the result that "the exclusivist argument remains a dominant feature of [Milton's] political theory." This is clear, Nelson argues, once we see that, drawing on rabbinical tradition, Milton cites and comments on 1 Samuel 8 in these texts to justify the view that "kingship per se is idolatry" and thus that "kingship is always illegitimate."[2]

While Milton is indeed more direct and passionate in criticizing monarchy in this tract than he is in the tyrannicide tracts, this criticism, I will show, is not an expression of a hardening belief that kingship is always illegitimate but part of a hyperbolic discourse that is in part intended to persuade various Englishmen that a Stuart monarchy is pernicious for their nation in 1660. That *The Readie and Easie Way* cannot be located in a story of growing commitment to republican exclusivism on Milton's part is, moreover, clear from his *Brief Notes upon a Late Sermon*, a short pamphlet published days after the appearance of the second edition of *The Readie and Easie Way*, and shortly before the Restoration in May 1660. Here Milton asserts the antiformalist constitutional principles that he had asserted in the *Defences* and that are consistent with his opposition to a Stuart monarchy in England in 1660. It is thus only on softer definitions of *republicanism* in terms of opposition to monarchy under some circumstances that Milton qualifies as a republican on the eve of the Restoration.

Such observations, however, hardly settle the issue of Milton's republicanism in *The Readie and Easie Way*. In recent years, the term *republicanism* has also been commonly used in scholarly discussions of Milton, seventeenth century English political thought, and Western political thought at large to refer to vocabularies that are used to express, endorse, and transform ideas about virtue, forms of government, property, civil liberty, history, empire, religion, and human nature. The complex usage of these vocabularies defines a *tradition* of political thought that runs from ancient Greeks (such as Plato, Aristotle, Polybius, and Plutarch) and ancient Romans (such as Cicero, Sallust, and Livy), through medieval Christian Aristotelians (such as Ptolemy of Lucca and Marsilius of Padua), up to Renaissance humanists (such as Leonardo Bruni and Niccolò Machiavelli), and beyond.[3] Little has been done in the way of assessing how *The Readie and Easie Way* stands in relation to this more complex and comprehensive definition of *republicanism*.

When we consider this issue, *The Readie and Easie Way* cannot fairly be seen as an expression of Milton's adherence to republicanism. This observation helps us to understand why in this tract Milton departs from and, indeed, argues against some of his contemporaries, such as Marchamont Nedham and James Harrington, who *were* seriously committed to many aspects of republicanism in this sense. It explains why one of the most acute satires on Milton and his tract was written and presented by someone who was pretending to be Harrington. And it shows how misleading it can be to lump Milton in with the "English republicans."

In the much enlarged second edition of *The Readie and Easie Way* (prepared some time after the first edition appeared near the end of February 1660 and published in early April), there are several passages in which Milton appears to be repudiating monarchy in principle. Thus, at the opening of the tract, he writes that when the Rump abolished "kingship" in 1649, it turned "regal bondage into a free Commonwealth."[4] And after providing a brief account of the conflict that preceded that abolition, and some of the actions of the government that followed it, he speaks of the "detested thraldom of Kingship" (YP 7:422). Such phrasings suggest that monarchy is always a form of government under which people are thralls, or as he frequently puts it in the tract, "slaves." After predicting the pernicious consequences of restoring monarchy in England, Milton then observes, "God in much displeasure gave a king to the *Israelites*, and imputed it a sin to them that they sought one" (424). Kingless government, he claims, is "planely commended, or rather enjoind by our Saviour himself, to all Christians, not without remarkable disallowance, and the brand of *gentilism* [is set] upon kingship" (424). This is clear from Christ's response to Zebedee's sons who wished to be exalted over their brethren: "but *Christ* apparently forbids his disciples to admitt of any such heathenish government: *the kings of the gentiles,* saith he, *exercise lordship over them;* and they that *exercise authoritie upon them, are call'd benefactors*" (424). The form of government that "coms neerer to this precept of Christ," Milton affirms, is obviously "a free Commonwealth" (425).

Milton proceeds to draw a graphic contrast between the leading men of commonwealths who "are perpetual servants and drudges to the public at thir own cost and charges," and a king who "must be ador'd like a Demigod" (YP 7:425) and who, at least in England, will have "a dissolute and haughtie court about him" (425). He then provides further grounds for rejecting monarchy in general: a king is often "a mischief, a pest, a scourge of the nation, and which is wors, not to be remov'd, not to be controul'd, much less accus'd or brought to punishment, without the danger of a common ruin, without the shaking and almost subversion of the whole land" (426). Another problem with monarchy is that kings can do so much damage: "that people must needs be madd or strangely infatuated, that build the chief hope of thir common happiness or safetie on a single person: who if he happen to be good, can do no more then another man, if to be bad, hath in his hands to do more evil without check, then millions of other men" (427). And since, under monarchy, a people comes to depend upon a single person for the management of their affairs and their safety and happiness, this form of government militates against self-reliance and reliance upon God and is therefore suited not for adults, but for boys, sluggards, and babies:

> And what madness is it, for them who might manage nobly thir own affairs themselves, sluggishly and we[a]kly to devolve all on a single person; and more like boyes under age then men, to committ all to his patronage and disposal, who neither can performe what he undertakes, and yet for undertaking it, though royally paid, will not be thir servant, but thir lord? how unmanly must it needs be, to count such a one the breath of our nostrils, to hang all our felicity on him, all our safetie, our well-being, for which if we were aught els but sluggards or babies, we

need depend on none but God and our own counsels, our own active vertue and industrie." (427)

If, moreover, the people suffer that single person "to pretend hereditarie right over them as thir lord," they "conclude themselves his servants and his vassals, and so renounce thir own freedom" (427–28).

Milton returns to his argument that kingship is un-Christian and repeats his charge that Christ "hath expressly declar'd, that...regal dominion is from the gentiles, not from him, and hath strictly charg'd us, not to imitate them therein" (YP 7:429). Monarchy, Milton adds, is also less stable than commonwealths: "Kingship it self is therefor counted the more safe and durable, because the king and, for the most part, his councel, is not chang'd during life: but a Commonwealth is held immortal; and therin firmest, safest and most above fortune" (436). "A single person," moreover, is "the natural adversarie and oppressor of libertie," and even if that person is good, he or she is "far easier corruptible by the excess of his singular power and exaltation, or at best, not comparably sufficient to bear the weight of government, nor equally dispos'd to make us happie in the enjoyment of our libertie under him" (449). "All kings," Milton later claims, have an antipathy "against Presbyterian and Independent discipline," for "they hear the gospel speaking much of libertie; a word which monarchie and her bishops both fear and hate, but a free Commonwealth both favors and promotes" (458). Finally, "monarchs will never permit" the establishment of schools that would promote knowledge, civility, and religion, for the aim of monarchs is "to make the people, wealthie indeed perhaps and well fleec't, for thir own shearing and the supplie of regal prodigalitie; but otherwise softest, basest, vitiousest, servilest, easiest to be kept under; and not only in fleece, but in minde also sheepishest" (460).

That one denounces monarchy does not necessarily mean one endorses a "free Commonwealth." Indeed, for many of the ancients, it was standard practice to observe the faults of both monarchical and nonmonarchical forms of government and then to recommend a specific form of government on the basis of these observations. But, as some of the passages cited above indicate, Milton's denunciation of monarchy goes hand in hand with a recommendation of a "free Commonwealth":

"I doubt not but all ingenuous and knowing men will easily agree with me, that a free Commonwealth without single person or house of lords, is by far the best government, if it can be had" (YP 7:429). And "the ground and basis of every just and free government (since men have smarted so oft for commiting all to one person) is a general councel of ablest men, chosen by the people to consult of public affairs from time to time for the common good" (432).

In *The Readie and Easie Way*, then, Milton has to an important extent overcome his impatience with talk of constitutional forms and his reluctance to denounce or endorse particular forms of government, which he displays in his earlier political writings. It is, however, important to observe some significant qualifications. First of all, as Milton indicates in the full title of the tract, he claims to observe the excellence of "*a free Commonwealth... compar'd with the inconveniencies and dangers of readmitting Kingship in this Nation.*" Given that the project is essentially comparative, it is not surprising to find that in many of the passages cited above, the values ascribed to different forms of government are relative. Kingless government, for example, comes "neerer" than monarchy to the teachings of Christ. Commonwealths are "safer and more thriving" than monarchies. "A frugal and self-governing democratie or Commonwealth," such as that exemplified by Solomon's ants, is "safer and more thriving in the joint providence and counsel of many industrious equals, then under the single domination of one imperious Lord" (427). A people may "with much better management and dispatch, with much more commendation of thir own worth and magnanimitie govern without" a king than with one, and they can do things "more easily, more effectually, more laudably" than a king can (448). A single person is "far easier corruptible" than councils, and neither "comparably sufficient" to govern, nor "equally disposed" to make the governed free and happy (449). "Our freedom and flourishing condition will be more ample and secure to us under a free Commonwealth then under kingship" (456). There is "no government more inclinable not to favor only but to protect" liberty of conscience "then a free Commonwealth" (456). The enjoyment of "civil rights and advancements of every person according to his merit" is "never more certain, and the access to these never more open, then in a free Commonwealth" (458). "Of all governments a Commonwealth aims most to make the people flourishing, vertuous, noble and high spirited" (460). The vocabulary of comparison and relativity pervades the tract, and it implies that monarchy differs from commonwealth not in kind but in degree: monarchy is not entirely without merit but has less merit than commonwealths, while commonwealths are not perfect but merely less prone to the problems that afflict monarchies.

The qualified version of republicanism Milton espouses in this tract is further evident when we take into account what Milton was attempting to achieve in writing and publishing it as he did. At the beginning of the second edition of the tract, he asserts that even if "those who are in power" be determined "to enthrall us" by reestablishing monarchy in England, he wishes nevertheless to be permitted, "before so long a Lent of Servitude," to speak freely, and thereby take his leave of liberty (YP 7:407–09). Near the end of this tract, he claims that he would have written what he did even if he had been sure he "should have spoken only to trees and stones; and had none to cry to, but with the Prophet, *O earth, earth, earth!* to tell the very soil it self, what her perverse inhabitants are deaf to" (462–63). Milton, at least by his own account, is bearing witness, denouncing, exhorting, venting passions of anger and disgust, lamenting in the manner of Old Testament prophets such as Jeremiah, and (though perhaps not entirely seriously) bidding farewell to something he highly values, in the manner of those approaching Lent.[5]

But however deeply he feared that this tract would indeed be a valediction to liberty and a prophecy that would fall on deaf ears, Milton also represents himself as one who is seriously engaged in the act of advising, counseling, and persuading his countrymen to take a particular course of action and to avoid others. Thus, in the second edition of the tract, he places a citation from Juvenal's first satire on the title page that suggests that, having advised Cromwell (or perhaps General George Monck), he is now advising the English people: "et nos consilium dedimus Syl'ae, demus populo nunc" (we have advised Sulla himself, advise we now the People) (YP 7:405). And in the introduction to the tract he expresses hope that what he says will be of "use and concernment" to those "whom it behoves to have all things represented to them that may direct thir judgement" concerning "Government" (408). He claims never to have "read of any State, scarce of any tyrant grown so incurable, as to refuse counsel from any in a time of public deliberation" (408). At the end of the tract, he asserts that he has followed his "duty to speak in season, and to forewarne my countrey in time" (462). He has spoken the language of "*the good Old Cause*" which he hopes will "not seem more strange...then convincing to backsliders" (462), and he trusts to "have spoken perswasion to abundance of sensible and ingenuous men: to som perhaps whom God may raise of these stones to become children of reviving libertie" (463).

Though the situation was, from his perspective, grim when he was composing the first version of the tract in February, and even grimmer as he revised it in March, it is nevertheless reasonable to think that Milton had not entirely given up hope and that he was, as he claims, making a genuine though desperate attempt to persuade at least some of his countrymen. Milton's unpublished writings of the period, in which he formulates and develops his proposals, display a genuine hope that a restoration might be avoided and exhibit a real urgency in composition, both of which bespeak a man making a last-ditch attempt to influence the situation. Sudden, unexpected changes in government, brought about by single persons, armies, or assemblies of men, were not unknown at the time. Monck's intentions were questionable even after he admitted the secluded members to Parliament in late February, and it was not entirely fanciful of Milton to draft a letter to him, urging him to prevent the return to Stuart monarchy (even after the first edition of *The Readie and Easie Way* had been published).[6] Popular opinion and sentiment, moreover, had hardly been the deciding factor in politics over the previous decade. As several scholars have observed, while in hindsight a restoration may appear to have been inevitable in the early months of 1660, it did not appear so to Milton and some others at the time.[7]

One of the things Milton claims to be doing in this tract is persuading (or attempting to persuade), but persuading whom of what? Was he aiming to persuade whoever might read the tract, any time, any place, that monarchy per se is pernicious and therefore ought never to be established? No. The principal polemical aims of the second edition were to dissuade various contingents of English society—the electorate for the elections to a new Parliament that would replace the Long Parliament, which had dissolved itself on March 16; members elected to that Parliament; Presbyterians; the army; sensible men; and perhaps even some waverers among the misguided multitude—from restoring monarchy, and to persuade these groups—along with Harrington and his followers, who from 1656 onward had been forwarding *their* proposals for a nonmonarchical constitution—to establish a specific type of "free Commonwealth" in England as it was following the civil wars of the 1640s and the sociopolitical instability of the 1650s.[8]

To return once more to the title page, Milton aims in this tract to show the English people *The readie and easie way to establish a free Commonwealth; and the excellence therof compar'd with the inconveniencies and dangers of readmitting Kingship* [not anywhere, but] *in this Nation*. And though, as we have seen, he on some occasions criticizes monarchy in principle, Milton emphasizes throughout the tract that, *given the history of England*, restoring monarchy would be "dangerous" and "inconvenient," whereas establishing a commonwealth would be safe and convenient in that place and at that time.

Indeed, even on those occasions when he appears to be inveighing against monarchy in principle, Milton often slides into a denunciation of monarchy in England. For example, in the passage cited above in which he describes "the madness" of devolving all on a single person, Milton begins with third-person pronouns that make it look as though he is talking about how detrimental monarchy is for everybody, but concludes the passage by using the first-person plural pronouns "we" and "our," which results in the much more limited observation of how unmanly monarchy would be for the English. After providing at the opening of the tract a brief history of England during the 1640s and 1650s, Milton writes that it is only "after our liberty and religion thus prosperously fought for, gaind and many years possessd, except in those unhappie interruptions, which God hath remov'd," that the restoration of monarchy in England would be so disastrous (YP 7:421). He continues:

> for this extolld and magnif'd nation, regardless both of honour wonn or deliverances voutsaf't from heaven, to fall back or rather to creep back so poorly as it seems the multitude would to thir once abjur'd and detested thraldom of Kingship, to be our selves the slanderers of our own just and religious deeds..., to throw away and forsake, or rather to betray a just and noble cause for the mixture of bad men who have ill manag'd and

> abus'd it... and by thus relapsing, to verifie all the bitter predictions of our
> triumphing enemies, who will now think they wisely discernd and justly
> censur'd both us and all our actions as rash, rebellious, hypocritical and
> impious, not only argues a strange degenerate contagion suddenly spread
> among us fitted and prepar'd for new slaverie, but will render us a scorn
> and derision to all our neighbours. (422)

The point is not that *any* nation that establishes monarchy would be
an ungrateful, rebellious, hypocritical, impious, rash, ignoble, shameful
slanderer and betrayer of itself that would merit the scorn of all Europe.
The point is that for *this* nation (England), which had *thus* achieved its
liberty (by taking up arms against and executing Charles I) *now* (in early
1660) to establish monarchy would be so.

Milton pursues this line of argument when he urges that "if *we* returne
to Kingship, and soon repent, as undoubtedly *we* shall," "*we*" shall find
"the old encroachments coming on by little and little upon our con-
sciences" and "may be forc'd perhaps to fight over again all that *we*
have fought, and spend over again all that *we* have spent" (YP 7:423;
my emphasis). For the English to restore monarchy in 1660, after the
civil wars, would be to make "vain and viler then dirt the blood of so
many thousand faithfull and valiant *English* men, who left us in this libertie, bought with thir lives; losing by a strange after game of folly, all
the battels we have wonn, together with all *Scotland* as to our conquest"
(423–24). For the English to return to monarchy now would, moreover,
be to tread "back again with lost labour all our happie steps in the
progress of reformation" (424; see also 428). After predicting that the
problems England had experienced under Charles I would recur "if ther
be a king" again in the nation (446–47), Milton continues to emphasize the dangers of restoring monarchy in England at this time. "But
admitt," he writes, "that monarchie of it self may be convenient to som
nations; yet *to us,* who have thrown it out, receivd back again, it cannot but prove pernicious" (449; my emphasis). This is because English
"kings to com" would never forget that they had been ejected earlier
and would therefore "fortifie and arm themselves" against any further
ejections and would monitor and oppress the people (449). Just as God
did not listen to the Israelites who complained to him after they had
rejected being "governd in a Commonwealth of God's own ordaining"

and had been given a king, so he would not hear English complaints should they restore monarchy after being "deliverd by him from a king" (449–50). Milton then provides another detailed catalog of the negative consequences for the English people should they restore monarchy in their country (450–58).

Much of the hostility and argumentation of the tract, then, is directed not against monarchy per se, but against a particular kind of monarchy in a particular place at a particular time: a Stuart monarchy in England in 1660. This aspect of the tract derives from the fact that, on this occasion, Milton was not writing a treatise of government, but attempting to dissuade various Englishmen from restoring a Stuart monarchy and to persuade them to establish a commonwealth *"in this Nation."* By bearing in mind that on this occasion Milton was, against the odds, attempting to persuade, but also venting his own anger and disappointment, we can also see many of his more extreme denigrations of monarchy for what they are: *hyperbole.* Milton knew that hyperbole was at the core of the impassioned lamentation and derision of Juvenal and Jeremiah. He knew that in his discussion of the stylistic dimension of persuasion in book 3 of the *Rhetoric*, Aristotle writes that hyperboles "betray vehemence. And so they are used, above all, by men in an angry passion."[9] And he knew that after discussing hyperboles that achieve the effect of sublimity, Longinus observes that, since the effect of this trope is amplification, it is also at the heart of vilification, for "vilification [is] in a sense an amplification of lowness."[10] Milton knew, in short, that hyperbole was the language of vehemence and vivid representation, which could be effectively used to persuade and to deride. Possessed of this knowledge, animated by his own passions and will to persuade, Milton in 1660 deploys rich metaphorical hyperbole to describe subjects of monarchs as boys and babies (YP 7:427), slaves (422, 428, 448, 455), thralls (422, 455), vassals (428), men in shackles (448), sheep for shearing (460), and cattle whose necks are in a yoke (428, 448, 449, 450, 452–53, 462); the condition of being subject to a restored Stuart monarchy as Lent (408); the subjects of an English monarchy as those who count a single person "the breath of our nostrils" and "hang all our felicity on him, all our safetie, our well-being" (427); those who oppose his proposal for a free commonwealth as men who are less intelligent than pismires (427) and "addicted to a single person or house of lords" (432); returning to monarchy as creeping (422); royalist pamphlets as "the spue of every drunkard, every ribald" (452) and their authors as "tigers of Bacchus, these new fanatics of not the preaching but the sweating-tub, inspir'd with nothing holier then the Veneral pox" (452–53); the English people in 1660 as a multitude infected with a "noxious humor" (407), "a strange degenerate contagion" (422), and madness of "epidemic" proportions (427, 446, 463); the English as the ancient Israelites who wanted to return to Egyptian bondage (463); and, I would add, all subjects of monarchs everywhere as false worshippers, adorers, idolators, and sinners (419, 425–26, 429, 448, 462).

Representing these things in this way, Milton is, as the author of a shrewd satire on the first edition of Milton's tract observes, not providing "a true account of things" but making them "worse then they really are," just as the "Declamers" of "the Ancient Commonwealths" did.[11] At the time he was writing, he no more really *believed* that all subjects of all monarchs everywhere and at all times were sinners than he believed that the English people were cattle and sheep, or that all English people who had lived under the ancient constitution were slaves, or that the supporters of a Stuart restoration were afflicted with an addiction and infected with a disease, or that their mental faculties were inferior to those of ants, or that they were all babies. Milton represents these people in these ways in order to *exaggerate* some of the faults he perceives them to have and thereby to serve God with zeal, vent his anger and disgust, deride the English people, but also persuade them (if he had not offended them too deeply) to establish a constitution in England that made no place for a single person or House of Lords.

It is, moreover, important to observe that even as he pursues his polemical aims, Milton displays some of the impatience with matters of constitutional form that he often displays in his earlier writings. Consider, for example, the cool generalization that "the happiness of a nation must needs be firmest and certainest in a full and free Councel of thir own electing, where no single person, but reason only swaies" (YP 7:427). It is difficult to understand this sentence because the referent of *where* is uncertain: is Milton saying that, even when a nation is a commonwealth, under a constitution that grants political powers to elected councils, its happiness may still be unfirm if that council itself is swayed by a single person within it rather than reason (as the happiness of England was when Cromwell swayed the Council of State from 1649 to 1653)? Is he saying that commonwealths are good only *where* you have councils of a certain kind? Perhaps not. Perhaps the claim is really just that a nation *where* no single person but reason only sways is happy. But if this is the claim, then at the very moment that Milton would seem to be recommending a specific constitutional form—one under which the few or the many would sway—he retreats and asserts that the main thing is just to ensure that reason sways. And if the main thing is just that *reason* sways, then it seems rather less important whether or not political powers are granted to one, few, or many.

Consider, too, the observation that "it may be well wonderd that any Nation styling themselves free, can suffer any man to pretend hereditarie right over them as thir lord; when as by acknowledging that right, they conclude themselves his servants and his vassals, and so renounce thir own freedom" (YP 7:427–28). The word *hereditarie* is an insertion in the second edition, and it introduces a significant qualification. As Robert Ayers observes of the passage in his notes to the first edition, "the implication is not strictly consonant with Milton's view clearly expressed elsewhere earlier, as in *Tenure*...where he concedes that a king may rule by right through delegation of powers by the people. Milton himself evidently recognized the inconsistency and so inserted 'hereditary' in the second edition" (363). "The insertion," Ayers observes in his notes to the second edition, "renders the revised version consistent with Milton's long-held belief that a king may rule by right through delegation of powers by the people" (427). A qualification of a slightly different nature is made later in the tract, after Milton claims that a Stuart restoration would result in another selfish king and another "endless tugging between petition of right and royal prerogative, especially about the negative voice, militia, or subsidies" (446): "I denie not," Milton writes, "but that ther may be such a king, who may regard the common good before his own, may have no vitious favorite, may hearken only to the wisest and incorruptest of his Parlament" (447–48). Government by this kind of king, Milton suggests, might not be so bad—the problem is just that "this rarely happens in a monarchie not elective" (448). But this way of putting it suggests that in elective monarchies, it is not so rare to have monarchs who take good counsel and govern with a view to the common good (as in fact the elected Roman kings, with the exception of Tarquin, did). After a diatribe against government by a single person (which was also inserted in the second edition), Milton again concedes that his case against monarchy in England holds, even if you "admitt, that monarchie of it self may be convenient to som nations" (449).

It is thus going too far to say that this tract amounts to an important document in the development and emergence of "republican exclusivism" in the political thought of Milton and western Europe at large, where this expression is taken to mean the doctrine that monarchy is always and in all circumstances an illegitimate form of government and that "republics are the only legitimate regimes." When in his earlier writings, including the *Commonplace Book*, Milton cites and comments on 1 Samuel 8, his main points are that kings are subject to civil laws and that humans have a natural and divine right to choose whatever form of government they wish, including monarchy, not that monarchy is a sin for all humans and always illegitimate for everyone.[12] Neither are these the points when, in *The Readie and Easie Way*, Milton simply notes in passing that "God in much displeasure gave a king to the *Israelites*, and imputed it a sin to them that they sought one" (YP 7:424), and that God did not listen to the Israelites when they complained to him about their first king, Saul (450). More importantly, Milton deploys a comparative vocabulary throughout the tract to describe and assess monarchies and commonwealths, a vocabulary that issues at best in the traditional republicanism defined by the view that republics are better than monarchies. The reading of this tract as a repudiation of monarchy in principle also fails to register the explicit concessions and qualifications Milton makes, and the way in which he directs his hostility mainly against a Stuart monarchy in England in 1660. This reading, moreover, takes as a literal expression of Milton's beliefs and "political thought" what is in fact a highly metaphorical and hyperbolic discourse that is driven mainly by his will to persuade and his disappointment and anger as his nation inclined toward restoring the Stuart monarchy.[13]

That *The Readie and Easie Way* is not a late step along Milton's way to republican exclusivism is, finally, clear from the tract that he published immediately following the appearance of the second edition. Responding to an incendiary royalist sermon that Matthew Griffith delivered on March 25 and published at the end of the month, Milton begins his *Brief Notes upon a Late Sermon* by identifying Griffith as one of those "deceivers" who, in *The Readie and Easie Way*, he had claimed was instilling "*the humor of returning to our old bondage.*"[14] Among the "many Notorious Wrestings of Scripture, and other Falsities" which Milton on the title page of the tract claims to find in Griffith's sermon, is the citation of 1 Samuel 8 to show that "so indissoluble is the Conjunction of God and the King" (YP 7:476). According to Milton, the Old Testament passage shows just that God was displeased with the Israelites for rejecting "a Commonwealth, wherein they might have livd happily under the Raign of God only, thir King" (476), and that "so unwilling was God to give them a King, So wide was the disjunction of God from a King" (476).

Milton then proceeds to discuss the main points he makes in connection with this passage in his earlier prose: "no form of Government" is dictated to the people by "the right of nature or right reason," and forms of government are therefore "but arbitrarie, and at all times in the choice of every free people, or thir representers" (YP 7:479). "This choice of Government," Milton again asserts, "is so essential to thir freedom, that longer then they have it, they are not free" (479). While arguing that "free Commonwealths" are "fittest and properest for civil, virtuous and industrious Nations," he also states that "monarchie" is in fact "fittest to curb degenerate, corrupt, idle, proud, luxurious people" (481–82). And if the English fall into this latter category, then, Milton concludes, they ought to choose "out of [their] own number one who hath best aided the people, and best merited against tyrannie the space of a raign or two" (482). This might permit them "to live happily anough, or tolerably" (482). Writing this shortly before the Restoration, Milton is not describing monarchy as idolatry and ruling it out for all peoples at all times. He is reaffirming his views that the value and legitimacy of the forms of government for any given people are relative to its moral condition, that peoples have a natural right to choose for themselves whatever form of government they wish, and that this freedom is the foundation of their civil freedom.

While Milton's critique of monarchy in *The Readie and Easie Way* thus does not measure up to the strict definition of *republicanism* in terms of the categorical repudiation of monarchy as a form of government, it does measure up to softer definitions of this word in terms of opposition to monarchy in one's own country at a certain time, or the view that a nonmonarchical constitution may be best for particular countries at particular times. But there is a different story to tell when it comes to the standing of this tract in relation to the more comprehensive definition of *republicanism* that I mentioned at the outset and which, as many have observed, strongly informs Milton's political writings of the 1650s.[15]

It seems that Milton would like those he is addressing to think that his proposals are in line with the practice of the great ancient and early modern republics, and the wisdom and prudence of those who described and celebrated them. He claims that, immediately following upon the creation of the Commonwealth in 1649, "the expressions both of armie and people, whether in thir publick declarations or several writings...testifi'd a spirit in this nation no less noble and well fitted to the liberty of a Commonwealth, then in the ancient *Greeks* or *Romans*" (YP 7:420). Recalling his own earlier prophetic visions of the English commonwealth as a new Roman republic, he cringes to think of how, if England did reestablish monarchy, all of Europe would scornfully ask, "where is this goodly tower of a Commonwealth, which the English boasted they would build to overshaddow kings, and be another *Rome* in the west?" (423).[16] He allies himself with Roman ideas of republican constitutional thought by frequently referring to the perpetual counsel he recommends as a "Senate" and its members as "Senators," and describing ancient Rome as well as other ancient political societies as ones that were governed by senates, the members of which sat for life (436, 442).

In Venice, too, Milton notes, "the true Senat, which upholds and sustains the government, is the whole aristocracie immovable" (YP 7:436). He claims an ancient Roman precedent for government without popular assembly (441–43), and lest his repudiation of single-person rule be thought "*Sectarian,*" he cites book 3 of Aristotle's *Politics* as a text that supports it (448–49). His proposal that "every countie in the land [be]...made a kinde of subordinate Commonaltie or Commonwealth" (458) within the federal commonwealth is, he argues, consistent with the practice of the ancient Athenians (460). And though he does not refer by name to Machiavelli, Milton deploys a vocabulary and mode of analysis that are, as some have noted, indebted to the early modern Florentine whose works he frequently cites in his *Commonplace Book.*[17]

These references and allusions to the Athenians, Spartans, Romans, Venetians, and Florentines, embodied by what Nicholas von Maltzahn calls "Milton's humanist rhetoric,"[18] define a discourse that is surely calculated to assuage the fears of the Harringtonians and other "republicans" and "commonwealthsmen." But this discourse conceals the extent to which in this tract Milton departs from and, indeed, challenges many major figures in republican tradition, especially those who are now widely seen as the primary sources of "English republicanism." This becomes clear if we recall what some of these figures say about monarchy, mixed constitutions, the tenure of political office, agrarian laws, civil liberty, religion, and human nature.

Milton's citation of book 3 of Aristotle's *Politics* as a text that supports his arguments must surely come as a surprise to anyone familiar with this purple passage of republican tradition and the ways in which Milton himself cites it in his earlier writings. For it is in this book of the *Politics* that Aristotle defines monarchy as the rule by one citizen of all other citizens of a political society, where these other citizens voluntarily submit to the rule of the one, that rule conforms with the principles of justice and the civil laws of the society, the armed guard of the one consists of his fellow citizens, and the one rules with the aim of serving the common interest. Defining monarchy in this way, and contrasting it with tyranny, Aristotle classifies it as a true form of government under which "freemen" may live the life of virtue and thus achieve the perfect and self-sufficing life that is the ultimate aim of all authentic political societies.[19] Aristotle also affirms in book 3 of the *Politics* the principle that "the good man has a right to rule because he is better" (1287b.11; see also 1325b.5–13). True, he observes that it was probably because "men of eminent virtue" were few "of old" that "the first governments were kingships," and that, in modern times when "cities have increased in size," "many persons equal in merit" are more commonly found (1286b.8–12). He nevertheless regards the existence of a man of preeminent virtue as a real possibility, one that poses a serious problem for political societies, and at the end of this book of the *Politics* he reasserts his view that rather than killing, ostracizing, or exiling such an individual, his fellow citizens ought to make him king (1288a.15–19; see also 1284b.25–34).

Milton, of course, knows all of this, and on earlier occasions he avails himself of this knowledge for entirely different purposes. In *A Defence*, for example, he cites book 3 of Aristotle's *Politics* not to denounce monarchy but to support views on natural law, meritocratic principle, the right of kings, and the punishment of tyrants, which in his mind justified those who killed the tyrant Charles Stuart.[20] In the *Second Defence*, Milton reasserts meritocratic principles (though without tying them explicitly to Aristotle's *Politics*), but this time with some other aims in mind: to defend the sway of the Independents in the lead-up to the tyrannicide and to justify the rule of the "single person" who assumed the office of Protector at the end of 1653.[21] Thus, though in *The Readie and Easie Way* Milton cites "the third of his [Aristotle's] Politics" to support his argument that since "a single person" is "the natural adversarie and oppressor of libertie," monarchy in England would be pernicious (YP 7:448–49), this argument in fact violates some of the major tenets of Aristotle's text, ones Milton explicitly cites in his earlier prose to justify the tyrannicide and the rule of various single persons.

Milton's proposals in *The Readie and Easie Way* are at odds with other passages in Aristotle that, along with writings of Plato and other ancient Greeks, stand at the origins of another idea that is central to republican tradition. Milton's "Grand Councel"

> must have the forces by sea and land committed to them for preservation of the common peace and libertie; must raise and manage the public revenue, at least with som inspectors deputed for satisfaction of the people, how it is imploid; must make or propose, as more expressly shall be said anon, civil laws; treat of commerce, peace, or warr with forein nations, and for the carrying on som particular affairs with more secrecie and expedition, must elect, as they have alreadie out of thir own number and others, a Councel of State. (YP 7:432–33)

True, Milton does not grant to this national council absolute judiciary and legislative powers. As he explains later in the tract, these powers are to be held mainly by "the nobilitie and chief gentry" in each county: they may "make thir own judicial laws, or use these that are, and execute them by thir own elected judicatures and judges without appeal, in all things of civil government between man and man. So they shall have justice in thir own hands, law executed fully and finally in thir own counties and precincts" (458–59). Though they may not propose legislation at a national level, a majority of counties may defeat legislation proposed by the grand council (459). The grand council will in some way be answerable to "inspectors," and there will be "certain limitations of thir power" (433, 444).

But these last two vague limitations on the power of the "Grand Councel" are both additions to the second edition and are clearly sops to the Harringtonians and others, such as Marchamont Nedham, who had or would have criticized Milton's proposals in the first edition: these limitations express not so much Milton's political thought as what he was willing to put up with in order to achieve consensus on the main issues of religious freedom and government without a single person and House of Lords. And even given these and the other limitations, "the administration of justice" in each county is not to be "supreme, but subordinate to the general power and union of the whole Republic" (YP 7:461); the "supreme autoritie" for legislation lies with the council (459), and each county will be "a kinde of subordinate Commonaltie or Commonwealth" (458) (another addition to the second edition). The political powers and activities of the counties, that is, will be subordinate to a unicameral governing body that will be elected on a limited franchise (459) and will have the lion's share of political powers.

Austin Woolrych and Martin Dzelzainis are quite right to challenge Zera Fink's view that these proposals conform to the idea of a mixed constitution (as presented by Aristotle, Polybius, Cicero, Machiavelli, and many others).[22] For though, in relation to the polemical aims of his earlier prose, Milton found the idea of the mixed constitution useful,[23] in relation to his aims in *The Readie and Easie Way* this idea was obviously rather inconvenient. In the first edition of this tract, Milton simply ignored the problem, but in the second, he acknowledges it: "it will be objected," he writes, "that in those places where they had perpetual Senats, they had also popular remedies against thir growing too imperious: as in *Athens*, besides *Areopagus*, another Senat of four or five hundred; in *Sparta*, the *Ephori*; in Rome, the Tribunes of the people" (YP 7:437–38). It would indeed have been objected by those who took republican tradition seriously that Milton's single "Grand Councel" unchecked by any popular assembly was dangerous. Many of the same people, moreover, would have objected that in political societies such as ancient Sparta and Rome, which had standing senates, there was also a single person, king, or magistracy (such as the consulship) that wielded "regal power" and that was a crucial component of the mix. Ignoring this second objection to his scheme, Milton moves to meet the first: "But the event tels us, that these remedies either little availd the people, or brought them to such a licentious and unbridl'd democratie, as in fine ruind themselves with thir own excessive power. So that the main reason urg'd why popular assemblies are to be trusted with the peoples libertie, rather then a Senat of principal men, because great men will be still endeavoring to inlarge thir power, but the common sort will be contented to maintain thir own libertie, is by experience found false" (438).

For Aristotle, Polybius, Cicero, Sallust, Machiavelli, and many others who are commonly considered members of republican tradition, "the event" and "experience" in fact did not show that popular assemblies or magistrates such as the Spartan ephors and the Roman tribunes led to ruin in short order. On the contrary, the strong consensus is that experience—what they also refer to as "history"—shows that such assemblies and magistrates are necessary in order to achieve long-term civil liberty and sociopolitical stability.[24] This is why both Harrington in *Oceana* (1656) and Nedham in *The Excellencie of a Free State* (1656) can so extensively cite this tradition in order to justify their opposition to unicameral government and their support for mixed constitutions that made a place for popular assemblies. And this is why the author of *The Censure of the Rota* can satirize Milton simply by impersonating Harrington and saying what Harrington would indeed have said of Milton's proposals for a single governing body: "you have really proposed the most ready and easie way to establish downright slavery upon the Nation that can possibly be contrived" (16).

Besides departing from book 3 of the *Politics* and the idea of a mixed constitution, Milton is at odds with the thinking of many figures in republican tradition when he proposes a "perpetual Senat," a powerful national governing council the members of which would hold office for life. It is true, as he observes, that the members of the Roman senate during the republican period (and the members of the Spartan *gerousia*) held office for life, and though they were often extremely critical of the way these bodies behaved, the ancient republicans did not object to them in principle. But this was because the members of the Roman senate were not strictly speaking magistrates but *ex*-magistrates and other prominent Roman citizens; its main job, in principle, was to advise the consuls and other magistrates; it exercised its power mainly by way of influencing and controlling in a variety of ways those magistrates who were formally granted specific political powers; and, most important of all, these other magistrates limited and checked in various ways the senate's exercise of power (it was the consuls, for example, who commanded the military). The ancient republicans, moreover, felt that it was of great importance that the tenure of those who did hold office was limited. When in the *Politics*, for example, Aristotle turns from considering the causes of revolution to consider "what means there are of preserving constitutions in general" (1307b26), he observes that "the short tenure of office" is among the most important (1308a18–24). After narrating the history of Rome during the regal period, from Romulus down to the expulsion of Tarquin the Proud in 509, Livy begins the second book of his great work by noting that the civil liberty which was established in 509 really depended not on the abolition of the regal power, but on the limited tenure of those two magistrates—the consuls—to whom that power was *transferred* upon the abolition of monarchy: "one might more correctly say that the birth of liberty was owing to the annual nature of the consuls' tenure than to any lessening of the power the kings had possessed." And in the preface to *The War with Catiline*, Sallust provides a similar description of this moment in Roman history: "when the rule of the kings, which at first had tended to preserve freedom and advance the state, had degenerated into a lawless tyranny, they altered their form of government and appointed two rulers with annual power, thinking that this device would prevent men's minds from growing arrogant through unlimited authority."[25]

Livy reasserts the importance of the limited tenure of magistrates' offices in his account of the decemvirate, the ten men who, after the Romans had suspended all other magistracies, were appointed for a period of one year in 451 BC to rule the country and codify its laws (3:33–39). In his great commentary on Livy's history of Rome, Machiavelli sees the decemvirate's rapid descent into arrogance and tyranny as just further evidence of what happens when you fail to have some kind of mixed constitutional arrangement.[26] But he also emphasizes that the granting of political powers to such a small number of men who were unchecked by other magistrates might not have been so detrimental had not the Roman populace permitted the office itself to exist beyond the one-year term they had initially set for it, and allowed some men to hold that office for more than one year (197). It turns out, moreover, that granting unchecked political powers even to good men will be dangerous, for as Machiavelli also observes, "absolute power will very soon corrupt" any material "by making friends and partisans" (196; see also 217). Machiavelli is thus forced to qualify his earlier statement that authority granted by free suffrage (such as that granted by the Romans to the decemvirs) never harms any republic by observing that this holds only so long as "a people is never persuaded to give it except under certain conditions and for a specified time" (198). Machiavelli returns to this theme of the dangers of unlimited or even prolonged tenure of office in his discussion of the censorship (230) and, indeed, the fall of Rome (473–74).

Milton knew perfectly well that Harrington and his followers, who took Machiavelli and his ancients more seriously than he did on this occasion, feared that "long continuance of power" (YP 7:434) would corrupt the members of anything like his unicameral governing body, and that they hence, at least since 1656 when *Oceana* appeared, were proposing mixed constitutions which granted only limited tenures of office.[27] He must have known, moreover, that in *The Excellencie of a Free State,* Nedham cites Aristotle, Plutarch, Cicero, Sallust, Livy, and Machiavelli to support the argument that since "long continuance in power" always results in corruption, faction, and tyranny, political societies ought to outlaw all "standing powers" and establish constitutions that call for continual "motion" in the holding of office.[28] Milton brushes these fears and arguments aside with a curt observation of resemblance: "but I could wish that this wheel or partial wheel in State, if it be possible, might be avoided; as having too much affinitie with the wheel of fortune" (435).

On a more serious note, he observes that there is no need to fear "a perpetual Senat" if "the well-affected either in a standing armie, or in a setled militia have thir arms in thir own hands" (YP 7:435), and if there are "ordinarie assemblies...in the chief towns of every countie" (443). Though, at the end of the tract, he suggests he might go along with some kind or rotation if others still feared "a perpetual sitting" (461), he clearly feels it is unnecessary. In saying all of this, Milton has it seems at least backed off from his earlier proposal (in *A Letter to a Friend* [written October 20, 1659] and *Proposalls of certaine expedients* [written some time between October 20 and December 26, 1659])[29] that life tenure be given to military commanders, a proposal that Machiavelli would have thought madness coming from anyone concerned with English civil liberties at the time. But neither would Machiavelli and the Romans have seen the limitations Milton places upon it as being anywhere near sufficient to prevent his powerful perpetual senate, unchecked by any other federal magistrates, from drifting toward arrogance and tyranny.

Milton is just as cavalier in his dismissal of another important aspect of the political thought which Harrington outlines in *Oceana* and which has deep roots in republican tradition. For one of the reasons Milton thinks his way of establishing a commonwealth in England is so ready and easy is that it requires "no perilous, no injurious alteration of circumscription of mens lands and proprieties; secure, that in this Commonwealth, temporal and spiritual lords remov'd, no man or number of men can attain to such wealth or vast possession, as will need the hedge of an Agrarian law (never succesful, but the cause rather of sedition, save only where it began seasonably with first possession) to confine them from endangering our public libertie" (YP 7:445–46).

Dismissing the need for laws that would limit the amount of land Englishmen could privately own once there were no "temporal and spiritual lords," Milton may reasonably be seen to follow Livy, Cicero, and other Romans whose sympathies lay with the patricians and who therefore opposed laws that decreased patrician or increased plebeian land ownership.[30] But there is a major difference of opinion *within* republican tradition on this issue, so that Milton's dismissal also diverges from many of the most powerful republicans. Thus, while observing that different property arrangements will suit different individuals and societies, Aristotle displays a strong inclination to favor societies in which private ownership of land is limited by law, and where existing inequities in the ownership of private property are "equalized." This is mainly because he holds that "civil troubles arise...out of the inequality of property" (1266b36–37), and that laws that ensure that citizens hold moderate and equal amounts of property are conducive to the life of moral virtue.[31] Polybius, too, supports laws that restrict the private ownership of land. In book 6 of the *Histories*, for example, he argues that in Sparta there were "land laws by which no citizen may own more than another, but all must possess an equal share of the public land."[32] "The equal division of landed property," he observes, "and the simple and common diet were calculated to produce temperance in the private lives of the citizens and to secure the commonwealth as a whole from civil strife" (6.48.3–4). In his life of Lycurgus, Plutarch confirms Polybius's view that these agrarian laws were effective in achieving these aims. It thus comes as no surprise that Plutarch also provides a favorable account of not only the Spartan kings, Agis and Cleomenes, who attempted to restore agrarian laws, but also Tiberius and Gaius Gracchus who attempted to establish such laws in Rome.[33]

Nelson plausibly argues that these authors form the foundation of an essentially "Greek tradition in republican thought," one that is distinct from the Roman republican tradition, which is grounded in Livy and Cicero and which, out of a conception of justice as the nonviolation of private property and a conception of the preservation of private property as the principal *rationale* of political society, is hostile to agrarian laws. There are in addition, as Nelson rightly observes, some notable exceptions to this way of discriminating between different strands in republican tradition, one of which is Milton's favorite ancient Roman historian.[34] In *The War with Jugurtha*, Sallust, who had himself been a tribune, expresses considerable sympathy for the Gracchi and their attempts at agrarian reform.[35] And though Machiavelli sees the *conflict* that arose over the agrarian reform laws championed by the Gracchi as one of the principal causes of the downfall of the republic, he by no means follows Cicero in condemning the Gracchi's commitment to these laws. On the contrary, he is closer to Sallust on this issue and clearly thinks that the Gracchi had the right idea, even if they went about implementing it in a way that was imprudent. Throughout the *Discourses*, Machiavelli asserts that preventing citizens from amassing large amounts of wealth and property—public lands or not—is essential to any republic's enjoying sociopolitical stability and civil freedom, and achieving empire.[36] Thus, though in dismissing the need for the "hedge of an Agrarian law" Milton may reasonably be seen to conform with Livy, Cicero, and their descendants, he diverges from another major strand of republican tradition, one that is grounded in the ancient Greek philosophers and historians but also one that includes two of the authors who are usually seen as major sources of "Milton's republicanism"—Sallust and Machiavelli.

Even if "the neo-Roman theory of liberty" identified by Philip Pettit, Quentin Skinner, and Dzelzainis informs Milton's thinking about civil liberty as these authors argue,[37] it is important to see that in *The Readie and Easie Way* Milton significantly departs from republican tradition on this issue. In proposing government by a national unicameral body, Milton proposes a form of government that many major figures in the tradition would have felt would in short order become an oligarchy that would rule in its own interests and deny the populace its civil liberties. That the members of this body sit for life would, in the eyes of most of these figures, only compound the problem and accelerate the progression to tyranny by the few. Milton thus differs in a fundamental way from republican tradition in his thinking about the constitutional conditions under which a populace may enjoy civil liberty over the long term.

Milton is also at odds with tradition on the question of how best to deal with a populace that has become immature or corrupt and therefore unfit for civil liberty. Though they might have been fit for liberty in the early 1650s, the English people, now inclined to restore monarchy, are in Milton's eyes no longer fit for it in 1660: "for this extold and magnif'd nation...to fall back or rather to creep back so poorly as it seems the multitude would to thir once abjur'd and detested thraldom of Kingship...argues a strange degenerate contagion suddenly spread among us fitted and prepar'd for new slaverie" (YP 7:422). True, not all are infected: "that part of the nation," Milton later writes, "which consents not" with those who would restore monarchy is, "of a great number, far worthier then by their means to be brought into the same bondage" (428). And, indeed, Milton writes and publishes in part with the aim of addressing these worthies. But he cannot conceal his pessimism on this count. At the opening of the tract, he observes "this noxious humor of returning to bondage, instilld of late by som deceivers and nourishd from bad principles and fals apprehensions among too many of the people" (407–08). One reason he opposes unrestricted popular elections to the senate is that when he listens to the populace now, he hears "the noise and shouting of a rude multitude" (442). At the end of the tract, he claims he does not doubt that, in his country, "ther be many wise men in all places and degrees, but am sorrie the effects of wisdom are so little seen among us" (462). Though he hopes to have persuaded an "abundance of sensible and ingenuous men," the English people are still like the Israelites who "chose them a captain back for *Egypt*." They are "rushing" back to captivity as a "torrent" that is "impetuous," and the virtuous few must avoid the "precipice of destruction the deluge of this epidemic madness would hurrie us through the general defection of a misguided and abus'd multitude" (463).

Thus, while Milton does not write off the English populace entirely, he hyperbolically depicts them as an immature, impetuous, servile, ignorant people who, demanding the return to "regal bondage," have become unfit for civil liberty. How does he propose to deal with this populace? By getting the virtuous minority to *deny* them their wish for regal bondage and *force* liberty upon them by establishing a free commonwealth in England. And he provides an explicit rationale for this course of action:

> if the greater part value not [freedom], but will degeneratly forgoe [it], is it just or reasonable, that most voices against the main end of government should enslave the less number that would be free? More just it is doubtless, if it com to force, that a less number compell a greater to retain, which can be no wrong to them, thir libertie, then that a greater number for the pleasure of thir baseness, compell a less most injuriously to be thir fellow slaves. They who seek nothing but thir own just libertie, have alwaies right to winn it and to keep it, when ever they have power, be the voices never so numerous that oppose it. (YP 7:455)

Such a statement runs counter to the thinking of some of the leading ancient Roman republicans. When, for example, in the second book of *On the Republic*, Cicero has Scipio provide an account of "the birth, growth, and maturity of our state,"[38] he provides a glowing account of the kings (with the exception of Tarquin the Proud, who was not really a king but a tyrant). This is because he sees monarchy as an appropriate form of government for an immature, uncivilized people (such as the first Romans) who are unprepared for the kind of civil liberty citizens enjoy under republican constitutions. Rather than lamenting that a Lucius Junius Brutus had not come along earlier to establish a republic, Scipio affirms the 244-year-long monarchy as a government that was appropriate for the immature and bellicose Romans and that enabled them to mature into a people who were ready for more extensive—but still very limited—civil liberties afforded by the early republic. Similarly, Livy observes that Lucius Junius Brutus "would have done a grievous wrong to the state if out of a premature desire for liberty he had wrested rule from one of the earlier kings" (2.1). Like Cicero, Livy clearly thinks that one *can* do wrong to others by forcing civil liberty upon them, and that anyone who had taken this course of action with the Roman populace when it was "immature" would have done such wrong to Rome (2.1).

There are many passages in the *Discourses* that indicate that Machiavelli, too, would have questioned both Milton's proposals for dealing with the immature or servile English multitude and the justification he provides for them. Though he sometimes seems to agree with the Ciceronian/Livian story of the development of the immature, uncivilized Roman populace during the regal period, Machiavelli also suggests that the achievement of civil liberty under the republic was an "accident" that was lucky to survive (153). His commentary on Livy's narrative highlights the *difficulty* with which Rome managed to maintain the nonmonarchical constitution that was established in 509, after the people had grown accustomed to living under monarchy. And when he considers a populace that has become corrupt, he is far from optimistic concerning the possibility of imposing civil liberties upon it: "if in a state which is on the decline owing to the corruption of its material a renaissance is ever to be brought about, it will be by the virtue of some one person who is then living, not by the virtue of the public as a whole, that good institutions are kept up, and, as soon as such a person is dead, they will relapse into their former habits" (159; see also 132, 246–47). Because "it is just as difficult and dangerous to try to free a people that wants to remain servile as it is to enslave a people that wants to remain free" (429), Machiavelli surmises that the chances of success in either enterprise is low, and suggests that it is foolhardy even to try.

True, when he was composing the first edition of *The Readie and Easie Way*, Milton may well have had General Monck in mind as part of his audience, and in the days following the publication of the first edition of the tract, he composed but apparently did not send a letter urging the general to bring about a free commonwealth by implementing his "faithful Veteran Army, so ready" if need be.[39] But by early April, when the second edition appeared, it seems likely, as Knoppers observes, that "Milton must have realized that Monck would not act to save the Commonwealth."[40] And neither the first nor the second edition of *The Readie and Easie Way* amounts to a call for "some one person" to seize absolute power and exercise it to establish a free commonwealth. On this occasion, that is, Milton is not about to follow Machiavelli who, at the end of *The Prince*, exhorts the Medici family to produce a single man, "a liberator," who would save his country, as Moses, Cyrus, and Theseus had saved theirs.[41] Neither does he follow Harrington, who imagines a single great man, Olphaus Megaletor, legislating the commonwealth of Oceana into existence. And his insistence that it would be *"easie"* to establish forever a free commonwealth for a populace that, for whatever reason, had become immature, mad, or servile flies in the face of those perceptions of the great *difficulty*, if not futility and destructiveness, of doing so which we find in Machiavelli and his ancients—though this insistence on how easy it could all be is surely just one more case of Miltonic hyperbole in the service of persuasion.

Milton also departs from some major republican thinkers on the issue of religion. Early in the tract, he observes in passing that "the best part of our libertie...is our religion" (YP 7:420); near the end of it, he refers to "this liberty of conscience which above all other things ought to be to all men dearest and most precious" (456). Why is this particular freedom so important? Because

> the whole freedom of man consists either in spiritual or civil libertie. As for spiritual, who can be at rest, who can enjoy any thing in this world with contentment, who hath not libertie to serve God and to save his own soul, according to the best light which God hath planted in him to that purpose, by the reading of his reveal'd will and the guidance of his holy spirit? That this is best pleasing to God, and that the whole Protestant Church allows no supream judge or rule in matters of religion, but the scriptures, and these to be interpreted by the scriptures themselves, which necessarily inferrs liberty of conscience, I have heretofore prov'd at large in another treatise. (456)

One might reasonably infer from this passage that Milton believes that the things of greatest value to humans are not only pleasing God and the salvation of their souls, but also peace and the enjoyment of things in this world. And he asserts that our peace and enjoyment in this world depend upon our serving God in the way we believe will please him and lead to the salvation of our own souls. These beliefs about God and salvation ought to be based solely on our own reading and understanding of Scripture, and these acts ought to be performed solely on the basis of our own intelligence and the guidance we receive from God. The freedom from other individuals, churches, judges, and governments to read Scripture in this way, to formulate beliefs about God solely on the basis of these acts, and to serve God on the basis of these beliefs is thus of great *instrumental* value. For this freedom is necessary to, though not sufficient for, our attainment of those things that are of the greatest value to humans. Any institution or individual that claims to be a judge in matters of religion and imposes rules that govern the reading and inter-pretation of Scripture, belief about God, or the act of worship impinges upon this freedom. Milton's proposals for a free commonwealth thus do not include proposals for any such institutions or judges, though they do include proposals for county "schools and academies" that would "spread much more knowledge and civilitie, yea religion through all parts of the land" (460). His proposals are thus consistent with his other "treatise," *A Treatise of Civil Power* (February 1659), in which he argued for limited separation of church and state.[42]

Again Milton runs counter to the prevailing view of the republicans we have so far considered. In book 6 of the *Histories,* Polybius points to not just the Romans' mixed constitution, but also their "religious convictions" in order to account for their achievement (6.56.6–7). It is "superstition," Polybius explains, "which maintains the cohesion of the Roman State. These matters are clothed in such pomp and introduced to such an extent into their public and private life that nothing could exceed it" (7–8). Polybius affirms this superstition on grounds that it "held in" the wild Roman populace "by invisible terrors and suchlike pageantry" (11–12), and made the Roman magistrates who dealt with money "maintain correct conduct just because they have pledged their faith by oath" (12–15).

Cicero, too, praises those political societies, such as ancient Rome, that, having understood the utility religion can have for the welfare of political societies, institutionalized and strictly regulated religious life and integrated it with citizenship and the government of the society at large. Thus, in *On the Republic*, Scipio praises Numa for introducing and arranging various ecclesiastical offices, introducing the laws that were to govern religious worship and ritual in Rome, and devising "many rituals which had to be learned by heart and adhered to" (2.26–27). Instituting "fairs and games" along with the state religion, Numa "established on a firm basis those two factors which, above all others, ensure that states will last, namely religion and humane behaviour" (2.27). In *On Laws*, Cicero again observes the importance of religious ideas, not because they are true or lead to salvation, but because they are so useful to the business of a thriving republic: "who would deny," he asks, "that these ideas are useful, bearing in mind how many contracts are strengthened by the swearing of oaths, how valuable religious scruples are for guaranteeing treaties, how many people are restrained from crime by the fear of divine retribution, and how sacred a thing a partnership of citizens is when the immortal gods are admitted to that company as judges or witnesses?"[43] And it is because he values religion for these reasons that Cicero includes extensive laws governing religious belief and practice when he outlines a legal code "not just for the Roman people, but for all good and stable communities" (2.18–69).

Though there is considerable difference of opinion concerning Machiavelli's own religious commitments and how they impinge upon his political thought,[44] it is clear that he endorses much of what Polybius and Cicero observe about the place of religion in a well-ordered republic. In the five sections on the religion of the ancient Romans in book 1 of the *Discourses*, Machiavelli, too, praises Numa for having "turned to religion as the instrument necessary above all others for the maintenance of a civilized state, and so constituted it that there was never for so many centuries so great a fear of God as there was in this republic" (139). It was this religion, detailed and favorable descriptions of which Machiavelli found in not just Polybius and Cicero but also Livy and Plutarch,[45] that "facilitated whatever enterprise the senate and the great men of Rome designed to undertake" (139), and that "helped in the control of armies, in encouraging the plebs, in producing good men, and in shaming the bad" (140). He clearly approves, moreover, of the ways in which the religious officials involved in auguries were also involved "in the election of consuls, in entering upon military enterprises, in leading forth their armies, on engaging in battles, and in all their important enterprises, whether civic or military" (148). In light of the Roman experience, Machiavelli strongly recommends that rulers enforce the national religion, whatever it happens to be, and regardless of whether or not it is true: "those princes and those republics which desire to remain free from corruption, should above all else maintain incorrupt the ceremonies of their religion, and should hold them always in veneration" (142); they "should uphold the basic principles of the religion which they practise in," even if "they be convinced that it is quite fallacious" (143).

Judging from the proposals he forwards in *The Readie and Easie Way*, Milton agrees with these republican thinkers that the religious beliefs and practices of a populace are of great importance to its ethical quality and, so, to its capacity for being a citizenry of a flourishing republic. But whereas earlier republicans stress the value of religious belief and practice in relation to the maintenance of a flourishing republic, Milton stresses the value of the establishment and maintenance of a republic in relation to the maintenance of freedom of religious belief and practice. Indeed, one of his principal arguments for the establishment of "a free Commonwealth" is that there is "no government more inclinable not to favor only but to protect" liberty of conscience (YP 7:456).

Polybius, Livy, Cicero, Plutarch, and Machiavelli generally hold that national institutions organized and operated by state-maintained officials who are empowered to impose significant penalties (including death) upon those who violate the religious beliefs and practices they promote and conduct are *effective* means of inculcating and maintaining those religious beliefs and practices in a populace. They hold, moreover, that it is *legitimate* for such institutions both to threaten to impose and to impose penalties to achieve these ends. At least in the other treatise to which he refers in *The Readie and Easie Way*, Milton holds that such institutions are both *ineffective* at doing so (indeed they promote only hypocrisy and heresy), and *illegitimate* means of controlling religious belief and practice. The republicans display little concern with the truth of the national religion and speak with equanimity of the prudent manipulation of superstition, fallacious religion, and the pretense to divine inspiration for ends of state. Milton ranks superstition and fallacious religion with tyranny as one of the principal "usurpers over mankinde" (YP 7:421) and will not contemplate their deployment, no matter how "useful" they might be to magistrates who want men to honor their contracts and fight well. For the republicans, the more pomp, pageantry, and public ceremony in religion the better; Milton finds such things repellent. The republicans generally view favourably political societies, such as Rome, in which ecclesiastical officials are involved in the running of the state; Milton wants church officials out of government. The republicans (and Harringtonians)[46] generally endorse national churches that define and promote the national religion; Milton repudiates them and therefore makes no place for them in his proposals for a free Christian commonwealth in England.

Many of the differences between Milton and the republicans we have been observing are grounded in a difference on a more fundamental issue. As many scholars have observed, an important, if not defining, element of republican tradition is the idea of man as a *zōon politikon*, a political animal that fulfills itself and lives the best, most fulfilling, and successful life it can only by way of participating in government and the administration of justice—only by way of living the life of citizenship as Aristotle defines it in book 3 of *Politics*. But they also think of this political animal as one who is highly mutable, one both educable in virtue, but also—even at his or her best—susceptible to arrogance and corruption. It is in part on the basis of this vision of human beings that they insist on mixed constitutions and limited tenure of office (the second of which not only counteracts human tendencies to corruption, but also provides the opportunity to all citizens to fulfill their nature).

There are several indications in *The Readie and Easie Way* that Milton does not share this vision of humanity. As we have seen, he asserts that the freedom to believe and worship as one sees fit, not the freedom to hold office, is the most important and valuable freedom for English men and women, and humans at large. This is because he believes that humans fulfill themselves and achieve what for them are the chief ends of existence (one of which is the salvation of one's soul) not through citizenship but through right religious belief and practice. Because he sees humanity in this way, he is not concerned that only "the nobilitie and chief gentry" in each county will "bear part in the government, make thir own judicial laws...and execute them" (YP 7:458–59). Responding to those who might object to being excluded from government at the national level, Milton testily concedes that "if the ambition of such as think themselves injur'd that they also partake not of the government, and are impatient till they be chosen, cannot brook the perpetuitie of others chosen before them," then there might be some kind of rotation (434). The idea that one might object to a perpetual senate on grounds that it would prevent one from partaking in activities that are essential to the fulfillment of one's nature and the achievement of the ends of human existence seems not to occur to Milton at this time.

True, one reason Milton endorses a unicameral and perpetual governing body is that "in a free Commonwealth, any governor or chief counselor offending, may be remov'd and punishd without the least commotion" (YP 7:426–27), though he is noticeably thin on the details of how this would be done. But another reason he endorses government by such a body is that, however unreliable and corrupt a populace may be, he does not really believe that good men go bad. Thus, he is obviously impatient with those who, fearing that "long continuance of power may corrupt sincerest men," insist on rotation (434). He presents a highly condensed, idiosyncratic history of the Roman republic to refute the view that "great men will be still endeavoring to inlarge thir power" (438) and to support the idea that "a Senat of principal men" can "be trusted with the peoples libertie" (438). Does not the entire tract make clear that, like the prophet Jeremiah and the sublime old railer Juvenal, he himself is incorruptible? Whereas the republicans tend to think of human beings as political animals and the virtuous men as men who are still susceptible to corruption, Milton thinks that humans achieve their ends by serving God well, and that virtuous men such as himself will stand fast, though worlds judge them perverse. It is because he differs from the republicans in this way that he is not so worried about granting so much power to so few, for so long.

In *The Readie and Easie Way*, then, Milton departs from many of the views expressed by Aristotle, Polybius, Cicero, Livy, Sallust, Plutarch, and their great early modern Florentine student and innovator, Machiavelli, on major issues such as monarchy, mixed constitutions, the tenure of political office, agrarian laws, civil liberty, religion, and human nature. This observation helps us to understand the rhetoric of this tract, the passions and beliefs that drive it, and some of the responses it provokes. Milton in many ways gives the impression that his proposals *are* in the spirit of the great ancient Spartan, Athenian, and Roman republics, as well as the early modern Venetian and Dutch republics. But this is merely a tactic he adopts in part to achieve some degree of persuasive power in relation to the various types of "republican" and "commonwealthsman" he is addressing. That he adopts such a tactic also further supports the view that, even in the second edition of the tract, Milton is still in the game of persuasion and is not simply bearing witness against a fallen people. Recognizing Milton's departures from republican tradition on major issues also helps us to understand the concessive but still argumentative stance he takes toward the Harringtonians, Nedhamites, and others whose proposals for settling a free commonwealth in England were more deeply informed by republican tradition than his were. Allied with them in opposing the restoration of a Stuart monarchy in England he may be, but because he does not take ancient Graeco-Roman and Machiavellian prudence on board as they do, Milton must oppose many of their central proposals, though without using the graphic and vehement vituperation he reserves for the royalists and the multitude. This recognition, finally, helps us to understand why the clever author of *The Censure of the Rota* could effectively satirize Milton simply by assuming the persona of Harrington and imagining what he and his followers at the Rota would have thought of *The Readie and Easie Way*. Part of the joke is that Milton's proposals would be rejected by royalists and republicans alike.

These observations also have significant consequences for the terms and categories we ought to adopt to describe and understand *The Readie and Easie Way*. If all we mean by *republican* is someone who repudiates monarchy in one's own country at a particular time, then it is fair enough to use this term to refer to the author of *The Readie and Easie Way*. While Milton's critique of monarchy is hyperbolic, and while he makes several important concessions, he is hostile to the reestablishment of monarchy in his own country in 1660. If, however, we use the term *republican* to refer to someone who has genuine and comprehensive commitments to a tradition of political thought that runs from Aristotle to Machiavelli and beyond, then the use of this term to refer to Milton on this occasion is highly misleading. For on the occasion that he comes out most strongly against monarchy, Milton also departs most sharply from this tradition. Our observations about how this tract is related to republican tradition, moreover, must surely give us pause before we lump it in with those texts that express the "body of ideas" which for Worden and others define "English republicanism."[47] For in opposing mixed constitutions, rotation, agrarian laws, national churches, popular elections, and popular participation in government, Milton in this tract opposes some of the main ideas of other English republicans of the time, such as Harrington and Nedham.

The University of New South Wales

Pirating Paradise: Alexander the Great, the Dutch East Indies, and Satanic Empire in *Paradise Lost*

Su Fang Ng

> But if it be only matter of conquest, then it is a great robbery; as a pirate said to Alexander that he was a great robber, he was but a petty robber.
>
> —Charles I, on the scaffold

It has been some years now since David Quint's groundbreaking monograph, *Epic and Empire,* which, among other things, considers Milton's allusions to Luís de Camões's *Os Lusíadas* that characterizes Satan as another Vasco da Gama.[1] The time seems ripe to take another look at Milton and empire in the context of European voyages of discovery to the East. Current scholarly interest in early modern England's transactions with Islam and the East, which has energized studies of Renaissance drama, has not had the same impact on Milton studies. Rather, Milton criticism tends to focus on the Americas, which though important do not pose an equal challenge to the narrative of an ascendant West as do Eastern empires. Early modernists "re-orienting" the Renaissance find Europeans threatened by the expansionist Ottoman Empire or playing supplicants at the Mughal court.[2] At least in terms of explicit reference, Milton's writings seem obdurate material for analyzing Asian and Islamic influences. Gerald MacLean finds Milton largely silent about both Islam and the Ottomans, while Robert Markley shows Milton rejecting evidence that China was populated before the Flood to insist on the higher authority of the Mosaic books. Nonetheless, Asia is crucial in Milton's views of empire: though focusing on the Asia of antiquity, primarily of Near Eastern biblical lands, John Archer argues, "*Paradise Lost*...places the Restoration within the cycle of [tyrannical] Asian empires...[and] criticizes commercial ambition as well as the hunger for territory."[3] In particular, Asia constitutes a major context for understanding Milton's Satan: for, as Quint has shown, Satan's epic journey reprises da Gama's celebrated discovery of the sea route to India.

Thus shaping Milton's view of empire, Asia is important in *Paradise Lost*, particularly since both Milton's characterization of Satan as Indies merchant and his relation to empire continue to raise questions. Puzzled by the seeming incompatibility of Satan's dual characterization as emperor and merchant, Blair Hoxby finds that "Satan wavers between warrior and merchant, sovereign and commoner."[4] Adding to the perplexity is the issue of God's resemblance to Satan, which makes problematic the argument that Milton is a poet against empire simply because Satan is an imperialist monarch. Milton famously depicts both God and Satan as monarchs. One approach to this difficulty is the Empsonian attack on Milton's God as wicked. However, a theodicy would be unlikely to reject God so thoroughly. Scholars wishing not to challenge Milton's God distinguish between good and bad kings, earthly and divine spheres.[5] Nevertheless, the many kings populating *Paradise Lost* make it difficult to separate God's monarchy from fallen ones: as David Norbrook comments, "Milton seems to go out of his way to blur distinctions."[6]

Empire too has divided critics, who cannot agree on whether Milton supports or opposes imperialism. Rome serves as both model and negative example as Milton distinguishes republican from imperial Rome; yet it was the Roman republic that expanded into a Mediterranean-wide empire. David Armitage argues that Milton's reading of Machiavelli and Roman historians and poets such as Sallust and Juvenal taught him that imperial expansion threatened liberty as the Romans became corrupted by luxury. But, as Blair Worden and Andrew Barnaby show, Milton shifted from seeing Rome as worthy of imitation to rejecting it completely in *Paradise Regained*. Nor are Milton's views on contemporary empires any clearer. Despite his support of Cromwell's Western Design and of the subjugation of Ireland, Milton seems critical of empire, even sympathetic to the plight of Native Americans.[7] Martin Evans's study of colonial imagery in *Paradise Lost* finds Milton thoroughly ambivalent, with Satan representing both Spanish conquistadors and duplicitous Indians, while Adam and Eve represent the positive images of English settlers and good-natured Indians. Paul Stevens attempts to resolve the issue of how *Paradise Lost* "authorizes colonial activity even while it satirizes the abuses of early modern colonialism" by arguing for a distinction between good and bad colonialism. Finding Milton's geographical imagination to be imperialist, Bruce McLeod argues that the "adventurer represented national endeavor, Protestant idealism, and bourgeois industry."[8]

Satan's link to Asia through Vasco da Gama, the negative exemplar of an adventurer, offers another perspective. I want to return to the context of Asia so fruitfully raised by Quint. In particular, I want to take up his suggestion that the new seventeenth century commercial rivalry between the United Provinces and England lies behind Milton's "indictment of European expansion and colonialism that includes his own countrymen and contemporaries" and that "Milton may be aware of the implication for epic poetry of the emergence of a merchant class whose interests had begun to shape the imperial destinies of the nation."[9] I argue that Satan's dual characterization as emperor and merchant is best understood within the context of early modern maritime empires, a context in which monarchs also acted as merchants in having a share of the overseas trade.

While warning against searching for Milton's views of empire in the imagery of *Paradise Lost*, Robert Fallon argues that in the 1650s Milton "kept his attention, like Cromwell's, eastward toward the Continent, where trade with wealthy and powerful neighbors was the prime concern of his superiors in government, leaving him little inclination to look over his shoulder at the relatively insignificant English colonies in the New World."[10] The eastward orientation of Milton's attention, I suggest, goes beyond Western Europe. During the Interregnum and into the Restoration, England looked to the Continent, to its sister republic the Low Countries, for a trade model of empire. This empire of trade was critiqued by Milton.[11] Milton's views of the East are inseparable from his concerns about European politics, especially the problem of monarchical tyranny: the status of Asia, the issue of the Dutch Indies trade, and the problem of tyrannical empire are intertwined. Asia was a significant context for intra-European relations. How deep Milton's interest was in the Indies is debatable, but European political relations mattered to him, and the Indies were a major sphere in which Europeans came into conflict not only with non-Europeans but also with one another. These fraught relations, played out in the foreign space of the Indian Ocean, are among the concerns of *Paradise Lost*.

At the same time, the classical tradition is never far from Milton's awareness. So it is with his depiction of Asia: while alluding to contemporary events, he reaches back to the ancient world for poetic images. The classical figure arguably most associated with Asia is Alexander the Great. Milton's source, Camões's *Os Lusíadas*, makes several allusions to Alexander, including two instances when the poet intrudes to emphasize the importance of poetry, recalling Alexander's envy of Achilles not for his deeds but for a Homer who memorialized them and in turn promising to be Homer to King Sebastião's Alexander.[12] Camões depicts Alexander's Indian conquests as forerunner to Portuguese exploration. Thus, Bacchus complains to Jove about the invasion of his domain of India:

> Unto the son of PHILIP it is true
> Such pow're the GODS did in those parts afford,
> 'Twas one with *Him*, to *See*, and to *subdue*,
> And MARS himself did homage to his *Sword*.
> But can it be indur'd, that to so *Few*
> FATE such stupendious puissance should accord,
> That *that* of MACEDON, of ROME, and MINE,
> The LUSITANIAN GLORY should *out-shine?*   (1.75)

Highlighting the contrast between Alexander, favored by the gods, and the unpromising Portuguese band, Bacchus is reconciled to Alexander's success but cannot bear that the small kingdom of Portugal would overshadow previous empires. Clearly, Alexander becomes a model for European exploration in the Indies.

Nonetheless, Alexander is an ambivalent figure—both model emperor and the moralist's exemplar of overweening ambition. He appears as the latter in *Paradise Regained*. Satan tries to goad Jesus into action by pointing out how far short of Alexander he falls: "Thy years are ripe, and over-ripe, the Son / Of *Macedonian Philip* had e're these / Won *Asia* and the Throne of *Cyrus* held / At his dispose" (*PR* 3.31–34). The ambivalence is perfectly captured by a much-repeated Ciceronian anecdote trans-mitted through Augustine about Alexander's encounter with a pirate, which, I argue, underlies the Satan of *Paradise Lost*. This classical anec-dote sharpens Milton's representation of Satan as merchant-adventurer, for it compares the conquests of Alexander—the archetypal conqueror of Asia—to robbery. The depiction of Satan as both oriental tyrant and Indies merchant, as emperor and pirate, are not two differing or contra-dictory characterizations but aspects of the same thing: tyranny.

Milton and the Dutch

For Milton, debates about empire were shaped by contact with Asia. He associated despotism with the East, stereotyping Asians as servile. In *Pro populo anglicano defensio,* Milton notes Aristotle's and Cicero's opinion "that the peoples of Asia easily endure servitude."[13] And he was con-cerned that the adventures of the new trading empires of East India companies would corrupt Europeans. While the memory of Portuguese exploration still haunts Milton's epic, in 1581 Portugal was absorbed into the kingdom of Spain (though the Portuguese Restoration War would begin in 1640 and Portugal would achieve independence in 1668), and Spanish-Portuguese power in Asia was under serious challenge. By 1605, the Dutch had displaced the Portuguese as the foremost European trad-ers in the celebrated Spice Islands, and in 1641 they captured the Por-tuguese base of operations in Southeast Asia, the port city of Melaka. The seventeenth century was the Dutch century. Jonathan Israel argues that from the 1590s onwards for about a century and a half, the Dutch established their primacy in world trade. Theirs was a maritime empire of trade, developed in contradistinction, even resistance, to territorial empires. Eli Heckscher notes that the "Netherlands were the most hated, and yet the most admired and envied commercial nation of the seventeenth century." While Satan has most often been interpreted as a Spanish conquistador, by the time Milton began to write *Paradise Lost* in 1658 and at its publication in 1667, it was the United Provinces who were the rising power, and English merchants had contended with the Dutch in Asia for at least half a century as they emulated the Dutch empire of trade.[14]

In the 1640s, after peace with Spain, the United Provinces greatly strengthened their position.[15] The 1647–48 treaty of Münster allowed the Dutch access to Spanish markets and lifted previous restraints on their growth. However, Dutch gains came at the expense of the English and Hanseatic states. This situation had been anticipated by the English: in 1641, parliamentarian Sir Thomas Roe had declared, "Now it is true that our great trade depends upon the troubles of our neighbours and we enjoy almost the trade of Christendom; but if a peace happen betwixt France, Spain, and the United Provinces, all these will share what we now possess alone."[16] When their fears came to pass, the English grew resentful. Not desiring war, leaders of the new English republic, including Cromwell, attempted to forge a political union with the United Provinces. Any union, though, meant subordination of the smaller United Provinces, much like Scotland's relation with England. Understandably, then, the Dutch were uninterested. Growing tensions led to the English passing the first Navigation Act; later the situation escalated into war. As Stephen Pincus notes, the proposed union was derailed when the English suspected the Dutch of having "forsaken the virtues of republicanism and Protestantism for absolute monarchy and the associated sins of pride and covetousness." Although Pincus argues that Anglo-Dutch conflicts arose out of ideological differences, he nonetheless acknowledges English fears that through trade the Dutch would follow the Spanish in aiming for universal dominion and would exclude all other trade in the Indies.[17]

In this context of growing Dutch maritime power, Milton served the Interregnum government. As Latin secretary, he was involved in negotiations for a settlement regarding the Dutch expulsion of English merchants from the Spice Islands. Milton composed a June 1652 state letter raising the issue of reparations for losses sustained from being "excluded from that Trade" as well as for the Amboyna massacre, and claiming,

"Damages by reason of our due part lost of the fruits in the *Molucca Islands*, *Banda* and *Amboyna*, from the time that by the slaughter of our men we were thence expell'd, till the time that we shall be satisfi'd for our Loss and Expences."[18] Milton's own views regarding Anglo-Dutch relations, however, are difficult to discern. In *Of Reformation*, while acknowledging trade as a point of conflict, Milton favors an alliance between the two states, "whose mutual interest is of such high consequence, though their Merchants bicker in the East Indies" (CM 3:51). In *Pro se defensio*, after the first Anglo-Dutch war, Milton hastens to declare himself a firm friend of the Dutch: "You are indeed greatly mistaken, if you think there is any Englishman more friendly, more willingly allied to the United Provinces than myself, anyone who thinks more highly of that republic, who prizes more or more often applauds their industry, their arts, ingenuity and liberty; who would less want a war begun with them, who would support it when begun with less enthusiasm, and when ended, who would more sincerely rejoice" (CM 9:104). That Milton spoke in favor of an Anglo-Dutch alliance, however, did not preclude criticisms of the Dutch. Leo Miller suggests that for Milton "the short-term goals of the Commonwealth merchants and shipowners were inseparable from his long-term goals of republican equality, of freedom of inquiry, freedom of speech and freedom of conscience."[19]

Milton's connection to the Netherlands was of a longer duration than his service to the republic and Protectorate. The traditional grammar school education would have included study of the international Dutch humanist Desiderius Erasmus, who had many English ties. Later, Milton's intellectual interests led to contacts with continental humanists, including those in the Low Countries. While in Paris on his grand tour of the Continent, the young Milton asked for and obtained an introduction to Hugo Grotius, then living in Paris as Swedish ambassador to France. Milton would later write favorably of Grotius in his early antiepiscopalian tracts, and *Paradise Lost* may have been influenced by Grotius's neo-Latin drama, *Adamus exul*.[20] The publication of *Defensio prima*, with copies circulating widely in the Netherlands, served to introduce Milton's work to Dutch humanists. Classicist Nicholas Heinsius, Claudius Salmasius's opponent at Leiden, corresponded with Isaac Vossius, court librarian to Queen Christina of Sweden, about Milton's work, and the philologist Jan van Vliet, secretary to the Dutch legation, even sought to meet him.[21]

Yet scholars have generally overlooked Anglo-Dutch interrelations. A recent exception is John Kerrigan, who makes a compelling case for the early modern triangulation of England, Scotland, and the Low Countries. Kerrigan points to wide Dutch influence in fields as varied as arts and engineering: "The English looked to Dutch models in painting, architecture, and such practical arts as fen drainage. The reclamation of large parts of East Anglia with Dutch help can only have made more evident what the marking of dykes, sandbanks, and sea-lanes on maps was imparting, that the British archipelago extended physically into the Netherlands."[22] Indeed, Kerrigan argues for redrawing our mental map to include the Netherlands as part of the cultural sphere of the British Isles: even in 1677, long after hopes of political union had dwindled, Marvell would claim that "the *Spanish Nether-land*...had always been considered as the natural Frontier of *England*."[23]

Furthermore, as Kerrigan notes, "the Scottish and the Dutch were drawn together by trade, higher education, Latin literacy, and religious affinity."[24] Both the English and Scots—particularly the latter, who shared their Calvinism with the Dutch—looked to the Protestant Dutch republic for the model of a prosperous commonwealth. In the later seventeenth century, Daniel Defoe would argue for Scotland's union with England on the model of the United Provinces, as well for imitating the strong Dutch economy by "expanding her trade overseas."[25] The close relationship between Britain and the Low Countries, however, did not preclude conflict, as the three Anglo-Dutch wars of the seventeenth century show. If the English admired and imitated Dutch trade, they also became economic competitors as well as political and religious allies. And the English might extend their anti-Scots prejudices to the Dutch. As Kerrigan notes, "The triangular matrix...was multibraided and full of conflicts," and "the links included so much contention as well as so much that was compatible."[26]

Milton's view of the Dutch likely depends on the segment of Dutch society in question. The United Provinces had their royalist faction in the supporters of the Princes of Orange, as one of Milton's royalist critics reminded him on the eve of the Restoration. Noting Milton's desire for England to become another Holland in *The Readie and Easie Way to Establish a Free Commonwealth* (1659), George Starkey wrote, "Such a *Common-wealth* (Mr. *Milton,*) as *Holland* is I suppose you could wish, and would help to make *England,* but there is among them something that you do not so well like and approve of, that is, the *house* of *Nassau* or *Orange family.*"[27] Blair Worden notes a number of anti-Orangist statements in Milton's earlier *Defensio secunda.* Worden speculates that as licenser of Marchamont Nedham's newsbook *Mercurius Politicus,* Milton may have written the Latin distich published by Nedham celebrating the death of the Prince of Orange just as Milton fabricated the 1652 letter from Leiden in *Politicus* that identified Alexander More as author of *Clamor regii sanguinis ad coelum.* Arguing for a close working relationship between Milton and Nedham in the context of Anglo-Dutch relations, Worden suggests, "it is artificial to detach [Milton] from the world of propaganda of which the tracts written in his own name in 1649–50, and his anonymous contributions to *Politicus* thereafter, were a part."[28]

If Worden is correct in seeing Milton as collaborating with Nedham and others on commonwealth propaganda, other writers during this period may offer clues on Milton's views. One such figure was John Hall, Milton's confessed admirer and part of a "Shadow Secretariat" called on for translation work that included Samuel Hartlib, Theodore Haak, John Dury, and John Hall. All of these men were or were to become Milton's familiars.[29] In 1651, Hall produced a propaganda piece on Anglo-Dutch disputes over Asian trade by republishing John Skinner's Jacobean tract on the Amboyna massacre.[30] The 1623 Amboyna massacre, wherein ten Englishmen were tortured and executed by the Dutch governors of the factory on the East Indies island, reentered public consciousness in the newsbooks as relations with the United Provinces worsened with the failure of the January 1651 embassy of Oliver St. John and Walter Strickland to the Hague. Hall's 1651 reprinted pamphlet was given a new republican frame. In a dedication to Cromwell, Hall criticizes James I and Charles I for not redressing their injuries but expresses hope for better under the republic "since that yoak of Kingship is taken off our necks, me thinks we should like men, whose shackles are taken off them while they are asleep, leap up nimbly, and make use of our Liberty." In a new coda, "Remarks upon the fore-going

"an embedded memory of the events of May 1652 that led to the out-break of the first Anglo-Dutch war."[36] These embedded memories of the 1650s, especially of the Anglo-Dutch conflict, would resonate with the immediate context of the poem's publication, which coincided with the conclusion of the second Anglo-Dutch war (1665–67), which the United Provinces decidedly won. There was a certain déjà vu effect to the second Anglo-Dutch war as pamphlets from the first Anglo-Dutch war were recycled, including Marvell's *Character of Holland*, which would be reprinted yet again during the third Anglo-Dutch war (1672–74).

But if Milton began writing *Paradise Lost* in earnest in 1658, one of his last tracts before the return of king, *The Readie and Easie Way*, may offer insight into Milton's thoughts at the time. John Kerrigan notes a positive assessment of the Dutch in this work: urging his fellow citizens to be steadfast, he uses the Dutch as an example of a model republic: "Which must needs redound the more to our shame, if we but look on our neighbours the United Provinces, to us inferiour in all outward advantages: who notwithstanding, in the midst of greater difficulties, courageously, wisely, constantly went through with the same work, and are settl'd in all the happie injoiments of a potent and flourishing Republick to this day."[37] Indeed, Milton's royalist critics mocked him for being an adherent of the Dutch. William Collinne found Milton's proposed constitution "borrowed in copy from the States of Holland," while George Starkey, as noted above, accused Milton of wishing to turn England into another Holland, which he described as a "*Hotch potch* of many *Independent Jurisdictions*, joyning forces together upon necessity, to keep them from being punished for their *Rebellion* against, and abjuring their lawfull *King*."[38] While Milton did not back down, producing a second edition of *The Readie and Easie Way* less than two months later, some of his revisions suggest a more complicated view of the Dutch than simple admiration.

In *The Readie and Easie Way*, Milton seems aware of the critique of the United Provinces as an unmanageable hodgepodge of independent entities. Robert W. Ayers notes, "Milton heightens and clarifies the difference between the government of the United Provinces and that which he proposes for England, to the clear disadvantage of the former" (YP 7:461n229). A careful examination of the revisions between the first and second editions shows how Milton tries to ensure that his proposal for England does not entail the sort of loose federation that made the political process in the Netherlands a quagmire of indecision. The first edition proposes, "every county in the land were made a little commonwealth, and thir chief town a city" (383). However, the second edition of *The Readie and Easie Way* subordinates the county to the authority of a central administration so that "every countie in the land were made a kinde of subordinate Commonaltie or Commonwealth, and one chief town or more, according as the shire is in circuit, made cities" (458). The second edition also adds that this arrangement means "fewer laws to expect or fear from the supreme autoritie," language missing from the first edition (459). The same passage from the second edition adds a comparison to the federal structure of the United Provinces precisely to emphasize difference: with such a political organization, the people

> may without much trouble in these commonalities or in more general assemblies call'd to thir cities from the whole territorie on such occasion, declare and publish their assent or dissent by deputies within a time limited sent to the Grand Councel: yet so as this thir judgment declar'd shal submitt to the greater number of other counties or commonalties, and not avail them to any exemption of themselves, or refusal of agreement with the rest, as it may in any of the United Provinces, being sovran within it self, oft times to the great disadvantage of that union. (459)

This new comparison highlights the disadvantages of the political system in the United Provinces. Political decisions there require unanimous agreement; in Milton's proposal for England, only a majority is needed.

In his revisions to *The Readie and Easie Way*, Milton signals awareness of some of the negative aspects of the Dutch government. Might he have been stung by some of the criticisms leveled by pamphleteers like Starkey? At the end of the first edition Milton already argues that his proposal for England is superior to the Dutch form of government: the English "shall also far exceed the United Provinces, by having, not many sovranties in one Commonwealth, but many Commonwealths under one sovrantie" (YP 7:385). Nonetheless, in the second edition he feels compelled to stress yet again the disadvantages of the Dutch system with a parenthetical insertion: "we shall also far exceed the United

Provinces, by having, not as they (to the retarding and distracting oft times of thir counsels on urgentest occasions) many Sovranties united in one Commonwealth, but many Commonwealths under one united and entrusted Sovrantie" (461). While these changes by no means indicate a loss of regard for Dutch republicanism, they nonetheless show Milton striving to distinguish his vision of England from the contemporary reality of the United Provinces, and in so doing distancing himself from the Dutch.

In the late 1650s, as Milton began composing *Paradise Lost*, England not only pursued war with Spain but also engaged in further conflict with the United Provinces in the Baltic crisis of 1658–60. When Sweden ignored Dutch demands to pull back their advance on Denmark and instead started besieging Copenhagen, the United Provinces entered the fray eventually to beat back the Swedes. In response to this victory, the English sent a fleet in support of Sweden early in 1659. While the United Provinces did not want another war with England, they nonetheless sent a second fleet to Denmark. Dutch forces waited on the other side of the Sound from Swedish and English navies, but the English ultimately withdrew. In the closing years of the Protectorate, Milton would have continued to be aware of Dutch power. Dutch control of the Baltic region was equally resented by Danes, Norwegians, Swedes, and the French. In the Restoration, the English sent an envoy, Sir Gilbert Talbot, in 1664 to Denmark to persuade them to break with the Dutch and to ally instead with the English.[39] This mission failed and soon the second Anglo-Dutch war broke out.

Piratical Satan

Whatever Milton's personal views, prevalent anti-Dutch discourse provided language to critique the dangerous tendency of trade to turn into oppressive mercantile empire. This language could be used to make broader points about just government and commercial endeavor. Several scholars note *Paradise Lost*'s critique of mercantilism. David Quint argues that Milton's depiction of Satan as a merchant-adventurer exposes false distinctions between martial heroism and mercantilism made in earlier epics. As noted earlier, Quint further suggests that in parodying da Gama's encounter with the king of Calicut in the episode of Satan in Chaos, Milton had the commercial wars between England and the Netherlands in mind.[40] Robert Markley, Timothy Morton, and Blair Hoxby extend this insight to suggest that Satan resembles a Dutch merchant. They all focus on similes comparing Satan to a fleet sailing to or returning from the Indies (*PL* 4.159–65, 2.638–40).[41] Upon reaching paradise, Satan is compared to sailors on East Indiamen ships headed for the East Indies:

> As when to them who saile
> Beyond the *Cape of Hope*, and now are past
> *Mozambic,* off at Sea North-East windes blow
> *Sabean* odours from the spicie shoare
> Of *Arabie* the blest, with such delay
> Well pleas'd they slack thir course, and many a League
> Chear'd with the grateful smell old Ocean smiles.   (*PL* 4.159–65)

The fleet is more than halfway to its destination, having passed the Cape of Good Hope on the southern tip of Africa, and having passed even Mozambique. Wafted by the perfume of spices, the sailors are "Well pleas'd" and even the ocean itself "smiles." But the pleasure of profit-seeking traders is linked to Satan's pleasure in approaching paradise where he seeks the destruction of God's work. Earlier, in book 2, as he travels to find his way out of hell, Satan is also compared to a fleet of East Indiamen:

> As when farr off a Fleet descri'd
> Hangs in the Clouds, by *Æquinoctial Winds*
> Close sailing from *Bengala,* or the Iles
> Of *Ternate* and *Tidore,* whence Merchants bring
> Thir spicie Drugs: they on the Trading Flood
> Through the wide *Ethiopian* to the Cape
> Ply stemming nightly toward the Pole.   (2.636–42)

Here, the ships laden with spices are returning to Europe. The place names were widely known in the period, even though Ternate and Tidore are tiny islands in eastern Indonesia. In book 2, Satan has just won the debate in hell, victorious like the East Indiamen with their rich stores of spice, won perhaps like Satan through deceit. Both similes firmly place Satan in Asia in the context of the spice trade.

Robert Markley argues that the passage in book 2 reveals "English anxieties about the Dutch monopoly in the East Indies" and that rather than being "an orientalist condemnation of the East," it is "a thinly veiled indictment of a European archrival." Building on Markley's point, Timothy Morton suggests, "In terms of the rhetoric of the spice trade, Satan is acting more like the Dutch as the English might have seen them...usurping the wondrous islands, possessing nothing of value himself but only recirculating others' goods, a master of tropological substitution." Blair Hoxby concurs with this reading of Satan as a Dutch merchant, but argues that Milton's comparison implicates both English and Dutch East India companies as he attacks the Restoration regime's expansionist commercial policies in *Paradise Lost*. Morton surmises, "This equation of Satan with the Dutch is carried out in spite of the sympathy which Milton's circle had for them during the war."[42]

While I argue that Milton implicates both Dutch and English merchants, it is interesting to note direct evidence linking Satan to the Dutch in the war in heaven. Discovering similar wording in the parliamentary *Declaration* of 1652, a document protesting Dutch tactics which Milton translated, and the second day of war in *Paradise Lost*, Martin Dzelzainis persuasively argues that the repeated use of the word *hollow* when Satan resorts to the use of cannons—his army marches "in hollow Cube / Training his devilish Enginrie, impal'd / On every side with shaddowing Squadrons Deep, / To hide the fraud" (*PL* 6.552–55) and when revealed the cannons with "hollow'd bodies" and "mouthes / With hideous orifice.../ Portending hollow truce" (6.574, 6.576–78)—recalls the failures of the 1652 Anglo-Dutch negotiations and the naval war that ensued.[43] In 1652 Milton made the same pun on Holland in the sonnet to Sir Henry Vane the Younger, praised for revealing "The drift of hollow states, hard to be spelled."[44] Dzelzainis further suggests that Milton's depiction of Satan's deceit in the war in heaven proffers an "implicit figuration of Satan as the Dutch commander Tromp," the commander who led the Dutch navy during the war; Milton identifies Satan "with one of the most notorious instances of state treachery [in the Anglo-Dutch negotiations] in living memory."[45] Like the deceptive diplomacy of the Dutch, Satan resorts to fraud.[46]

Given the evidence of war polemic in *Paradise Lost*, it is tempting to read anti-Dutch satire in the water imagery for Satan. The geographical meaning of *hollow*, from the sonnet to Vane, is also present in *Paradise Lost*. In his edition, Merritt Hughes glosses line 6 in the sonnet to Vane thus: "Holland is *hollow* both in character and in its situation, with much of its land below sea level." In *Paradise Lost*, Satan, like the Dutch, is a creature of marshy places. The geography associated with Satan is marked by amorphousness and blurred boundaries. Hell's division into land and water is undermined by the sameness of both: Satan lights on "dry Land / ... if it were Land that ever burn'd / With solid, as the Lake with liquid fire" (*PL* 1.227–29). When crossing chaos, Satan is "Quencht in a Boggie *Syrtis*, neither Sea, / Nor good dry Land: nigh founderd" (2.939–40). When approaching earth, he rests in a stormy place, later to become the paradise of fools, described as a "windie Sea of Land" (3.440). Finally leading Eve to the tree of knowledge, he is compared to phosphorescent swamp gas thought to be "some evil Spirit" that "Misleads th' amaz'd Night-wanderer from his way / To Boggs and Mires, and oft through Pond or Poole" (9.638, 640–41). These descriptions of boggy marshes, land not firmly defined as earth nor truly water, are reminiscent of anti-Dutch satires that mock the watery, "windie Sea of Land" of the Low Countries. In "The Character of Holland" Marvell not only makes fun of Dutch geography, but also indicts the Dutch for lack of political commitment; they reject monarchy but are unwilling to be thorough republicans: "For these *Half-anders*, half wet, and half dry, / Nor bear strict service, nor pure liberty."[47] This political amorphousness is akin to Satan's hypocritical combination of republican rhetoric and tyrannical rule.

Milton's imagery might have been recognizable as anti-Dutch stereotyping to seventeenth century readers of polemical pamphlets. Yet such terms were also applicable to the English. Milton himself associates English changeability and political instability with their own proximity to the sea. Arguing for a settled Parliament in *The Readie and Easie Way*, he complains, "I know not therefor what should be peculiar in *England* to make successive Parlaments thought safest, or convenient heer more then in all other nations, unless it be the fick'lness which is attributed to us as we are Ilanders. But good education and acquisite wisdom ought to correct the fluxible fault, if any such be, of our watrie situation" (YP 7:372–73, 437).

While scholars have so far identified Satan as a foreign merchant, whether Portuguese or Dutch, the epic similes that link Satan with the Indies may indicate that he is also English. Following David Quint, Roy Flannagan glosses the simile in book 2 as pertaining largely to the Dutch United East Indies Company, or the VOC (Verenigde Oost-Indische Compagnie). Hence, Flannagan suggests, "Ternate and Tidore are two of the Moluccas or 'Spice Islands,' both of which were ports of call for the Dutch East India Company. Milton may be drawing on his diplomatic experience as a civil servant in dealing with various merchants of the Low Countries. The entire simile is a living picture of East Indian trade in Milton's era, with some suggestion of evil in the dangerous conquest of expensive and exotic spices and in the choice of the word 'Drugs.'"[48] However, Ternate and Tidore were not simply VOC ports of call. Their importance in the early modern era can be gauged from the two pages devoted to the map of the Maluku (Moluccas) islands, despite their comparatively small size, in Joan Blaeu's *Atlas*.[49] This is the very atlas that Milton considered purchasing when in 1656 he asked Peter Heimbach to look for one for him in Amsterdam: "Be good enough to take so much farther trouble as to be able to inform me, when you return, how many volumes there are in the complete work, and which of the two issues, that of the Blaeu or that of Jansen, is the larger and more correct" (CM 12:83, 85). Milton might also have known the islands' history of conflict with one another, and how Europeans aided in their wars. In 1522 the Sultan of Ternate allied with the Portuguese; in response the Sultan of Tidore requested Spanish help. After the union of the Spain and Portugal, the Dutch perpetuated these conflicts by assisting Ternate in fighting against the Spanish-backed Tidore.[50]

While English involvement in the Maluku was minimal despite early contact through Francis Drake's 1579 landfall there, they remembered well their exclusion from the Maluku through Dutch actions, including the 1623 massacre of East India Company factors in Amboyna. But from the start the English were at a disadvantage: when in 1605 Henry Middleton arrived in Ternate requesting trading privileges, Sultan Said was skeptical of his ability to help, preferring to deal with the Dutch. In fact, the sultan had written to Prince Maurits offering an exclusive trading partnership in return for guns. As historian Leonard Andaya notes,

"Sultan Said was confidently maneuvering among the Europeans and exhibited an aplomb in his relationship, secure in the knowledge that there were many foreign groups now eagerly competing to obtain the cloves."[51] Milton's invocation of the names Ternate and Tidore conjured up for readers not only the romance of spices but also warfare among Europeans in Asia in order to procure the "spicie Drugs" (*PL* 2.640).

Both the war in heaven and Satan's voyage through Chaos show, along the lines of Quint's argument, the partnership of war and mercantile imperialism. By depicting Satan and crew as hollow merchants, politicians, and soldiers, Milton comments on Dutch and English unjust use of force in the service of an expansionist empire. But he makes Satan not just a merchant but also a pirate, and he does so by seizing on the definitional instability of piracy. In the early modern period, armed trading meant that mercantilism shaded into privateering, and privateering into piracy. Bona fide merchants were easily mistaken for pirates. In 1608, the fleet Peter Mundy was sailing on nearly got into a skirmish for taking the king of Spain's armada for Turkish pirates.[52] Pirates can also be intimately connected to the enforcers of maritime law. In the 1580s, while Sir John Killigrew was Queen Elizabeth's vice-admiral of Cornwall, his own mother led a force that seized a Spanish ship in Falmouth harbor. The owners sought restitution through the Commissioners of Piracy for Cornwall, a body presided over by Lady Killigrew's son.[53] Europeans engaged in piracy and tolerated it when they could not suppress it.

Despite local successes, European attempts at monopolies in Asia were largely unsuccessful; preexisting networks of trade remained intact and sufficiently powerful to resist European incursions. Portuguese control over the Malabar pepper trade is one well-known example of the permeability of such European monopolies where so-called "pirating" in the form of theft and armed resistance long persisted.[54] Moreover, East India companies used piracy to intimidate local rulers into trading or to punish them for not doing so. Janice Thomson finds that the distinction between piracy—defined as non-state-authorized violence—and privateering cannot be maintained in the case of mercantile companies, acting as sovereign entities while not being actual states, and thus breaking down distinctions "between the economic and political, nonstate and state, property rights and sovereignty, the public and private."[55]

Europeans also engaged in piracy upon one another. An act can be viewed as piracy by one party and as legalized war by the other, as in the famed case of the 1603 Dutch capture of the Portuguese carrack, *Sta. Catarina*, which Hugo Grotius defends in *De jure praedae* as the right of seizing war booty. The aggressive freebooting methods adopted by the VOC thus shaded into illegal acts of war. Although mainly aimed at the Portuguese, Dutch privateering was also directed against other Europeans and Asians, even against the English before the VOC and East India Company came to an agreement in 1619.[56] The English East India Company tried to imitate the VOC, though with less success. Around 1600, the statesman Thomas Wilson claimed that English merchants plundering to enrich their queen and themselves were imitating the Dutch: "They have one pollicy which all the world cryes out of which, notwithstanding, is but newe and lerned from the Hollanders: videlicet, to desire to continue in warres with Spayne, and Enmity with some other Countryes; that haveing so great store of shipping marriners and force by sea, . . . by this in robbing and takeing purchase by sea they doe greately enrich the Queen, the Admirall and themselves."[57] The Dutch East India Company had no qualms about allying with those they called pirates and were willing to use piracy as a tool of empire, including an attempt to organize Chinese pirates into a maritime coalition to force the Ming empire to allow free trade.[58]

The thin dividing lines between merchants and pirates and between pirates and privateers are thematized in Milton's source for *Paradise Lost*, Camões's *Os Lusíadas*, as well. When he pleads with Chaos, Satan is figured as Vasco da Gama speaking to the sultan of Calicut: "I come no Spy, / With purpose to explore or to disturb / The secrets of your Realm" (2.970–72). As David Quint notes, the word *spy* has no precedent in ancient epics but recalls Richard Fanshawe's 1655 translation of Camões: Vasco da Gama says to the Muslim king, "*We* are not Men, who spying a weak *Town* / Or careless, as wee pass along the shore, / Murther the *Folks*, and burn the *Houses* down / To make a *booty* of their thirsted store" (*Lusiad* 2.633–36).[59] But *spy* is not the only term for da Gama in the *Lusiad*. In canto 1, a disguised Bacchus sets the Muslims of eastern Africa against the Portuguese by accusing them of piracy: "These bloody CHRISTIANS (as I understand) / With *Flames* and *Pyracies* have fill'd the *Sea*, / As well as with their *Robberies* the *Land*" (1.626–28). The stanza above from canto 2 portrays pirates opportunistically robbing and pillaging coastal towns. Instead of *spy*, the word Camões uses in the stanza from canto 2 above is *roubadores*, in other words, plunderers; Fanshawe's "*Pyracies*" (1.627) translates Camões's *roubos*, or theft.[60] In both, da Gama's crew is depicted as marauding pirates.

The depiction of da Gama as a piratical robber is Bacchus's slander. But just as he parodies other aspects of da Gama to debunk Camões's mercantile epic, Milton also makes robbery and piracy fundamental characteristics of Satan. Satan is compared to "a Thief bent to unhoord the cash / Of some rich Burgher" (*PL* 4.188–89) and to a "prowling Wolfe" who "Leaps o're the fence with ease into the Fould" (4.183, 187), a conventional image for hypocrisy but one that perhaps also echoes Dutch pamphlet literature depicting Cromwell as "Protecteur Weerwolf."[61] At the same time, Satan is associated with the sea. Besides the similes comparing Satan to an Indies fleet that brackets his voyage through Chaos (2.638–39, 4.159–65), an opening extended simile depicts Satan as a monstrous creature of the sea, a Leviathan mistaken for an island (2.195–210). Later, when Satan finally makes the safe crossing across Chaos, he is described as "glad that now his Sea should find a shore" (2.1011) and compared to a ship much the worse for wear from surviving a storm: "And like a weather-beaten Vessel holds / Gladly the port, though Shrouds and Tackle torn" (2.1043–44).

The devils too are associated with the sea. When they are not hissing like snakes, the voices of the devils in Pandaemonium sound like the ocean—"such murmur filld / Th' Assembly, as when hollow Rocks retain / The sound of blustring winds, which all night long / Had rous'd the Sea" (*PL* 2.284–87)—with perhaps another allusion to Dutch "hollow States." Book 1 of *Paradise Lost* opens with a view of shipwrecked fallen angels lying in the "vast and boundless Deep" (1.177) until Satan urges them to seek "harbour" (1.185) on land. The image of shipwreck is reinforced in book 2 when Belial fears God's retaliation, worrying that they "Caught in a fierie Tempest shall be hurl'd / Each on his rock transfixt, the sport and prey / Of racking whirlwinds, or for ever sunk / Under yon boyling Ocean, wrapt in Chains" (2.180–83). These images of shipwreck again link Satan and his devils to pirates whose fortunes are made or lost at sea. Satan's piratical nature, moreover, comes from his specific orientation to the sea. Camões's da Gama tries to reassure the Indians that they are not there to plunder and to colonize. In moving from sea to shore in book 1, Satan and his devils colonize hell like the pirates the Portuguese are accused of being. In significant contrast, the account of Creation in book 7 reverses this orientation. Surrounded by the angels, the Son calms the waters to create new worlds from the shores of heaven: "On heav'nly ground they stood, and from the shore / They view'd the vast immeasurable Abyss / Outrageous as a Sea, dark, wasteful, wilde" (7.210–12). In his divine act of Creation, God colonizes the sea, unlike Satan, who arises out of the sea to colonize land.

The depiction of Satan as a pirate was already available in contemporary sermons. Using the analogy of the ship of state for the church, Stephen Gosson vividly imagines a chase on the high seas: "There is another ship at sea which hath this ship in chace, that is the Pyracy of hel, a hot ship and full of wild-fire, where the Divell is maister, pride the mast, impurity the saile, the wisdome of flesh the Card, the mysterie of iniquity the compasse, Diagoras the Atheist, Iudas ye traytor, and the whole rabble of hel the Marriners: two type of Ordnance planted in her, one mixt of hereticks & schismatiks, another of persecuting heathen princes, that spit smoke & sulphur at the church of God."[62] By the end of the seventeenth century, Thomas Watson easily made the analogy between Satan and pirates: "Satan tempts after some *Discoveries* of God's Love. Satan like a Pyrat, sets on a ship that is richly laden: So when a Soul hath been laden with spiritual Comforts; now the Devil will be shooting at him to rob him of all."[63]

Finally, Milton extends the implications of the analogy to portray Satan as a pirate who has lost all former communal identity. Sir Edward Coke calls the pirate *hostis humani generis* (an enemy to the human race), derived from Cicero's *De officiis*, which says, "nam pirata non est perduellium numero definitus, sed communis hostis omnium" (for a pirate is not included in the number of lawful enemies, but is the common foe of all the world).[64] Similarly, Satan and his devils lose their heavenly citizenship to become the universal enemy of all humankind. The enmity between Satan and God's empire is like the total war between the pirate and the state. The loss of citizenship from this state of war against all is one acutely felt by Satan and the devils. Like stateless pirates, the devils are "Heav'ns fugitives" (*PL* 2.57) but nonetheless desirous to "repossess thir native seat" (1.634).

Emperor and Pirate

Milton's characterization of Satan as pirate sharpens the critique of mercantile imperialism. But the critique is more pointed than a simple charge of robbery. Milton is influenced by a classical anecdote transmitted through Augustine linking pirates to emperors and so to tyranny. In book 4, chapter 4, "Kingdoms without justice are similar to robber bands," of *De civitate dei*, Augustine ends with an anecdote about Alexander the Great:

> Eleganter enim et veraciter Alexandro illi Magno quidam comprehensus pirata respondit. Nam cum idem rex hominem interrogaret, quid ei videretur, ut mare haberet infestum, ille libera contumacia: Quod tibi, inquit, ut orbem terrarum; sed quia id ego exiguo navigio facio, latro vocor; quia tu magna classe, imperator.

> [For it was an elegant and true reply that was made to Alexander the Great by a certain pirate whom he had captured. When the king asked him what he was thinking of, that he should molest the sea, he said with defiant independence: "The same as you when you molest the world! Since I do this with a little ship I am called a pirate. You do it with a great fleet and are called an emperor."][65]

The pirate's defiant reply equates imperialism with robbery. For Milton, both are acts of tyrants. Tyranny is the key that ties together the disparate portrayals of Satan.

The divergent characterizations of Satan as merchant and as king have been difficult for scholars to reconcile. Thus, for instance, Blair Hoxby attempts to explain it by arguing, "Neither open war nor sheer industry, Satan's bold enterprise lacks its own terms; therefore it must waver between the courses recommended by Moloch and Mammon. This is one of the reasons that Satan wavers between warrior and merchant, sovereign and commoner."[66] I contend, however, that these characterizations of Satan are by no means a wavering between two terms. By showing how easily they can be viewed as pirates, Milton critiques

the heroic posturing of merchants, but it is not just because piracy constitutes the dark side of merchant adventuring. When we recognize
Milton's use of this anecdote regarding Alexander, which Augustine took
from a lost section of Cicero's *De republica*, we can make better sense
of the dual characterizations of Satan, piratical merchant and Eastern
tyrant, as inextricably linked. Having surprising currency in the political discourse of the 1650s, the anecdote relates to the debates over the
formation of the republic, and Milton weaves it into his depiction of a
monarchist Satan making republican speeches.

In *Defensio prima*, Milton himself uses the passage from Augustine to
respond to Salmasius's claim that Augustine equated "the power of a
master over slaves and of a king over subjects" (146). Milton argues
that, on the contrary, "concerning the power of a bad king over his
subjects and that of a robber over every one he meets, he [Augustine]
has certainly proclaimed them the same" (146), for Augustine says that
"'with the removal of justice, what are kingdoms,' except 'great robbers'
dens; for what are robbers' dens themselves, except little kingdoms?"
(146).[67] Both emperor and pirate plunder by force. The robber band is
a microcosm of empire. Indeed, the word Augustine uses, *latro*, meaning
brigand, robber, or pirate, refers also to a hired soldier or mercenary;
in classical Latin the latter is the primary meaning of the word. While
Alexander's interlocutor is identified as *pirata* (pirate), in his reply the
pirate calls himself *latro*. The original Greek *peirates* initially referred simply to sailors; the word later came to refer to brigands on the high seas.[68]
In *Defensio prima*, Milton uses the word *praedoni* for robbers but more
often he uses Augustine's *latronum* (CM 7:176, 288, 262). The power
of both emperor and pirate/robber is exactly the same: force without
justice.[69] Moreover, Augustine's warning that "to rejoice in the extant
of empire is not the characteristic of good men," would be repeated in
an edition of Suetonius by the Dutch humanist Erasmus, whose works
formed the grammar school curriculum of Milton's childhood.[70]

Milton's use of Alexander was not unmotivated, but likely a response
to Charles I's scaffold speech, published in Samuel Pecke's newsbook on
parliamentary affairs, in which Charles rebuked his executors for what
he considered an act of conquest, saying, "But if it be only matter of
conquest, then it is a great robbery; as a pirate said to Alexander that

he was a great robber, he was but a petty robber."[71] In *Defensio prima*, Milton turns Augustine against Charles: using the pirate to deflate the emperor, Milton exposes Charles's injustices, showing how in reducing his people to slavery Charles committed crimes against humanity. A later piratical encounter must have also emphasized for Milton the link to bad Stuart kings. On May 14, 1656, he composed a state letter to Louis XIV on behalf of John Dethicke, lord mayor of London (who presided over Milton's marriage to Katherine Woodcock), and William Wakefield, who claimed that in October 1649 their ship was captured by a pirate in the employ of the exiled Prince Charles: "a ship of theirs, called *The Jonas of London*, was taken at the mouth of the Thames by one White of Barking, acting under a commission from the son of the late King, and then taken into Dunkirk."[72] Not receiving a reply, in November 1656 Milton wrote another strongly worded letter on the same subject of royal piracy. It probably did not surprise Milton to find Charles Stuart, the son of a tyrant, an *imperator*, consorting with pirates and indeed employing them to make war on his former country.

During the Interregnum, Milton's collaborators used Alexander as a figure for sovereign power: Marchamont Nedham and Andrew Marvell compared Cromwell to Alexander, though to praise Cromwell's military successes.[73] But another close associate, James Harrington, used the anecdote to critique Cromwell for tyranny. In the "Corollary" to *Oceana*, Harrington imagines an ideal legislator, Lord Archon, who in abdicating from power acts in an exemplary manner, unlike Cromwell. Harrington questions what good Alexander's "sword of war" has brought, for "Of this kind of empire, the throne of ambition, the quarry of a mighty hunter, it hath been truly said that it is but a great robbery."[74] Harrington wrote *Oceana* in 1655 when it was expected that Cromwell would assume the crown, at which time it was debated whether he would adopt the name of king or take on the title of emperor with expanded powers (which some members of the Council of State were advocating).[75] Since "mighty hunter" is the Bible's term for Nimrod,[76] Harrington brings together biblical and classical tyranny.

Milton too references both Nimrod, his prime example of the archetypal tyrant and empire-builder in *Paradise Lost*, and Alexander. When Satan tempts Eve, he is compared to serpents of classical mythology, including the god Ammon seducing Olympia:

> pleasing was his shape,
> And lovely, never since of Serpent kind
> Lovelier, not those that in *Illyria* chang'd
> *Hermione* and *Cadmus,* or the God
> In *Epidaurus;* nor to which transformd
> *Ammonian Jove,* or *Capitoline* was seen,
> Hee with *Olympias,* this with her who bore
> *Scipio* the highth of *Rome.*   (*PL* 9.503–10)

The serpentine passage impressively compresses a wide range of allusions in a short space. All the stories tell of serpents that are actually
gods, including the Ammon who supposedly fathered Alexander. Taken
together, the allusions suggest tyrannical empire-building. The reference
to Asklepios of Epidaurus, deified by Zeus for his ability to raise the
dead to life, speaks to the false promise of life beyond death that Satan
makes to Eve. The story of Cadmus is of the founding of Thebes through
horrific bloodshed—first Cadmus's mistaken killing of the serpent-
guardian of a spring and then the mutual slaughter of armed men who
sprout from the dragon's teeth sown by Cadmus.

Finally, as Ammon and as Jupiter Capitolinus in the aspect of serpents,
Jove begets two great military figures, one Greek (properly Macedonian)
and the other Roman. Both Alexander and Scipio are commanders who
won empires outside of Europe, in Asia and in Africa, respectively. Both
are also ultimately associated, like Asklepios and Cadmus, with death.
Alexander's life offers only the false promise of immortality through
imperial fame, built on the false foundation of piratical plunder. In fash-
ioning Satan as both monarch and his double the pirate, Milton points
back to the Augustinian passage from *Defensio prima* where pirate and
emperor are fundamentally the same. And if Milton recalls the language
of the parliamentary *Declaration* of 1652 in his depiction of the war in
heaven, as Dzelzainis argues, he may also be looking back to 1654 when
there was the possibility of Cromwell's elevation to emperor.

The term *emperor* has particular import in *Paradise Lost.* That Milton
depicts both Satan and God as monarchs has troubled critics. An examination of the titles Milton uses for kings in the poem offers a way to
reconsider the question of kingship. Milton uses the term *king* liberally,
applying it to heavenly, earthly, and hellish figures without distinction. In
contrast, his use of the word *emperor* is notably restricted. Three instances

of the word in *Paradise Lost* refer to Satan alone. When denouncing God's tyranny, Satan may speak of God's "Empire" (2.327), but he names God "Almighty" (1.259), "Thunderer" (2.28) or "Conqueror" (2.338), never emperor. While modern readers may automatically associate empire and emperor, early modern understanding of these terms was more complex. The name of *emperor*, in particular, was debated not just in the case of Cromwell's potential enthronement but also when James VI of Scotland took the crown of England, a part of Stuart history that Milton would probably have known.

The title of emperor and idea of empire did not begin with James. From the fourteenth century, the kings of France declared themselves "imperator in regno suo,"[77] though they refrained from claiming universal *imperium*. Nicholas Canny comments, "During the sixteenth century England was sometimes described as an empire, but always with a view to emphasizing the long tradition of independence from foreign potentates.... The word 'empire,' which was particularly favoured by Henry VIII after his breach with Rome, therefore called to mind the relative isolation of England through the centuries rather than its dominion over foreign territories." The concept of a sovereign state as an empire was borrowed from the Romans, but rulers of such territorially limited states did necessarily not make claims to be emperors. David Armitage notes: "Late medieval and early modern rulers made increasingly frequent claims to independent *imperium*. Such claims were particular, rather than universal; they did not suggest any intention to compete with the emperor or the pope for supremacy, but asserted both independence from external interference and ascendancy over internal competitors."[78]

The English might have understood their kingdom as an empire but did not necessarily consider their monarch an emperor: in about 1600, Thomas Wilson defined England as "an absolute Imperiall Monarchy held neither of Pope, Emperor but God alone," asserting national sovereignty apart from that of the Holy Roman Emperor.[79] However, English kings certainly aspired to imperial dignity: Henry VIII affected the title "The Imperial Crown of this Realm." Fond of Arthurian legend, Henry had his seal engraved with the title *imperator* and commissioned Polydore Vergil to write a history that traced the origins of his kingship to the

British-born Emperor Constantine, although his aspirations were not recognized abroad.[80] The idea of an empire of Great Britain was developed in the 1540s by proponents of the union of England and Scotland harking back to the time of Constantine when "al Britayn, was under one Emperor, and beeyng under one Emperor, then was Scotlande and Englande but one Empire."[81] Talk of both union and Great Britain as empire revived with James I's ascension. In a 1604 parliamentary session, the Welsh MP Sir William Maurice proposed the title of emperor for the king, but his suggestion was thus rejected: "The Name of Emperor is impossible—No particular Kingdom can make their King an Emperor.—The Name of a King a sweet Name:—Plentitude of Power in it:—A Name, which God taketh upon him."[82] The wrangling over the name *emperor* says more about English and Scots nationalist biases than anything else. Tellingly, English opponents of the proposal to call James *emperor* insisted on the worth of the name of *king*, and they did so by reference to a higher authority: God too takes the sweet name of *king*.

While it is difficult to say whether Milton was aware of a debate conducted before he was born, English squeamishness about the title *emperor* persisted long after the project of union was once again dropped. If Milton had known of the earlier debates, he would probably have thought of the title *emperor* as yet another Stuart pretension. Regardless, the pattern in *Paradise Lost* is suggestive. By confining his use of the term *emperor* to merely three instances, Milton carefully focuses its impact. The first is applied to Satan when he rises from the burning lake to gather together his demon legions, roused by "thir great Emperors call" (1.378). The second comes at the end of the council of hell, when Satan, about to embark on his adventures, "seemd / Alone th'Antagonist of Heav'n, nor less / Than Hells dread Emperour" (2.508–10). The last occurs when the grand council of hell waits for news of Satan's success, sitting "sollicitous what chance / Might intercept thir Emperour sent" (10.428–29). The only other figure to be similarly addressed is Eve, extolled as "Empress" by Satan in the guise of the serpent (9.568, 626). While the term *king* has a range of connotations, Milton uses the term *emperor* only in negative contexts.[83] Outside *Paradise Lost*, the word appears three other times in *Paradise Regain'd*, each instance referring to Roman emperors (*PR* 4.81, 90, 126). Milton's distinction between king and emperor, *rex* and *imperator,* is the difference between just and unjust rule.[84]

The story of Alexander and the pirate resolves a key crux of *Paradise Lost,* bringing together merchant adventuring in Asia with ideas of empire. Imperial tyranny in *Paradise Lost* is exposed as piratical robbery. The imagery of colonization, mercantilism, and plunder associated with Satan works together as an integrated whole. The depictions of Satan as emperor and pirate are but two sides of the same coin. The pirate functions as a *doppelgänger* for the tyrant. Moreover, this tyranny is cast as both Eastern and hollowly mercantile: for Satan is not simply represented as an oriental despot but uses republican rhetoric to conceal imperial ambitions. Just as the Dutch were thought to aim at universal monarchy while pretending to negotiate a republican alliance, or indeed just as the English slavishly desired a return of the monarchy despite their earlier embrace of republicanism, Satan's republicanism is a tool of his expansionist "nether Empire" (2.296). In Satan, Milton explores the pride and hollow ambition of an expansionist maritime empire whose reach exceeds its grasp. *Paradise Lost* shows a persistent concern with issues driving the Anglo-Dutch wars: sovereignty and international relations in the oceanic world of the Indies.

Satan in the East

Satan's adventure in Chaos is particularly interesting in regard to the issue of freedom of the seas. Milton's geographical imagination responds to the debate between Hugo Grotius and John Selden over the sovereignty of the sea. Of the three pre-Creation regions of *Paradise Lost,* Chaos is the one that resembles a sea. When Sin opens the gates of hell, Satan finds himself standing in front of "a dark / Illimitable Ocean without bound" (*PL* 2.891–92). But as he crosses this oceanic chaos, he finds it not to be *terra nullius,* or more accurately *mare nullius,* empty, unoccupied space, but rather one teeming with inhabitants:

> At length a universal hubbub wilde
> Of stunning sounds and voices all confus'd
> Born through the hollow dark assaults his eare
> With loudest vehemence.   (2.951–54)

Chaos and his consort Night claim dominion of this ocean. Though Satan does not recognize it, he is subject to the foreign ruler. Milton recalls the experience of European visitors to the Indies who found themselves poor and seeking preferment in these wealthy civilizations. While searching for the way to paradise, Satan presumptuously offers to recover Chaos's lands even though he is but a lost, bedraggled traveler:

> Thither to arrive
> I travel this profound, direct my course;
> Directed no mean recompense it brings
> To your behoof, if I that Region lost,
> All usurpation thence expell'd, reduce
> To her original darkness and your sway.   (2.979–84)

Likewise, the Portuguese were a small contingent when they first arrived in India and were laughed at for their poverty. Europeans subsequently insinuated themselves into the rich Indies trade by taking sides in local political conflicts, just as Satan tries to do here.

Satan's discovery that the ocean without limit is in fact occupied and ruled by its own sovereign resonates with Grotius's argument in *Mare liberum* against Portuguese claim to dominion in the Indies. As Grotius argues, the Portuguese have no right of dominion in the Indies because those lands already have their rulers: "But that the Portugals are not lords of those parts whither the Hollanders go—to wit, of Java, Taprobana and the greatest part of the Moluccas—we gather by a most certain argument, because no man is lord of that thing which neither he himself ever possessed nor any other in his name. These islands we speak of have, and always had, their kings, their commonwealth, their laws and their liberties."[85] The "Indians" have the right to rule themselves and to own property, even if they are infidels: "it is a point of heresy to believe that infidels are not lords of their own goods, and to take from them their goods which they possess for this very cause is theft and robbery no less than if the same be done to Christians."[86] Grotius unmasks European imperialism as nothing more than robbery. Likewise, Chaos and Night have the right to rule the space between hell and heaven, even if their kingdom is a discordant one. For Satan, Chaos is a foreign jurisdiction from whose sovereign he must secure permission to travel and to conduct his business.

One other aspect of Chaos evokes the Indian Ocean: its association with warfare. For with their entry into the Indian Ocean the Portuguese initiated armed trading. Such trade warfare erupted not just between Europeans and Asians but also among Europeans themselves. The immediate occasion for the writing of Grotius's *Mare liberum* was the Dutch seizure of the Portuguese carrack *Sta. Catarina*, which carried a rich cargo and yielded enormous profit. Grotius treated the capture of the ship as booty taken in a just war, but from the Spanish perspective it was piracy, even though the Spanish themselves engaged in similar actions. As Anne Pérotin-Dumon notes, "Iberians declared pirates other Western Europeans with whom they came into conflict in regions where they had asserted initial imperial dominion." The debate over definitions of pirates and piracy turned into warfare, for piracy had an economic impetus and political implications. Pérotin-Dumon points out that piracy arose from "either the will of a state to establish commercial hegemony over an area where it had previously been weak or nonexistent, or from the conflict between two political entities, one an established trading power and the other a newcomer."[87] In many ways, state formation and commercial expansion (including privateering and piracy) were mutually constitutive for the early maritime nation-states of England and the Low Countries. This symbiotic relationship can perhaps be seen in the kingdom of death that Milton's Satan tries to build through his acts of piracy. In that regard, the numerous maritime allusions in Milton's depiction of Satan are suggestive.

Fearing the corrupting effects of Eastern wealth, Milton also links Europeans to orientalist imagery in *Paradise Lost* in a critique of mercantile imperialism. Even an obviously orientalist allusion such as the reference to "the barren Plaines / Of *Sericana* where *Chineses* drive / With Sails and Wind thir canie Waggons light" (3.437–39) is triangulated by the Dutch and hints at their monarchical ambitions. Wind-propelled Chinese land yachts, described in sixteenth century European print accounts (and illustrated in Abraham Ortelius's 1583 map of China) inspired the *zeilwagen* built by Dutch engineer Simon Stevin for Prince Maurits.[88] In the spring 1602 test ride, Stevin's land yacht carried 28 passengers (including the prince, the French ambassador, and the brother of the Danish king) along the beach from Scheveningen to Petten for a distance of almost 60 miles in under two hours. The drawing of the event by the Antwerp-born Jacques (or Jacob) de Gheyn II (1565–1625) was subsequently engraved by Willem van Swanenburg, and its publication as a large print in 1603 helped broadcast Stevin's invention.[89] It was subsequently satirized in a number of Dutch prints, including the 1637 *Floraes Mallewagen* (Flora's Car of Fools) by Crispijn van de Pas Jr., which uses the wind chariot to reference the greed, folly, and ambition driving the speculative frenzy of tulip mania.[90]

Stevin's land yacht was popularized in England by John Wilkins's *Mathematicall Magick* (1648). Sidney Gottlieb suggests that Milton might have been satirizing Wilkins's argument for harnessing wind as a source of energy in the section on the paradise of fools: "Far from being a sign of cosmic vigor tamed by rational husbandry, wind here is a comic sign of intellectual folly, even flatulence."[91] As symbol of foolishness, wind is prominently featured in the passage in *Paradise Lost* on land yachts. An epic simile comparing Satan's unbounded flight to that of a vulture's from north to south over India and China is followed by the section on the paradise of fools, climaxing in the vanities and material corruption of friars that thematize the vices of pride, greed, and ambition. Another of Milton's multilayered allusions, the "cany wagons light" points to the Indies trade and to the ambitions of the House of Orange. Certainly, by the 1650s, Milton would have become aware of the developing Orange and Stuart alliance, which threatened the English republic.[92]

Milton's pattern of allusions linking East and West does not show a straightforwardly imperial stance toward Asia. With this in mind, we need to reconsider readings of Satan's encounter with Adam and Eve that view the scene as colonial. David Quint argues, "Adam and Eve...assume the roles of innocent natives victimized by their European conquerors."[93] However, Satan's offer to Eve of an exotic fruit with powerful medicinal qualities is more reminiscent of merchants peddling Eastern spices in Europe than of European trade in Asia, where they had to pay bullion for Asian products. Given the propaganda depicting the Dutch as devils in response to the 1623 Amboyna massacre, it might even be possible to see Satan's relation to Adam and Eve as reflecting the struggle between the English and the Dutch for preeminence in the Indies. It is misleading to argue that Europeans were conquerors in

Asia. Satan's encounter with Chaos, as I have noted, is more typical of European experience in Asia. We cannot frame Asian-European relations of the period in terms of inferior Indians and superior Europeans. Rival Europeans courted native princes and merchants as allies in their struggles with each other much as Satan involves Adam and Eve in his war against God. Milton's contemporaries did not make the mistake of assuming a colonial paradigm. Arguing that the Portuguese were not able to subject Asians to their rule, Hugo Grotius gave a rather different picture of the islanders of Southeast Asia: "Nor truly are the Indians out of their wits and unsensible but ingenious and sharp-witted."[94] Grotius's thinking on Asia would change. Initially open-minded about Asian rulers, he became more hostile over time, with exposure to practical politics and greater awareness of the formidable trading skills of Arabs and Asians.[95] Yet he remained very much aware of their claim to self-sovereignty.

Rather than reading Milton's comparison of Adam and Eve to Indians as colonial, I would suggest that the comparison of Adam and Eve to both kinds of Indians in book 9 is part of Milton's larger strategy to depict a unified world about to become fractured by sin. The ambiguity of Milton's postlapsarian landscape—neither new world nor old—is replicated in the ambiguity of his famed comparison of Adam and Eve to both East Indians and Amerindians. The fig tree with whose leaves they clothe themselves is that "as at this day to *Indians* known / In *Malabar* or *Decan*" (*PL* 9.1102–03), and underneath it "the *Indian* Herdsman shunning heate / Shelters" (9.1108–09). But they are also compared to Amerindians: "Such of late / *Columbus* found th' *American* so girt / With featherd Cincture, naked else and wilde" (9.1115–17). Neither East Indians nor Native Americans, Adam and Eve encompass both. Moreover, they represent Europeans as well. Karen Edwards argues, "Adam and Eve's history is written on the bodies of all their children. The American's feathered cincture and the Indian herdsman's tree-shelter do not point to the difference between natives and Europeans but to their common ancestry."[96]

Even contemporaries saw commonalities. In their sixteenth century struggle for independence from Spain, the Dutch compared themselves to Native Americans, seeing in them fellow victims of the Spanish empire.[97] Thus, the Dutch are represented by both Satan and his victims. One offers a typical English demonization of the Dutch while the other presents the Dutch's own ideal self-image. Rather than presenting a colonial encounter, Milton juxtaposes two contrary views of the Dutch to explore the contradictions, the possibilities, and the failures of the kind of trading empire that the Dutch were successfully building and that the English were attempting to imitate, an empire he condemns for theft and tyranny.

Milton's opposition to monarchical tyranny is not merely domestic but also international as he frames the issues of *Paradise Lost* in terms of European piratical attacks on each other in Asia. The Dutch and developing English seaborne empires become targets of his criticism and a focus for his concerns about sovereignty at home and abroad. Trade networks facilitate both the transportation of exotic fruit and war among Protestants. The Indies trade and tyranny become linked in *Paradise Lost*. There Milton offers a terrifying vision of what travel between distant places can bring, for Death and Sin build a bridge from the world to hell, a thoroughfare comparable to the one Xerxes built to enthrall Greece when he "Came to the Sea, and over Hellespont / Bridging his way, Europe with Asia joyn'd" (*PL* 10.309–10). The bridge is the result of Sin and Death's ambition to extend their dominion, an ambition incited by Death's taste for new foods. Telling Sin to lead the way, Death sniffs the smell of human flesh in the air, saying, "such a scent I draw / Of carnage, prey innumerable, and taste / The savour of Death from all things there that live" (10.267–69). This empire of piracy and death is no sanguine view of trade networks. Offering instead a picture of European depredations of each other, Milton reminds us that robbers who turn emperors are still no better than pirates.

University of Oklahoma

Theology

"Greedily she ingorg'd":
Eve and the Bread of Life

Christopher Baker

After his elaborate temptation speech in *Paradise Lost*, Satan offers Eve the forbidden fruit by saying, "Goddess humane, reach then, and freely taste."[1] Addressing Eve with dubious logic as both divine and human, he encourages her to "reach then," casually implying that this act of hers is only to be expected after he, as she later says, "Persuasively hath so prevail'd" (*PL* 9.873). Satan's invitation to "freely taste" is just as dissembling, as if her choice to do so were at this point completely unencumbered by his "glozing lies" (3.93). The language of the temptation recalls that of the creature in Eve's dream in book 5, who had also "pluckt" and "tasted" (5.65), but Eve's own action is even bolder, as the narrator's final verb asserts: "Forth reaching to the Fruit, she pluck'd, she eat" (9.781). Ten lines later, a still stronger verb, at the very center of its line, degrades Eve even more dramatically: "Greedily she ingorg'd without restraint" (9.791).[2] The forceful adverb propels the line forward, conveying the all-consuming intensity of Eve's fateful meal. Forms of the verb "to gorge" occur only three times in *Paradise Lost* and once in *Samson Agonistes,* and they are consistently sinister. Apart from Eve's statement, Satan in book 3 walks like a "Vulture" who seeks "To gorge the flesh of Lambs or yeanling Kids" (3.434), while in book 10, God graphically describes Sin and Death as his "Hell-hounds" (10.630), who

95

> lick up the draff and filth
> Which man's polluting Sin with taint hath shed
> On what was pure, till cramm'd and gorg'd, nigh burst
> With suckt and glutted offal.   (10.630–33)

The idolatrous Philistines in *Samson Agonistes* are similarly "drunk with Wine, / And fat regorg'd of Bulls and Goats" (*SA* 1670–71).

Milton's use of "ingorg'd" at the moment of the Fall documents his well-known skill in exploiting the full lexical range of his words; as Christopher Ricks remarks, "the inspiration of words that would otherwise be half-dead is inseparable from Milton's famous liking for using words with their original Latin meaning."[3] The linguistic connection between *ingorge* and the Latin *gurges* (whirlpool) is not straightforward, but Milton may well have assumed that his verb derived from the Latin word owing to their similar roots, making his diction poetically apt.[4] Unlike Milton's other ingorging creatures, Eve voraciously ingests the fruit only after first weighing Satan's temptation, and her mouth is rendered a devouring maw reminiscent of the theatrical hell-mouth that consumed sinners in the medieval cycle plays or in the illuminations of prayer books.[5]

If, however, Eve's eating of the fruit is, as others have suggested, a parody of the Roman Catholic Eucharist, then Milton's arresting verb may carry more specific theological and scriptural weight than it typically holds in conventional readings as a marker of her spiritual collapse. I want to argue that Milton's use of the word *ingorge* may derive from his recollection of a similarly forceful word employed in John's Gospel at the point when Jesus impresses upon listening Jews their need to consume physically the bread of life, a passage central to both the Roman Catholic doctrine of transubstantiation and to the contrasting Calvinist belief in the Real Presence. Milton's critique of prelacy and sacramentalism is often couched in language that emphasizes a grotesquely physical devouring of the Communion wafer, and Eve's own verb acquires greater thematic import when read as a Puritan burlesque based on John 6:54, mocking the central doctrine of Catholic eucharistic theology by exaggerating the sense of Christ's emphatic diction as it appears in the Greek New Testament. Satan is an accomplished rhetor, so we are not surprised that what Jamie Ferguson terms the "Eucharistic travesty" by which he entraps Eve employs a sophisticated classical figure such as antanaclasis to destabilize the natural language of Eden.[6] But Milton's narrator is equally adept at shaping his own great argument by means of satire, and the roots of his parody reach beyond traditional rhetorical schemes to a reminiscence of Gospel language that condemns Eve's participation in Satan's specious sacrament.

"Ingorg'd" reminds us that we are far indeed from the decorous meal of book 5 or the earlier snack of "savory pulp" that Adam and Eve innocently "chew" in Eden (*PL* 4.335). Eve has now cast off any hint of moderation; the verb stresses her utter lack of hospitality as she, Satan-like, unrestrainedly gratifies only herself.[7] Commentators, with good reason, have typically read the word *ingorge* as an indicator of Eve's moral and spiritual demise. It expresses the sin of gluttony mingled with lust to which Michael Lieb has pointed, her "vulgarity and brutality" as identified by Glenda Jacobs, and "the full play of her appetitive self" as she takes on a new, illusory identity, as noted by Jun Harada. Anne Cotterill contends that "The frenzied greed around 'ingorg'd' reflects the restless and self-consuming quality of the act to which Eve has allowed herself to be led," and in Ovidian terms Milton's verb discloses that Eve, according to Mandy Green, "becomes like one of the Circean herd, a creature of excessive appetite."[8]

Yet the word *ingorge* at this juncture, owing to its placement in a scene infused with Roman Catholic resonances, connotes more than the gratification of pride, hunger, and libidinal desire or the tragic alteration of Eve's identity. Like an eager catechist, Satan has prepared Eve for this act with careful instruction, offering himself (that is, the transformed serpent) as an apparent example of the fruit's efficacy. Eve finds such delight "as seem'd, / In Fruit she never tasted" (*PL* 9.787–88). And she eagerly devours "this Fruit Divine" (9.776), convinced that with it she will "grow mature / In knowledge, as the Gods who all things know" (9.803–04). For John King, Eve's eating is a perversion of the eucharistic ritual; it "seems to take on the character of a parodic Mass that recalls insatiable clerical appetites condemned in Milton's antiprelatical tracts and the gluttony of hell-dogs," and "the representation of Eve's sin in terms of intoxication 'as with wine' [9.793] is analogous to misuse of sacramental wine." Thomas Stroup characterizes Eve's "low

Reverence" (9.835) to the tree after she has eaten the fruit as "possibly a genuflection…intended to be associated, no doubt, with papistry," while Anne Barbeau Gardiner situates Satan's fraudulent praise of Eve more precisely within a fulsome mariolatry, her adoration of the tree mocking Catholic eucharistic hymns such as the *Vexilla regis* of Venantius Fortunatus.[9]

Such a satiric contextualization of Eve's action points Milton's parody as much toward the theology of the Mass as toward what the Archangel Michael will later call its "outward Rites and specious forms" (*PL* 12.534). I want to add that Milton's critique of sacramentalism at the moment of Eve's eating appears to draw upon his revisiting of the bread of life discourse in John's Gospel (6:22–71).[10] In these verses, Jesus proclaims himself as the true spiritual food of his believers after he has satisfied the physical hunger of the 5,000 on the shore of Galilee. Announcing "I am the bread of life" (John 6:35), he declares that he "came down from heaven, not to do mine own will, but the will of him that sent me" (John 6:38).[11] In an exchange that anticipates Satan's dialogue with the skeptical Eve prior to her fall, Jesus tells the murmuring crowd that they should prefer him as the bread of life to the bread they have just eaten for their bodily nourishment. Everyone who "believeth on him, may have everlasting life" (John 6:40), for he is "the bread which cometh down from heaven, that a man may eat thereof, and not die" (John 6:50). As the Geneva gloss on verse 32 states, "He denies that manna was the true heavenly bread and says that he himself is the true bread, because he feeds the true and everlasting life."[12] Satan seeks to repeat a similar promise of immortality to Eve but for the wrong reason:

> do not believe
> Those rigid threats of Death; ye shall not Die:
> How should ye? By the Fruit? it gives you Life
> To Knowledge.   (*PL* 9.684–87)

Like the hesitant Jews, Eve does not at first accept what she is being told, noting that Satan's "overpraising leaves in doubt / The virtue of that Fruit" (9.615–16). Satan will convince Eve to fall by presenting himself as the reality of a new life enabled by the fruit, misconceived by her as beneficial, just as the bread and wine, from a Catholic perspective, embody rather than act as a sign of a contrasting salvation through Christ, who tells the crowd, "Whoso eateth my flesh, and drinketh my blood, hath eternal life; and I will raise him up at the last day" (John 6:54).[13]

John's bread of life discourse is, along with the synoptic accounts of the Lord's Supper (Matt. 26:26–28, Mark 14:24–25, Luke 22:9–20), a primary scriptural basis for the doctrine of transubstantiation as formally adopted by the Fourth Lateran Council of 1215 (the sacramental ritual is again described in 1 Cor. 11:23–26). This doctrine held that the bread and wine of the Mass do become the body and blood of Christ at the moment of consecration by the priest while the physical appearance and material composition of these elements remain unchanged. The first of Henry VIII's Six Articles (1539) had affirmed "that in the most blessed sacrament of the altar, by the strength and efficacy of Christ's mighty word...is present really, under the form of bread and wine, the natural body and blood of our Savior Jesus Christ...and that after the consecration there remaineth no substance of bread and wine, nor any other substance, but the substance of Christ, God and man."[14] This doctrine is expressly rejected by Elizabethan and later English Protestant theology, as, for example, in one of the most explicit statements of reformed theology in the Anglican Thirty-Nine Articles (1563). Article 28 ("Of the Lord's Supper") asserts, "Transubstantiation (or the change of the substance of the Bread and Wine) in the Supper of the Lord, cannot be proved by Holy Writ; but is repugnant to the plain words of scripture, overthroweth the nature of a sacrament, and hath given occasion to many superstitions."[15] Fourteen years before the publication of *Paradise Lost,* Jeremy Taylor likewise contended that "the doctrine of Transubstantiation is infinitely useless, and to no purpose." The result of such a belief for the communicant is dire: "this corporal union of our bodies to the body of God incarnate which these great and witty dreamers dream of, would make man to be God. For that which has a real and substantial unity with God, is consubstantial with the true God, that is, he is really, substantially, and truly God, which to affirm were highest blasphemy."[16]

The blasphemy of such an errant understanding of the Eucharist accords with the blasphemy of Satan's fraudulent appeal to Eve, by

which he persuades her to believe in the capability of a wisdom-endow-
ing fruit to effect in her a divine metamorphosis:

> ye shall be as Gods,
> Knowing both Good and Evil as they know.
> That ye should be as Gods, since I as Man,
> Internal Man, is but proportion meet,
> I of brute human, yee of human Gods.   (*PL* 9.708–12)

As shaped by Satan, Eve's understanding of the fruit distorts the Protestant conception of the Communion bread as a sign or figure for a larger
divine reality beyond itself in contrast to the Roman Catholic perception
of it as a material substance that retains a localized spiritual potency.
Her "ingorging" of this fruit is a hyperbolic version of what Taylor
(along with Milton and other reformers) argued as Christ's intending of
a "spiritual manducation"[17] rather than a carnal consumption.

The Greek text of John 6 uses as synonyms two words that in classical
Greek had distinguished different categories of eating. One is a conventional verb denoting the generic act of eating to satisfy bodily hunger.
The other is a more vigorous verb expressing the energetic biting and
mastication of food; it later helped affirm for Catholics what the Six Acts
called "the substance of Christ, God and man" and hence the doctrine
of transubstantiation. Luther and Calvin, however, read both words as
metaphors for the believer's faithful allegiance to the words and presence of Christ, an eating that was spiritually understood. In the Geneva
and King James translations, Jesus' use of *eat* in John 6:54 repeats the
same verb he uses in verses 50–53, but this is not the reading of that
verse in Greek texts upon which Milton is likely to have relied, nor did
he probably construe these two verbs as casual synonyms.

As Stella Revard and Ira Clark demonstrate, Milton had a close
knowledge of John's Gospel, a text of central importance for *Paradise
Regained*.[18] Milton refers to the sixth chapter of John often in *De doctrina
Christiana*, twice quoting directly from the Greek text of John in his comments on "divine glory," including "vi.46: not that anyone has seen the
Father, except him who is from God, ὁ ὢν παρὰ τοῦ Θεόυ." He may
have seen the 1521 Greek New Testament of Erasmus or, more likely,
the 1569 *textus receptus* of Robert Estienne or the 1587 edition of Robert's
son Henri (who styled himself Stephanus), in all of which Jesus employs a

stronger verb in verse 54.[19] Instead of forms of the verb φαγεῖν (*phagein,* "to eat"), which he speaks in verses 49–53, he shifts to τρώγων (*trōgon*), a more intensive verb, which in classical texts meant "to *gnaw, nibble, munch,* [especially] of herbivorous animals, as mules." In such authors as Aristophanes, Homer, Theocritus, Herodotus, and Xenophon the word was applied to cattle, swine, and dogs, and, in regard to humans, it pertained to "human beings in disease" (Hippocrates) as well as humans eating "vegetables or fruit."[20] Liddell and Scott note that in postclassical texts it meant "simply *eat*" and could function as the present tense of ἔφαγον; they cite the opening portion of John 6:54: ὁ τρώγων μου τὴν σάρκα καὶ πίνων μου τὸ αἷμα (Whoso **eateth** my flesh and drinketh my blood; my emphasis). The verb also carries a participial meaning relevant to Eve's voracity of "a continuing appropriation."[21] This word, like Milton's verb, is somewhat uncommon in its text (it does not appear in the Septuagint and only five times in the New Testament) and carries a similarly emphatic lexical force not unlike *ingorge* in conveying the masticating, physical consumption of food.[22] F. F. Bruce suggests that the difference between *phagein* and *trōgein* "could well be conveyed in German by using the verbs *essen* and *fressen* respectively," *essen* referring to the act of human eating and *fressen* being the crude way in which animals consume their food.[23] Although Rudolph Schnackenburg argues that "the word used in the Greek for 'eat' (τρώγειν) does not have to be understood in an extreme realistic sense ('chew')," a more vigorous connotation for the verb gains support from Rudolph Bultmann, who notes that "it is possible that in colloquial usage τρώγειν took on the meaning of 'eat' = 'devour,' which it has in modern Greek."[24]

By the time of its use in John's Gospel, the verb may have lost its earlier meaning of animals and humans hungrily devouring herbs and fruits, but its classical connotations so fittingly amplify the debased quality of Eve's fall that it seems unlikely for Milton not to have intended knowledgeable readers to recall them; such echoes are part of an "answerable style" (*PL* 9.20) for his "fit audience" (7.31). Jesus also employs *trōgon* (as *trogontes,* τρώγοντες) in Matthew 24:38 to describe the lives of those before the Flood who were "eating and drinking, marrying and giving in marriage." Their indulgence in a thoughtless, pleasure-loving life has overtones of Eve's own heedlessness, for it conveys an eating "without concern and without any forboding of an impending catastrophe."[25] This verse is the basis of Edward Leigh's definition of the word in his lexicon of biblical Hebrew and Greek, *Critica sacra* (1662): "They gave themselves to eating as brute beasts; so the word signifieth; for otherwise it is no fault to eat. The word is properly used of beasts, so *Homer* useth it; and the Hebrew phrase of eating being in the present time, noteth a continuance of eating, as brute beasts will eat all day, & some part of the night: yet this word is used also of men eating spiritually, John 6.v 54, 56, 57, 58 and 13.18."[26] Leigh's first sentence in this entry is a brief paraphrase of a Latin comment by Theodore Beza included as a marginal note: "Quum illud propriè de brutis de dici, videtur magna esse hujus verbi emphasis, quo significatur homines brutorum instat fore ventrit deditos nam alioqui edere & bibere per se non est vitium, *Beza*" (Grammarians emphasize this verb to describe an irrational creature or men without reason who are dedicated to the urging of their stomachs; aside from this, eating or drinking per se is not a vice).

Leigh's opening statement is a helpful gloss on Eve's "ingorging" of the fruit, which she is certainly not "eating spiritually." Jesus' use of *trogontes* sharpens his pointed warning against thoughtless antediluvian indulgence, and the word's conjunction of animal and spiritual contexts lends it a possible pejorative meaning that Milton could have found useful, as Eve thinks she is acting in a godly fashion while in fact she is behaving bestially in eating the apple. Milton had also used *gorge* in an image rather similar to Homer's—in this case referring to hungrily feeding birds of prey—in an acerbic passage in *Animadversions* (1641), citing lucrative church positions that were "the very garbage that drawes together all the fowles of prey and ravin in the land to come, and gorge upon the Church" (YP 1:718).[27] In contrast to the otherwise theologically exalted language of John's Gospel, in John 6:54, Christ bluntly underscores for his audience the fact of his truly human nature, thus countering any possible Gnostic or Docetic views of himself; he is a physical man, not merely some spiritual phantom.[28] Yet, as Calvin and other reformers had (following Augustine) emphasized, though Christ is truly present his truth can be apprehended only by a faithful eating and not by a mere physical gratification alone, which is all that Eve's ingorging can provide her.[29]

For Puritan readers, the energy of Christ's diction conveys the active belief in his spiritual presence required of his followers, neither an ideational knowledge of his body somehow circumscribed within a material object nor the satisfaction of a merely human hunger. Unlike Jesus, who identifies himself as the heavenly food and offers himself to serve his father's will (compare 3.236–56), Satan shrewdly does not actually claim to be the fruit itself but encourages Eve to believe in its autonomous agency, through which he alleges he has attained a "life more perfet…than Fate / Meant mee, by vent'ring higher than my Lot" (*PL* 9.689–90). Satan has of course come to earth to do his own will and no one else's, and the fruit's purpose is likewise entirely self-referential: it is to be eaten not as a sign of devotion to any higher reality but solely for the aggrandizement of whoever eats it. When Satan exclaims of the apple, "Now I feel thy Power / Within me clear" (9.680–81), he would have sounded like a Catholic to Puritan ears. As Bruce Gerrish comments, "against the Romanists…Calvin denies that the sacraments [themselves, apart from Christ] are endowed with 'I know not what secret powers.'"[30]

For Eve in *Paradise Lost,* the fruit Satan proffers appears to hold the potential of the person she hopes to become, a reality seemingly coexistent with the apple itself, while behind his offer of "reach…and…taste" echoes the *Accipite et manducate* (take and eat) of the Mass. The promise of a heightened identity in her earlier dream — "among the Gods / Thyself a Goddess" (*PL* 5.77–78) — now seems literally within reach, so that in grasping for the apple she is reaching for her projected sense of an exalted self. The gesture also echoes her earlier mesmerizing encounter with her own reflection: "What there thou seest fair Creature is thyself" (4.468). Her greedy "ingorging" thus becomes a feast of oblivious egoism: "*Eve* / Intent now wholly on her taste, naught else / Regarded" (9.785–87). Adam later mimics her in both attitude and act: "*Adam* took no thought, / Eating his fill" (9.1004–05). After Satan has returned to hell, his fallen angels similarly enact the meaning of *trōgo* and recall Eve's fallen state: "they fondly thinking to allay / Thir appetite with gust, instead of Fruit / Chew'd bitter Ashes" (10.564–66) and "writh'd their jaws / With soot and cinders fill'd" (10.569–70).

By disdaining God's command, Eve has rejected that prior and necessary attitude of faith, which for the reformers underlay the validity of Communion. Her obsession with the apple only for her own sake is clearly at odds with Calvin's understanding of the nature of the sacrament, as Ronald Wallace explains: "In participating in the Supper faith connects itself with something outside of itself and other than mere idea, and, in so doing, effects in the spiritual realm a real communication between itself and the earthly reality such as that figured in the act of eating the bread. Thus Calvin says that the eating is more than simply believing. Eating is for him the effect or fruit of faith."[31] Furthermore, from Calvin's point of view, it would be significant that Eve "ingorg'd" the apple alone, Satan having "Back to the Thicket slunk" (*PL* 9.784), before she feeds "without restraint" (9.791). William Bouwsma comments, "The way in which the sacrament was celebrated in the Roman church offended [Calvin's] sense of community. Private masses, in which 'one person withdraws and gulps alone and there is no sharing among the faithful,' seemed to him a mockery of communion."[32] (Calvin too was not above using extravagant language to describe Catholic worship.)

Faith in God, manifested prior to Christ's birth in Eve's obedience to the divine warning to avoid the tree, has been replaced by her false faith in the special transformation supposedly to be gained by chewing its fruit. Reading Eve's "ingorging" through Augustine's comments on John 6:54 highlights the enormity of what Satan hopes she will regard as merely a "petty Trespass" (*PL* 9.693) and facilitates our vision of her sin within this specific scriptural context.[33] Calvin, certain of Christ's real presence in the Communion, though modestly less sure of how to explain it, devotes an entire section of chapter 17 of his *Institutes* to John 6:54, drawing approvingly upon the Augustinian distinction between physical and spiritual eating, of which Eve is unaware. Calvin cites several of Augustine's pejorative references to "teeth" that consistently imply the rejection of a literal reading of *trōgo*, contending instead that the word signifies the inward, faithful appropriation of Christ, something far different from Eve's carnal act of eating.[34] John's Gospel verse, according to Augustine, refers to "the virtue of the sacrament, and not merely the visible sacrament: the sacrament of him who eats inwardly, not of him who eats outwardly, or merely with the teeth."[35] Furthermore, "he who remains not in Christ, and in whom Christ remains not, without doubt neither spiritually eats his flesh, nor drinks his blood, though with his teeth he may carnally and visibly press the symbol of his body and blood" (921). Lastly, Augustine instructs, "Prepare not the jaws, but the heart; for which alone the Supper is appointed.... It is not therefore that which is seen, but that which is believed, which feeds" (922).[36]

Jesus' replacement of the more generic verb (*phago*) with a more emphatic one (*trōgo*) has the effect of dispelling misconceptions about his physical being and, from a Puritan perspective, of signifying the thorough, yet spiritual, incorporation of his reality by the believer in faith; as Luther quipped in his sermon on John 6:51, "it will not be the sort of flesh from which red sausages are made."[37] And as Beza writes in his marginal commentary on John 6:52, "Fleshe can not put a difference betweene fleshly eating, which is done by the helpe of the teeth, and spirituall eating which consisteth in faith: and therefore it condemneth that which it understandeth not."[38]

Milton's epic narrator too intensifies his language from "eat" to "ingorge," but to emphasize instead Eve's misplaced obsession with the fruit that has obviated her obedience to God. Christ's description of an eager and faithful chewing of the true bread is degraded by Eve to the merely physical feeding upon a forbidden food, wrongly assumed to possess a spiritual vitality. If Eve's "ingoring" of the apple is read as a Miltonic rewriting of the Johannine *trōgo*, enhanced by Milton's recollection of feeding animals in the *Odyssey* and similar classical uses of the verb, we are better able to appreciate how his poetic diction fuses pagan and Christian connotations of the word to mock the bestial physicality of her eating and her misconceived, satanic theology of Communion.

Such an allusion to John's Greek diction would not be out of place in a dramatic scene that has been recognized for its carefully wrought language, such as the unique rhyming couplet at 9.781–82, the Latin pun on "Sapience" as both "wisdom" and "taste" (*PL* 9.797), and especially the famous ending of the statement under discussion: "And knew not eating Death" (9.792). Eve both eats and is (unknowingly) eaten by Death.[39] Annabel Patterson finds this "a very strange and clever locution; it requires a degree of abstract thought that is certainly beyond

Eve, and perhaps some readers too."[40] Yet Milton's intentional use of Greek syntax here serves a larger literary and theological purpose. Kenneth Haynes points out that "the strangeness of the expression bears witness to a foreign element, which in this case is both Greek and Latin, Virgil having imitated the grecism and introduced it into his Latin (*Aeneid* 2.377). Participating in the Renaissance aspiration to recreate authority and deliberate magnificence, Milton imitates both languages at once."[41]

A Miltonic recollection of *trōgo* broadens the scope of this "grecism" by associating Eve's eating with that of animals (an appropriate denigration of her Edenic status) and extends the line's thematic reach beyond a reflection of pagan antiquity to suggest a topic of reformation doctrinal debate. By focusing Eve's attention and ours upon her physical consumption of the apple and its inherent power, Milton implies that her eating of a food she is convinced will lift her to a godlike knowledge casts her as a misguided communicant whose devouring perverts Christ's command to "eat" his flesh. She crudely parodies the gesture and misses the faith that defines it, thus committing what all reformers regarded as a radical theological error. As Timothy Rosendale rightly states, Satan's "entire argument in terms of knowledge contained within the Tree itself…is a fundamental (and, in a Miltonic context, distinctly Catholic) misreading."[42]

While Zwinglians believed Communion to be essentially a memorial event and Lutherans favored consubstantiation (according to which Christ's body and blood were with, rather than in, the elements), for Calvinists and Anglicans there existed in the Lord's Supper a Real Presence of Christ that was legitimized only through the believing assent of the faithful, and that was not to be understood in the Roman Catholic terms of Aristotelian "substance" and "accidents" as these were adapted by Thomistic theology. As Calvin writes in his commentary on John 6:47, "I acknowledge that Christ is not eaten but by faith, that he may dwell in us.…To *eat* him, therefore, is an effect or work of faith."[43] Milton's position on the nature of the Communion is stated unequivocally in *De doctrina:* "Consubstantiation and particularly transubstantiation and papal ἀνθρωποφάγια or cannibalism are utterly alien to reason, common sense and human behavior.…The papist Mass is not at all the same as the Lord's Supper" (YP 6:554, 559). Transubstantiation was believed to occur *ex opere operato,* by "the work worked," or in the very operation of the sacrament itself. Milton's dismissive attitude toward this mechanism of transubstantiation is reflected in a derogatory pun. After eating the fruit, Eve praises the tree for its intrinsic ability to grant wisdom by its very nature, "of *operation* blest / To Sapience" (*PL* 9.796–97; emphasis added). But when we next meet the word after Adam has eaten the fruit, what had seemed a beneficial "operation" is now cast more ominously by the narrator:

> As with new Wine intoxicated both
> They swim in mirth, and fancy that they feel
> Divinity within them breeding wings
> Wherewith to scorn the Earth: but that false Fruit
> Far other operation first display'd,
> Carnal desire inflaming.   (*PL* 9.1008–13)

As if at Mass, Adam and Eve have been betrayed by the two Communion "species" they have eaten and drunk. "Far other operation" reveals that the fruit has had a result far worse than they expected; but equally as important is Milton's satiric implication concerning the false fruit's "*other* operation." Its presumed agency resembling *ex opere operato*—to offer "Life / to Knowledge" (9.686–87) under the guise of "fair Apples" (9.585)—is in fact inoperable; those who believe such a doctrine confront "the force of that fallacious Fruit" (9.1046).[44]

Milton's conviction here places him in the company of reformers who emphasized the figural nature of Christ's language when explicating the meaning of the Eucharist, by which "a thing which in any way illustrates or signifies another thing is mentioned not so much for what it really is as for what it illustrates or signifies" (YP 6:555). The Jews had, after all, asked for a *sign*—"What sign shewest thou then, that we may see, and believe thee?" (John 6:30)—and Jesus had reminded them, "It is the spirit that quickeneth; the flesh profiteth nothing" (John 6:63).[45] The Henrician martyr John Frith, for example, stated, "the Sacrament figureth a holy thing"; "I am sure there is no man so childlike but that he knoweth that the figure of a thing is not the thing itself."[46] Eve's inadequate hermeneutic of childlike credulity leads her to "ingorge" Satan's story of his own transformation. Milton's dramatic irony reveals that she cannot rightly read his story because she is unable to distinguish false signs from true ones, to tell the difference between a godly food and a "God-like food" (*PL* 9.717) or the word of God by which she should live from an apple whose only power is that of a rhetorical ploy — "the bait of *Eve*" (10.551).

Typologically, Eve's "ingorging" frames her as one of those Jews in the sixth chapter of John who misunderstand what it means to consume the true bread of life ("How can this man give us his flesh to eat?" [6:52]), as well as the papist who, from a Reformed perspective, respects a delimited existence of Christ's body within the bread over the defining faith in a real presence which variously linked Frith, Calvin, Cranmer, and Taylor.[47] Erasmus had emphasized this misperception of the Jews in his paraphrase of John 6:52–56: "Jesus beyng not ignoraunt about what matter they contended, did not declare unto them by what way [and] meanes that flesh might be eaten in steade of breade, but here now confirmeth [the] thing to be nedeful, [and] a very necessary thing, which they judged but a vayne thing and a plain absurditie, and that it could not be doen."[48] From the skewed perspective of Eve and Satan, it is a "plaine absurditie" *not* to consume the fruit as being anything but a physical food of tangible power, and Milton's denoting of Eve's theological error by reference to her crude, unrefined eating echoes Augustine's unfavorable comments about chewing Christ's flesh with one's teeth.

Consistent with his practice outside *Paradise Lost,* Milton's reference contributes to what Susannah B. Mintz terms, in her discussion of his images of eating, "a grotesquerie in which the spiritually corrupt luxuriate."[49] The "Blind mouths" in *Lycidas* (line 119) come to mind, as well as the "hireling wolves whose Gospel is their maw" in the sonnet on Cromwell (line 14). In *Of Reformation,* Milton castigates the "many-benefice-gaping mouth of a Prelate" with "his canary-sucking, and swan-eating palat" (YP 1:549), not to mention "the obscene, and surfeted Priest [who] scruples not to paw, and mammock the sacramental bread, as familiarly as His Tavern Bisket" (YP 1:548).[50] The masticating language of Milton's criticism of the Mass in *De doctrina* stresses that the words of Christ at the feeding of the 5,000 in John 6 "show us quite clearly" that "the mere flesh is of no use here any more than it was in feeding the five thousand: also that not teeth but faith is needed to eat his flesh" (YP 6:553).

Not surprisingly, animal imagery again makes an appearance: "The Papists hold that it is Christ's actual flesh which is eaten by all in the Mass. But if this were so, even the most wicked of the communicants, not to mention the mice and worms which often eat the eucharist, would attain eternal life by virtue of that heavenly bread" (YP 6:553). And in one of the most famous examples of Miltonic polemic, we read that the Mass "drags" the body of Christ "back to the earth," "to be broken once more and crushed and ground, even by the fangs of brutes" (YP 6:560). I do not suggest that these references to the chewing of the Communion bread all spring from Milton's remembrance of the unique Greek verb in John 6:54, but rather that Milton's predisposition to link theological error with a devouring orality could have made the Gospel writer's diction an attractive linguistic model for his own satiric language.

Regina Schwartz argues that Raphael's banquet in book 5 of *Paradise Lost* announces a Miltonic definition of transubstantiation: Milton's only use of *transubstantiate* occurs at 5.438, in which all of created nature would become transmuted into spirit. "It is not about the wafer turning into the body of Christ or the wine turning into the blood of Christ," Schwartz contends, "it is about man turning into God."[51] Conversely, Eve's ingorging of the apple and Milton's language of gnawing in the antiprelatical tracts proclaim that humans are equally as capable of turning into Satan if they only mimic the action of Christ's command to his Galilean audience without inwardly assenting to his authority.[52]

Denise Gigante describes Eve's situation concisely when she says that for "Milton, as for other Protestants, the symbolic nature of [the Communion] meal is crucial. If flesh is literally eaten, one is transported out of the sacramental and into the superstitious, the irrational sphere of sheer idolatry."[53] Eve has in effect misinterpreted John 6:54, assuming that she need only chew up a seemingly unique fruit to gain a kind of self-gratifying divinity: "dieted by thee I grow mature / In knowledge, as the Gods who all things know" (*PL* 9.803–04). Her voracious eating of the fruit is an adroit Miltonic caricature that employs a kind of transubstantiation to mock that very concept, for it is Eve herself who is transubstantiated from Edenic to fallen being. Her essential, unfallen nature—the radical identity of innocence she enjoyed while in an obedient relationship with God (in Thomistic or Aristotelian terms her "substance")—is perversely transformed by her ingorging of the fruit, while her physical, corporeal self (her "accidents") remains unchanged. Eve's blushing discloses her sudden awareness of this profound change: "But in her Cheek distemper flushing glow'd" (9.887). The "Sapience" she desired has now become instead Adam's knowledge that she is "on a sudden lost, / Defac't, deflow'r'd, and now to Death devote" (9.900–01).[54]

By grounding Eve's parodic consumption of the sacred host in a scriptural passage that addresses both the meaning of the bread of life and the manner in which it is to be consumed, Milton invites his audience to characterize Eve's eating in terms of Paul's statement in 1 Corinthians 11:27 condemning the faithless taking of the sacrament (cited as a marginal gloss on John 6:54 by Beza, the Geneva translation, and in Henri Estienne's 1587 Greek New Testament): "Wherefore whosoever shall eat this bread, and drink this cup of the Lord, unworthily, shall be guilty of the body and blood of the Lord." Her act also confirms Paul's assertion that "he that eateth and drinketh unworthily, eateth and drinketh damnation to himself, not discerning the Lord's body" (1 Cor. 11:29).

Initially unaware of her tragic mistake, Eve becomes "jocund and boon" (*PL* 9.793), like a communicant joyfully grateful at having received the wine and the wafer. But, like the unbelieving Jews at Capernaum who had been fed with loaves and fishes and assumed that salvation was only a matter of menu, she has mortally confused the divine reality of an indwelling God with the mere substance of an ingorged apple. Her misconceived gorging is the dramatic and even grotesquely comic climax of Milton's epic and a preview of Satan's own error when he later seeks to tempt Christ with bread in the desert, only to experience a summary rejection as he too misconstrues the living bread (Matt. 4:1–11, Mark 1:12, Luke 4:1–13, and *Paradise Regained* 1.342–45).[55] By evoking in the reader that "grim laughter...in an austere visage" that Milton believed "hath oft-times a strong and sinewy force in teaching and confuting" (YP 1:663–64), Eve's ingorging mocks the poet's contemporaries who fail to grasp the proper meaning of the bread of life celebrated in Communion. An awareness of Eve's action within its Johannine context enhances our perception "of a new referential aptness in a long familiar line" so that Milton's intent to have the "*viva vox Christi* breaking through the text" can be more fully realized.[56]

Armstrong Atlantic State University

The Trinity in Milton's Hell

Neil Graves

Milton's *Paradise Lost* dramatizes the doctrinally orthodox Trinity of Father, only-begotten Son, and Holy Spirit as it was developed by the patristic fathers of the early Christian church. This statement may seem surprising, given that many Miltonists now consider the poem to manifest a thoroughgoing subordinationism, if not outright Arianism. But this essay will argue that in *Paradise Lost* the orthodox Trinity is found not in heaven, but in hell—a suitable place for such a monstrously perverse notion.

The wheel has come full circle in the interpretative history of Milton's portrayal of the Trinity. Notwithstanding the publication of the stridently Arian *De doctrina Christiana* in 1825, Milton critics long viewed the Godhead in *Paradise Lost* as orthodox and Trinitarian, and to use Ben Jonson's label from *The Alchemist*, adjudged the infernal "venture tripartite" to be a parodic inversion of this Trinity, contributing to the structural opposition of good and evil in the poem.[1] However, critics have come to recognize that the portrayal of the Godhead in Milton's epic is not Trinitarian, given the subordination seen in the Son of God. Yet the view of the infernal triad as a simple and direct inversion of the divine Godhead continues.[2] I want to suggest that the disappearance of the Trinity from the epic's heaven is coupled with its reappearance in hell, for in this great poetic affirmation of faith the whole concept of the Trinity is condemned to the region of the damned;[3] yet hitherto no scholar-pilgrim has undertaken this Dantean trip to the infernal realm to elucidate its precise nature.[4] I will present that evidence in a novel thesis.

Michael Lieb remarks that the debate over the nature of the Miltonic "Trinity" is as vibrant as ever.[5] I will not attempt to define "yet once more" the subordinationist or Arian portrayal of the Miltonic Godhead upon which so much has been written since the 1970s, but it does rest upon the now generally accepted premise that no orthodox divine Trinity exists in *Paradise Lost*.[6] Milton's Satan denounces his offspring, claiming never to have witnessed "Sight more detestable than him and thee";[7] in light of modern Milton scholarship, the same conclusion can be extrapolated from the epic poet's writings about the Trinitarian off-spring of God.

The Son of God in *Paradise Lost* is a subordinate being who lacks the essential Trinitarian attributes of omniscience, ubiquity, immutability, and existence from eternity. Notwithstanding the twofold begetting of the Son in 3.305–41 and 5.600–15, which "By merit more than birthright" (3.309) declares the Son's lack of essential consubstantiality with the Father, the epic's Son demonstrates precisely the subordinationist argu-ment that Athanasius (ca. 296–373), Bishop of Alexandria and renowned as the father of orthodoxy, attacks as heretical in *Contra Arianos:* "whether the Word is alterable,...Has He free will, or has he not? Is He good from choice according to free will, and can He, if He will, alter, being of an alterable nature?"[8] Milton's Son exhibits precisely these Arian quali-ties—specifically named and refuted in the "anathema" of the original Nicene Creed in 325 AD as possessing ἀλλοιωτός ("changeable") and τρεπτός ("alterable") essence—which Arians understood as not only ontological modulation, but also implying "of a moral nature capable of improvement,"[9] making possible filial peccability. Milton's dramatiza-tion in the epic accords with this most strongly maintained Arian belief: "Some one asked of them whether the Son of God could change even as the devil changed; and they feared not to answer that He can; for since He was made and created, He is of mutable nature."[10] Concerning the Holy Spirit in *Paradise Lost,* there is not much to say because the epic does not say much: the Holy Ghost is simply truant. The great celestial council in book 3, like all conversations between members of the poem's Godhead, is a dialogue between Father and Son only, in which even the angels participate, and critics have gone so far as to argue that the apparent invocations of the Holy Spirit refer to the Father rather than to an individuated third member of the Trinity.[11]

It is in the infernal triad that we perceive the rehearsal of specific Trinitarian dogmas that are absent from the poem's divine Godhead; accordingly, I argue that Milton's satanic allegory is a composite polemical satire upon both the Eastern and Western traditions of Trinitarian orthodoxy as developed from the patristic theologians of the early Christian church. This is unsurprising, for Milton had ridiculed the convoluted interpretive endeavors of the patristic church fathers since his earliest prose writings in *Of Reformation* in 1641: "Who is ignorant of the foul errors, the ridiculous wresting of Scripture, the Heresies, the vanities thick sown through the volumes of *Justin Martyr, Clemens, Origen, Tertullian* and others of eldest time?"[12] This essay proposes that Milton's infernal triad is modeled on the Trinitarian doctrines of the Western Christian church and posits Milton's Sin and Death as the Trinitarian Son and Holy Spirit, respectively.

I will demonstrate that the sexual coupling of the father Satan and his offspring Sin, which creates Death, replicates in all its convoluted parentage the Athanasian doctrine of the double procession of the Holy Spirit, facilitated through what Augustine of Hippo (354–430), the most influential theologian in the development of the Western church, terms the "mutual love" of the Father for the Son. The belief that the Holy Spirit proceeds from the Son as well as from the Father was attacked by the Pneumatomachians ("people who make war against the Spirit"),[13] who ridiculed a doctrine which made the Holy Spirit the brother of the Son, or even the Son's son and thereby the grandson of the Father. Likewise, many Arians had accused Trinitarian theologians of establishing the Son as a "brother" to the Father. Such, as we shall see, is the lineage of the incestuous infernal Trinity in *Paradise Lost*. Furthermore, we will examine how the cephalic generation of Sin, modeled on the parthenogenetic birth of the Greek goddess of wisdom, Athena, dramatizes the begetting of the Son as the divine Wisdom of God. This female Old Testament Wisdom figure was typologically interpreted as the Second Person of the Trinity by the central patristic tradition of early Christian apologists from Justin Martyr (ca. 100–65) to Tertullian (ca. 160–225). The Word and Wisdom of God is figured in countless patristic explanations as "springing" out from the Father, and by the time of Augustine in the late fourth century AD as proceeding from the intellect of God. The only begotten Son is generated directly from the substance of the Father, sharing homogeneity of being, which is manifested in their identity of purpose—of crucial importance to the Trinitarian defense of divine unity in the Godhead.

Paradise Lost satirizes the confusion and contrariety of orthodox Trinitarian doctrines of both West and East. Having considered Satan, Sin, and Death as satire on Western Trinitarian doctrine, I will go on to examine how Milton's infernal allegory also replicates the Eastern doctrine of the Trinity, which depicts the person of Death and not Sin as the only-begotten Son of the Father, with Sin now figuring as the Holy Spirit. Milton's Death is a true offspring by nature and not in title only, whose procreative birth is dramatized in *Paradise Lost* in terms of the analogy expounded by the Eastern patristic writers of Seth's genera-tion from Adam and Eve. This is the Son Death who in his confronta-tion with his Father is revealed as unsubordinated in power or rank but truly equal—a key point of conflict for the Arians, who denied the ὁμοούσιος, or unity of essence of the Son with God. Accordingly, Sin appears as the Holy Spirit of the orthodox Trinity, not begotten but "proceeding" from the Father alone according to Eastern Trinitarian dogma, and issuing forth "as the breath of God's mouth," in the words of Saint Basil (ca. 329–79), bishop of Caesarea and preeminent member of the influential Cappadocian triumvirate of theologians. Understood in this manner, the cephalic birth of the Wisdom figure recalls the ulti-mately subsumed early patristic tradition of his identification with the Holy Spirit, and not with the Son of God.

The primary cause of this division of the Christian church into East and West concerned the precise formation of the Trinity. Specifically, the *filioque* clause ("and the Son") originated in a letter from Pope Leo I to members of the Synod of Toledo in Spain in 447 AD and was added to the Nicene Creed at the Third Council of Toledo in 589 AD, thereby involving the Son causally in the procession of the Holy Spirit from God the Father.[14] The result became two orthodox theories of the Trinity, with the Eastern church following primarily the Greek patristic writers, who placed a strong emphasis upon the distinct identity of each person of the Godhead, and the Western church based upon the Latin fathers, who stressed the unity of the Godhead. This disagreement over the procession of the Holy Spirit originated from vigorous fourth century patristic discussions regarding the ontological nature of the Logos or Son of God, but both Eastern and Western Trinitarian doctrines were grounded in the concept of ὁμοούσιος, which expressed the diversity of the three persons while retaining the unity of their essentially common nature. The two doctrines of the hypostatic procession of the Holy Spirit were termed "a Patre Filioque tanquam ab uno principio" (from the Father and the Son as from one principle) and ἐκ τοῦ Πατρός μόνου ("from the Father alone"), and represented two different triadological solutions to the question of personal diversity in the Trinity.[15] The Western doctrine became known as the "double procession of the Holy Spirit" due to the causal agency of both God and the Son, while the Eastern doctrine endorsed the ἐκπόρευσις, or single procession of the Third Person from the Father alone. This essay will show that the allegory of Satan, Sin, and Death in *Paradise Lost* combines elements from both orthodox doctrines to form a comprehensive satire upon Christian Trinitarian theology.

The Trinity of Satan, Sin, and Death in *Paradise Lost*

It is indisputable that the allegory of Satan, Sin, and Death that appears in two extended scenes in *Paradise Lost* (2.629–889, and mentioned in 2.1024–33, and 10.229–409) portrays a Trinity. The first allegorical scene in which Satan confronts his hitherto unknown apologetic daughter, Sin, and aggressively autonomous son, Death, and the second scene in which they venture forth from hell to colonize creation, are replete with allusions to the Nicene Creed—the creed whose primary function in 325 AD was to enforce Trinitarian orthodoxy, which had been under threat from Sabellian modalism and Arian subordinationism.[16] Additionally, there are the numerous biblical allusions and quotations referring to the Godhead, and the dramatic and ontological relationships between the three characters. Imitating the Nicene Creed, Sin, the "offspring dear... [of] Satan our great author" (10.236–38), describes herself as "thy perfect image" (2.764), who "shall reign / At thy right hand... without end" (2.868–70), for "Thou art my father, thou my author, thou / My being gav'st me" (2.864–65). Death is "Thine own begotten" (2.782), "only son" (2.728) to the "Father" (2.810) Satan, who as "monarch reign[s]" (10.375) and "unites us three" (10.364). Evident among these biblical allusions are those that were traditionally interpreted as evidence of the Trinitarian Godhead in the Old Testament. For instance, Sin's outcry to Satan, "O Father, what intends thy hand, she cried, / Against thy only son?" (2.727–28), echoes Abraham's proffered sacrifice of his son Isaac in Genesis 22, interpreted typologically by Christian readers as God's sacrifice of his Son Jesus on the cross[17] and in the epic applied to the father Satan and his son, Death.

Furthermore, Sin and Death duplicate the creative power of the Godhead found in the Creation account of Genesis by building in the "Wide anarchy of chaos damp and dark" (*PL* 10.283), and described in the poem as a typological reference to the Holy Spirit in Genesis 1:2, "with power (their power was great) / Hovering upon the waters" (10.284–85). This analogy is supported in the divine Creation scene in *Paradise Lost*, book 7, where "darkness profound / Covered the abyss: but on the watery calm / His brooding wings the spirit of God outspread" (233–35).[18] Sin and Death are the agents of satanic creativity with their construction of the demonic bridge that links hell with earth, imitating the creative roles of the orthodox Son and Spirit. One critic claims that "Satan's confrontation with Sin and Death is a recognition scene to end all recognition scenes,"[19] and this powerful drama provides a detailed description of the precise relationships among the triad as well as their ontological formation. These can both be seen as clearly Trinitarian. Ontologically, Sin and Death are "double-formed" (*PL* 2.741) directly from the very substance of Satan himself. Concerning their interrelations, Sin continually comments on the inseparability (10.250) and essential harmony (10.358) that binds her and Death together with Satan, a

> sympathy, or some connatural force
> Powerful at greatest distance to unite

With secret amity things of like kind
By secretest conveyance.   (10.246–49)

The satanic triad also demonstrates the harmony of unitary action found
in the persons of the orthodox Trinity due to their consubstantiality.
Death is confirmed as truly coequal with his father, Satan, during a
thrilling scene in which the thorny question of filial subordination is
explored and repudiated; while Sin, "Likest to thee [Satan] in shape
and countenance bright" (2.756), recognizes instinctively the interre-
lated ontological nature that binds the persons of the infernal Trinity
together.[20]

Satan, Sin, and Death are, furthermore, invested with a host of
famous iconographic accoutrements of the infernal Trinity—for
example, Death's "trident" (*PL* 10.295), Sin figured as the tricephalous
infernal goddess Hecate whose womb encompasses Cerberus, the triple-
headed dog (2.662–66, 655), and Scylla of the "Trinacrian," or three-
pointed island of Sicily (2.661). Artistically, the tricephalous figure was
the perfect icon: The Trinitarian deity was μία οὐσία, τρεῖς ὑπόστασεῖς
("one person in three hypostases"), and Satan could be depicted as
one person in three, or rather with three faces.[21] Augustine had sanc-
tioned the search for *vestigia Trinitatis*—"we must needs understand the
Trinity of whom there appear traces in the creature, as is fitting."[22]
And Renaissance Neoplatonists found divine emanations even in these
pagan trinities of Hades.[23] As contemporaneous as 1655, in an English
poem addressed to Pope Alexander VII (and ironically discovered next
to a letter of Milton's), the Chigi coat of arms is thus described: "Whose
threefold scutchian from the Trinitie / Displays three mightie powers *Heav'n Earth* and *Hell*."[24] Regarded in this sense, the infernal trinity
in *Paradise Lost* is indeed *vestigia Trinitatis*, but a vestige emanating not
from the true Godhead but from the erroneous Trinitarian ramblings
of the patristic fathers. Indeed, we are told by modern historians that
"it is a fact that the earliest representations of a tricephalous Christian
Trinity which we have found are chronologically later than those of the
tricephalous devil."[25] Accordingly, it seems that Milton's location of the
orthodox Christian Trinity in hell may be not only doctrinally motivated, but also historically accurate.

The "Double Procession" of Death

The incestuous generative relationships among Satan, Sin, and Death can be seen, more precisely, to dramatize the Western doctrine of the double procession. In the account in book 2, Satan generates Sin and they then procreate together to produce Death, who in turn rapes Sin. Accordingly, Satan is both the father and lover of Sin and the father and grandfather of Death. In turn, Sin is the daughter and lover of Satan and the mother, sister, and lover of Death, while Death is the "son and grandchild both" (*PL* 10.384) of Satan and son, brother, and lover of Sin. The account is related by Sin to Satan while Death listens, and is replete with specific and commonplace Trinitarian phraseology: Sin is "likest to thee in shape and countenance bright" (2.756), "shining heavenly fair" (2.757), "thy perfect image" (2.764), "offspring" (2.781), "thine own begotten" (2.782), "his mother" (2.792), "my son" (2.804), "me his parent" (2.805), "thou, O Father" (2.810). In our context, we can see that the perversely confused Oedipal couplings of the infernal geniture[26] duplicate the patristic refutations to contemporary attacks upon this Trinitarian dogma of the double procession, while its explicitly sexual, incestuous, and transgendered nature suggests a pointed attack upon what Augustine termed the "mutual love" of the Father and Son in this double procession.

The orthodox doctrine, although derived from pseudosubordinationist writings of Origen (ca. 185–ca. 254), influential theologian and biblical scholar of the early Greek church, paradoxically "contributed to the strengthening of the divine unity by binding into a coherent and organic relation the conceptions entertained of the three divine Persons."[27] Eusebius of Caesarea (ca. 260; d. before 341), bishop, theologian, and historian, followed Origen's subordinationist lead and taught that the Father created all things through the Son, including the Holy Spirit who is thereby γενητός, or "created." But this developed into orthodox Trinitarian doctrine in the hands of Basil of Caesarea and his younger brother and fellow Cappadocian bishop, Gregory of Nyssa (d. after 385), as well as Epiphanius (born after 310–403), bishop of Salamis (Cyprus), ascetic and monk, the latter teaching that the Spirit is from both Father and Son. Similarly, Augustine argues that "He, who in the Trinity is

styled the Holy Spirit, is the Spirit both of the Father and of the Son";
Athanasius contends that "the Son of God is also the source of the
Spirit"; and Cyril the Patriarch of Alexandria (ca. 375–444), famous
anti-Nestorian defender of orthodoxy and prolific exegete, concisely
argues that the Spirit "proceeds from the Father and the Son."[28]

Ultimately, the expression "*out of* the Father *through* the Son" became
the regular formula for the procession of the Holy Spirit, who derives
intrinsically and substantially from the Father in the Son. Such a doctrine firmly linked the Holy Spirit to the Father through the intermediary Son, and was a major step in solving the paradox of a monotheistic
Trinity. Accordingly, the Western Trinity was a strongly organic triplic-
ity with the act of procession being the completion of the act of generation, retaining for all three persons of the Trinity the fundamental
quality of ἀγένητος, meaning "uncreated"—the term reserved only for
God. It is this concept of ἀγένητος, which Satan famously takes for himself; he argues he is "self-begot" (*PL* 5.860)—his ontological claim as a
Trinitarian unbegotten begetter of Sin and Death.

This double procession of the Spirit might be orthodox Trinitarian
doctrine, but it was the subject of a great number of Arian critiques
that seized on its potentially unbiblical and sometimes perverse implications. And it is these that the reader can perceive in the satanic family
in *Paradise Lost*. Prominent among them is the criticism that the Father
must have two Sons. Early on, Origen noted this problem and hesi-
tantly ruminated that it is because of the Son's agency that "perhaps,
is the reason why the Spirit is not said to be God's own Son. The
Only-begotten only is by nature and from the beginning a Son, and
the Holy Spirit seems to have need of the Son, to minister to Him His
essence."[29] But by the fourth century, this aspect of dual sonship, and
indeed brotherhood, was a common jibe by the Arians, such that it was
one of Athanasius's central refutations in his *Letters to Serapion on the Holy
Spirit*. Athanasius defends against those whom he styles the "Tropici"
for their figurative mode of exegesis—a sect with similar beliefs to the
fourth century Pneumatomachians—who argue that if the Holy Spirit
"is not a creature nor one of the angels, but proceeds from the Father,
then he is himself also a son, and he and the Word are two brothers.
And if he is a brother, how is the Word only begotten?"[30] In *Contra*

Arianos, Athanasius had countered similar accusations of ἀδελφοί, or "brotherhood," between Father and Son, for if "He is eternal, and coexists with the Father, you call him no more the Father's Son, but brother." The theologian is forced to grapple in the same mire of perverse paternity and brotherhood that the reader discovers in Milton's infernal Trinity: "it is madness to envisage a brother to the Son, or to ascribe to the Father the name of grandfather. For the Spirit is not given the name of son in the Scriptures, lest he be taken for a brother; nor the son of the Son, lest the Father be thought to be a grandfather. But the Son is called Son of the Father, and the Spirit of the Father is called Spirit of the Son. Thus the Godhead of the Holy Triad and faith therein is one."[31]

Such attacks on the illogical ramifications of the divine μοναρξία, or Monarchy, are endemic in the formative period of Trinitarian theology. Far earlier in his *Treatise against Praxeas,* the influential ecclesiastical writer Tertullian had been forced to combat a twisted modalism that concluded, that as the Father and Son were one identical person, so when the Father entered the Virgin at the Incarnation he becomes, as it were, his own Son: "the Father can make Himself a Son to Himself, and the Son render Himself a Father to Himself." This, according to Tertullian, "must be the device of the devil."[32] Augustine battled against the conclusion that the double procession inferred two Fathers, for the Holy Spirit "would be called the Son of the Father and of the Son, if—a thing abhorrent to the feeling of all sound minds—both had *begotten* Him." Remarkably, Augustine defends the procession by arguing that the Son does not operate in the manner of a mother[33]—precisely the role of Milton's Sin, whose "womb conceived / A growing burden" (*PL* 2.766–67). The burden in *Paradise Lost* of the doctrine of the double procession is "this odious offspring" (2.781) of the "father" (2.743) Satan and "mother" (2.792) Sin, a Trinitarian "phantasm callst my son" (2.743), a Holy Spirit or "shadow" (2.669) of the Godhead "that shape had none / Distinguishable in member, joint, or limb, / Or substance" (2.667–69).

The traditional defense against accusations of dual sonship was to differentiate between the modes of hyparxis or generation of the Son and the Spirit. In its final Trinitarian form, the Eastern Cappadocian

Settlement defined the individuality of the divine persons not according to their οὐσία, or ontological composition, but in terms of these modes, labeling the Father as ἀγεννησία ("ingenerate"), the Son as γέννησις ("begotten"), and the Spirit as ἔκπεμψις ("promission") or ἐκπόρευσις ("procession"). The concept of procession or spiration, derived from the Greek πνεῦμα—meaning the Holy Spirit but with its root meaning of "breath"—is the result of the mutual love between the Father and Son. This procession became known as *per modum amoris,* or "in the manner of love," and Western patristic theologians used a number of amorous metaphors such as "the kiss of the Father and Son" and "the kiss of love" to describe the mutual gratification and reciprocal love that terminates in the Holy Spirit, who is in Trinitarian theology thereby coeternal and consubstantial with both Father and Son. The doctrine was originally propagated by Augustine as the *modus operandi* of the double procession of the Holy Spirit, who "is neither of the Father alone, nor of the Son alone, but of both; and so intimates to us a mutual love, wherewith the Father and the Son reciprocally love one another."[34] By the time of Thomas Aquinas (ca. 1225–74), it had become standard Catholic dogma, for "from this very fact that the Father and the Son mutually love each other, it is behooving that the mutual love, who is the Holy Spirit, proceed from both."[35]

It is this procreative mutual love that we see satirized in the epic's sexual coupling of Satan with Sin, which produces Death. The double procession becomes a double incest, for Death also shares his "love" with his mother, Sin. Using Trinitarian language, Sin relates how Satan, "full oft / Thyself in me thy perfect image viewing / Becam'st enamoured, and such joy thou tookst / With me in secret, that my womb conceived / A growing burden" (2.763–67). Satan's incestuous love for Sin is the self-love for his perfect image that the Trinitarian Father expresses for his Son. Milton's scene dramatizes the famous Augustinian analogy from *De Trinitate* which "is so even in outward and carnal love," conceiving of the persons of the Trinity as "three things: he that loves [*amans*], and that which is loved [*quod amatur*], and love [*amor*]."[36] The Miltonic allegory expresses this Augustinian Trinity precisely: the lover, the object loved, and the love that unites. In the poem's Trinitarian and therefore satanic terms, the result of this divine and protosexual "mutual love" is "my fair son here...the dear pledge / Of dalliance had with thee in heaven, and joys / Then sweet" (2.818–20). The Miltonic Sin/Son "shall reign / At thy right hand voluptuous, as beseems / Thy daughter and thy darling, without end" (2.868–70). In this sense the Miltonic supplement of "voluptuous" does not suggest an ironic travesty of the Nicene Creed,[37] but functions as a satire of the Trinitarian *per modum amoris*.

The Transsexual Son Sin

This satiric sexualizing of internal Trinitarian relations identifies the "male" Son of God as the female Sin, a gender reversal that also has roots in patristic biblical exegesis. *Paradise Lost* figures the generation of Sin in terms of the parthenogenesis of Athena, the Greek goddess of wisdom, from the head of her father Zeus:

> the left side opening wide,
> Likest to thee in shape and countenance bright,
> Then shining heavenly fair, a goddess armed,
> Out of thy head I sprung.   (*PL* 2.755–58)

Church father and Christian apologist Justin Martyr specifically condemns the gender obfuscation of the classical and Christian wisdom figures of Minerva (Athena) and the Son of God (the Word), arguing that the pagans "craftily feigned that Minerva was the daughter of Jupiter, not by sexual union, but, knowing that God conceived and made the world by the Word, they say that Minerva is the first conception; which we consider very absurd, bringing forward the form of the conception in a female shape."[38] But there are many precedents for patristic theologians transforming pagan fantasy into Christian "truth" despite such gender incongruities. Merritt Hughes calls this exegetical reinterpretative process "true icastic mimesis," and cites as an example early Greek theologian Clement of Alexandria (died ca. 215), who views Homer's myth of the expulsion of the female character Strife from Olympian heaven as an image of Satan and his devils' expulsion from the Christian heaven.[39] This continued into the fifteenth and sixteenth centuries, with the gender change ignored by Trinitarian reinterpretations of the birth of Athena. For example, we see the commonplace pun on Sun/Son in the standard reference work on classical mythology during the Renaissance, Natale Conti's *Mythologiae:* "Wisdom was born out of Jupiter's head, which is the topmost or purest part of the ether. Jupiter shared his powers with Minerva on an equal basis, because the Sun is second only to God in the influence it exerts on man's business."[40] In the Middle Ages the Roman Catholic Church had figured Death as the queen of hell and spouse of Satan,[41] and by Milton's own time, the Counter-Reformation was sanctioning the cult of the "Trinity on Earth" comprised of Joseph, Mary, and Christ, again ignoring the transsexuality of the orthodox Second Person. Milton's contemporary poet Abraham Cowley confronts without apparent heed the Oedipal paradox of the Virgin Mary, "who must *God's wife, God's mother* be!" in his biblical epic *Davideis.*[42] Naturally the satanic account in *Paradise Lost* employs this "true" icastic mimesis with its perverse gender inversion as an element of its satiric attack on orthodox doctrine.

One school of patristic commentators interpreted the female Old Testament Wisdom figure Hokmah typologically as an adumbration of the Second Person of the Trinity—a Son and not a daughter—while also eliding the gender discrepancy. Proverbs 8:22–25 became a favorite Trinitarian proof-text for the eternal generation of the Son under the name of Wisdom, and predictably Milton in *De doctrina Christiana* forms an Antitrinitarian interpretation of the text, arguing that "the figure introduced as a speaker there is not the Son of God but a poetical personification of Wisdom" (YP 6:304). Following orthodox tradition, Origen states that "the only-begotten Son of God is His wisdom hypostatically existing," while Tertullian argues that "Σοφία,...Wisdom herself, constituted in the character of a Second Person...is the perfect nativity of the Word, when he proceeds forth from God—*formed*—by Him first to devise and think out *all things* under the name of Wisdom."[43] Indeed, this typological exegesis may well have been fertile ground for Milton's satanic account of the Trinity. Sin relates how "familiar grown, / I pleased...with attractive graces," so that Satan with his cephalic Wisdom child "Becam'st enamoured, and such joy thou tookst / With me in secret" (*PL* 2.761–66). Tertullian goes on to note the same reciprocal pleasure between Father and Son/Wisdom/daughter, articulating the feminine gender of Wisdom, and quotes the Septuagint translation of Psalm 110.3, which proclaims the begetting of the typological Word as prior to that of the Morning Star, the prelapsarian name of Satan:[44]

The father took pleasure evermore in Him, who equally rejoiced with a reciprocal gladness in the Father's presence: "Thou art my Son, to-day have I begotten Thee;"—even before the morning star did I beget Thee. The Son likewise acknowledges the Father, speaking in His own person, under the name of Wisdom: "The Lord formed Me as the beginning of His ways, with a view to His own works; before all the hills did He beget Me." For if indeed Wisdom in this passage seems to say that She was created by the Lord.[45]

Critics of *Paradise Lost* have hitherto failed to explain convincingly why the poem figures the birth of Sin in terms of the birth of Athena.[46] But the suitability of this allusion is made clearer by understanding it as a satiric attack on the eternal begetting of the Word as the Old Testament female Wisdom figure.

The Begetting of Sin

The genesis of Sin is further elucidated in light of the orthodox belief of the Son being begotten specifically from the "intellect" of the Father. The begetting of Sin is the material embodiment of Satan's intellectual error which literally ruptures his head—he "thought himself impaired" (*PL* 5.665) and therefore aspired "To set himself in glory above his peers" (1.39). The moment recalls the intellectual overreacher or *sapientia* topos—which is understood as a satire upon the birth of classical wisdom but also as an attack upon the doctrine of the generation of the Word from the Father's intellect. The sixteenth century English churchman and theologian Richard Hooker argued that the original creation of sin could only be intellective, for "*There was no other way for angels to sin, but by reflex of their understanding upon themselves.*"[47] But the Son's generation is also intellectual according to a later series of medieval biblical scholars, and this doctrine was utilized to buttress the Trinitarian belief that the Son was begotten from eternity. From as early as the second century, bishop and Christian apologist Theophilus of Antioch (ca. 115–81) equates the increate Word with God's reason, arguing that "before anything came into being He had Him as a counsellor, being His own mind and thought."[48] By the time of Aquinas, the argument that "The procession of the Word is by way of an intelligible operation"[49] was orthodox doctrine and ironically formed part of the defense against

Antitrinitarian scoffing at dual Sonship by differentiating it from the mode of the Holy Spirit's hyparxis (or generation), which was by way of an operation of the "will" of the Father.

The patristic fathers developed the identity of the Son of God as a person of the Trinity from the Greek Logos or Word, the Hebrew Wisdom, and the intellective reason among others, all of which they used to support their crucial contention that the Son of God was begotten from eternity and to counter the famous Arian jibe that "the time was when He was not." Tertullian had argued that "even then before the creation of the universe God was not alone, since He had within Himself both Reason, and, inherent in Reason, His Word, which He made second to Himself by agitating it within Himself," explaining this idea of eternal generation through a human analogy: "Thus, in a certain sense, the word is a second *person* within you, through which in thinking you utter speech, and through which also, (by reciprocity of process), in uttering speech you generate thought."[50] This idea developed into the distinction between ἐνδιάθετος, or "logos-imminent," and προφορικός, or "logos-expressed," first developed by Theophilus. It sought to safeguard the eternal existence of the Son by explaining two stages of existence: from eternity he inhered unexpressed in the Father as thought or reason in the mind, only later to issue forth into external self-expression as thought does into words. This distinction was later rejected for its suggestion that the Son was merely an impersonal function of the Father,[51] but as originally formulated it was intended to counter Antitrinitarian subordination of the Son as a being created within time. Theophilus draws this distinction while making reference to the Septuagint translation of Psalm 45:1, another favorite anti-Arian proof-text, arguing that "God, then, having His own Word internal within His own bowels, begat Him, emitting Him along with His own wisdom before all things."[52]

So, too, the primordial procession of Sin from Milton's Satan is not dramatized in "real time" during the action of the epic, but retrospectively related as a dimly remembered primeval event, one that Satan has forgotten. As the personification of her father's pride and envy, Sin was imminent within Satan from the very beginning, only to be uttered forth into external existence as the expression of his reason or thought. She is in fact Satan's Logos or Word. Sin lay forever dormant within Lucifer, the morning star "great in power, / In favour and pre-eminence," until she was uttered forth by "Satan, so call him now, his former name / Is heard no more in heaven" (*PL* 5.658–61) at the moment of cephalic emanation. Sin was truly begotten "in the beginning" of satanic existence. Perhaps the hell-hounds which are "hourly conceived / And hourly born" (2.796–97) in the womb of Sin are suggestive of this eternal generation. The same can be said for Satan's offspring Death, who exists *in potentia* within Satan from the beginning; like God the Father who generates the Son and Spirit from eternity through the voluntary exercise of his intellect and his will, Sin and Death are forever imminent within Satan and, crucial to Milton's theodicy, they are the products of his free will.

Such material metaphors as Tertullian's agitation of the divine innards and Theophilus's emission from the sacred bowels are typical of patristic descriptions of the act of filial generation, in contrast with the pneumatic spiration of the Holy Spirit that we have already considered. In fact, Theophilus, quoting the Septuagint Greek to describe the process of begetting—ἐχηρεύχατο ἡ καρδία μου λόγον ἀγαθόν—suggests in literal translation the more violent and offensive meaning of "vomiting" or "belching" rather than that of "emission."[53] In another early patristic account, second century apologist Tatian describes the Son's begetting as "by His simple will the Logos springs forth; and the Logos, not coming forth in vain, becomes the first-begotten work of the Father."[54] This is the "sprung" (*PL* 2.758) that Sin in the epic describes as the mode of her own hyparxis (or beginning): her being vomited ("threw forth" [2.755]) from the head of her father Satan causes a very understandable reaction from the surrounding angels, who "recoiled afraid" (2.759). They are naturally afraid for Sin is naturally monstrous and deformed although apparently pleasing when "familiar grown" (2.761). So Trinitarianism is presented as alluring "with attractive graces" (2.762), yet in fact is a distorted perversion residing in Miltonic hell. According to Sin, she sprang from "the left side" (2.755) of Satan's head when it split open, a detail absent from Hesiod's *Theogony* and perhaps suggesting more than merely the etymology of "sinister."

Milton is known to have made use of rabbinical texts,[55] and one of the most famous characteristics of Jewish kabbalistic thought is the creation of fallen angels through "left-side emanations," an example being *A Treatise on the Left Emanation* authored by Rabbi Isaac ben Jacob ha-Kohen in the thirteenth century. In some accounts, these demons belong to the patrimony of Samael, which is the primary name of Satan in Judaism. In keeping with the allegorical account in *Paradise Lost* precisely, Samael copulates with his concubine Lilith, the queen of evil, to bring the poison of death into the world. And Milton's Sin even possesses the defining characteristic of the child-murderer Lilith — "Lured with the smell of infant blood" (*PL* 2.664).[56] The *Zohar*, which was known to Milton, in places identifies Old Testament characters with Samael, whom Christian typological exegesis interprets as the Son of God: for example, the "man" who wrestles with Jacob in Genesis 32:24–32.[57] I do not claim that the source for Milton's left-side emanation of Sin from Satan is necessarily from the Kabbalah, or that those rabbinical accounts of Samael necessarily suggest typological exegesis of the Son of God. But certainly the connection is not difficult to make, and a primary concern of *A Treatise on the Left Emanation* is the "mythology of evil expressing a messianic apocalypse."[58]

Milton's cosmogony is famously of the *creation ex Deo* variety; he vigorously rejected orthodox *creatio ex nihilo* doctrine in *De doctrina Christiana* (YP 6:305–11) and dramatized aspects of his dynamic monist materialist form of *ex Deo* creation in a much-debated passage in *Paradise Lost* (7.165–73). But Satan's creation of Sin is, according to Marshall Grossman, curiously *ex nihilo*, an anomaly in Milton's epic: "As the thought of negation joined to the absence of material, she is the phenomenal appearance of nothing — the reified form of the negative — a generation from Satan's thought exemplifying the *creatio ex nihilo* Milton otherwise seems at such pains to reject."[59] I believe that the reasons are twofold. On the one hand, the satanic Trinity is, paradoxically, a doctrinally orthodox dramatization in *Paradise Lost,* and accordingly it is possible to postulate it in terms of a form of *ex nihilo* ontology. Yet, on the other hand, the composition of an orthodox Trinity is not the province of cosmogony. It is not *creatio* in the proper sense at all, but what the patristic writers variously call "generation" or "emanation" or "begetting," and all nonsubordinationist theologians distinguish sharply between γενητός (*genetos,* derivative creature, and therefore not God) and ἀγένητος (*agenetos,* uncreated, and therefore God).[60] In its final statement by Athanasius, the Trinitarian Son is γεννητός (*gennetos,* "begotten") yet ἀγένητος (*agenetos,* "uncreated"), possessing an ἀρξή (*arche,* "cause"), yet ἀναρξία (*anarchia,* "without a beginning"), γέννημα (*gennema,* "offspring") but not γενητός (*genetos,* "derivative being") or ποίημα (*poiema,* "thing made") or κτίσμα (*ktisma,* "creature"). Contrary to Grossman's account, the satanic production of Sin is not truly analogous to the creation of Eve from Adam's rib, which would contrast *creatio ex nihilo* with *creatio ex materia,* but to God's begetting of the Son from his own *essentia,* which is in a sense a form of *ex Deo* production.[61] Sin was begotten directly from the hypostasis of the father "in the beginning" of Satan's existence (from Lucifer), and is not independently preexistent or derived from any other source.

This is demonstrable in the internal relations of the infernal trinity, which are sharply contrasted to those of the poem's Edenic lovers Adam and Eve, who increasingly demonstrate independence from God and from each other consequent upon the exercise of their free will. Basil writes of the Godhead, "we perceive the operation of Father, Son and Holy Ghost to be one and the same, in no respect showing difference or variation; from this identity of operation we necessarily infer the unity of the nature."[62] The Trinity in *Paradise Lost* is bound together "With secret amity things of like kind" that "no power can separate" (10.248, 251), and this ontological homogeneity is reflected in their singular mode of behavior, which is essentially Trinitarian. For instance, according to Gregory of Nyssa, "every operation which extends from God to the Creation, and is named according to our variable conceptions of it, has its origin from the Father [Satan], and proceeds through the Son [Sin], and is completed in the Holy Spirit [Death]."[63] In *Paradise Lost,* this homogeneous identity of action originates in satanic choice, proceeds to sinful behavior, and is completed in the punishment of death. Sin offers a paean to Satan regarding his work with humankind and their own messianic redemption from "Hell [which] could no longer hold us in her bounds" (10.365), recalling the eulogy by the Son of God to his "author and prime architect" (10.356) in the celestial council of *Paradise Lost,* 3.227–65. But Sin's account rehearses the fundamental Trinitarian principles that "unite us three" (10.364)—the identity of operation ("joint vigour," 10.405) and identity of being ("things of like kind," 10.248) between Satan, Sin, and Death—even punning on Sin's/Son's most crucial ontological attribute of ἀγένητος or deity in her "heart *divined*" (10.357):

> O parent, these are thy magnific deeds,
> Thy trophies, which thou viewst as not thine own,
> Thou art their author and prime architect:
> For I no sooner in my heart divined,
> My heart, which by a secret harmony
> Still moves with thine, joined in connection sweet,
> That thou on earth hadst prospered, which thy looks
> Now also evidence, but straight I felt
> Thou distant from thee worlds between, yet felt
> That I must after thee with this thy son;
> Such fatal consequence unites us three:
> Hell could no longer hold us in her bounds,
> Nor this unvoyageable gulf obscure
> Detain from following thy illustrious track.
> Thou hast achieved our liberty, confined
> Within hell gates till now, thou us empowered.   (10.354–69)

Satan, Sin, and Death demonstrate the identity of activity consequent upon the unity of being found in patristic defenses of the Trinity.

The Eastern Trinitarian Formulation in Hell

But this satanic Trinity is a composite satire, damning the Eastern as well as the Western version of the doctrine. The Eastern church never accepted the addition of the *filioque* to the Nicene Creed, or the doctrine of the double procession, which developed from it, objecting to the Western reduction of the divine persons to mere relations. The Son of God is the Father's only begotten while the Holy Spirit proceeds directly from the Father alone, the divine μοναρξία ("Monarchy") being expressed as μία οὐσία, τρεῖς ὑπόστασεῖς, or "one essence in three hypostases." One can understand the satanic triad in *Paradise Lost* incorporating this Eastern conception in its design by reversing the attributions of Sin and Death with the Second and Third Persons of the Trinity. Death is first introduced to Satan as "thy only son" (*PL* 2.728), his identity revealed as "this odious offspring whom thou seest, / Thine own begotten" (2.781–82), and Satan is named as "thy father" (2.730), and he claims Death as "my fair son" (2.818). This is a direct reference to the Son of God's unique status as γέννημα or "only begotten offspring" of God the Father, and in book 10 Death is specifically named as "son" (10.235, 363) and "his offspring dear" (10.238, 349).

While the creation of the Son/son Death is related as a true begetting, Sin proceeds directly from Satan in a parthenogenetic Father/father only emission—"Out of thy head I sprung" (*PL* 2.758)—which suggests the doctrine of the spiration of the Holy Spirit by ἔκπεμψις ("promission") or ἐκπόρευσις ("procession") and the Eastern Trinitarian belief in the agency of the Father alone.[64] Basil, as one of the Eastern Cappadocian fathers, describes the Holy Spirit "proceeding out of God, not by generation, like the Son, but as Breath of His mouth," and when talking of the Spirit's emanation, only the Father is ever given as cause: "It is called 'Spirit of God,' 'Spirit of truth which proceedeth from the Father.'"[65] Another Cappadocian, Gregory of Nazianzen (ca. 325–89), suggests similarly that the Father alone is the source of "The Holy Ghost, which proceedeth from the Father; Who, inasmuch as He proceedeth from That Source, is no Creature; and inasmuch as He is not Begotten is no Son; and inasmuch as He is between the Unbegotten and the Begotten is God."[66]

So also the designation of Milton's Sin as the "perfect image" (*PL* 2.764) of her father, the mother of the Second Person of the Trinity, and modeled in terms of the Hebrew feminine Wisdom figure, all appear in patristic accounts not only with reference to the Son but also to the Holy Spirit. Orthodox doctrine on these issues was not finalized until at least the fourth century with the establishment of creedal authority. Indeed, Πνεῦμα, the neuter Greek noun for Holy Spirit, which was translated from the feminine Hebrew *Ruah*, meaning YHWH's breath or motion of breathing, legitimated early patristic as well as Gnostic and Platonist feminine conceptions of the Third Person.[67] Regarding Christology, the prolific Greek theologian Origen struggles with "the difficulty of explaining how the Holy Spirit can be the mother of Christ" according to the book of Hebrews, and the second century church father Irenaeus, bishop and author of the originally Greek *Adversus haereses*, describes how

"His offspring and His similitude do minister to Him in every respect; that is, the Son and the Holy Spirit, the Word and Wisdom."[68] Irenaeus had followed the Eastern writer Theophilus, the first writer to apply the term Τριάδος or "Triad" to the Godhead, by identifying the Spirit as Σοφία in his "Trinity, of God, and His Word, and His Wisdom."[69] There was a concerted but ultimately futile effort in the early centuries after Christ to associate the Spirit with the Wisdom of God, which continued with Tatian, the martyr and presbyter Hippolytus (died ca. 236) and Gregory Thaumaturgus (ca. 213–70), known as the miracle-worker bishop.[70] Milton seems to point to this tradition directly in his invocation to the heavenly muse Urania in *Paradise Lost*, book 7 — often identified by critics as the Holy Spirit — who "with Eternal Wisdom didst converse, / Wisdom thy Sister, and with her didst play / In the presence of the Almighty Father" (7.9–11).

One analogy favored by the Eastern Trinitarian theologians to illuminate the mode of hyparxis of the triadic Godhead was that of the generative relationships between Adam, Eve, and their son Seth from the book of Genesis. The satanic trinity in *Paradise Lost* consisting of father, daughter/wife, and mutual son recreates these relations. It was developed from Origen, who in his defense of the divine generation of the Son from the substance of God argues that "'Adam begat Seth in his own likeness, and after his own image.' Now this image contains the unity of nature and substance belonging to Father and Son."[71] Eve was subsequently added to the equation and it was used as a "proof" for the substantial unity of the three persons of the Trinity, as Gregory of Nazianzen argues: "What was Adam? A creature of God. What then was Eve? A fragment of the creature. And what was Seth? The begotten of both. Does it then seem to you that Creature and Fragment and Begotten are the same thing? Of course it does not. But were not these persons consubstantial? Of course they were." This Adamic triad is particularly fitting as a Trinitarian analogy for the different modes of hyparxis of Eve, and Seth is analogous to that of the Spirit and the Son: "For is not the one an offspring [Son], and the other a something else [Spirit] of the One [Father]? Did not both Eve and Seth come from the one Adam? And were they both begotten by him? No; but the one was a fragment of him, and the other was begotten by him. And yet the two were one and the same thing; both were human beings; no one will deny that."[72]

It is clear how this Adamic Trinitarian analogy is reproduced in Milton's infernal Trinity, with Father/Adam/Satan emanating Spirit/ Eve/Sin, who together beget Son/Seth/Death. Ironically and crucially, this analogy breaks down for the orthodox Trinity, which does not posit the Holy Spirit as the feminine co-begetter of the Son—an important facet obfuscated by the patristic theologians, but which the poem satirizes in the overt sexuality and procreative function of Sin. It is true that some of the Cappadocian writers were aware that any comparison between the consubstantiality of the triadic persons, and different human beings possessing the same essence of humanhood, is highly problematic, as Gregory of Nyssa discusses in *Ad Ablabium quod non sint tres dei*. But the analogy, as seen in this argument by John of Damascus (ca. 676–787), the last of the Greek fathers of the church, to support the Eastern Trinitarian doctrine of "one essence in three hypostases" while differentiating between the modes of hyparxis, is teased out fully in Milton's satanic dramatization and revealed as spurious:

> For though the Holy Spirit proceedeth from the Father, yet this is not generative in character but processional. This is a different mode of existence, alike incomprehensible and unknown, just as is the generation of the Son. Wherefore all the qualities the Father has are the Son's, save that the Father is unbegotten, and this exception involves no difference in essence nor dignity, but only a different mode of coming into existence. We have an analogy in Adam, who was not begotten (for God Himself moulded him), and Seth, who was begotten (for he is Adam's son), and Eve, who proceeded out of Adam's rib (for she was not begotten). These do not differ from each other in nature, for they are human beings: but they differ in the mode of coming into existence.[73]

But the clearest evidence of satire within the Eastern Trinitarian model, which posits Death as the Son of God, concerns the arch-heresy of Arianism or the question of filial subordination. Death is the only son dramatized in *Paradise Lost* who is demonstrably unsubordinated to his father. The biggest threat to the establishment of the doctrine of the Trinity as orthodox church doctrine came from a number of different heretical strategies, all of which sought to establish a hierarchy in the Godhead with the Father elevated above the Son. According to these heresies the equality of the Son with the Father threatens the absolute μοναρξία, or "Monarchy of God," the primary sense of which is that of omnipotence: "Monarchia" is by definition—the heretics argue—wielded by only one ultimate power and is therefore essentially a monotheistic concept. If the subordination of the Son could be established, that of the Holy Spirit was taken for granted.

In Milton's epic, the only son who is clearly dramatized as coequal with his father is Death; he is truly equal in power, in status, in kingship, and in the substance from which he is directly begotten—a natural son as opposed to adoptive. We see this dramatized in a thrilling clash between father and son that obviously has no biblical precedent, a fact that strongly suggests that it is an important theological tenet in the poem. It is claimed in the epic's first invocation and elsewhere that *Paradise Lost* is a divinely inspired text, and accordingly it is unlikely that this passage should be considered merely entertaining fiction. So how do we interpret this father and son confrontation? For the reader is distracted from seeking any theological meaning by the sheer emotional tension of the violent encounter. Simply put, the scene depicts the strict Trinitarian equality of father and son, an idea that is condemned to hell. This is why Milton depicts the pair fighting. They are battling for sovereignty—an attempt to subordinate one member of the divine unity to the other—and the result is a stand-off. "So matched they stood" (*PL* 2.720) declares the Miltonic narrator; they are a pair genuinely matched in equality as they stand opposed—the verb "stand" being one that resonates throughout Milton's verse with moral and theological implications. As genuine relatives, and orthodox Trinitarian ὑπόστασεις, or *personae*, this is a fight that neither side can win, as distinct from the mock standoff between angels and devils, dissolved by the Son of God in book 6.

Death sports "The likeness of a kingly crown" (*PL* 2.673) and challenges the sovereignty of Satan that we remember in the archfiend's famous lines, "To reign is worth ambition though in hell" (1.262). The deathly son threatens his father, who in turn "breath'st defiance here and scorn / Where I reign king, and to enrage thee more, / Thy king and lord?" (2.697–99). So begins the clash of father and son, who are insistently and appropriately described as mirror images of each other:

> Each at the head
> Levelled his deadly aim; their fatal hands
> No second stroke intend, and such a frown
> Each cast at the other.   (2.711–14)

The climax is marked by the oppositional dialectic of father-son and son-father, combining chiasmus and anaphora:

> O Father, what intends thy hand, she cried
> Against thy only son? What fury, O son,
> Possesses thee to bend that mortal dart
> Against thy father's head?   (2.727–30)

There can be no victor in this battle of equals, a clash repeated in both form (epic simile) and meaning by the confrontation between the co-archangels and former "brothers" Satan and Gabriel in *Paradise Lost* 4.977–1015, who are so evenly matched that a stalemate promises to ensue; it is only with the intervention of heaven that Gabriel is granted superior power. By nature, all is equal. John Shawcross notes that "the subordinationism of not only the Son to the Father but of Adam to Eve, and on through all generations, supernal or human. Significantly and ironically, of course, Death is not subordinate to *his* father."[74] Significant indeed, but what is this irony Shawcross claims to recognize? It is too simplistic to read this extended and exhilarating scene as merely another platitudinous inversion of heaven and hell. The scene is not ironic, but satiric. The doctrinal battle for the consubstantiality of the Trinitarian *personae* is one that can only be won in hell, as father and son in the epic discover.

Miltonic Allegory as Satire

Understanding Milton's allegory as a satire provides an answer to a long history of negative criticism of the scenes with Satan, Sin, and Death. From early influential scholars such as Joseph Addison and Samuel Johnson until the present day, the central criticism of these episodes has been aesthetic, based on the poet's inappropriate use of genre.[75] J. B. Broadbent is typical in his condemnation of Milton's depiction of Satan, Sin, and Death, arguing that "narrative allegory is essentially a polemical or didactic technique, so that when a poet who is trained in pragmatic polemic uses allegory for a literary purpose he is almost bound to write more coarsely than in his straightforward narrative."[76] Milton's bold use seems incongruous, notwithstanding the biblical source from James 1:15 of an allegorical lust begetting sin and sin begetting death, coupled with the account from Basil in his *Sixth Homily on the Hexaemeron* of Sin being the first born of the evil spirit Satan.[77] The publication in 1906 of this source has spawned the "discovery" by scholars of a multitude of sources from biblical texts, patristic commentary, classical myth, and Greek, Latin, and Renaissance poetry, all essentially unverifiable, and most of which leave the reader unsatisfied as aids to what these episodes mean.[78]

For example, the most obvious of all the mythic allusions is the cephalic birth of Sin, derived from the birth of Athena from the head of Zeus and usually attributed to the *Theogony* of Hesiod. But why does the epic incorporate such an allusion? What is it meant to mean? Miltonists have proposed various rationales for associating the Greek myth with Satan, but all are too generalized to be convincing: to criticize classical heroism, to castigate classical myth as inferior to Christian truth, as a diabolic reworking of biblical history, as an explanation of the origin of classical myth.[79] Nor can one propose the commonplace interpretation of satanic behavior in *Paradise Lost:* as counterpoint to analogous divine actions that thereby manifest the structural division between good and evil in the epic. This is because there is no cephalic birth of the Son or Holy Spirit dramatized in the poem; but more importantly critics are coming to appreciate that *Paradise Lost* does not operate in such simple binary terms of parodic opposition. The depiction of good and evil, divine and satanic, is far more subtle and challenging. According to two Milton critics, the God of *Paradise Lost* is a liar who dwells in a heaven where there is genuine fear and greed, and a study of the epic's typology reveals that Satan is identified surprisingly with the patriarchs Moses, Jacob, and David, while the Son of God is described shockingly in term of the Egyptian Pharaoh, Esau, and the sexually licentious Alexander the Great.[80]

Ironically though, Broadbent's criticism of allegory in *Paradise Lost* as "essentially a polemical or didactic technique" is inadvertently pertinent. Milton was (in)famous for his "pragmatic polemic" in his public pamphleteering long before his fame as a poet, and if it is generally accepted by literary scholars that narrative allegory of the type in Milton's epic is best suited to a "polemic" or "didactic" purpose, it is normally one that is indirect and couched in "a subtle and penetrating symbolic fable."[81] But Broadbent is incorrect when he states that Milton's literary use of allegory is not polemical or didactic, causing it to appear "coarse." On the contrary, it is overtly and pointedly belligerent, and therefore in a sense deliberately coarse. If, as I contend, the primary function of satanic infernal allegory in *Paradise Lost* is satiric, rather than what Balachandra Rajan described as the diabolic distortion of Milton's heavenly composition, then this explains and validates the shift in generic modes that has upset so many critics.[82] As a satire upon patristic Trinitarian theology, which was the bedrock of orthodox Christian belief in the seventeenth century,[83] the satanic allegory in *Paradise Lost* is thereby appropriately polemical and didactic.

Monmouth University

Reading Milton

Monism and Metaphor
in *Paradise Lost*

Stephen Hequembourg

In *Paradise Regained*, Satan claims to read the Son of God's future in the
stars: "A Kingdom they portend thee, but what Kingdom, / Real or
Allegoric I discern not" (*PR* 4.389–90).[1] Satan's ambivalence points to a
question Milton and other monist thinkers of the period were constantly
asking: How do we separate the real from the metaphoric? What do
metaphors mean, and how does a monist worldview allow us to reinterpret inherited metaphors (whether scriptural, philosophical, or poetic) as
literal descriptions of the physical world?

Thomas Hobbes claimed that everything in the cosmos was ultimately reducible to matter in motion. Even mental states could be
so understood: "All Fancies are motions within us, reliques of those
made in the Sense."[2] This materialist understanding of mental events
allowed Hobbes to reread scholastic descriptions of internal motion
(those "Metaphoricall Motions" of the mind, soul, and will) as literally
taking place. The Schoolmen believed they were only speaking figura-
tively — "yet that doth not hinder, but that such Motions are" (*Leviathan*
38). In reducing all forms of motion to local motion, Hobbes discovered
that some of what Aristotle claimed "hath bene metaphorically taken,
but is properly true."[3] Margaret Cavendish, though she opposed her

own animist monism to Hobbes's mechanical materialism, agreed: "for knowledge lives in motion, as motion lives in matter." In the context of such a worldview, the metaphor of the "intellectual touch" (made popular by the Cambridge Platonists) can be boldly literalized: "for thought is onely a strong *touch*, and *touch* a weak *thought*."[4] Anne Conway, who comes closer than either Hobbes or Cavendish to Milton's mature philosophy, uses her monism to reinterpret the scriptural metaphor of "hard-heartedness" in terms that are at once moral and mineral: "From these examples one may easily understand how the heart or spirit of a wicked man is called hard and stony because his spirit has indeed real hardness in it like that found in those small, stony particles of water." From this perspective, we can read Scripture in a way that is almost perversely literal—"without taking refuge in some forced metaphor."[5]

In this more general form, Satan's question is one that the attentive reader of Milton will face in a number of different contexts across his poetry and prose—what is real and what is meant only metaphorically, or in "mysterious terms"? *Paradise Lost* is riddled with interpretive cruxes of this sort, from God's assertion, "This day I have begot whom I declare / My only Son" (the chronological beginning of the poem) to Adam's struggle to understand the protoevangelium (its narrative end); from the narrator's assertion that "God is light" to Raphael's suggestion that earth is merely the shadow of heaven.[6] In addition to these isolated moments of interpretive ambiguity, there are those troublesome key words ("wanton," "wandering," "error," "luxuriant") that ask the reader at every turn to parcel out the moral from the merely physical meanings in attempting to make sense of the poem's cosmos.[7] Literal or metaphorical—the question threads its way through the poem, weaving together in the process the experiences of reader and narrator, our first parents, and the hosts of angels and demons as all are caught up in the intricate problem of finding and making meaning. It is as if Milton formulates some of his key ideas in such an ambiguous way as to be able constantly to ask the readers to reflect on their own interpretive acts, to demand at each instance: But how do you understand this? Is it a guiding metaphor that uses the physical to gesture to an immaterial truth, or can you read it more literally, the truth inhering in the very material nature of things?

The critical reaction to these cruxes bears out this intuition. So David Masson and Herbert Grierson insist that "begot" be read metaphorically (in a way consistent with Milton's claims in *De doctrina Christiana*), while Denis Saurat responds that for narrative purposes Milton meant it literally.[8] Likewise, Maurice Kelley's claim that the proem to the third book of *Paradise Lost* is an invocation "to light in a physical sense" provokes Albert Cirillo's objection that light is meant only "as the traditional metaphor for the higher, nonphysical light."[9] Finally, Stanley Fish's response to the many readers who see intimations of the Fall in words like *wanton* and *wandering* is to claim that Milton is only tempting us to read these as moral metaphors, while they can and should be understood only physically.[10]

Against this critical tendency to choose sides between literal and figurative senses, I want to explore the more dynamic aspect of the tropology of *Paradise Lost*—the ways in which a single image can slide between metonymic, metaphoric, or even purely ironic figurations. These different interpretive possibilities imply different understandings of the material organization of the cosmos in *Paradise Lost*. Monism favors synecdoche and the kinds of surprisingly literal readings described above, while metaphor and ontological dualism develop through and alongside each other over the course of the poem—becoming increasingly prominent as the reader approaches the moment of original sin. The end point of this progression is satanic irony or antiphrasis, the pure divorce of the mental and physical, of tenor and vehicle. The poem's figurative strategies as a whole create a kind of spectrum, ranging from the "beyond compare" of satanic rhetoric to the angelic "as may compare," and finally to Adam's urgent question: "Yet what compare?" Moving along this spectrum, the reader of *Paradise Lost* is asked at every turn to distinguish between the literal and the figurative—to resist the temptation to read metaphorically what Milton is insisting can be understood as literally and physically true. This is a particularly monist kind of hermeneutic, as the above examples from Hobbes, Cavendish, and Conway illustrate. Ultimately, I argue, the success or failure of Milton's animist materialism in the poem rests on these moments of readerly decision.

Satan and Hobbes

Satan's confusion as to the meaning of the kingdom of God is primarily a hermeneutic one, but the words he finds for his dichotomy, "Real or Allegoric," have ontological implications as well. The opposite of "allegoric" here is not "literal" as one might expect, but "real"—hinting that whatever may be signified under a dark conceit is *immaterial* (which for Hobbes and Satan is synonymous with "nonexistent"). In *Leviathan,* Hobbes too wonders how "Kingdom of God" is to be understood. He ultimately decides that it is both real *and* allegoric, drawing an important distinction. If by *kingdom* we mean God's covenant with a people and his institution of a divine commonwealth (as of old with Israel, or to come at the end of days), then this "is a reall, not a metaphoricall kingdom" (*Leviathan* 283). But if we mean simply God's irresistible power as it extends itself over the whole of creation, then *kingdom* in this sense "is but a metaphoricall use of the word" (*Leviathan* 245). Typically for Hobbes, the metaphoric use is simply an illegitimate one. *Kingdom* by irresistible power and without any contracting parties is not a kingdom in any true sense. But such is the nature of metaphors—"seeing they openly profess deceipt" (*Leviathan* 52). For a monist, Hobbes has a rigidly dualistic approach to metaphors. In some cases they can be revealed on closer inspection to be literal truths (as in the examples of Scholastic motion); the rest of the time they are entirely without significance: a misapplication of terms that properly signify in other contexts. The metaphoric is the realm of the nonsensical—though such nonsense is (as Hobbes often repeats and Satan implicitly understands) potentially dangerous and deceptive.

A reading of those long and intricate epic similes in the description of hell in the opening books of *Paradise Lost* supports this alignment of infernal rhetoric with Hobbes's theory of metaphor. From this perspective, the reader can appreciate how fitting it is that the poem's first epic simile is the famous comparison of Satan and the Leviathan:

> or that sea-beast
> Leviathan which God of all His works
> Created hugest that swim th'ocean stream.
> Him haply slumb'ring on the Norway foam
> The pilot of some small night-foundered skiff

> Deeming some island, oft, as seamen tell,
> With fixèd anchor in his scaly rind
> Moors by his side.   (1.200–07)

Milton draws his great sea-beast from the book of Job, but in its immediate context the biblical monster would naturally invoke "the monster
of Malmsbury," as Hobbes was sometimes called.[11] Metaphors openly
deceive, says Hobbes, and Milton appropriately begins his engagement
with epic simile by digesting Hobbes's great emblem and exposing its
rhetorical deceit in his narrative. As the simile digresses beyond the comparison of its two immediate terms (Satan is like the beast in terms of size
and posture), the figure of the pilot enters, only to be deceived and led
astray by Leviathan's "likeness" to a land mass. The simile itself sprawls
over several lines ("stretched out huge in length") encompassing Satan,
the biblical Leviathan, Hobbes's *Leviathan,* and metaphors generally (as
understood and used by Hobbes and Satan)—all under the common
denominator of "deceit."

But Hobbes is not always exclusively critical of metaphor. His
"Answer" to William Davenant's preface to *Gondibert* praises the poetic
use of fancy in creating vivid analogies and similes. Even in political
council he admits that "sometimes the understanding" may "have need
to be opened by some apt similitude" (*Leviathan* 52).[12] By this criterion
of "aptness" and illustrative ability, the epic similes in hell fail almost
consistently, as critics have long observed. The illustration of Satan's
spear is a favorite example: "to equal which the tallest pine / Hewn
on Norwegian hills to be the mast / Of some great admiral were but a
wand" (1.292–94). The reader is tempted into assuming an easy ratio, as
the phrase "to equal which" seems to encourage. But this assumption is
rudely upset by the final line, in which the tree or mast (for a moment
the equal of the satanic spear) is abruptly reduced to a mere wand, leaving the reader without any firm sense of relative magnitudes.

Stanley Fish sees the same process at work in another satanic simile, in which the archfiend resting on the sun appears as "a spot like
which perhaps / Astronomer in the sun's lucent orb / Through his
glazed optic tube yet never saw" (*PL* 3.588–90).[13] Again, the comparison
is overturned just as it reaches for its conclusion. While the pine was
only *reduced* to a wand, the sunspot meant to illustrate Satan disappears

completely in the final "yet never saw." Sometimes the process takes only a single word, as when Satan's army is described as

> A multitude like which the populous north
> Poured never from her frozen loins to pass
> Rhene or the Danaw when her barbarous sons
> Came like a deluge on the south and spread
> Beneath Gibraltar to the Libyan sands.   (1.351–55)

The reader is left with the fallen host on the one hand and the vivid description of barbarian hordes on the other, while it becomes all too easy to overlook the one word that overturns all relation—"poured *never* from her frozen loins." Fish explains, "the components of a simile often do not have a point of contact that makes their comparison possible in a meaningful (relatable or comprehensible) way."[14] Borrowing one of Milton's favorite terms, we might describe this failure of contact as the poem's technique of "beyond compare." The satanic hosts, we are told, could be compared to all the glorious knights and armies of human history—if only we remember that compared to the fallen angels these mortal warriors would be mere pygmies. "Thus far these beyond / Compare of mortal prowess" (1.587–88). Satanic similes constantly tempt us with the illusion of relation and ratio, only to abruptly refuse any such alignment. Like Leviathan's body, they offer a deceptive appearance of stability, masking the failure of their component parts to achieve any final relation.

If these similes enact a kind of epistemological tease—always just about to illuminate a resemblance or set of correspondences and always abruptly canceling it—Satan's own words profess deceit more openly and concisely. His long punning speeches during the war in heaven (a point of mild embarrassment for some eighteenth century readers) perform at the level of the single word what the satanic similes do more diffusely. When Raphael describes the archfiend as "scoffing in ambiguous words," we are meant to take "ambiguity" not simply as vagueness but as literally offering two clear and distinct ways of meaning:

> Vanguard to right and left the front unfold
> That all may see who hate us how we seek
> Peace and composure and with open breast
> Stand ready to receive them if they like

Our overture and turn not back perverse!
But that I doubt. However, witness Heaven,
Heav'n witness thou anon while we discharge
Freely our part! Ye who appointed stand
Do as ye have in charge and briefly touch
What we propound—and loud, that all may hear!   (*PL* 6.558–67)

Satan's rhetoric works by forcing an absolute severance of the physical and more abstract or moral senses of the key words—overture, perverse, discharge, touch, propound. In one sense it is starkly literal. If the words are understood as inflected in any sense by their common metaphoric associations, then the message is lost. Belial's punning description of their artillery as "terms of weight" is a precise description of the inert physicality of the speech itself.

But, in a larger sense, satanic rhetoric is deeply ironic, as it purposely invokes the metaphoric associations it means to exclude. Satan revels in showing the incommensurability between the physical and moral senses of words, their lack of any "point of contact." So the loyal angels become "perverse"—physically turning or falling backward while yet remaining unswerving in their service to God. Satanic artillery, says Belial, can "show us when our foes walk not upright."

Satanic rhetoric forces the reader or hearer to make absolute distinctions between literal and metaphorical meanings—between the movements of matter and morality. Words such as "upright" and "perverse" in this context designate simultaneously a presence and an absence, a semantic either/or. The reader registers at once the physical and moral senses that so often cohere in the poem's other speakers, only to find that in satanic speech they are finally beyond compare. Jonathan Richardson observed that "as Ridiculous as This Kind of Wit may be Thought Now," it nonetheless had a long classical pedigree, and that as an "Intire collection of what was thought Excellent," the poem would be incomplete without it.[15] It may be more true to say that the poem would be incomplete because it would lack one of its linguistic polarities. How could we appreciate the narrator's fusion of literal and metaphoric senses (in such words as "fruit" and "taste") if we did not have before us an illustration of how easy it is to sever them, to emphasize one or the other exclusively and so lose sight of that elusive point of contact that allows them to cohere?

In reducing moral metaphors to the collisions of matter in motion, Milton's Satan is indebted to Hobbes's mechanistic monism—a philosophy that Milton is anxious to differentiate from his own animist materialism. Stephen Fallon has written persuasively of Satan's "mechanist descent" over the course of the epic, falling from a state of heavenly monism first into a rigid Cartesian dualism and finally into outright "Hobbism"—a world of inert Cartesian matter explicable without the postulate of immaterial minds (a machine without a ghost). "In turning from spirit to matter," Fallon writes, the fallen angels "migrate toward the pole at which Hobbes found all reality."[16] At this pole the universe is entirely corporeal, and nothing which is not body can be said to exist in any sense. The sovereign may decree that words like *upright* and *perverse* signify moral or immoral acts, but there will not be any necessary logic behind the transfer—no physical point of contact between the two senses. The attempt to find any such rational connection, our natural expectation that the two senses will cohere in our experience of the world, leads to confusion and deception—in Hobbes's civil society as in heaven's civil war. So Hobbes, in a strikingly metaphoric passage, describes the dangers of metaphor: "The Light of humane minds is Perspicuous Words, but by exact definitions first snuffed, and purged from ambiguity; *Reason* is the *pace;* Encrease of *Science,* the *way;* and the Benefit of man-kind, the *end.* And on the contrary, Metaphors, and sense-lesse and ambiguous words, are like *ignes fatui;* and reasoning upon them, is wandering amongst innumerable absurdities; and their end, contention, and sedition, or contempt" (*Leviathan* 36). If Hobbes made his first appearance in the poem through the opening simile of Satan and the deceptive Leviathan, it is these equally deceptive metaphoric lights that allow Satan to lead Eve into temptation in a much later simile:

> As when a wand'ring fire,
> Compact of unctuous vapor which the night
> Condenses and the cold environs round,
> Kindled through agitation to a flame
> Which oft, they say, some evil spirit attends,
> Hovering and blazing with delusive light,
> Misleads th' amazed night-wanderer from his way
> To bogs and mires and oft through pond or pool,
> There swallowed up and lost from succor far,

So glistered the dire snake and into fraud
Led Eve our credulous mother to the Tree
Of Prohibition, root of all our woe.   (*PL* 9.634–45)

Reading these two similes together offers a fairly concise account of Milton's engagement with Hobbes's language — in terms of both his theory and practice. Satan is both Leviathan and *ignis fatuus*, Hobbes's great work and the metaphors he explicitly rejects but constantly employs in his masterpiece. Both are ultimately deceptive, as the night-foundered pilot and the amazed night-wanderer testify.

Part of Hobbes's distrust of metaphor was that it encouraged belief in immaterial substances, which led to superstition among the vulgar (who were then more easily swayed by the clergy to the detriment of the sovereign). The temptation simile also encodes this particular Hobbesian problem, as the purely physical description of the foolish fires ("compact of unctuous vapor which the night / Condenses and the cold environs round") slides into the superstitious explanation based on the spirit world ("Which oft, they say, some evil spirit attends"). As in the infernal similes and satanic puns, what Milton illustrates here is the incommensurability of the two terms — a physical and spiritual explanation, again without a point of contact. As a monist, Milton was likely to associate Satan, his artillery, the temptation, and the Fall with such dualistic imagery. But even here we see Milton working to undermine the rigid dichotomies (physical and spiritual, literal and metaphoric) that satanic rhetoric attempts to establish. In describing how the dire snake "into fraud / Led Eve our credulous mother to the Tree," Milton (as Christopher Ricks observes) makes the word "Led" serve as a hinge between both literal and moral senses — as "into fraud / Led Eve" moves seamlessly into "Led Eve…to the Tree." In this short verb, Milton subtly provides what has been missing in the various examples of Hobbesian linguistics and infernal rhetoric — the elusive point of contact that holds together moral and physical senses always on the verge of falling apart. Ricks describes the result: "what begins as a moving and ancient moral metaphor (lead us not into temptation) crystallizes with terrifying literalness."[17] This easy, often barely perceptible movement from the metaphoric to the literal characterizes Milton's own poetic technique throughout *Paradise Lost* and takes a number of complex and fascinating shapes. But we should read an important qualification into Ricks's observation: it is a process that depends for its success on the careful attention of the audience. If the movement from the allegoric to the real is to occur, it will take place not so much on the page as in the mind of the fit reader, always ready to respond to the poet's implicit question—how do you understand this?

Milton's Monist Poetics

W. K. Wimsatt describes a poem as "a structure of verbal meaning which keeps a metaphor alive, that is, which holds the focal terms A and B in such a way that they remain distinct and illuminate each other, instead of collapsing into literalness."[18] As we have seen, satanic rhetoric keeps the terms of its comparisons distinct to the point that mutual illumination becomes impossible. In the case of similes, we are teased with a point of contact, a commensurability, that abruptly disappears; in the case of satanic puns the terms simply oppose rather than illumine each other—angels are most "upright" when knocked down, most obedient when blown back "perverse." Ricks's subtle reading of the temptation simile points to a different understanding of metaphor in Milton's epic, in which the terms are allowed to interact while the physical and moral, literal, and metaphoric gradually shade into each other—differing in degree perhaps, but of kind the same (cf. *PL* 5.490). This too disturbs Wimsatt's ideal metaphoric balance, the fruitful tension between its two terms, but in this case by not keeping them distinct *enough*.

Wimsatt and Ricks both describe the potential for literalization of the figurative, but while Wimsatt sees it as the figure's failure, Ricks captures something of the urgency and excitement of this movement in the context of *Paradise Lost* (and I would argue, in monist writing of the period more generally). We should read Wimsatt's "collapse" into dead metaphor against Rick's idea of a metaphor's "crystallization" into literalness. This crystallization takes a number of different forms in *Paradise Lost*, but all involve the same kind of engagement with the reader, who is tempted at every turn to understand metaphorically what can and should be read as somehow literally true, as physically unfolding in the time and space of the poem. In this way, Milton frequently asks us to correct our first impressions, to literalize retroactively what appeared as a figure of speech, or a mere vehicle of comparison. Some aspects of this literalizing tendency have been observed by Milton's readers (from his earliest editors to his most recent critics); but what has not been thoroughly understood is the extent of the process and its larger relation to the poet's philosophy of matter. Milton does not allow metaphors simply to die off into literalness. *Paradise Lost* provides a context in which they are resurrected into a new literal life—a space in which metaphors, like everything that exists in a monist materialist cosmos, *take place*.

This spatial realization of the poem's imagery occurs even in the infernal similes, through Milton's frequent addition of a third-person human perspective. Many of the examples are well known—Satan's shield is like a moon, as seen by Galileo; the devils are as large as sea-beasts (as seen by sailors) or as small as fairy elves (as seen by the belated peasant); the spears of the angelic hosts wave like "a field / Of Ceres ripe for harvest," as anxiously observed by the "careful ploughman" (*PL* 4.980–83). Modern critics have found various ways to defend these seemingly extraneous additions, arguing that the space of the epic simile is not simply a "poetic holiday," but is in fact integral to the poem's structure and themes.[19] But surely this sense of their relevance does not necessitate that (like William Empson)[20] we search for a set of strict correspondences between narrative and simile (the ploughman must be either God or Satan). The importance of the observer is more simply the mild surprise he (or she) provokes in the reader, who discovers that the vehicle of the simile is not an immaterial point of comparison but something embodied by a human gaze. The two-term formula, "A is like B," is a flat line: A is real, present, acting in the poem before our eyes, while B is not. Milton's "A is like B as seen by C" changes the shape of things. Three points create narrative space; analogy becomes story, and the third term makes all three seem to exist equally, interdependently.

This aspect of the epic simile is closely related to Milton's technique, at the level of the individual word, of using a common (often Latinate) term in an unexpectedly literal sense. His eighteenth century editors were fond of pointing out instances of this—the "hideous ruin" of the rebel angels is in fact a literal fall; Abdiel's verbal response to Satan is part of his physical gesture: "And with *retorted* scorn his back he turned"

(*PL* 5.906; my emphasis). Whenever Satan is described as "transported" with emotion, we are asked to look beneath the metaphor and see his actual motion—to discover, as Ricks suggests, that "after all it is literally true that rage *transports* Satan."[21] The challenge for the reader in such cases is to find the concealed physical element, to see words normally descriptive of intentional or emotional states as equally spatial and physical. In this sense, we must read them as Hobbes read the "metaphorical motions" of the will as described by the Scholastics: "And although unstudied men, doe not conceive any motion at all to be there, where the thing moved is invisible; or the space it is moved in, is (for the shortnesse of it) insensible; yet that doth not hinder, but that such Motions are" (*Leviathan* 38). Milton makes the process easier for us by showing inner and outer motions as coinciding—making the physical and moral senses of the word a "both/and" in place of the satanic "either/or." The mind in a monist cosmos does not move independently of the body, and Milton's use of such words insists that we pay attention to their interaction. For the reader who understands Milton's strategy, "the litteral meaning," as Newton wrote, "appears more new and striking than the metaphor itself."[22]

In the third-person observer of the epic similes and in the unusually literal aspect of these Latin verbs, we have examples of Milton's tendency to realize the abstract, to give definite shape and presence both to vehicles of comparison and to mental or moral attributes. The reader is constantly surprised by *space*—as the outlines of the seemingly immaterial become clearer and condense into physical objects. Jonathan Richardson discovered long ago that Milton's sense "is Crouded so Close" that his readers "must Attend Dilligently, or Something Material will pass away."[23] I suggest that we take Richardson as literally as possible and see him as offering an important warning to readers of the poem. If our ways of thinking are too stubbornly dualistic, and if we do not attend carefully enough to Milton's words, we are likely to overlook the subtle physical elements and the unexpected spatiality of many of the poem's objects, actions, and events—and that precarious "something material" will indeed pass away. Milton tempts the reader into complacently accepting many of his descriptions as merely metaphoric, but the dynamics of the reading process often involves (or encourages) a second, more literal reinterpretation.

As Adam returns to meet Eve just after her first taste of sin, Milton describes how "Yet oft his heart, divine of something ill, / Misgave him" (*PL* 9.845–46). Just as we are likely to understand this as a purely mental or spiritual form of apprehension on Adam's part, Milton adds a half-line that reinvests these moral misgivings with shape and substance—"he the falt'ring measure felt" (9.846). "Heart" is not simply a figure for an immaterial inner state, as the first line seems to hint; the second insists that we see the thing itself—the irregular beating of an actual heart (in all its complex splendor of valves and veins) as it senses the approach of something wicked. The reader's experience of words like *transport* or *ruin*, which collapse literal and metaphoric into a single sense, is here dilated over two lines. It is impossible to understand what exactly is meant by "heart," until the following line retroactively literalizes it. John Guillory describes how Ithuriel's spear has the power to perform just this kind of magic in the poem. We are told in book 4 that Satan is found "squat like a toad" at the ear of the sleeping Eve, but are left uncertain as to whether this is a simile or whether he has in fact taken the physical shape of a toad—that is, until Ithuriel touches him with his spear and Satan "started up in his own shape" (4.800, 819). Guillory writes, "The simile is undone by Ithuriel, or revealed as literal."[24] The reader's challenge in *Paradise Lost* is to incorporate this action into the reading experience, to perform the same surprising literalizations without the aid of the angel's spear—to notice, as in the case of Adam's heart, that "something material" always on the verge of passing away.

This technique of retroactive literalization finds its counterpart in the narrator's ability to anticipate through the vehicles of his similes the objects and events soon to materialize in the space of the poem. Satan's transformation (under the literalizing touch of Ithuriel's spear) is described:

> As when a spark
> Lights on a heap of nitrous powder laid
> Fit for the tun (some magazine to store
> Against a rumored war) the smutty grain
> With sudden blaze diffused inflames the air,
> So started up in his own shape the Fiend.   (*PL* 4.814–9)

The "rumored war" of the simile is soon to become the very real war in heaven, where Satan invents gunpowder from "sulfurous and nitrous foam" (6.512). So Satan's inner turmoil upon first arriving in Eden, when he recoils upon himself "like a dev'lish engine," anticipates the later moment when he can be seen literally "training his dev'lish engin'ry" on the angelic hosts (4.17, 6.553). One of the epic similes of book 1 begins: "As when the potent rod / Of Amram's son" (1.338–39) and goes on to compare the swarming of the fallen angels to the locusts summoned by Moses. In book 12 Michael tells Adam, "Moses once more his potent rod extends" (12.211). The story is freed of its metaphoric association with Satan and incorporated into the plot, while the "once more" is a subtle reminder to the reader that this material should be familiar—that the "potent rod" has been extended once already in the poem.

Of the many disastrous natural events in the infernal similes, we find two mentions of the eclipse: the "dim eclipse disastrous," which is like Satan's diminished brightness, and the "labouring moon" that eclipses during the flight of the Night-hag, likened to the hell-hounds around Sin's waist (*PL* 1.597, 2.665). As if aiming for perfect symmetry, Milton offers two literal eclipses in the final books of *Paradise Lost*. Awaking for the first time to postlapsarian nature, Adam and Eve see "air suddenly eclipsed / After short blush of morn" (11.183–84). More remarkable is the description of the entrance of Sin and Death into this world: "the blasted stars looked wan / And planets, planet-strook, real eclipse / Then suffered" (10.412–14). The specification "real eclipse," like the "once more" of Moses' rod, reminds the reader that this is another act of poetic recurrence—first as figure, then as fact.

Raphael, Adam's first angelic instructor, first arrives in the poem in book 5. But his appearance is anticipated by an earlier simile, where Milton describes Satan's experience of the pleasant odors of Eden by comparison with sailors rounding the Cape of Hope toward "the spicy shore" (*PL* 4.162). Satan, he adds, was

> with them better pleased
> Than Asmodeus with the fishy fume,
> That drove him, though enamoured, from the spouse
> Of Tobit's son and with a vengeance sent
> From Media post to Egypt, there fast bound.   (4.167–71)

This is the reader's first introduction to Raphael—the angel who, in the apocryphal book of Tobit, instructed Tobias to create the "fishy fume" that forced Asmodeus to flee. The angel literally enters the poem in the following book, just as Adam and Eve begin their morning labors:

> They led the vine
> To wed her elm: she spoused about him twines
> Her marriageable arms and with her brings
> Her dow'r, th' adopted clusters, to adorn
> His barren leaves. Them thus employed beheld
> With pity Heav'n's high King and to Him called
> Raphael the sociable spirit that deigned
> To travel with Tobias and secured
> His marriage with the sev'n-times-wedded maid.   (5.215–23)

The same story appears, again free of its previous metaphorical (and satanic) context. Milton's angel *materializes*—starting up, as it were, in the flesh from the nebulous vehicle of a previous simile. But even within the passage itself another quick collapse of the literal and figurative (or "crystallization of the literal") takes place in just a few short lines, as the heavily loaded nuptial imagery of the garden work ("wed," "spoused," "marriageable," "dower") subtly merges with the real marriage of Tobias and Sara, the "sev'n-times-wedded maid." Just as the third-person observer allows the vehicle to unfold in space, so this proleptic imagery allows it to unfold temporally in the poem. And just as the principle of Ithuriel's spear insists that the reader look back and see the material something lurking beneath a metaphor, so Milton urges us to hold on to the vehicles of his similes as we look forward, as this is often the physical "stuff" that events to come are made of.

In Hobbes's understanding, metaphor can usually be revealed (when read carefully) as essentially meaningless—inexplicable in terms of the matter and motion of which everything that truly exists in his materialist cosmos is ultimately constituted. Metaphor flirts dangerously with the immaterial, leading the vulgar into superstitious or rebellious acts. Milton's metaphors, by contrast, only *seem* to designate objects and events not physically existing in the world of the poem, while in fact they often subtly lead the reader (through Milton's various literalizing strategies) back to the thing itself—the material vehicle realized and purged of its satanic associations. Even the Leviathan, so troublesome and deceptive in the first epic simile, reappears later in Raphael's account of Creation:

> There Leviathan,
> Hugest of living creatures, on the deep
> Stretched like a promontory sleeps or swims
> And seems a moving land and at his gills
> Draws in and at his trunk spouts out a sea.   (*PL* 7.412–16)

The literal description closely echoes the earlier simile (Leviathan still *seems* "a moving land"), but this time no night-foundered sailors are taken in by the resemblance. Milton has purified Hobbes's deceptive metaphoric beast — "king over all the children of pride" — by literalizing it. For all its dangerous bulk we are left with a real Leviathan that is as harmless as the Edenic elephant wreathing his lithe proboscis.

The predominant characteristic of both Hobbesian metaphor and infernal rhetoric is the lack of commensurability in the terms it attempts to compare or bring together — the loss of that "point of contact" that allows one term to illuminate the other. By contrast, the proleptic nature of Milton's similes creates innumerable minor points of contact throughout the poem, as vehicles lean forward into the developing action as if struggling for their own realization. The narrator's technique in this respect is nearly symmetrical with the way his unfallen characters make their own analogies. Prelapsarian similes are drawn directly from the speaker's physical surroundings, from the immediately visible or tangible objects and events of the natural world. So Adam and Eve end their morning orisons: "And if the night / Have gathered aught of evil or concealed, / Disperse it as now light dispels the dark!" (*PL* 5.206–08). Stanley Fish is right to assert that light and dark here are not moral metaphors and that "Adam is merely reaching for an analogy in nature (he looks up and sees it happening; had it been evening the thought might have been reversed)."[25] This is how metaphors are made in paradise — almost as if they are a part of the lush natural world unfolding on every side, ready to be plucked. At times they reach slightly backward or forward temporally, as when Adam tells Eve the descending angel "seems another morn / Ris'n on mid-noon," or when Raphael himself describes how the angels pass the time in song and mystical dance, "which *yonder* starry sphere...resembles nearest" (5.310–11, 620–22; my emphasis). It may be too light to see them as he speaks, but the subtle addition of "yonder" allows us to imagine the archangel actually gesturing toward the space where the stars will soon be visible.

As Milton's similes anticipate later objects and events in the poem, so reciprocally in Eden the future can only be described by things at hand, as they readily offer themselves as vehicles for things to come. So Raphael addresses Eve:

> Hail Mother of Mankind whose fruitful womb
> Shall fill the world more numerous with thy sons
> Than with these various fruits the trees of God
> Have heaped this table! (*PL* 5.388–91)

Such a technique favors contiguity over substitution. Edenic metaphors can often be seen at a second glance to shade into metonymy (or borrowing Gérard Genette's terminology, we might call these "diegetic" metaphor or metonymy, as mirroring Milton's proleptic similes).[26] But the narrator at least once employs the Edenic technique himself, describing Eve tending her flowers: "Herself though fairest unsupported flow'r" (9.432). This brief metaphor is actually at once diegetic and the realization of a much earlier proleptic simile, in which Eden is contrasted to Enna, "Where Prosérpine gath'ring flow'rs, / Herself a fairer flow'r, by gloomy Dis / Was gathered" (4.269–71). In a single line, we can observe what intricate patterns the poem's metaphors make in their proliferating points of contact—as vehicles lean forward into literalization and objects immediately at hand present themselves (almost willingly) as the material of illustration. Such is a monist cosmos: a space in which tenor and vehicle, body and soul, mind and matter all partake of the same richly varied physical existence, all differing but in degree, of kind the same—on earth "*as may compare* with Heaven."

Knowledge and Food

Milton's most explicit formulation of his animist materialism can be found in *De doctrina Christiana:* "Man is a living being, intrinsically and properly one and individual. He is not double or separable: not, as is commonly thought, produced from and composed of two different and distinct elements, soul and body. On the contrary, the whole man is the soul, and the soul the man: a body, in other words, or individual substance, animated, sensitive, and rational."[27] But the great literary expression of this philosophy of matter and the centerpiece of Milton's monist poetics is Raphael's speech to Adam in book 5, where the archangel explains the gradual ontological refinement of that "one first matter all" by his famous illustration of the unfolding plant:

> O Adam! one Almighty is, from whom
> All things proceed and up to Him return
> If not depraved from good, created all
> Such to perfection, one first matter all
> Endued with various forms, various degrees
> Of substance and in things that live of life,
> But more refined, more spiritous and pure
> As nearer to Him placed or nearer tending,
> Each in their several active spheres assigned
> Till body up to spirit work in bounds
> Proportioned to each kind. So from the root
> Springs lighter the green stalk, from thence the leaves
> More airy, last the bright consummate flower
> Spirits odorous breathes.   (*PL* 5.469–82)

While critics tend to agree that this is the closest the poem comes to the explicit materialism of the treatise, there is considerably less consensus on the nature of Raphael's imagery. The passage (and in fact Raphael's entire discourse) constitutes one of those many interpretative cruxes that can be understood either literally or metaphorically, as Milton encourages the reader actively to reflect on the process of his or her interpretation. The plant or tree has often been described as a metaphor. Walter Curry goes so far as to offer a point-for-point reading of the correspondences between world and plant: "The root of the tree is prime matter, the green stalk and the leaves constitute the corruptible creation (including perhaps the vital and animal spirits of living creatures), the flower is the intellectual or rational soul of man, and the fruit is the rational-intuitive soul of angels."[28] But in positing these various points of contact, Curry eludes the question of whether it is possible, in such a monist universe as the passage describes, to isolate any single element, to remove it momentarily from the great mobile chain of being and make it stand in relation to that cosmos merely as a vehicle to tenor. It is perhaps this difficulty that led Isabel MacCaffrey to insist that "the plant with its bright consummate flower is at once a stage in the argument and an epitome of the whole subject."[29] On this reading, we might say, the plant hovers vaguely somewhere between metaphor and metonymy—at once part and larger illustration of the monist cosmos.

Stephen Fallon goes a step further in this direction, stressing the dynamic nature of the imagery: "In Raphael's speech the plant begins as a metaphor for the steps of the hierarchy of matter only to become a synecdoche for the process by which creatures ascend the hierarchy."[30] Fallon describes exactly the kind of readerly temptation that I argue is crucial to the experience of *Paradise Lost*—the temptation to understand as metaphor what Milton is subtly insisting that we understand somehow more literally, as physically inhering in the matter of illustration. Reading this passage for the first time, we inevitably understand "So from the root" as signaling the move into metaphor, only to become aware that what Raphael describes is in fact taking place in the plant itself, as in all of creation "not depraved from good." The narrator sets the stage for Raphael's speech by his own act of literalizing an inherited metaphor:

> So down they sat
> And to their viands fell, nor seemingly
> The angel nor in mist (the common gloss
> Of theologians) but with keen dispatch
> Of real hunger.   (*PL* 5.433–37)

The real hunger of his angels is a particularly striking instance of Milton's monist poetics and that hunger for the real underlying the urge to literalize figures—to give shape and substance to the abstract, to allow metaphors to take place.

It is worth remembering that within the narrative of *Paradise Lost* Raphael's ontological discourse arises more or less incidentally. It was not an explicit part of his heavenly commission, and comes about only because Adam cannot quite accept the kind of angelic digestion Milton has described in his literal reading of the Scholastic gloss. Adam knows that angels must eat, but between earthly and heavenly nourishment "yet what compare?" (*PL* 5.467). So Raphael describes the gradual refinement of the plant from the root to its fruit and flowers. But he does not stop there:

> flow'rs and their fruit,
> Man's nourishment, by gradual scale sublimed
> To vital spirits aspire, to animal,
> To intellectual, give both life and sense,
> Fancy and understanding, whence the soul
> Reason receives, and reason is her being,
> Discursive or intuitive: discourse
> Is oftest yours, the latter most is ours,
> Differing but in degree, of kind the same.
> Wonder not then what God for you saw good
> If I refuse not but convert as you
> To proper substance.   (5.482–93)

Understanding the speech not as a philosophical set-piece but as a response to a specific (and perhaps urgent) question on Adam's part makes Raphael's rhetorical strategy clearer. His employment of the plant imagery is intended to illustrate the material continuity between the highest faculties of men and angels and the food they consume—as these are arranged on a monist spectrum stretching from roots and soil to the soul and its "intellectual spirits" (Milton's own innovation on the Galenic system). The idea that "knowledge is as food" appears, at least in this first instance, as true in a more than metaphoric sense—food literally is the substance which, when transformed by unfallen man's concoctive heat, is gradually refined into intellectual matter. In this brief preface to his thousands of lines of direct narration, Raphael establishes at once a monist ontology and the proper way of speaking, reading, and understanding it. This is the heart of Milton's monist poetics—in which body and spirit, heaven and earth, tenor and vehicle, are all relative designations of the same substance. Raphael's claim that his discourse will proceed by "lik'ning spiritual to corporal forms" is already in a sense authorized by the fact that bodies are constantly working their way up to spirit. As William Kerrigan puts it, "As spiritual is to corporeal in the nature of things, so spiritual is to corporeal in the names of things."[31]

As a description of the ontological and semantic processes of book 5, Kerrigan is certainly right. From Raphael's confident proem to his long narration, we are indeed led to suppose that his act of "likening" heaven to earth, the spiritual to the corporeal, is a matter only of slight degrees of difference rather than "flimsy similes...thrown across the void separating two worlds distinct in essence."[32] But to take this as a final description of Raphael's instruction as a whole is to ignore the gradual process by which this initial confidence is undermined, as heaven and earth seem slowly (and troublingly) to pull away from each other in the narrative dialectics of the poem's middle books. Like many of the textual cruxes I have been exploring, Raphael's narrative is not simply *either* literal or metaphoric; as readers we should closely attend the subtle movements (both in the poem's speakers and in our own responses to them) between these two possible understandings. Gordon Teskey notes in his edition of the poem that Raphael's words "are at once figurative and literal."[33] I would call attention only to the process by which they *seem* much more literal in book 5 and more like accommodations to our limited earthly minds by books 7 and 8.

Raphael's initial suggestion that the things of heaven and earth are "each to other like more than on Earth is thought" gives way slowly, punctuated by such moments of doubt as:

> For who though with the tongue
> Of angels can relate or to what things
> Liken on Earth conspicuous that may lift
> Human imagination to such height
> Of godlike pow'r!   (*PL* 6.297–301)

As readers we feel the strain as Raphael's similes move slowly away from the earlier diegetic mode, becoming both more elaborate and more distant from the immediate physical surroundings of speaker and listener. So he illustrates Satan's clash with Abdiel:

> As if on Earth
> Winds under ground or waters forcing way
> Sidelong had pushed a mountain from his seat
> Half sunk with all his pines.   (6.195–98)

In this and his later request that Adam imagine two planets colliding in the sky as if "nature's concord broke," we could certainly forgive our first parent if his experiences in Eden make such conceits seem rather dark indeed (6.311). The strain becomes more palpable in the Creation narrative as Raphael, comparing the gathering waters to armies, hastily adds, "for of armies thou hast heard" (7.296). All sense of the less and more familiar is lost, as something Adam has only heard of (and which may itself be a linguistic accommodation of something *even more* remote) is here supposed to illustrate yet another phenomenon he has never seen. As the narrative proceeds, the reader has the sense that Raphael's words gradually become precisely what Kerrigan claims they are not in book 5 — "flimsy similes" attempting to span an ever-widening chasm between worlds. Both Adam and the reader may be somewhat skeptical of the archangel's claim at the end of book 6 to have measured things in heaven by things on earth, especially when he later tells Adam, "Heav'n is for thee too high / To know what passes there" (8.172–73).

Whether "real or allegoric" we cannot finally say, but the narrative certainly appears to have drifted more from the one to the other. To borrow a phrase from Herbert, we might describe the development of Raphael's narrative as a gradual "curling of metaphors" around the "plain intention" of his proem in book 5. Yet sinless, Adam and Raphael remain on this side of satanic irony. But their dialogue inaugurates the steady tropological drift from Raphael's monist synecdoche and Edenic metonymy (as well as the poet's various literalizing strategies) to the reliance on a metaphor whose terms become ever more tenuously related. Critics of Milton have a tendency to ignore this drift in favor of either Raphael's initial pronouncements or his later hesitations. So while W. B. C. Watkins claims that the "absolutely unbroken" material continuum of *Paradise Lost* allows Milton to speak of all orders of being "in identical sensuous terms," N. K. Sugimura insists that Raphael in fact makes no sincere effort to "render things more intelligible as [his] technique intends but instead reminds us of the fissure existing between the reality we receive in narrative — itself a sort of 'sensory image' — and the celestial reality it claims to depict."[34] By insisting that the narrative as a whole is either monist and (more or less) literal or dualist and metaphoric, both critics overlook the more interesting story of how the story itself changes as it unfolds. The "fissure" between our sensuous imagery and celestial realities should not be understood simply as a datum of the poem's cosmos but rather as something actively carved out by its various speakers over the course of Raphael's visit — in all its fascinating and sometimes desperate tension ("yet *what* compare?").

The narrative act of carving out this fissure can be seen nowhere more clearly than in the vicissitudes of Raphael's alignment of food and

knowledge — first formulated in the description of the plant and its progress from gross material roots to tenuously material odors and finally
rational matter. At Fallon's urging we can read Raphael's plant as a
metaphor that slides imperceptibly into a synecdoche for the process
it describes, or as Kerrigan more simply puts it — as a metaphor that
"comes true."[35] In this, the monist centerpiece of Milton's epic, food is
simply matter waiting to become "intellectual spirits" by a process that
is at once material, moral, and metabolic. Angelic and earthly food is
different only in degree, as grosser and lighter fare. So we see the angels
celebrating the elevation of the Son by feasting on "angels' food...the
growth of Heav'n," all of which sounds scarcely different from Edenic
nourishment — "rubied nectar," "fruit of delicious vines" (*PL* 5.633–
35). After the narration of the war in heaven, Adam asks Raphael to
describe the creation of the heavens and earth — "What cause / Moved
the Creator in His holy rest / Through all eternity so late to build / In
chaos" (7.90–93). Raphael prefaces his account with a mild warning on
the limitations of the human intellect:

> But knowledge is as food and needs no less
> Her temperance over appetite to know
> In measure what the mind may well contain,
> Oppresses else with surfeit and soon turns
> Wisdom to folly as nourishment to wind.　　　　　　(7.126–30)

While this is in some sense a condensed repetition of the claims of
book 5, it is a repetition with a difference. The key terms and ideas
are the same, but the rhetorical formulation has moved a few degrees
from the initial synecdoche to more straightforward metaphor. Knowledge now is "as" or like food, rather than its sublimation in the human
composite or "living soul." Points of contact between vehicle and tenor
remain, but they are more abstract and schematic, less physical and
immediate. Even within the passage itself food and knowledge seem to
grow further apart, forcing Raphael to end with a four-term analogy that
sounds even more tenuous, more a mental exercise than a description of
the nature of things: "Wisdom to folly as nourishment to wind."

As the original monist formulation unravels, the mind (now figured
as "container" of knowledge) seems suddenly more remote from the
body and its metabolic activity. This is less a reflection of any change

in the poem's ontology than of the context of speech. The whole of Raphael's narrative, he tells Adam at its outset, is "for thy good...dispensed" (*PL* 5.570–71). Adam's question in this case is somewhat carelessly expressed, as critics have noted—implying a slight questioning of divine providence in that "what cause...*so late* to build." It is for his good then that Raphael clarifies the moral implications of "food and knowledge." The metaphoric revision makes paramount the ethical imperative only loosely adjoined to the original synecdoche ("Meanwhile enjoy / Your fill what happiness this happy state / Can comprehend, incapable of more" (5.503–05). As the poem progresses and the moral situation becomes more urgent, the unfallen speakers (Adam, Eve, and Raphael) increasingly figure the relation of food and knowledge as moral metaphor—gradually prying apart the monist imagery and using the body in an abstract way as an emblem to illustrate the acts and responsibilities of the mind or soul. So Adam, troubled by Eve's suggestion that they divide their labor, responds,

> Yet not so strictly hath our Lord imposed
> Labor as to debar us when we need
> Refreshment, whether food or talk between,
> Food of the mind or this sweet intercourse
> Of looks and smiles, for smiles from reason flow,
> To brute denied, and are of love the food,
> Love not the lowest end of human life.   (9.235–41)

Eve's suggestion is, of course, not in itself immoral. But Adam senses the strain it may place on their moral fortitude, and so responds with another (more domestic) variation on the "food and knowledge" theme. The quick repetitions of "food" and the somewhat abrupt transitions into and between metaphors (as "food or talk" becomes food first "of the mind" and then of "love") betray some anxiety on Adam's part. If a semblance of relation to the great monist imagery of book 5 still lingered in Raphael's later "knowledge is as food" metaphor, the reader is unlikely to make any such connection here. Adam is not in the least concerned at this point with the ontological mobility of the cosmos; his metaphors are intended to clarify his and Eve's duties to each other and to God. Accordingly, he imitates Raphael in removing the life of the mind a step further from the corporeal—from the brute beasts and the lower ends of human life.

In the tasting of the forbidden fruit, this process of unraveling the poem's monist imagery reaches its natural conclusion. Under the influence of Satan's glozing words, Eve begins to describe the fruit as "this intellectual food," as if forgetting that, according to Raphael's depiction in book 5, all fruit in Eden is potentially intellectual and every tree is heavily laden with "food of the mind." In her final unfallen words, we see the archangel's great image hanging on by its very last and slenderest thread:

> Here grows the cure of all: this fruit divine,
> Fair to the eye, inviting to the taste,
> Of virtue to make wise. What hinders then
> To reach and feed at once *both body and mind?*
>
> (*PL* 9.776–79; my emphasis)

Eve speaks as though she has just discovered (to her surprise and delight) a clever point of contact between mind and body, when she should have learned from Raphael that in Eden to eat is *always* to feed at once both body and mind, through the material continuum that unites them both. Her ominous note of ontological dualism reflects the final dualism of tenor and vehicle in the great conceit of "knowledge as food." And if these overlapping dichotomies were not remarkable enough in Eve's last unfallen words, Milton makes them painfully clear in Adam's first fallen words:

> Eve, now I see thou art exact of taste
> And elegant of sapience no small part
> Since to each meaning savor we apply
> And palate call judicious.   (9.1017–20)

That Adam and Eve should be lustful, wrathful, even suicidal as a consequence of original sin all seems perfectly appropriate, perhaps even predictable. But that they should take pleasure in pedantically elaborating the different senses of one of the poem's key words is almost beyond belief. When read, however, as the end point in the slow process of unraveling Raphael's brilliant monist synecdoche, we can appreciate that as terrible as these lines are, the universe of *Paradise Lost* would be incomplete without them. If, as Ricks claims, what happens in the narrative of the Fall "is reflected in what happens to the words," how could we possibly measure the Fall semantically if not in terms of the distance between the "mortal taste" of the introductory proem and Adam's "exact of taste," with its severance of the physical and mental dimensions of "sapience"?[36] Having clearly and distinctly conceived these separate senses, Adam is now equipped to understand satanic rhetoric and its devious "either/ or"—the mutual exclusion of physical and moral meanings. Eve comes dangerously close to this point in describing the fruit as being "of *virtue* to make wise," and Adam himself is already a novice in satanic irony, telling Eve just moments before his own mortal taste: "If death / Consort with thee death is to me as life" (9.953–54). As a theological event, the Fall may indeed be instantaneous and inexplicable, but as a linguistic phenomenon innocence is lost inch by semantic inch, in the long lapse from Edenic metonymy to anxious metaphor to diabolic irony—as may compare, yet what compare, beyond compare.

Three Trees

Like the whole of Raphael's narrative in which it forms a kind of leitmotif, this idea that "knowledge is as food" becomes in its unfolding one of those interpretive cruxes where the reader is asked to discern, like the Satan of *Paradise Regained*, whether it is real or metaphorically meant. Fallon and Kerrigan argue convincingly for the "real," but in doing so they place more emphasis on the formulation of book 5 and less on the later modifications. Sugimura's claim that it is only by metaphor that "physical 'food' becomes 'food for thought'" seems right on the evidence of these later usages, but her insistence that even Raphael's tree is ultimately "a type of metaphor" is less persuasive.[37] As I have been arguing, it is the movement that matters—the figurative shift from the initial surprising synecdoche to those increasingly stilted metaphors, from the seemingly complete physical coincidence of terms to their increasingly precarious point of contact.

The end point of this trajectory is the tree of knowledge, in whose presence Eve finally distinguishes body from mind just as Adam distinguishes physical taste from sapience. But the tree itself, more than just the end point, is in a sense the source of the problem. According to the orthodox understanding, which Milton espouses in *De doctrina*, the fruit of this particular tree was not evil per se: "It was necessary that one thing at least should be either forbidden or commanded, and above all

something which was in itself neither good nor evil, so that man's obedience might in this way be made evident. For man was by nature good
and holy, and was naturally disposed to do right, so it was certainly not
necessary to bind him by the requirements of any covenant to something
which he would do of his own accord" (YP 6:351–52). The effect of
the fruit—knowledge of good and evil, mortality, imposed labor, and
pains in childbirth—is ultimately from God. The fruit itself is an empty
vehicle, providing the occasion for God to act in the imposition of these
penalties, but not containing them materially in any sense. A vitalist
like J. B. van Helmont could, in fact, see the fruit in this latter sense, as
in itself contaminated—original sin inhering in its very sap, rind, and
seed.[38] The problem is that this would reduce the prohibition from a
moral prescription to a kind of "peculiarly compelling" case of "doc-
tor's orders" (to adapt J. W. N. Watkins's description of Hobbes's ethical imperatives).[39] In any event, as Milton writes, such an order would
be pointless because unfallen creatures were "naturally disposed to do
right" and would have avoided contaminated food without needing to
be commanded to do so. "It was called the tree of knowledge of good
and evil," Milton continues, "because of what happened afterwards" (YP
6:352). And what happens afterwards is an act of God, not a natural
effect of any physical cause.

The fruit, one might say, does nothing. But in saying this, one should
suggest something of the strangeness of this fact in a monist cosmos,
where all food is potentially "intellectual" according to Raphael, capable
of working its spiritual effects by virtue of its own material substance.
The fruit of the tree of knowledge does *nothing*—that is, its effect is not
its own. Kerrigan observes that "the first monist effect of the poem is
the 'fruit' dangling at the end of the opening line, both victual and
consequence."[40] The tree of knowledge is the one point in Eden where
this coherence is lost both semantically and ontologically—where the
fruit is not in the fruit. So Eve intimates when Satan first brings her
to it: "Serpent, we might have spared our coming hither, / Fruitless
to me though fruit be here t'excess" (*PL* 9.647–48). What Adam in his
first fallen speech does to Milton's opening use of "taste" is precisely
what Eve does to "fruit" in this rather lame pun, offering two clear
and distinct senses and emphasizing (like satanic puns) the presence of
the physical without the more abstract: "without consequence to me

though fruit be here to excess." This is the linguistic effect of forbidden fruit—the absolute separation of the semantic coherence of the "fruit" of the poem's opening line. This is the tree of knowledge—the stillpoint of difference around which a universe of sameness turns.

Between the tree of knowledge and the anonymous tree that Raphael describes to Adam, where do we place the other, less famous tree of Milton's epic—the tree of life? In *De doctrina*, Milton is noticeably more cautious on the subject than he was in his explanation of the tree of knowledge: "I do not know whether the tree of life ought to be called a sacrament, rather than a symbol of eternal life" (YP 6:353). Milton's distinction in this case is less than clear, since his own uses of *sacrament* and *symbol* later in the treatise overlap:

> In the so-called sacrament, as in most matters where the question of anal-ogy arises, it is to be noted that a certain trope or figure of speech was fre-quently employed. By this I mean that a thing which in any way illustrates or signifies another thing is mentioned not so much for what it really is as for what it illustrates or signifies. Failure to recognize this figure of speech in the sacraments, where the relation between the symbol and the things symbolized is very close, has been a widespread source of error, and still is today. (YP 6:555)

Sacrament seems to be a special subclass of symbolism in which sign and signified remain "very close," though they never in fact touch each other or overlap. Even in the sacrament we are left to catch the sense at some remove. But Milton allows yet another possibility: "I do not know whether the tree of life ought to be called a sacrament, rather than a symbol of eternal life *or even perhaps the food of eternal life*" (my emphasis). In its entirety this sentence creates a spectrum of proximity for its terms and their degree of contact, from *symbol* to *sacrament* to the food itself—at which point symbolism breaks down, and the metaphor (like so much else in Milton's work) becomes true.

In *Paradise Lost* we encounter this mysterious tree at our first entrance into Eden, as Satan perches on top of it to view the garden:

> Thence up he flew and on the Tree of Life,
> The middle tree and highest there that grew,
> Sat like a cormorant. Yet not true life
> Thereby regained but sat devising death

> To them who lived. Nor on the virtue thought
> Of that life-giving plant but only used
> For prospect what well used had been the pledge
> Of immortality.   (*PL* 4.194–201)

Combining this with the passage from *De doctrina*, we can see in the tree of life a symbol not so much of immortality as of the interpretive options constantly available to the reader of *Paradise Lost*. We can read it in the more orthodox manner as sacrament or symbol, using the tree for the prospect it offers in the understanding of something else—as in Kenneth Burke's description of metaphor as perspective ("to consider A from the point of view of B is, of course, to use B as a *perspective* upon A").[41] Reading it in this sense—"not so much for what it really is as for what it illustrates or signifies"— is not in itself wrong. But as the reading experience of the poem and the dialectic experience of its speakers constantly testify, there is always the danger that metaphor will lapse slowly into irony and antiphrasis, as it does for Satan, who perches on the tree of life only to sit "devising death." There remains the more difficult possibility of meditating on the physical virtues of the "live-giving plant," understanding it metonymically as the true and material cause (rather than simply the occasion) of its effect, as the pure coincidence of victual and consequence. "Perhaps" even the food itself: as the material nourishment concocts and sublimes in the body, the fruit itself becomes a small physical part of the immortal being it feeds—synecdoche and "pledge" rather than metaphoric "prospect."

At the foot of the tree of life, this baffling tree of master tropes, stands Milton's reader. Satan and his diabolic irony perch ominously on top, a cruel anticipation of Adam's fallen profession: "death is to me as life" (*PL* 9.954). At our backs we have the poet with all his literalizing strategies, surprising us at every turn with the spatial and physical aspects of what seemed empty vehicles, whispering that this just *might* be the thing itself, "even perhaps the food of eternal life." The interpretive possibilities ramify in front of our eyes, with the figure of Milton always somewhere in the background, confronting the reader with his incessant question—but how will *you* choose to understand this?

Harvard University

"Pardon may be found in time besought": Time Structures of the Mind in *Paradise Lost*

Ayelet C. Langer

R ecently, there has been a shift of focus from the traditional consideration of time in *Paradise Lost sub specie aeternitatis* to an interpretation of time as a significant component represented in the poem in its own right.[1] Though in some commentaries time is still seen as a part of eternity, it is not anymore considered as an inferior phenomenon.[2] Catherine Gimelli Martin, for example, maintains that in Milton's epic time is "not [regarded] as the traditional enemy but rather as an ultimately *benign* ingredient of eternity." For Martin this is expressed, *inter alia*, in Milton's portrayal of Eden as profoundly mutable and temporal.[3] That time is central to the poem's representation of paradise is also acknowledged by Anthony Welch. In his account of the chronology in *Paradise Lost*, Welch argues, "only in Paradise before the Fall does a conventional chronology operate." By contrast, hell has been identified as a changeless, static space, in which time is a "duration without sequence."[4] Though in these readings the temporal and the static structures of paradise and hell have been linked to the fallen and unfallen conditions, respectively, little has been said of the significance of time for the representation of the transitions from one condition to another. I believe that an interpretation of these transitions in terms of time and stasis may provide us with a deeper understanding of the poem's representation not only of the fallen and unfallen condition of Adam and Eve but also of the process of their recovery from sin.

In this essay I propose that in *Paradise Lost* there exist two distinct time structures, static and dynamic, which are fully intelligible and concrete. Yet these time structures are not the properties of either paradise or hell; rather, they reflect the two time structures of the human mind, fallen and unfallen. I will show that this representation of time as a conceptual form allows for the transitions from the unfallen to the fallen condition and vice versa. This is significant because the poem's representation of time as unreal implies that the fallen condition is not predetermined and fixed but rather a state from which the mind can recover. I will show that once fallen, the mind loses its capacity for grasping time and starts viewing the world in static terms. It is only when this capacity for time is recovered that regeneration is made possible and humankind may start its way back to God.

Milton's emphasis on time as the indispensable form in and through which regeneration may be achieved is very similar to the role that the concept of time plays in the metaphysical system of the twentieth century philosopher J. M. E. McTaggart. I will explore the two time structures of the mind that are represented in *Paradise Lost* through McTaggart's distinction between two time series, the A-series and the B-series of time. This examination will show how profoundly significant time is to Milton's representation of the process of regeneration in the poem. Using McTaggart's distinction as a gloss, I will show that in Milton's epic it is only by an A-structured mind that a transition from a fallen to an unfallen condition is made possible. Once the fallen mind has recovered its dynamic structure a free act of repentance is performed which may ultimately lead to regeneration. Satan, who is trapped within the fixity of his B-structured mind, is incapable of achieving a free act of repentance and, consequently, doomed to an eternal fall.

The question of time in *Paradise Lost* comes into sharp focus when we reach the first descriptions of paradisian life in book 4. There, in lines 5–7, Milton strikingly announces that time *now* is, that is, time now exists: "*now*, / *While time was*, our first parents had been warned / The coming of their secret foe" (emphasis mine).[5] If, one may ask, time indeed begins now, what should we call the chronology of events that unfolded in books 1–3? And if time does exist prior to book 4, why does the poem find it necessary to declare that time *now* exists?

I propose that the adverb "now" (*PL* 4.5) defines a boundary between two durations that the poem represents as the time structures of the postlapsarian and prelapsarian mind, respectively. In *Paradise Lost* time is not represented as a real, objective phenomenon that exists in the world independently of the mind. Rather, in Milton's epic time is a conceptual structure or form that reflects, facilitates, or perhaps even enables the capacity for freedom and moral choice.[6] The temporal duration that starts in book 4 is not a property of paradise but rather a representation of the time structure of the unfallen mind. By contrast, in books 1–2, which describe the whereabouts of the fallen angels, there exists a duration that is insufficient for time since it provides an experience that does not entail change. Gordon Teskey insightfully identifies this lack of time with forms of paralysis: "When error is carried over...into 'apostasy,'" says Teskey, "it...must be represented *apart from the movement of narrative* in forms of paralysis: logically as self-contradiction, psychologically as blind perversity, and existentially, when the devils compulsively take ashes for fruit, as absurd repetition."[7] Following Teskey I propose that these static forms are but a reflection of the static time structure of the fallen mind itself. Significantly, both the fallen and the unfallen time structures are represented in *Paradise Lost* as illusory forms that equally hide the true nature of reality. Yet, in Milton's epic the misperception of reality through the temporal form of the unfallen mind is represented as significantly more fundamental to the process of recovery from sin.

To demonstrate the difference between these two mindsets, fallen and unfallen, I make use of the distinction between two series of time, the A-series and the B-series, as suggested by the twentieth century philosopher J. M. E. McTaggart. In *Paradise Lost* the time structure of the prelapsarian mind corresponds to the A-series of time in which interchangeability of past, present, and future is possible, whereas the time structure of the postlapsarian mind parallels the B-series of time, in which relations between events are perceived as fixed. Though change and immobility are the hallmarks of the unfallen and fallen minds, respectively, Milton's epic allows for a transition from one to the other and vice versa. After the Fall the time structure of the prelapsarian mind of Adam and Eve changes from the A-series to the B-series. This change, too, is not irreversible. By the beginning of book 11 the fallen minds of the human pair regain their full structure of the A-series of time. The exact turning point is Adam's postlapsarian soliloquy in book 10, when Adam experiences two significant moments in his mind's life: death and rebirth. This experience of coming into being *ex nihilo* marks the regeneration of the postlapsarian mind, and this regeneration must take place in time. Satan, who fails to make the transition from the B-series to the A-series of time is incapable of repentance and therefore is doomed to be "forever fallen."

McTaggart's Theory of Time

In "The Unreality of Time," J. M. E. McTaggart maintains that we observe positions in time in two distinct ways: "each position is Earlier than some, and Later than some, of the other positions. And each position is either Past, Present, or Future."[8] McTaggart defines the first series of positions as the B-series. The relationship formed between events in this series is fixed. An event that was *once* will always remain earlier in relation to an event which is *now*, even when this *now* becomes a near-past event and that *once* becomes a distant-past event.[9]

This fixed relationship between events does not hold for the ever-changing positions McTaggart describes as the A-series. On the contrary, events on the A-series are always changing their positions. An event in the future will become a present event and then a past event. This constant changeability of positions on the A-series is for McTaggart at any one moment self-contradictory, since it forces us to admit that an event can belong to different moments in time. On the basis of this contradiction McTaggart maintains that the A-series is unreal.[10] According to McTaggart, this leads to the conclusion that time itself is unreal. If the A-series is unreal, there can be no B-series, for the latter depends on temporal direction, which only the former can provide.

In McTaggart's metaphysical system time is, in Peter Geach's words, "the most pervasive form of error."[11] Yet though illusory, time is still the only form by which reality can be inferred. According to McTaggart, underlying both series of time is a real, timeless series he terms the C-series. "There is a series," says McTaggart, "of the permanent relations to one another of those realities which in time are events.... But this other series—let us call it the C-series—is not temporal, for it involves no change, but only an order."[12] McTaggart maintains that the C-series holds an inclusion relation between its terms. Thus, a C-term can be either *included in* or *inclusive of* other terms in the series. The final term of the C-series is all-inclusive and is the only place where there is no misperception.[13] Since the human mind perceives everything through the illusory form of time, the all-inclusive term of a C-series is misperceived by the mind as being in the future. From this point of view, the eternal is the last term of the timeless C-series, which can only be inferred through our misperceptions of time. In "The Relation of Time to Eternity," McTaggart defines this state of affairs: "we must look on the Eternal as the end of Time; and on Time as essentially the process by which we reach to the Eternal and its perfection."[14]

For Milton, as for McTaggart, time is not an inferior creature but rather the indispensable means by which the mind may reach to God. This is true as regards both the fallen and unfallen conditions of human existence. As we learn from Raphael in book 5, prelapsarian Adam and Eve can improve their human position and turn, at last, all to spirit, "by tract of time" (*PL* 5.498). Having sinned, it is again by persisting through time that humankind may attain a sequence of lights—"light after light"—and, finally, "safe arrive" (3.196–97).[15] Milton builds the idea of time as a necessary means of regeneration into the text of *Paradise Lost.*

The Time Structure of the Prelapsarian Mind

In contrast to the events described in books 1–3 both in heaven and in hell, the events from book 4 onward are continuous and ordered in definite temporal categories such as mornings, evenings, and nights. Continuity also allows for the creation of perspective in the story. When events are anchored in specific points in time and then ordered successively, they create a foreground and background. The continuous nature of prelapsarian time enables the construction of complex relationships between past, present, and future events. The present moment, for example, is never presented as if it were severed from past events. A link between past and present events is formed in the mind of the prelapsarian self through memory. This leads to a consciousness of an existence in time created by the relationship between different points of existence in time and the understanding of these points as successive and causal.

Textual evidence for the representation of time in book 4 and after is ample. Here I quote two examples, each of which demonstrates the conception of time for each of our "first parents." In their first dialogue in the poem, Eve relates to Adam the details of her dream. The dream is contextualized in a day, the memory of which Eve says often returns to her:

> *That day* I oft remember, when from sleep
> I first awaked, and found myself reposed
> Under a shade on flowers, *much wondering where*
> *And what I was, whence thither brought, and how.*
>
> (*PL* 4.449–52; emphases mine)

Eve forms a relationship of continuity between the present moment, in which she relates her story to Adam, and the past event she describes. She does this by linking the two events in memory: "that day I oft remember" (4.449). Eve's expression of her existence in different yet related positions in time testifies to her dynamic perception of reality. As we shall see later, this passage also describes Eve's contemplation of her own beginning in time. Such a question, "whence thither brought" (4.452), triggers the regeneration of the fallen mind.

The time structure of the prelapsarian mind is reflected also in the language of Adam:

> Fair consort, *the hour*
> *Of night,* and all things now retired to rest
> Mind us of like repose, since God hath set
> Labour and rest, as day and night to men

> *Successive*, and the timely dew of sleep
> Now falling, with soft slumbrous weight inclines
> Our eyelids.   (4.610–16; emphases mine)

Expressions of specific time markers that designate continuity — "hour of night," "day and night" — dominate Adam's suggestion of a night repose. His perception of reality as continuous is therefore similar to Eve's.

I propose that the time that begins in the opening lines of book 4 of *Paradise Lost* is compatible with McTaggart's A-series of time. A definition of time that is very close to McTaggart's description of the A-series appears also in Milton's *Art of Logic*. There, Milton defines time as the duration of things past, present, and future.[16] As I understand McTaggart, the transitory relation between events in time parallels the way time is represented in the speech of prelapsarian Adam and Eve. Both Adam and Eve position events in a successive, continuous manner within a changeable temporal context along the lines of McTaggart's definition of the A-series of time. Change, which is the condition of the A-series, is expressed in Eve's speech both in her contextualization of her narrative within a specific day in the past and in her wish to know her origin, a wish that points to a perception of a continuous existence in time. Time is successive also for Adam, which is evident from his use of the phrase "day and night to men / Successive" (*PL* 4.613–14). In contrast to the time structure of the minds of prelapsarian Adam and Eve, the time structure of the postlapsarian mind reflects the fixed relationship between events of McTaggart's B-series of time, as I will show below.

The Time Structure of the Postlapsarian Mind

Change is conspicuously absent from the events described by Satan and the fallen angels. This is evident from the absence of time markers such as day and night, and diurnal markers such as morning, noon, and evening, in the language of postlapsarian creatures (as we shall see later, the language of fixed relations in time also characterizes the speech of postlapsarian Adam). Instead, vague time markers such as "once" and "now" are used by the postlapsarian fallen creatures to describe the fixed relationship of events in time. This representation parallels McTaggart's description of the B-series of time as a series of permanent relations between events.[17] The ordering of events as earlier or later would always be fixed in the B-series, in contrast to the A-series, in which events can change their positions from being future, through being present, to being past. According to McTaggart, the fixity of the B-series renders it insufficient for an experience of time, since time is conditioned by change.

There are numerous descriptions in which fixed relations of *earlier* and *later* are used in books 1 and 2. Of many examples I will mention four.[18] The first example is taken from Satan's soliloquy in book 4. Turning to the sun, Satan divides his existence into two distinct temporal domains, prelapsarian and postlapsarian "once" and "now":

> O sun, to tell thee how I hate thy beams
> That bring to my remembrance from what state
> I fell, how glorious *once* above thy sphere;
> *Till* pride and worse ambition threw me down
> Warring in heaven against heaven's matchless king.
>   (*PL* 4.37–41; emphases mine)

In line with McTaggart's description of the B-series of time, the point in time at which Satan's state was "glorious…above [the sun's] sphere" (4.39) will always remain earlier to the point in time when "pride and worse ambition threw [Satan] down" (4.40).

The second example is *Paradise Lost* 1.84–91, where Satan places Beelzebub's change of appearance within the *once-now* formula:

> If thou beest he; but oh how fallen! how changed
> From him, who in the happy realms of light
> Clothed with transcendent brightness didst outshine
> Myriads though bright.
>
>   . . . .
>
> Joined with me *once, now* misery hath joined
> In equal ruin.   (1.84–87, 90–91; emphases mine)

In this passage "once" and "now" are related to each other as absolute time levels. They function as two termini of the change discussed, yet they form no impression of the motion that led from one point to another. "Once" and "now" are thus presented as two static points in time that are related to each other in the sense that one precedes the other, yet they do not form a causal chain in that the former causes the latter. In this presentation of the situation, the joining together of Satan and Beelzebub in the past seems to have nothing to do with the misery they now share. Further, it will always be true that the relationship between the first event, when Beelzebub joined with Satan in their prelapsarian existence, will be earlier than their existence in postlapsarian hell.

A similar fixed relationship between events is formed in Satan's speech to his peers in hell. In his opening words Satan draws a fixed relationship between the fallen angels' possession and loss of heaven: "Princes, potentates, / Warriors, the flower of heaven, *once* yours, *now* lost" (1.315–16; emphases mine). In this passage the possession and loss of heaven are equally treated as neutral positions in time. But a sense of the motion that might have actualized the potentiality of the first to become the second, that is the potentiality of the angels to exercise their free will and, consequently, become fallen angels, is missing. In terms of perspective, the laconic phrase "once yours" provides us with no background for the situation of what is "now lost" (1.316).

The lack of any perspectival relationship between events past and present is so dominant in the time structure of the postlapsarian mind that sometimes the boundaries between past and present are entirely blurred to create an impression of a complete stillness. This is demonstrated in my final example. In *Paradise Lost* 1.777–79, where the devils in Pandaemonium are likened to bees in their hive, both the present and the moments that precede it are referred to as "now." Consequently, the temporal difference between events is made indistinct. The two different moments are transformed into one homogeneous time level that is devoid of change:

> So thick the airy crowd
> Swarmed and were straitened; till the signal given,
> Behold a wonder! they but *now* who seemed
> In bigness to surpass Earth's giant sons
> *Now* less than smallest dwarfs, in narrow room
> Throng numberless.   (1.775–80; emphases mine)

The dramatic transformation from giants to dwarfs fails to leave any traces in time. It is the same fixed "now" that forms the temporal context for both ends of the change discussed. In what follows we shall see that this inability—or refusal—to perceive reality through the A-series is precisely what prevents Satan from achieving a free act of repentance and receiving God's grace.

The B-series of time can be traced also in Adam's first postlapsarian monologue. This means that no time markers that designate successiveness and continuity can be found in his speech. Instead, events are expressed as permanently earlier or later than other events. In the opening lines of the monologue Adam uses a variation on Satan's *once-now* formula: "and me *so late* / The glory of that glory, who *now become* / Accursed of blessed" (*PL* 10.721–23; emphases mine). "So late" and "now become" do not specify two points on a continuous line of time but rather a fixed relationship between events, the former permanently earlier than the latter.

The same fixed relationship between an earlier and later event is expressed later in Adam's soliloquy: "Oh voice *once* heard / Delightfully, Increase and multiply, / *Now* death to hear! (10.729–31; emphases mine). Here, too, Adam uses the *once-now* formula that is characteristic of Satan's speech in books 1–2, presenting a fixed temporal difference between past and present events.

Regeneration of the Fallen Mind

Paradoxically, Adam's postlapsarian monologue is also the context within which he regains the A-structure of his prelapsarian mind. I propose that in *Paradise Lost* the transition from the B-series to the A-series is conditioned by two significant moments in the mind's life: an experience of one's own death and an experience of one's own creation. Ordered successively, the poem's two conditions of regeneration form the moment of becoming or, to be more precise, the moment at which one's conscious life begins.

The death and rebirth of consciousness are fully represented on the passage's diachronic level. First, Adam considers his death. Then, still in despair, he contemplates the moment of his own creation. References to death are made already in the opening lines of the monologue. In *Paradise Lost* 10.720–22, Adam wonders whether "this [is] the end / Of this new glorious world," and of himself, "so late / The glory of that glory." This experience of death is burdened with shame ("hide me from the face / Of God") and guilt ("yet well, if here would end / The misery, I deserved it, and would bear / My own deservings" (10.723–24, 10.725–27). Adam's feelings of despair, shame, and guilt amount to a deep sense of unworthiness to the point of self-annihilation.

It is only after Adam has experienced the death of what was heretofore his prominent place in Creation that his mind undergoes a transition from the B-series to the A-series of time and his regeneration begins. The precise turning point is 10.743, where Adam turns to God, his "maker," and begins contemplating the moment of his creation:

> Did I request thee, *Maker*, from my clay
> To mould me man, did I solicit thee
> *From darkness to promote me*, or here place
> In this delicious garden?   (*PL* 10.743–46; emphases mine)

Though Adam is convinced that he can find "no way, from deep to deeper [plunged]!" (10.844), his recovery begins with his acknowledging of the moment of his becoming "from darkness," and with the assertion that he is a creature created by God. Though these two statements consist of no specific time markers they nevertheless point to a budding experience of time. Both the words "Maker" and "promote" testify to a temporal process that is necessarily successive and dependent on change. By contrast, when Satan toys with the possibility of repentance in his monologue in book 4, he refers to God not as his creator but rather as his "punisher":

> But say I could repent and could obtain
> By act of grace my former state.
>
> . . . .
>
> This knows my *punisher;* therefore as far
> From granting he, as I from begging peace.
>   (4.93–94, 103–04; emphasis mine)

In contrast to Adam's temporal concept of God—his Maker—as the author of the dynamic process of the Creation, Satan's use of the word "punisher" betrays no understanding—and perhaps even a denial—of God as the source and origin of his own creatureliness.

Adam is not the first in the poem to refer to his beginning. In contemplating his origin in time Adam repeats the language used by prelapsarian Eve in her relation of her first dream. Lying still on the ground, Eve sets in motion a chain of questions in which she examines, first, the essence of her new existence—"what I am"—and then the dynamics of her becoming—"whence thither brought" (*PL* 4.452). That Eve contemplates the moment of her becoming in temporal terms so early in her conscious life may suggest that time is an *a priori* form in the prelapsarian mind. As we shall see later, when asked by Satan, the same question, "what I was" (4.452), triggers no such chain of questions. Satan's fixed, self-concentrated mind is interested only in the final, fixed product of Creation, and misses completely the dynamic process of coming into being.

Both Adam and Eve acknowledge the moment of creation, which takes place between the lifeless immobility of nonbeing and the dynamic vigor of being. This is significant, because in Milton's epic becoming is often imagined as a sequence of these two instances—nonbeing and being. Thus, for example, in Raphael's account of Creation light comes into being with a moment of stillness that is immediately followed by a rapid movement designated by the adverb "forthwith" and the verb "sprung":

> Let there be light, said God, and *forthwith* light
> Ethereal, first of things, quintessence pure
> *Sprung* from the deep, and from her native east
> To journey through the airy gloom began,
> Sphered in a radiant cloud, for yet the sun
> Was not.   (*PL* 7.243–48; emphases mine)

Both "forthwith" and "sprung" have a feeling of immediacy about them, and jointly they produce a sense of a sudden and powerful movement, which begins an everlasting journey through the "airy gloom" (7.246). The moment of immobility is written into line 7.244: separated by commas, the three modifiers of the noun "light" bring the powerful movement suggested by "forthwith" to a momentary halt. Such a moment of immobility that is suddenly transformed into a powerful motion underlies also Adam's account of his own creation in book 8:

> As new waked from soundest sleep
> Soft on the flowery herb I found me laid
> In balmy sweat, which with his beams the sun
> Soon dried, and on the reeking moisture fed.
> Straight toward heaven my wondering eyes I turned,
> And gazed a while the ample sky, *till raised*
> *By quick instinctive motion up I sprung.*   (8.253–59; emphases mine)

In this passage, too, the moment of creation, symbolized by movement, follows the moment of death, symbolized by immobility: a sudden motion brings Adam's motionless position "in balmy sweat" to an abrupt end with a "quick instinctive motion."

Significantly, after Adam has acknowledged the moment of his becoming, there are no further occurrences of the language of the B-series in his speech. Instead, Adam's language testifies that his mind has fully regained its prelapsarian A-structure. One example is Adam's repeated association of himself with posterity. I will cite three such instances successively:

> Nor I on my part single, in me all
> *Posterity* stands cursed.   (10.817–18; emphasis mine)

> But from me what can *proceed,*
> But all corrupt, both mind and will depraved.
>   (10.824–25; emphasis mine)

> first and last
> On me, me only, as *the source and spring*
> Of all corruption.   (10.831–33; emphasis mine)

In all three passages, when Adam contemplates his direct responsibility for the fate of future generations, he assumes an everlasting temporal chain of which he himself is the "source and spring" (10.832). This chain is necessarily successive and dynamic and thus corresponds to McTaggart's definition of the A-series of time. The transformation that Adam's mind undergoes from the B-series to the A-series of time allows him to repent and accept God's grace. Adam's contemplation of posterity in terms of the bipartite movement of becoming which is built into the descriptions of both the creation of light and that of himself invests his monologue with the regenerative power of Creation.

In contrast to Adam, Satan experiences neither the death nor the re-creation of his mind. More significant still, a contemplation of the moment of becoming, which the poem offers as the trigger to Adam's transformation of mind, is conspicuously missing from Satan's speech. Even when Satan acknowledges the two termini of his own creation, that is, a creator (God) and a creature (Satan himself), he fails to mention the process of creation itself: "He [God] deserved no such return / From *me, whom he created what I was* / In that bright eminence" (4.42–44; emphasis mine). This failure renders line 4.43 paradoxical: God seems to have created what Satan already was. In Satan's B-structured mind there is no place left for the concept of Creation, which is necessarily a process that takes place in time.

This failure to acknowledge the Creation becomes an explicit denial in Satan's confrontation with Abdiel in book 5. "Who saw," asks the archangel, "When this creation was?":

> Rememberst thou
> Thy making, while the maker gave thee being?
> We know no time when we were not as now;
> Know none before us, self-begot, self-raised
> By our own quickening power.   (*PL* 5.856–61)

By claiming that he is self-begot, self-raised, and possessing no memory of his own creation, Satan, paraphrasing ironically the famous words of God to Job, denies his own creation. Quoting the same passage, Geoffrey Hartman discusses the implications of this forgetting of creation: "[The] denial of creatureliness," says Hartman, "[the] forgetting of creation is the origin and type of all sin."[19] What Hartman calls the denial of creatureliness is, I suggest, the denial of that form in the prelapsarian mind that is represented in *Paradise Lost* as time. The assertion that life has always existed in a fixed present independently of a creation is preceded in this passage by a rejection of any knowledge of time: "*we know no time* when we were not as now…self-begot, self raised" (5.859–60; emphasis mine). Underlying Satan's denial of Creation is not a mere incapability of grasping the idea of change but rather an explicit resistance to view reality through the dynamic form of time.

I believe that it is precisely this resistance to time that is at the heart of Satan's sin. Adam and Eve, who form a clear temporal concept of

Creation very early in their existence and do not at any time deny time are capable of regaining the A-series of their prelapsarian mind, repent, and start their way back to God. In Milton's epic time may be represented as unreal, a mere illusory form, yet it is the only way by which any understanding of reality may be achieved. This is evident from Abdiel's explicit advice to Satan that pardon should be achieved in and through time: "pardon may be found *in time besought*" (5.848; emphasis mine). Satan, who denies time, cannot help but understand the process of regeneration in static terms. Thus, for example, when the archangel toys with the possibility of repentance he locates both repentance and pardon in space rather than in time: "is there no *place* / Left for repentance, none for pardon left?" (4.79–80; emphasis mine). Satan's question betrays the static form of his fixed mind, which can only view repentance as a concept fixed in space. Curiously, his association of repentance with pardon reflects the Father's plan of regeneration delineated in *Paradise Lost* 3.173–97. Yet whereas the Father describes a temporal process in which "prayer, repentance, and obedience due" (3.191) may ultimately lead to regeneration, Satan draws no sequential relationship between the two. Satan is incapable of repentance and therefore receives no pardon because he denies the dynamic temporal form through which the former should be achieved and the latter besought. As I have attempted to show, in *Paradise Lost* it is only by an A-structured mind that a free act of repentance can be made. Satan, who is trapped within his fixed B-structured mind, "self-tempted, self-depraved," is doomed to be forever fallen.

University of London

Milton Reading

Reconstructing Milton's Lost *Index theologicus:* The Genesis and Usage of an Anti-Bellarmine, Theological Commonplace Book

Jeffrey Alan Miller

In addition to his commonplace book in moral philosophy, which survives in the British Library and which we now refer to simply as Milton's Commonplace Book, Milton also maintained a theological commonplace book, which has never been found.[1] The latter he referred to as his *Index theologicus,* and everything that we know about this lost *Index* comes from the 12 cross-references that Milton made to it in his surviving Commonplace Book.[2] As with the Commonplace Book's other, internal cross-references—such as the instruction "vide de Divortio," appended to the heading atop page 109, "Matrimonium," and referring to the heading on page 112—Milton always directed the reader (who, primarily, was himself) to see specific headings in the *Index theologicus,* rather than specific entries (CPB 109, 112). In total, references to six different headings from the *Index* appear, all in Latin: "de bonis Ecclesiasticis" (Of Ecclesiastical Goods); "de Idololatria" (Of Idolatry); "de Conciliis" (Of Councils); "de Religione non cogenda" (Of Religion not being something to be Forced, or Coerced); "Papa" (The Pope); and "Ecclesia" (The Church).[3]

Since the discovery of Milton's Commonplace Book in 1874, when the fact that Milton had also maintained a separate *Index theologicus* first became known to modern scholars, there have been two major advances in our understanding of this mysterious "other index."[4] The first came in 1977, when Gordon Campbell recognized that Milton's *Index theologicus* appeared to have been organized according to headings that targeted not only Roman Catholicism, but its greatest, most extensive, and so most notorious, early modern defender: the Jesuit Cardinal Roberto Bellarmino (1542–1621), anglicized as Bellarmine. Specifically, Campbell discerned that Milton's *Index* seemed structurally pitched against Bellarmine's magnum opus, *Disputationes de controversiis Christianae fidei, adversus huius temporis haereticos* (Disputations concerning the Controversies of the Christian Faith, Against the Heretics of this Time [i.e., the Protestants]).[5] Bellarmine's *Disputationes* began appearing in 1586 and ultimately swelled to three very heavy folio volumes.[6] Together these volumes covered 15 broad "Controversies," ranging from "De Summo Pontifice" and "De Conciliis, & Ecclesia," to "De Sacramento Eucharistiae" and "De Reparatione Gratiae" (this last divided into a volatile trilogy of sub-controversies, "De Gratia & libero arbitrio," "De Justificatione," and "De bonis operibus") (*Disputationes* 1.3.584–1087, 1.4.1–286, 2.3.448–1159, 3.3.503–1515). Most controversies and sub-controversies comprised a number of individually entitled books. Thus, for example, the controversy "De Membris Ecclesiae Militantis" contained the books "De Clericis," "De Monachis," and "De Laicis" (*Disputationes* 1.5.287–694). And each book was then further subdivided into numerous, individually entitled chapters. The work sought to parry, or rather to demolish one by one, every last claim of the Protestant cause. For decades, Protestant scholars regarded confuting Bellarmine's *Disputationes* as a matter of international importance, and many of the most celebrated of Milton's day set out to compose point-by-point animadversions on Bellarmine himself, frequently under expressly anti-Bellarmine titles.[7]

Milton's *De doctrina Christiana* is not his lost *Index theologicus,* nor in any direct sense can *De doctrina* have grown out of it. Many of the *Index*'s cross-referenced headings find no analogue in *De doctrina.* Moreover, Milton conceived *De doctrina* from the first as a work of systematic theology, and as therefore belonging to a different genre, one entailing a very different method of organization, than polemical theology, the broad genre governing an anti-Bellarmine, or anti-anything, commonplace book.[8] The difference between two important works by William Ames (1576–1633)—Ames's work of anti-Bellarmine polemical theology, *Bellarminus enervatus,* subtitled *Disputationes anti-Bellarminianae,* and Ames's work of systematic theology, *Medulla ss. theologiae,* which served as one of the two primary sources for *De doctrina* itself—throws the divergence between the two genres into particular relief.[9] In systematics, the headings establish the fundamental topics for building a complete body of positive theology: "Of God," "Of the Holy Scripture," and so on. In polemical theology, the headings by contrast almost always lock onto targets, or onto specific matters of controversy, such as "The Pope" or "Idolatry" (to name two classics evidently present in Milton's own *Index theologicus*). A work of polemical theology might still aim to produce a complete body of theological doctrine, but it went about generating that body negatively, through the catalyst of opposition.

In the absence of a Miltonic work conforming to the anti-Bellarmine design of the *Index,* whether *De doctrina* or any other, Campbell thus concluded that Milton "had at some time planned to write a polemical work directed against Bellarmine," but had ultimately abandoned the project.[10] William Poole's revision of that conclusion stands as the second major advance in our understanding of Milton's lost *Index theologicus.* In his work on "The Genres of Milton's Commonplace Book," Poole determines that theological commonplace books organized under anti-Bellarmine headings constituted a prevalent and recognizable genre of commonplace book in Milton's day. The fact that Milton began keeping a commonplace book aimed at Bellarmine's *Disputationes,* in other words, need not mean that Milton ever planned to compose a refutation of Bellarmine's *Disputationes.*[11] In compiling pro-Protestant and anti-Catholic notes or *adversaria* under headings that accorded with the thorough structure that Bellarmine supplied, Milton may simply have been doing what many bright and aspiring Protestants did by widespread convention, and likely by instruction. (Students at Cambridge may have been especially encouraged to do so, as many of the most notable English anti-Bellarminists of the period had at one point been fellows there: among of Richard Stock (1568/9–1626), Milton's boyhood preacher — and Thomas Young (ca. 1587–1655) — eventual Smectymnuan and Milton's revered boyhood tutor — also corresponded with Ward during the 1620s and 1630s.[17] Milton himself remained intimately in contact with Young over the same period of time.[18]

For the purposes of this essay, two consistent features of Ward's anti-Bellarmine commonplace books bear noting. First, while several of them are fairly thick — one totals 346 folio-sized pages[19] — they are all predominately blank. Many pages affixed with a heading at top remain otherwise unannotated, and these neglected headings do not represent mere minor points of anti-Catholic or anti-Bellarmine contention: the pages that Ward reserved for material "De Ceremoniis," "De Transubstantione," "De Causa Reprobationis," "De Nomine Sacramenti," and "De Necessitate operu*m* ad salute*m*," for instance, contain not a single entry between them.[20] A page set aside for recording "Objectiones Pontificioru*m*" contains only one entry.[21] However, while Ward may have hardly touched many of their pages, that is not to say that Ward's anti-Bellarmine commonplace books were little used in general. Indeed, certain headings accumulated a great deal of material beneath them.

The designated concerns of these more heavily trafficked pages correspond, almost without exception, to the concerns of Ward's *published* theological output: those foci being baptism, justification, and grace (particularly with regard to the matter of predestination).[22] As that list alone would indicate, the theological controversies that animated Ward most were not those of paramount importance between Protestants and Catholics, but rather those that became increasingly central between Protestants and other Protestants, namely between Calvinists (like Ward) and the ascendant Arminians of his day. In 1618, Ward in fact served as one of the five British delegates to the Synod of Dort.[23] Nevertheless — and this is the second key thing to note — Ward maintained several anti-Bellarmine commonplace books *after* Dort and through the changing urgencies of English Protestant polemic signaled by the synod. Thinking in terms of opposition to Bellarmine infused the structure and substance of much Protestant polemic, along with many Protestant commonplace books, and it was not simply relinquished as a mental habit the moment one realized that there were now blacker beasts to stalk than the cardinal himself. In a variety of ways and to a variety of purposes, Bellarmine endured as a foil for far longer than he did as a threat. John Selden (1584–1654) continued to incorporate scattered references to Bellarmine in the major works of Hebraic scholarship that he published during the 1640s and 1650s, despite the fact that the confutation of Bellarmine could hardly be said to have been one of his objectives.[24] Hobbes's *Leviathan* (1651) famously contains an extended confutation of Bellarmine's "De Summo Pontifice": "yet because the Pope of Romes challenge to that Power universally [ecclesiastical power], hath been maintained chiefly, and I think as strongly as is possible, by Cardinall Bellarmine, in his Controversie *De Summo Pontifice;* I have thought it necessary, as briefly as I can, to examine the grounds, and strength of his Discourse." Far from brief, that examination occupies the bulk of chapter 42.[25]

Even as Ward's primary target shifted definitively from Roman Catholics to Arminians, Ward did not abandon his anti-Bellarmine commonplace books. Neither did he abandon the practice of citing and confuting Bellarmine throughout them, nor throughout the published works those commonplace books helped to cultivate. As with the anti-Bellarmine polemic that permeates his anti-Arminian *Opera*, Ward simply bent his anti-Bellarmine commonplace books in the direction of intra-Protestant controversies. This, doubtless coupled with the fact that Ward's handwriting could be exceptionally poor, perhaps most explains why the genre and the life spans of these largely blank *adversaria* have proven so difficult for scholars to place, these notebooks devoted to anti-Arminian topics but structured according to anti-Catholic headings and primarily busied with confuting Catholic authors. One of Ward's commonplace books, indeed, had the following scrawled into the back of it by an early classifier of his papers, sometime in the second half of the seventeenth century: "Sevveral mss chiefly in Dr. Ward's hand, and relating to the points canvassed at *the* Synod of Dort, scarce legible, and of very little value I believe." The commonplace book in question appears, in fact, to have been begun almost a decade before Dort.[26]

Many of the defining characteristics of Ward's anti-Bellarmine commonplace books seem to have been shared by Milton's lost *Index theologicus*. The fact that Milton cross-referenced only six different headings, when the *Index* would have contained dozens at minimum, bespeaks quite targeted use. Thanks to the one exact page reference to the *Index theologicus* recorded in the Commonplace Book, we know that a page headed "Pope" in the *Index* was numerated as page 42 (CPB 221; appendix no. 9). That would have left room for quite a few preceding headings. Moreover, if Milton was indeed following the structure of Bellarmine's *Disputationes*—or the structure of a work of anti-Bellarminiana such as Ames's renowned *Bellarminus enervatus* (a crucial possibility to which I will return)—there would have been many more headings left to cover. Bellarmine's "De Summo Pontifice" appears in the first volume of three, and Ames's refutation of it in the first of four.[27] Milton's surviving Commonplace Book itself remains two-thirds blank, despite decades of use.[28] The fact that Milton felt drawn to cross-reference only a very small percentage of the headings present in the *Index theologicus* may intimate that it, too, like Ward's own anti-Bellarmine commonplace books, remained largely blank.

However, as with Ward's anti-Bellarmine commonplace books, suggesting that Milton's use of his *Index theologicus* may have been quite *targeted* is not to propose that such use was insubstantial, or confined to a narrow period of his life. Indeed, that appears to have been far from the case. In 1641, in his antiprelatical *Animadversions* (1641) against Bishop Joseph Hall (1574–1656), another former British delegate at Dort, Milton jeeringly referred to Hall as "a swashbuckler against the Pope," and he derided the bishop and his like for "all this careering with speare in rest and thundering upon the steele cap of *Baronius* or *Bellarmine*" (YP 1:731). Professed exasperation with English anti-Bellarminiana even prompted what appears to have been a Miltonic neologism, albeit not exactly one of Milton's more enduring efforts. In an equally explicit (and in this case exclusive) reference to the countless anti-Bellarmine works pitched against the *Disputationes*, Milton declared that all those "Hecatontomes of controversies"—that is, all those hundreds of volumes of controversies—penned in "confutation of the Pope and Masse" constituted nothing more than a pernicious, and often duplicitous, distraction (YP 1:731).[29] They made a show of confuting popery's international spread while nonetheless allowing it to be sown at home.

Campbell considered this moment as marking, definitively, the "*terminus ad quem*" for Milton's abandonment of his plans to write an anti-Bellarmine work.[30] Poole, as noted, shrewdly doubts whether Milton ever seriously saw himself as embarked on such an undertaking in the first place. But regardless of the exact reason that Milton *began* keeping an anti-Bellarmine commonplace book at some point prior to 1641, the most important thing to stress is the fact that Milton did not stop keeping it, or at least he did not stop using it, *after* 1641, even if he had by then abandoned whatever anti-Bellarmine or anti-Catholic ambitions he initially may have harbored. After the passage from *Animadversions,* Milton never again mentioned Bellarmine in print; indeed, that line constitutes the only explicit reference to Bellarmine to be found in Milton's extant writings. Yet for all his anti-anti-Bellarmine bluster, Milton still continued to employ, and crucially to draw upon in composing some of his most famous prose works, a theological commonplace book organized under anti-Bellarmine headings.

Many of the cross-references to the *Index theologicus* that Milton added to the Commonplace Book postdate 1641 with certainty. With only two exceptions, these references appear either directly beside a page's heading at top, or *in the margin* beside specific entries (as opposed to being built-in parts of those entries, a distinction occluded in the Yale edition). Moreover, the majority of the entries to which Milton appended these cross-references are the last or second to last entries on their respective pages (see appendix). As this would suggest, and as the often divergent ink and handwriting further confirms, by and large these cross-references represent later additions to the pages on which they appear, often later even than the entries, much less the headings, that they adjoin. The cross-reference that Milton tagged to the Commonplace Book's heading for "Alms" (*Eleemosynae*) provides one clear example of this: between the time that Milton recorded the heading, and the time that he added the cross-reference to "de bonis Ecclesiasticis," his minuscule "e" had undergone the famous shift from Greek (ε) to italic (*e*).[31]

Each of the items in the Commonplace Book that Milton cross-referenced with the *Index theologicus* recurs (often quite precisely) in one or another of Milton's *post*-1641 works. To provide one clear example, the Commonplace Book contains a short entry on the supremacy of church councils over popes, a position strenuously contested by Bellarmine's *Disputationes.* Found near the bottom of the page headed "Subject" (*Subditus*), the entry includes an appended cross-reference to the *Index's* heading "de Conciliis." In full, the entry reads, along with the cross-reference: "If *the* pope be not greater then a councel, then is no K*ing* to be thought greater then *the* Parlament [/] see de Conciliis" (CPB 183; appendix no. 7). Significantly, this exact antimonarchical argument—built upon precisely the same antipopish, anti-Bellarmine argument-turned-premise—first surfaces within one of Milton's published works in the last chapter of *Eikonoklastes:* "Certainly if whole Councels of the Romish Church have in the midst of their dimness discern'd so much of Truth, as to Decree at *Constance,* and at *Basil,* and many of them to avouch at *Trent* also, that a Councel is above the Pope, and may judge him, though by them not deni'd to be the Vicar of Christ, we in our clearer light may be asham'd not to discern furder, that a Parlament is, by all equity, and right, above a King, and may judge him" (YP 3:588–89). *Eikonoklastes,* one of the most important works of Milton's life, was of course not even begun until 1649.

Correspondences such as this do not simply provide confirmation of Milton's protracted use of his anti-Bellarmine *Index.* They offer a vivid picture of the *way* in which Milton used both the *Index theologicus* and the Commonplace Book throughout the bulk of his career as a prose writer. We may assume that (as in the Commonplace Book itself, and as in Ward's own anti-Bellarmine commonplace books) the headings that would have received the most attention in Milton's *Index theologicus* would have been those most bound up with the intra-*Protestant* controversies about which Milton wrote and published over the course of his life, notwithstanding the *Index*'s anti-Catholic structure and (presumably) its substantially anti-Catholic content. More significantly, however, the cross-references appear to indicate that we need to imagine Milton, as he prepared to compose his antiprelatical, divorce, and regicidal tracts (at least), combing back over a long-assembled collection of theological notes and quotes structured according to, and likely with many entries devoted to, the confutation of Cardinal Robert Bellarmine. Scholars have long been exercised by Milton's protracted use of his surviving Commonplace Book in this capacity, as a repository of material later culled and imported, often with striking immediacy, into his prose writing of the 1640s and 1650s.[32] It may well be that Milton's habit on those occasions was to page through his Commonplace Book and *Index theologicus* in parallel, looking for relevant material. But regardless, most of the cross-references to the *Index theologicus* within the Commonplace Book bespeak their having been added during precisely such a later stage of mobilization: as Milton quite literally went about gathering his thoughts in preparation to compose, or perhaps while already in the middle of composing, specific prose works.

This explains why, among other things, certain cross-references separated by hundreds of pages, or set alongside variously dated entries and headings, nonetheless appear to have been added at virtually the same moment. Take the cross-references to "de bonis Ecclesiasticis" found on page 12 under "Avarice" (*Avaritia*), and the aforementioned cross-reference to "de bonis Ecclesiasticis" found on page 151 under "Alms" (CPB 12, 151; appendix nos. 1, 2, and 5). In this case, Milton would seem to have been consulting his Commonplace Book—in addition to, or even alongside, his *Index theologicus*—with the specific idea of collating whatever dispersed material he had amassed there related or relatable to clerical abuses of tithing, or of power more broadly. As we shall see, *avarice* and *alms* possessed sharp polemical connotations when it came to the matters of tithing and clerical authority. One might even say that they functioned as Protestant keywords or, when paired together, as a kind of argument in shorthand. And so it was to the (initially quite disparate) pages devoted to *avarice* and *alms* in the Commonplace Book that Milton added, during what I propose was the same targeted sitting, the cluster of cross-references to the place in the *Index theologicus*—"de bonis Ecclesiasticis"—where material on tithing must have been centrally gathered.

Such cross-references may have enabled Milton to access the cross-referenced passages or pages in the Commonplace Book with even greater speed when subsequently looking to draw upon them in writing. Most were indeed positioned in such a way as to be spotted at a glance, and all draw attention to entries (for example, the entry regarding councils and parliaments) or concerns (such as clerical avarice) that can be tightly correlated with moments in Milton's published prose, something that is by no means true of all the Commonplace Book's entries in general. That being said, Milton well might have had other reasons for adding the cross-references beyond flagging things for use. He was clearly quite capable of retrieving material from the Commonplace Book without relying upon any kind of paratextual cue, as evidenced by the relative scarcity of such finding-devices in the Commonplace Book, save of course for each page's heading itself. Likewise, a cross-reference to the *Index* recorded in the Commonplace Book by an amanuensis, and so potentially (though not necessarily) scribed when Milton was blind, would perhaps argue against assuming that Milton meant these cross-references to serve visual purposes for his own benefit (CPB 197; appendix no. 8). Milton may have added the cross-references merely for the sake of knitting the *Index theologicus* and the Commonplace Book more closely together into a kind of whole, and so with the less utilitarian but very early modern idea of making those paired manuscripts, however private, more "complete."

Yet whatever the precise function of the cross-references, the way in which the majority of them came to be inserted into the Commonplace Book signals something beyond Milton's continued use of the *Index* as part of his *reading* practice.[33] What the cross-references seem primarily to have been a product of, and what they collectively denote, is Milton's continued use of the *Index theologicus* as part of his *writing* practice.

Campbell's groundbreaking identification of the anti-Bellarmine structure of Milton's *Index theologicus* has tended to lead scholars to regard the *Index* as therefore having been an object of both brief and marginal importance to Milton.[34] If Milton himself had abandoned it by 1641—or, even if Milton retained it, if the *Index* still simply served as a repository of material designed for the confuting of Catholics whom Milton never really bothered to confute—how important could the lost *Index theologicus* have been to him, and should it therefore be to us? Of course, until the actual *Index* is recovered, a recovered sense of the *Index*'s importance leaves us with a much bigger blank in the canvas of Milton studies than we have traditionally assumed that its loss entailed. However, if we ever do find Milton's anti-Bellarmine *Index,* the traces of it left behind in the Commonplace Book, and the points of contact between those traces and Milton's published works, suggest that we will have found an object whose longevity, and whose centrality to Milton's writing practice, has hitherto been greatly underestimated.

Milton's Reading Practice and His *Index theologicus*

One thing that the anti-anti-Bellarmine swipe at Bishop Hall in *Animadversions* may bespeak is Milton's awareness and remembrance of Hall's own anti-Bellarmine work.[35] That work, Hall's 1609 *The Peace of Rome Proclaimed to All the World by her famous Cardinall Bellarmine,* consisted almost entirely of English translations and detailed paraphrasings of Bellarmine's *Disputationes:* it is something like a Bartlett's of Bellarmine. "Understand (good reader)," Hall's prefatory "ADVERTISEMENTS *to the Reader*" begins, "that in all these passages following, I have brought in C. *Bellarm.* speaking in his owne words."[36] *The Peace of Rome* appears to have been expressly designed to provide its readers with reams of exact references to the *Disputationes* for use as anti-Bellarmine fodder, down to the very page number of the *Disputationes,* without those readers ever needing to consult further (or at all) Bellarmine's weighty "hecatontomes" themselves.[37] All works of anti-Bellarminiana came replete with lengthy and frequent references to the *Disputationes,* even if usually not formatted as a catalogue of them. Milton's jab at Hall's engagement with Bellarmine does not mark the abandonment of the *Index theologicus,* but it might reveal something important about Milton's own engagement with Bellarmine. Naturally, given the *Index*'s anti-Bellarmine structure, scholars have tended to imagine Milton sifting through the weighty, bi-columned folios of the *Disputationes* itself in order to compile it,[38] and have tended to take the measure of what the Commonplace Book witnesses about the *Index* in relation to the *Disputationes.* Bellarmine, however, could be confronted and confuted in other, more readily available ways. Perhaps works of anti-Bellarmine polemic, like Hall's, functioned as the primary sources upon which Milton drew, even if (or, rather, though) these intermediaries largely went unacknowledged.

Examples are not lacking of other anti-Bellarmine commonplacers practicing exactly this form of mediated engagement. The Bodleian Library contains a copy of Richard Stock's virulently antipapist *Sermon Preached at Paules Crosse* (London, 1609), which has been annotated in a telling fashion by an early modern hand. Nearly every one of the sermon's references to Bellarmine has been underlined, and an ominous-looking capital *B* has been additionally inscribed in the margin alongside several of them. The sermon is otherwise unannotated.[39] This reader, it would seem, was primarily not engaging with Stock's argument, but rather culling Stock for shards of Bellarmine — perhaps precisely for the purposes of later insertion into an anti-Bellarmine commonplace book. Hence the marginal *B*, facilitating quicker retrieval during that later task. And when it came to recording the references to Bellarmine provided by Stock, specifically in this case to Bellarmine's *"De Pontifice Romano"* (the other, more polemical name of the *Disputationes*'s "De Summo Pontifice"),[40] or even when it came to adducing those references in a later published work of the commonplacer's own, there is little doubt that one would not have found the commonplacer writing, "as Richard Stock saith 'Here saith *Bellarmine.*'"[41]

It is unlikely that even Stock's engagement with Bellarmine was entirely unmediated. A committed anti-Bellarmine polemicist throughout his extant works, Stock had been mentored as a student at St. John's College, Cambridge, by the man regarded as having been perhaps the greatest rebutter of Bellarmine in English history, William Whitaker. Numerous early modern authors, in fact, circulated the report, though it was no doubt spurious, that visitors of Bellarmine had found hanging in his study a picture of Whitaker, in honor of Whitaker's being in Bellarmine's own estimation the best of all his heretical adversaries.[42] Whitaker had "favoured Mr *Stock* very much for his ingenuity, industry and proficiency in his Studies," Stock's contemporary biographer recalled, and it was Whitaker's implacable brand of anti-Catholicism, and the very moderate brand of puritanism to which it was scrupulously alloyed, that Stock emulated for the rest of his life.[43] Stock's own first published work, indeed, was a translation of Whitaker.[44] Twice a Sunday, Stock delivered to his parishioners at All Hallows (in Breadstreet, London) sermons suffused with anti-Bellarmine polemic. Milton, throughout his youth, of course, would have been one of those parishioners before leaving to attend Cambridge in 1625.[45] As with so much about Stock, it would hardly be surprising if careful analysis revealed Stock's anti-Bellarmine material itself to be directly indebted to Whitaker to a significant degree, especially to Whitaker's various *Praelectiones contra pontificios, inprimis Robertum Bellarminum*, versions of which Stock would have witnessed Whitaker deliver and which were later accessible in many editions published in England and on the Continent.[46]

One example of an anti-Bellarmine commonplace book listed by Poole
in demonstration of the genre's prevalence is Bodleian MS Rawlinson
D 1425.[47] Maintained by an anonymous author, it postdates 1618 (at
least in part), though it would seem not by much.[48] Beneath a section
headed "princeps civilis jure divino supremam habet authoritatem in
personas et res ecclesiasticas" (the civil ruler holds supreme authority by
divine right over ecclesiastical persons and things), the commonplacer
cited Bellarmine's notorious, dissenting conviction in the following manner: "Bell. 1..Tom..contra illum Berclay. Amesius Chamier" [spaces all
sic].[49] As can be seen, it is clearly not Bellarmine but anti-Bellarmine
sources (one of them, notably, being Ames's *Bellarminus enervatus*) that
were being used, at least for this particular entry. Working from a source
that had apparently neglected to provide a full citation for Bellarmine's
position—Ames, as an example, often gave exact quotations from
Bellarmine without noting exactly where in the *Disputationes* the quota-
tion might be found—the unknown commonplacer left spaces in the
reference where the precise book and volume number of the *Disputationes*
might be later inserted, though they ultimately never were. Had they
been, of course, it would have appeared as if the commonplacer had
been reading Bellarmine all along. The pervasiveness of this very phenomenon, of references to Bellarmine being happily derived at some
number of removes from the actual source itself, no doubt contributed
to John Dove's grim observation that many "*name* Beza *before them which
have onely heard of his name, but knowe not how to spell it,* (*for they call him* Bezer,
as also Bellarmine *they call* Bellamye)." When it came to the majority of
those people referencing Beza, indeed, Dove doubted if "*it is likely they
have read his workes*" at all. It shows the extent to which that must have
been true of the majority referencing Bellarmine that the comparison
immediately suggested itself, and needed no elaboration.[50]

Much about Milton's lost *Index* (and surviving Commonplace Book)
snaps into focus when one interposes intermediary sources between him
and the points of Catholic controversy to which he appears to refer.
Instead of trying to squint at the *Disputationes* to see which of Bellarmine's
headings Milton might have had in mind when crafting his own on
"Religion not being something to be coerced," a title that is obviously
not replicated in the *Disputationes*, why not simply look to a work like

Ames's *Disputationes anti-Bellarminianae* (that is, *Bellarminus enervatus*), where an entire chapter entitled "Of the Coercive Power of the Pope" does in fact appear?[51] The *Index*'s "de Idololatria" similarly lacks an exact correspondent among the headings found in Bellarmine's work. Milton, of course, would hardly have been the first Protestant to find in the *Disputationes* a prompt for such a title, notwithstanding. One thinks especially of John Rainolds (1549–1607) and his *De Romanae ecclesiae idololatria*, in whose two books, according to the work's extended title, "*cum alia multa variorum Papismi patronorum errata patefiunt: tûm inprimis Bellarmini... calumniae in Calvinum ac ceteros Protestantes, argutiaeque pro Papistico idolorum cultu discutiuntur & ventilantur*" (the many other errors of the various defenders of papistry are discovered, and chiefly Bellarmine's calumnies against Calvin and the rest of the Protestants, and his subtleties on behalf of the papist worship of idols, are dashed to pieces and blown away).[52] Andrew Willet, in his influential and anti-Bellarmine *Synopsis Papismi*, also framed a number of his work's polemical "questions" as discussions of the papists' idolatry, each taking a different section of the *Disputationes* as its targeted counterpart.[53] Nor, it should be said, did making idolatry a titular point of contention begin with or ever become restricted to the genre of anti-Bellarmine polemic. If one broadens the scope to include the more generally anti-Catholic works of Reformed theology that Milton likely would have encountered (at the latest) during his student days at Cambridge, one finds a surplus of matching headings on idolatry. The *Opera theologica* of Hieronymus Zanchius (1516–90), for instance, a work which Milton displays both a broad and detailed knowledge of in *De doctrina*, contains a lengthy section entitled "*DE IDOLOLATRIA*."[54]

It certainly could be that Milton, basing the *Index*'s headings on Bellarmine's *Disputationes*, simply made choices that paralleled those made previously by Protestant luminaries such as Rainolds and Willet, as Campbell suggested.[55] But perhaps the fact that direct equivalents for all of the *Index*'s known headings can be found in major Reformed works of anti-Catholic and anti-Bellarmine polemical theology, while ones for only some of the *Index*'s headings occur in the *Disputationes* itself, suggests instead that Milton was actually working from the former, and not (or at least not primarily) the latter. Why did Milton repeatedly cross-reference the subjects of marriage and divorce with "Of Ecclesiastical Goods," when any number of other potential headings in Milton's *Index* might seem to have been more pertinent, when that correlation does not seem prompted by Bellarmine's own treatment of those issues, and when the *Disputationes* does not even contain a heading on ecclesiastical goods?[56] Perhaps because in the famous *Loci communes theologiae sacrae* of Wolfgang Musculus (1497–1563), Musculus's section entitled "DE CAUSIS MATRI-MONIALIBUS"—which covered the various sums of money required by the pope in order for special allowances of marriage and divorce to be granted—appeared beneath the running header of "Nundinatio Romani Pontificis": the trafficking (as if in goods) of the Roman pontiff. Or, as it was translated during the period, "The Popes Merchandises."[57]

Unacknowledged intermediary sources may indeed hold the key to what has long been one of the most perplexing items in Milton's Commonplace Book. Under "Avarice," Milton wrote, with inscrutable brevity, "Martino quarto. vide de bonis Eccl*iasticis*" (CPB 12; appendix no. 2): on (Pope) Martin IV, see "Of Ecclesiastical Goods." The entry is the last on the page. Milton made no note of the source that prompted it, nor did he leave any indication of what exactly about Martin IV he had in mind, beyond the fact of his having placed Martin IV under "Avarice" and his having cross-referenced Martin with the section on "Ecclesiastical Goods" in the *Index theologicus*. It remains, to my knowledge, the only entry in the Commonplace Book that scholars have been unable to trace backward to a befitting source. Tracing it forward has proven just as difficult. Martin IV appears nowhere else in Milton's extant writings, which has only deepened the confusion. The entry seems a dead end in either direction. That is, until one considers it in relation to works of anti-Catholic polemical theology.

Milton's "Martino Quarto"

Only two other entries appear in Milton's Commonplace Book under "Avarice." In the first entry on the page, Milton noted (in Latin) Dante's censure of clerical avarice in canto 7 of the *Inferno*.[58] In the second entry, located between the reference to Dante and the reference to Martin IV, Milton recorded (in Italian) a passage taken from the celebrated *Croniche* of Dante's Florentine contemporary, Giovanni Villani, concerning the avaricious, mid-thirteenth century Caliph of Baldac (Baghdad) (see CPB 12). Understandably—if, I hope to show, misguidedly—scholars have traditionally looked to attribute Milton's reference to Martin IV to one or another of those authors. With regard to Dante, it has been noted that Milton would have encountered Martin IV in his reading of the *Purgatorio,* a work cited elsewhere in the Commonplace Book (see YP 1:367n6). Villani devotes an entire sequence of short chapters in the *Croniche* to the papacy of Martin IV, from Martin IV's ascension to the throne of St. Peter in 1281 to his death in 1285.[59] This section in the *Croniche,* moreover, appears only 20 folios after the passage that Milton extracted for his entry on the Caliph of Baldac.[60] Milton owned a copy of the *Croniche,* and his familiarity with and estimation of it must have been high: Milton's nephew Edward Phillips (1630–96?) recalled that Milton had used it to teach Italian to Phillips's brother John and him when the two were being schooled by Milton during the 1640s.[61]

Neither Dante nor Villani quite fits, however, as a source for Milton's entry on the avarice of Pope Martin IV. In the *Purgatorio,* Dante only mentions two popes, Martin IV being one of them; yet Dante offers Martin IV as an example of gluttony, not avarice. Martin IV, or rather the pope "from Tours"—it is perhaps not irrelevant to note that Dante never refers to Martin IV by name—appears fasting in purgatory after a life of feasting on eels *alla vernaccia.*[62] Had the *Purgatorio* been Milton's source, he should then have slotted Martin IV under "Gluttony" (*Gula*), which is in fact the heading atop the very next page in the Commonplace Book.[63] Furthermore, Milton's reference under "Avarice" to Dante's *Inferno* was scribed in a noticeably earlier hand than was the reference beneath it to Martin IV.[64] The idea that Milton's reading of Dante some years prior led Milton to adduce the lone name of Martin IV under "Avarice," years later and under the wrong heading according to Dante's poem, can be safely retired.

The *Croniche* represents a more tantalizing possibility. Villani's Martin IV engaged in a number of practices that one imagines Milton would have found repugnant, perhaps especially when it came to Martin IV's untrammeled efforts to support Charles of Anjou, the overthrown king of Sicily. As Villani shows, Martin IV's means of furthering the wars and claims of Charles included, among other persuasions, excommunication and deprivation of property. However, based solely on Villani's account, Martin IV seems largely to have *spent* the spiritual and temporal capital he acquired, primarily on Charles and other crusades, which is precisely the opposite approach to the accumulation of wealth evinced by the Caliph of Baldac and censured by Villani as avaricious. (Villani claimed that the Caliph would not even spend part of his hoarded treasure on battle, leading to his defeat.) If anything, Villani's Martin IV might appear to merit praise for his support of Charles. On his deathbed in 1285, according to Villani, Charles prayed to God "con molta reverenza" that his attempts to seize the kingdom of Sicily were made "plus por servir saint eglise que por mon profit uoltre [*sc.* ou autre] covertise [*sic*]" (more to serve the holy church than for my own gain or out of some other covetousness). That Charles is shown praying in his native French only deepens the authenticity, and the pathos, of the scene. Martin IV died shortly thereafter, and when in the *Croniche* Villani paused to remark upon the "grandi signori de christiana" who had died between 1284 and 1285, he listed Martin IV and Charles first and second, respectively.[65]

Milton may have found this King Charles as repellent as he would come to find that other Caroline monarch, and Villani's Martin IV might well have seemed to Milton like a textbook illustration of clerical over-reach, and of the papacy's habit of supporting, by all available means, something that may have struck Milton as attempted civil suppression. Nevertheless, Villani's Martin IV simply does not cut a good figure of exemplary avarice, at least no more than any pope might in Milton's view. Other, more minor features of Milton's reference to Martin IV in the Commonplace Book likewise argue against tracing it back to Villani. While, in calling Martin IV "Martino quarto," Milton may have been writing Martin's name in Italian, it could instead be in the Latin ablative, as in "[de] Martino quarto" (on Martin the fourth), which might make greater sense and which is indeed how it has always been taken by modern editors of the Commonplace Book (YP 1:367n6).[66] Milton's entry from Villani on the Caliph of Baldac, by contrast, is entirely in Italian, and Milton cites the entry's derivation with care, recording that it comes from "Gian Villani. l. 6. c. 61" (CPB 12). This compared to the way that the entry on Martin IV is handled, which would seem to have fallen into the Commonplace Book out of the sky for all the attribution that Milton gives it.

In a way, however, Milton did attribute the entry on Martin IV to a source: the *Index theologicus*. It is important to note that Milton scribed the entry on Martin IV and the cross-reference to the *Index* at the same time. "Martino quarto. vide de bonis Eccl*iasticis*" is, thus, not so much an entry with a cross-reference attached to it as it is a cross-reference to the *Index* unto itself. It explicitly asks to be seen in relation not to other entries in the Commonplace Book but to an entry or entries located in the *Index theologicus*. And many, perhaps most, of *those* entries, as I have been suggesting, would have been derived from anti-Bellarmine or, more broadly, anti-Catholic sources, sources abundant in early modern England and much more likely, of course, to traduce a pope by name for avariciousness. Overwhelmingly, those sources point to the conclusion that Milton indeed made a mistake in placing Martin IV under "Avarice" after all. Not that, misrecalling Dante, Milton should have put Martin IV elsewhere. But rather that Milton meant to record the name of Martin V and simply got the number wrong.

The Commonplace Book contains additional clues as to what sort of material Milton might have been keeping in the *Index* under "de bonis Ecclesiasticis," besides material on (a) Pope Martin, and thereby contains clues as to the sources that Milton might have been consulting in the process. As we have seen, Milton also cross-referenced the headings of "Avarice" and "Alms" themselves with the topic of "Ecclesiastical Goods." (Indeed, I propose that all three of these cross-references to the *Index*—those adjoining "Avarice," "Alms," and "Martin IV"—were added to the Commonplace Book in the same sitting, a proposition the manuscript supports.) Associating the subjects of avarice and alms with church property, and with material compiled on the latter according to an expressly anti-Catholic rubric, Milton can only have had one thing in mind: tithes, and specifically Wyclif's famous contention that tithes were not due *jure divino* but were rather "alms." Wyclif (d. 1384), in other words, had maintained that tithes could be bestowed (or, crucially, withheld) voluntarily and were not to be compelled by church authority, which of course in England during Wyclif's time meant papal authority.[67] In the *Disputationes*'s chapter "De decimis," appearing in the book "De Clericis," Bellarmine sourced to Wyclif specifically the first two of four major "errors" regarding tithes: "Primus error fuit Joan. Wiclefi, qui...docebat decimas esse puras eleemosynas, & nullo jure deberi

Sacerdotibus" (The first error was John Wyclif's, who taught tithes to be pure alms, and not to be due by any right to priests). "Alter error est eiusdem Wiclefi, quod scilicet decimae non modò sint purae eleemosynae, sed etiam nullo modo dandae sint malis Sacerdotibus" (The second error is also Wyclif's, namely that tithes are not only pure alms but that they also should in no wise be paid to wicked priests).[68] Wyclif's position on tithes could obviously be mobilized in judgment against more than one pope, and more than one pope condemned him. Pope Gregory XI was the first to do so, via the five bulls issued against Wyclif in May of 1377.[69] In Milton's time, though, the pope most often and most damningly associated with Wyclif and with abuses of tithing was Pope Martin. Not Pope Martin the *fourth*, however, but Pope Martin the *fifth*.

George Downame's *Treatise concerning Antichrist*—"Proving that the Pope is Antichrist," its title page proclaimed, "against all the *objections* of Robert Bellarmine"—contained an entire section devoted to demonstrating "the insatiable avarice of the Pope." The papacy's "extraordinary exactions were intollerable," Downame wrote: "*For* he [the pope] hath not beene ashamed to demaund the tenths of all spirituall livings, in some whole realmes, for many yeares together." Downame's primary example of such avariciousness in tithing was Martin V. "Out of *Fraunce* alone in the time of *Martin* 5," Downame declared, "the Pope and court of Rome received 9. millions."[70] Martin V was, in fact, the only pope in Downame's section on papal "avarice" mentioned by name.

Downame found this testimony of Martin V's insatiable demand for tithes in *Brutum fulmen Papae Sixti V*, an incendiary blast of antipopery by the French Protestant and lawyer François Hotman (1524–90). Hotman's *Brutum fulmen*, a sustained attack on the pope's alleged authority, was an *ad hominem* litany of the "crimes" perpetrated by the various Roman pontiffs. Therein, Hotman decried "the summe of monie"—the "grosse summe," as the work's contemporary English translator added—"that during the time of pope Martin the fifts popedome, was caried [*sic*] to Rome out of France alone, which is said to have amounted to ninetie hundred thousande crownes."[71] Argumentatively, *Brutum fulmen* is slight, but as a source for anecdotes of papal atrocities, it is an anti-Catholic polemicist's, and an anti-Bellarmine commonplacer's, dream. It even came appended with a brief refutation of Bellarmine's "disputatio" on papal supremacy, an anti-Bellarmine addendum that was heralded on *Brutum fulmen*'s title page — reflecting, perhaps, the marketing as well as the polemical pressures created by Bellarmine's omnipresence.[72]

Foxe also recorded from "Fraunce lykewise, what floudes of money were swalowed up in this sea of Rome," when "in the time of Pope Martine, there came out of France to the court of Rome, 9. millions of golde."[73] Indeed, in the *Acts and Monuments*, Martin V appears as the pope who most evinces "the prety shiftes of the Pope to hooke in the English money by all manner of pretences possible" (AM1583, 1:642). "In the first year of his popedome," Foxe relates, "Pope Martin 5…sent two Cardinals to the Archbishop [of Canterbury] to cause a tenth to be gathered of all spirituall and Religious men" (AM1583, vol. 1, sig. *5r). Foxe provides a full translation of Martin V's "bloudy and abhominable" bull "directed foorth against the Followers of John Wickliffe of England, [and] of John Husse of Boheme," issued "about the latter end & breaking up of the councel of Constance, an. 1418." The bull reaffirmed the Council of Constance's "condemnation of 45. articles of John Wickleffe," one of those articles being Wyclif's position on tithes.[74] And further, in the bull, Martin ordered everyone "suspected in the foresayd articles, or else otherwise found with assertion of them" — including all "such takers away & incrochers upo*n* ecclesiastical goods" — to be hunted down and "punished as committers of sacriledge" (AM1583, 1:648–52).

Foxe presented Martin V as arguably the most indelibly vicious pope in history. It was Martin V who, in 1427, notoriously ordered Wyclif's body disinterred, his bones burned, and the ashes scattered.[75] First and foremost of all the past bishops of Rome, Foxe identified Martin V with the two-horned beast of Revelation 13:11 ("And I beheld another beast coming up out of the earth, and he had two horns like a lamb, and he spake as a dragon").[76] He spoke of Martin being "hatched" at the Council of Constance and specifically called Martin himself "the great antechrist" (AM1583, 1:595, 65[3]). Yet Foxe often referred to the hated Martin V simply as "Pope Martine," sans numeral — as he did in the above rebuke of the tithes exacted out of France during "the time of Pope Martine" — leaving ample room for a reader to mistake Martin's regnal number. Indeed, at one point in the *Acts and Monuments*, Foxe himself mistook it! Discussing the Council of Basel, Foxe reminded his readers of his previous discussion regarding the time when "Pope Martine the 4. being yet at Constance, under the licence of *the* Councell, sent out his bulles [against the Wycliffites and Hussites], which d[id] recken up the Articles, whereupon they ought to be examined, which had falle*n* into any heresy" (AM1583, 1:677). The edition of *Acts and Monuments* that Milton himself appears to have used retained this error (London, 1631–32), and it is perhaps not a coincidence that, in the 1631–32 edition, Milton would have come upon this confused reference to the bulls of "pope Martine the fourth" within a section whose pages bore large, thematic headings at top such as *"The Councell of Constance decreeth the Pope to be under the Councell"* and *"The Councell of Basill: The Councell and the Church above the Pope."*[77]

If we consider Milton's reference to Martin IV in relation to the context of anti-Catholic polemic—and, in cross-referencing the *Index theologicus,* Milton directed himself to do precisely that—the evidence both within and (pervasively) outside of the Commonplace Book argues that this is in fact a garbled reference to Pope Martin V. Suddenly, there exist scores of perfectly plausible sources for what was hitherto the Commonplace Book's most orphaned item. Indeed, we can now even find in Milton's documented reading a source from which the very mis-numbering of Pope Martin itself might have been derived. Moreover, as with all of the other parts of the Commonplace Book cross-referenced with the *Index theologicus,* the reference to Pope Martin can now be rec-ognized as intimately coordinated with Milton's *writing.*

In *Of Reformation* (1641), Milton referenced "avarice," "almes," and "tithes" within a single paragraph. The paragraph begins with Milton railing against bishops "whose mouths cannot open without the strong breath, and loud stench of avarice, Simony, and Sacrilege, embezling the treasury of the Church." From there, Milton further attacks the bish-ops for "warming their Palace Kitchins, and from thence their unctu-ous, and epicurean paunches, with the almes of the blind, the lame, the impotent, the aged, the orfan, the widow, for with these the treasury of Christ ought to be" (YP 1:610–11). Note the Wycliffite contention, which would not have been lost, that the avaricious clergy were "embezzling alms"—as opposed to lawfully compelling tithes rightfully theirs—and that those alms would be best redirected to other recipients. Driving the point home, Milton concludes the paragraph by calling for an end to "the ignoble Hucsterage of pidling *Tithes*" (YP 1:613). Elsewhere in *Of Reformation*, Milton refers pointedly to "the almes due to *Christs* living members," and he praises "our *Wicklefs* preaching, at which all the succeeding *Reformers* more effectually lighted their Tapers." He laments, however, that in England Wyclif's "blaze" was "soon dampt and stifl'd by the *Pope*, and *Prelates*" (YP 1:547, 525–26). At the forefront of Milton's mind must have been Pope Martin V (or, perhaps I should say, "Martin IV") and Archbishop Courtenay, who by all medieval and early modern accounts were the pope and prelate respectively most responsible for crushing the spread of Wyclif's influence in England.[78]

In *Areopagitica* (1644), Milton mentioned Martin V by name. "*Martin* the 5," Milton declares, "by his Bull not only prohibited, but was the first that excommunicated the reading of hereticall Books; for about that time *Wicklef* and *Husse* growing terrible, were they who first drove the Papall Court to a stricter policy of prohibiting" (YP 2:502). This mention of Martin V appears to have been prompted by Paolo Sarpi (1552–1623), specifically Sarpi's *Historia del Concilio Tridentino* (1619). In the preceding sentence in *Areopagitica*, Milton claims that, initially, "the primitive Councels and Bishops were wont only to declare what Books were not commendable, passing no furder, but leaving it to each ones conscience to read or to lay by, till after the yeare 800. [as] is observ'd already by *Padre Paolo* the great unmasker of the *Trentine* Councel." It was only after that time, according to Milton, that "the Popes of *Rome*" descended to "burning and prohibiting to be read, what they fansied not," before finally reaching, with Martin V, the extreme of excommunicating people on the grounds alone of their having read something (YP 2:501–02). The passage in Sarpi's *Historia* that Milton references, and that he closely parallels, follows much the same trajectory. Sarpi begins by noting the papacy's transition to burning books and condemning reading "Dopo l'anno 800," and then quickly moves into discussing "Martino 5" and the pope's bull against "tutte le sette d'heretici, Viglefisti massime, & Ussiti" (all the sects of heretics, the Wycliffites chief among them, and the Hussites).[79]

Sarpi's *Historia*, therefore, represents yet another anti-Catholic source from which the Commonplace Book's reference to Pope Martin might have been derived. (Though he mentions Martin V multiple times, Sarpi mentions Martin IV only once, and then only in a fleeting aside.)[80] Milton, indeed, had also extolled Sarpi by name in *Of Reformation*—"You know Sir what was the judgement of *Padre Paolo* the great Venetian Antagonist of the *Pope*" (YP 1:581)—and Sarpi is one of the more highly represented sources in the Commonplace Book.[81] However, as Ernest Sirluck notes, Milton actually *contradicts* what Sarpi says about Martin V and his efforts against the Wycliffites and Hussites. Sarpi adduced Martin V to show that not even the brutal Martin proposed excommunicating those who had simply *read* the works of Wyclif or Hus. Milton, as we have just seen, claimed precisely the opposite. Consequently, Sirluck took the discrepancy as an indication that Milton must have been counterbalancing what Sarpi had said about Martin V with the claims of some other source: Foxe was proposed as the uncited, mediating influence.[82]

Although *Areopagitica* is the only work in which Milton mentions Martin V by name, it remains more probable that the Commonplace Book's reference to Pope Martin was a product of, or preparative for, Milton's composing *Of Reformation*. "Avarice" and "Ecclesiastical Goods," the two headings with which Milton specifically triangulated "Martino quarto," do not figure even as fleeting concerns in *Areopagitica*, nor do alms or tithes. This in contrast to *Of Reformation*, where not only are all of those subjects present, but where they all appear tightly bound up with one another, as intertwined aspects of a single concern. It is also unlikely that the Commonplace Book's reference to "Martino quarto" derived from Sarpi. The *Historia* always includes Martin V's regnal number when referring to him (and, unlike Foxe's *Acts and Monuments*, it always numerates Martin V accurately), which is doubtless one of the reasons Milton himself gets Martin V's regnal number right in *Areopagitica*. Moreover, Sarpi was not interested in Martin V as an example of avarice, nor indeed was Milton interested in Sarpi's Martin V as such. Milton placed the following entry in the Commonplace Book under not "Avarice" or "Alms," but "Gentleness" (*Lenitas*): "Prohibition of books when first us'd. The storie thereof is in *the* Councel of Trent l. 6. strait from *the* beginning p. 457. *etc.*" (CPB 184).

As we have observed, that story in Sarpi's *Historia* specifically featured Martin V; indeed, in the edition that Milton used (London, 1619), Martin V appears on the verso side of the very page there cited by Milton. Yet the Commonplace Book takes no note of that story's relation to Martin V, nor did Milton key the entry with either the reference to Martin under "Avarice" or to the place in the *Index theologicus* where further material on Martin could be found. I suspect that this particular reference to Sarpi in the Commonplace Book postdates both *Of Reformation* and the reference to "Martin IV" under "Avarice." At the very least, it reflects that when Milton added the cross-reference to Pope Martin under "Avarice," his mind was on matters other than censorship, and so almost certainly on passages other than the one from Sarpi's *Historia* that would later occasion the mention of Martin V in *Areopagitica*. The Commonplace Book's reference to Pope Martin bespeaks Milton's reading of the very unacknowledged source — a source, Foxe or otherwise, that offered Martin V as an example of avarice — whose mediating presence Sirluck intuitively sensed at work in *Areopagitica*. And, in turn, *Areopagitica* reveals that material first stored in Milton's *Index theologicus*, both in general and on Martin V specifically, was continuing to infiltrate Milton's writing, even if Milton kept his reliance on the *Index*, and on the anti-Catholic, anti-Bellarmine sources that filled it, almost always out of his audience's view — though only barely. Close by his side throughout much of his career, the *Index theologicus* can be detected whispering lines to him from just offstage.

Milton's cross-reference to his material "on Martin IV" in the *Index theologicus* serves as a kind of microcosm of the *Index* as a whole. Like the *Index* itself, the reference has long been treated as a dead end, or, maximally, as a stray curiosity, something neither significantly related to any of the most important works that Milton read nor to any of the most important works that he himself went on to write. Yet, as with the product of an enigma machine, once one attempts to run the *Index* back through the very thing Milton appears to have used to generate it — anti-Bellarmine, anti-Catholic polemical theology — something else entirely takes shape, something far more significant. Milton's reference to the avaricious Martin IV, a reference seemingly out of nowhere and going nowhere, becomes a reference to the most reviled pope in English antipapist history, Martin V, and to content stored in the *Index theologicus* concerning *that* Pope Martin which Milton brought to bear upon his prose works again and again.

Even the aforementioned entry in the Commonplace Book on councils being above popes, which Milton cross-referenced with the *Index*'s "de Conciliis," bears a strong relation to Milton's (polemical) interest in Martin V (CPB 183; appendix no. 7). As we have seen, in 1649 Milton drew upon that entry, doubtless together with the correlated entries in the *Index*, for the passage in *Eikonoklastes* in which he declared that as "a Councel is above the Pope" so must Parliaments be, "by all equity, and right, above a King" (YP 3:588–89). In the Commonplace Book, Milton gave no specific examples of councils evincing that supremacy. In *Eikonoklastes*, he gave three, the first two of them being the Council of Constance and the Council of Basel. It was at the Council of Constance that Martin V, notoriously, was made pontiff over the entire schismed church, and in the immediate aftermath of Constance that Martin issued his merciless bulls against the Wycliffites. And as no shortage of anti-Catholic polemicists emphasized, it was at the Council of Basel, called by Martin V (though he died before it opened), that Martin V's "avaricious" exaction of tithes across Europe emerged as a major point of complaint. Indeed, Foxe's mistaken reference to Martin V as "Pope Martine the 4" occurred, as we have seen, within Foxe's very discussion of the Council of Basel, and specifically in a section on Basel heralded by the paratext as demonstrating that church councils held ultimate authority over popes.

If we feed what little the Commonplace Book tells us about the *Index theologicus* back through the context of anti-Catholic polemical theology, the significance of the *Index* as a whole becomes similarly clarified and transformed. The commonplace book that Milton kept arranged in opposition to Cardinal Robert Bellarmine—an already vanquished author whom Milton only ever mentioned once and whose *Disputationes* Milton gives no indication of ever having read[83]—reveals itself to have been one of Milton's most vital storehouses, and weapons.

Conclusion

"*I vent to you nothing quoted at second hand,*" John Selden assured his readers in the preface to *Titles of Honor*, "*but ever lov'd the Fountain, and, when I could come at it, usd that* Medium *only.*"[84] This was not a governing principle that Milton always appears to have shared, perhaps especially when it came to reading, and subsequently drawing upon works of theology and religious polemic. It may be disappointing to relinquish the belief that Milton had actually turned over the pages, much less "all the pages," of everything that he referenced, cited, or targeted.[85] Yet if a readily available intermediary author, however unacknowledged, could easily have supplied Milton with the material that he adduced in a given instance, particularly if it could have been supplied by an author whom Milton trusted (or would have wanted to trust), it might be little more than wishful to assume that the material in question must nevertheless have been more laboriously or more directly won.

In the revised second edition of *The Doctrine and Discipline of Divorce* (1644), Milton declared, "Jesuits, and that sect among us which is nam'd of *Arminius*, are wont to charge us of making God the author of sinne" (YP 2:293). At the time he penned those words, as we have seen, Milton still retained in his possession, and was continuing to draw upon, a theological commonplace book structured according to the most notorious early modern Jesuit work of them all. Do we really believe, however, that Milton bothered to consult enough Jesuit sources, the *Disputationes* or any other, to be able to verify that Jesuits were actually "wont" to say that? Maybe; but he obviously need not have, and *The Doctrine & Discipline* itself gives no indication that he did. In the same tract, Milton supplemented a passage from Grotius's *Annotationes in libros Evangeliorum* (Amsterdam, 1641) with some further rabbinic examples: "to this I adde," offered Milton, "that *Kimchi* and the two other Rabbies who glosse the text, are in the same opinion" (YP 2:335). Milton could read Hebrew, and primary sources of rabbinic materials were increasingly available in England. He himself, in fact, owned a Hebrew Bible, sent to him by Thomas Young.[86] However, fewer than 15 pages prior in *The Doctrine & Discipline*, Milton explicitly sources his knowledge of "the testimony of some Rabbies" to what certain unnamed "antiquaries [like Selden?] affirm" (YP 2:317). With regard to Milton's citation of "*Kimchi* and the two other Rabbies," even the Yale Prose, despite the general inclination of its editors to assume that Milton read anything and everything cover to cover, notes "that rabbinical glosses were available at second hand," that is, available via intermediary sources (YP 2:336n4). Jason Rosenblatt goes even further, positing that moment in *The Doctrine & Discipline* as an indication of Milton's specific use of Selden's *De jure naturali & gentium* (London, 1640): "as if Selden were a primary rather than secondary source."[87] Milton often drew upon Foxe, yet he almost never attributed anything to his reading of Foxe. Nowhere is this more in evidence than in *Of Reformation*, which, famously, makes no mention of Foxe or Foxe's work whatsoever, despite *Of Reformation*'s being the tract of Milton's most indebted to the *Acts and Monuments* (See YP 1:524n24).

According to the ideals (if not always the habits) of modern scholarship, Milton might seem the less for even occasionally evincing this mediated approach. Critiquing him on the basis of it, however, would be to judge Milton by standards that, while advocated by Selden, not only were evidently far from the norm in practice, but may have been quite alien to Milton's own ideals, and to the ideals of many of his contemporaries, regarding what was truly worthwhile to read and how one might profitably (and scrupulously) go about drawing upon that reading in writing. It has been observed about no less a figure than Grotius that, "while most authors have mistakenly assumed that the mention of a source by Grotius presupposes first-hand knowledge of the author concerned," closer inspection frequently reveals Grotius to have been handling "'intermediate' sources" instead.[88] Hobbes's "constant reluctance to refer to his sources" is famous.[89]

Milton, in fact, was only using Foxe in the very way that Foxe himself had used his own "primary" sources. When relating the "grosse summe" of tithes extracted out of France by Martin V, both Foxe and Hotman cite the commonplace book of the Magdeburg Canon Heinrich Toke (or Token, d. 1454), who had been at the Council of Basel to witness the moment when that protest against the late Martin V was first voiced.[90] The title of Toke's commonplace book was *Rapularius*, though it was alternately referred to as Toke's *Sylva locorum communium*. Foxe cited it by the former name, Hotman by the latter. What is clear, however, is that neither Foxe nor Hotman had actually derived that fact about Martin V from it. Instead, both took it from Matthias Flacius's landmark *Catalogus testium veritatis, qui ante nostram aetatem reclamarunt Papae* (The Catalogue of Witnesses of Truth, who before our age cried out against the Pope) (Basel, 1556). Therein Flacius influentially recorded "quòd tempore Martini Papae venerunt ad curiam Romanam de Francia novem milliones auri" (that in the time of Pope Martin there came to the court of Rome out of France nine millions of gold), and he identified the passage as a quote from the commonplace book of *Henricus Token*, "qui in concilio Basiliensi Madeburgensis Archiepiscopi legatus fuit" (who was

the legate of the Archbishop of Magdeburg at the Council of Basel).[91]
Foxe and Hotman both simply took Flacius's word for it, and, when
subsequently referencing what Toke had allegedly written, neither Foxe
nor Hotman felt it necessary to mention the name of the man whose
word they were taking. Downame, who gleaned that vivid example of
Martin V's avarice from Hotman's *Brutum fulmen* and so at an additional
remove from Toke, seems neither to have known, nor to have thought it
essential to know, what the *Sylva locorum communium* even was, or who was
responsible for it. Hotman, when citing Toke's work, recorded simply
that he had drawn "ex libello, cui titulus est, Sylva locorum communium,
sub exitum Concilii Basiliensis edito" (from the notebook whose title is
Sylva locorum communium, which was published upon the conclusion of
the Council of Basel), absenting Toke's name altogether.[92] Accordingly,
Downame contented himself with citing the work merely as the nebulous "*Sylva locorum commun.,*" without attributing it to any author at all.[93]
Given the indistinct title, he might as well have cited "Book."

The story of Milton's *Index theologicus,* and of his engagement with
Bellarmine and Roman Catholic theology, may in fact be the story
of Milton's engagement with some of the most notable founts of anti-
Bellarmine and anti-Catholic polemic of his day: Musculus, Zanchius,
Foxe, Hotman, Whitaker, Rainolds, Andrewes, Willet, Downame, Stock,
Hall, and Ames among them. All of those aforementioned authors had
a special significance for Milton, and he cited nearly every one of them
at one point or another by name in his extant writings.[94] So many of
Milton's countrymen who had ultimately earned a place in the pantheon
of great English theologians over the course of the generations immediately preceding Milton's had engaged in the confutation of Bellarmine
in some form or fashion. Milton long aspired to merit inclusion in that
same pantheon, if increasingly not on anti-Bellarmine grounds. While
admittedly belonging to a standard genre of commonplace book, perhaps
Milton's *Index theologicus* should nonetheless be seen as a testimony to that
aspiration: not to compose a work of anti-Bellarmine polemic himself,
but to join the ranks of the men who had. Milton, in other words, may
have filled his anti-Bellarmine commonplace book with material culled
from the very sources that had inspired it after all. Yet if the relationship of Milton's reading and writing to Bellarmine and to Catholicism
appears to have been far more mediated, or layered, than we have

Headings from Milton's *Index theologicus* Referenced in His Commonplace Book

Note: The page numbers are those of the CPB manuscript (BL, Add. MS 36354). The cross-references are numbered according to the order in which they now appear within the CPB and do *not* necessarily correspond to the order in which they were added to the manuscript. Abbreviations have not been expanded, nor superscripts lowered.

"De bonis Ecclesiasticis" (Of Ecclesiastical Goods)

(1) reference: "vide de bonis Ecclesiasticis"
location: p. 12, beside the heading "Avaritia" (Avarice), at the top of the page.

(2) reference: "vide de bonis Eccles."
location: p. 12, the page headed "Avaritia"; in the text of an entry, with the entry in full reading, "Martino quarto. vide de bonis Eccles." The entry is the last on the page.

(3) reference: "vide titul. de bonis Ecclesiasticis"
location: p. 109, the page headed "Matrimonium"; in the margin, beside the last entry at the bottom of a very full page. The entry to which it is appended is a reference, by book and chapter, to John Selden's *Uxor Ebraica* (London, 1646), stating (in Latin) "That the ministers of the Church had no right, among the earliest Christians, to share in the celebration of either contracts or nuptials," but that "the popes and pontiffs quite improperly involved themselves with those matters, seeking from that source profit and mastery" (translation YP 1:403, with minor alterations).

(4) reference: "vide de bonis Ecclesiasticis"

location: p. 112, the page headed "De Divortio"; in the margin, beside an entry that appears in the middle of a very full page. The entry is a reference, by page number, to Paolo Sarpi's *Historia del Concilio Tridentino* (London, 1619), stating (in Latin) that "Cases related to marriage initially belonged to the civil magistrate before the ecclesiastics...seized the courts that tried such cases" (translation YP 1:407).

(5) reference: "vide de bonis Ecclesiasticis"

location: p. 151, beside the heading "Eleemosynae" (Alms), at the top of the page.

"De Idololatria" (Of Idolatry)

(6) reference: "vide de Idolatriâ [*sic*]"

location: p. 183, beside the heading "Subditus" (Subject), at the top of the page.

(11) reference "vide Idololatria. et Ecclesia." (see also number 12, below)

location: p. 246, beside the heading "De Seditione" (Of sedition), at the top of the page.

"De Conciliis" (Of Councils)

(7) reference: "see de Conciliis"

location: p. 183, the page headed "Subditus"; in the text of an entry, with the entry in full reading, "If ye pope be not greater then a councel, then is no K. to be thought greater then ye Parlament [/] see de Conciliis." The entry is the second to last on the page.

"De Religione non cogenda" (Of Religion not being something to be Coerced)

(8) reference: "Vide Indicem Theologicum de Religione non cogenda"

location: p. 197, the page headed "De Religione quatenus ad Rempub: spectat" (Of Religion, to what extent it pertains to the State); in the margin, beside the second to last entry on the page. The entry is a reference to Machiavelli's *Discorsi*, by book and chapter, stating (in Latin),

"The opinions of men concerning religion should be free in a republic, or indeed under good princes" (translation YP 1:476). Both the entry and the cross-reference are in the hand of an amanuensis, identified as that of Edward Phillips.

"Papa" (The Pope)

(9) reference: "vide Papa 42. in indice altero"

location: p. 221, beside the heading "Rapina seu extorsio pub." (Official Robbery or Extortion), at the top of the page.

"Ecclesia" (The Church)

(10) reference: "vide Ecclesia."

location: p. 244, the page headed "De bello Civili" (Of Civil War); in the margin, beside the second to last entry on the page. The entry is a reference, by page number, to Sarpi's *Historia*, recording (in Latin) that "Tyrants pretend that they do not make war on anyone because of religion, but on certain ones who under that pretext are rebels against their rulers," specifically with regard to the Emperor Charles V (translation YP 1:501).

(12) reference: "vide Idololatria. et Ecclesia." (see number 11, above)

location: p. 246, beside the heading "De Seditione," at the top of the page.

Milton's Aristotelian Experiments: Tragedy, *Lustratio,* and "Secret refreshings" in *Samson Agonistes* (1671)

Russ Leo

Machina cum Deo, nihil usitatius.
[Nothing is as common as a device involving a god.]
—Daniel Heinsius, *De Constitutione Tragoediae*

In the 1671 epistle preceding *Samson Agonistes,* "Of that sort of Dramatic Poem which is call'd Tragedy," John Milton announces the degree to which his work is "much different from what among us passes for best."[1] Heretofore many scholars have taken this to confirm Milton's strict Aristotelian formalism, as if *Samson Agonistes* is different because his contemporaries were ignorant or negligent of Aristotle's formal rules and thereby failed to produce or recognize great tragedy—as if *Samson Agonistes* rather than, say, John Dryden's *Tyrannick Love; or, The Royal Martyr* (1669/70) ranks among those truly exemplary works with roots in the most ancient of aesthetic theories and models. Milton invokes Aristotle directly on the title page of the work: he reproduces the Greek

221

text from *Poetics* 6 and duly renders the locus, the definition of tragedy itself, in Latin: "Tragoedia est imitatio actionis seriae, &c. Per misericordiam & metum perficiens talium affectuum lustrationem" (Tragedy is the imitation of an action that is serious, etc., perfecting, through pity and fear, the purification, by sacrifice, of such affects). Milton only translates the beginning of the sentence and the final clause, substituting "*&c*" for many of the characteristics Aristotle lists as essential to tragedy. Nevertheless, both this invocation and the material given in the epistle direct the reader's attention to the *Poetics,* a text that bore considerable influence on humanist philosophy and poetics following the diffusion of several monumental editions printed in Greek and Latin, beginning with publication of the Aldine Aristotle in 1495–98.[2] But it is nonetheless wrong to assume that *Samson Agonistes* is a slavishly Aristotelian work. On the contrary, both the epistle and the body of the work suggest otherwise. *Samson Agonistes* is no mere application of Aristotelian formal principles; Milton, rather, actively and imaginatively engages with Aristotle and Aristotle's early modern editors and commentators. Taking Milton's experimentation with Aristotelian aesthetics as the subject of this essay, I attend to his engagement with the *Poetics* and with two prominent seventeenth century commentators, Daniel Heinsius (Daniel Heins) (1580–1655) and Gerardus Joannes Vossius (Gerrit Janszoon Vos/Voskens) (1577–1649), tracing Milton's deviation from the Aristotelian determination of tragedy as well as the purchase of his occasional adherence to ancient rules and methods. Milton's treatment of *lustratio* as well as the operation of "Secret refreshings" in *Samson Agonistes* complicates even the most prominent and celebrated early modern retrievals of Aristotelian poetics. By placing the text of Judges in direct conversation with Aristotle's *Poetics,* Milton challenges the typographical and christological conventions of the Samson story as well as the efficacy and limits of Aristotelian formalism. It is thus through experimentation *with,* not adherence *to* the *Poetics* that Milton demonstrates and indeed dramatizes the intimate and often illegible work of the Spirit.

This essay first examines how seventeenth century theorists of tragedy translated and glossed Aristotle's *Poetics* to explore and map the affective and political dimensions of tragedy; moreover, I will show how Milton extends these investigations of tragedy to address providence, faith, and assurance. Next, I will explain the importance of *constitutio*—also translated as arrangement, plot, or disposition—as well as its pertinence to the philosophical integrity of Aristotelian tragedy. Milton seems to have followed Heinsius and Vossius closely, and his is a careful engagement with preceding seventeenth century versions of tragedy, even if ultimately a departure. Lastly, I will illustrate how Milton exploits the resources Heinsius and Vossius make available for understanding tragedy. The important question is not whether *Samson Agonistes* is or is not truly an example of Aristotelian tragedy but, rather, how Milton draws on certain formal and theoretical conventions regarding *constitutio,* necessity, and *machinae* in an attempt to pose exacting, suggestive, and unorthodox questions regarding the work of the Spirit in history. Milton suspends our judgment on the formal character of *Samson Agonistes* in order to investigate our most hallowed assumptions about God in everyday life and the terms of miraculous causality. Milton's most radical revision of early modern theory concerning Aristotelian tragedy is, in fact, his replacement of the Latin *lustratio* for the Greek κάθαρσις, or *catharsis*—a translation that is singular among editions and redactions of Aristotle's *Poetics,* before and after 1671.

The Affective Register of Tragedy in Early Modern Editions of the *Poetics*

Samson Agonistes effectively begins with Aristotle's definition of tragedy from the *Poetics,* a reference given (in an abbreviated version) in both Greek and Latin on the second title page of the 1671 poems. Milton, a talented and experienced reader of Greek, certainly translated the phrase from the original language into Latin himself. In order to understand the scope of Milton's project it is thus crucial to consider how his Latinization of the Greek text differs from other formidable early modern versions. The Greek text of *De poetica* was available in multiple editions printed during the sixteenth and seventeenth centuries.[3] Relatively few editions of any of Aristotle's works were published in London during the sixteenth or early seventeenth centuries. In his comprehensive bibliography, F. Edward Cranz does not list a single edition of Aristotle's *Poetics* in England in the sixteenth century, nor does Omert J. Schrier list any edition of the *Poetics* printed in England before 1623, before Theodore Goulston's Latin *Aristotelis De Poetica liber, latine conversus et analytica methodo illustratus,* printed in London.[4] While Milton may have certainly used another continental version of the *Poetics*—perhaps Casaubon's 1590 Genevan edition, or any number of Italian editions available to him on his tour during the late 1630s[5]—Goulston's important translation was likely a resource for his 1671 commentary and poem. Milton, like Goulston, would no doubt have consulted the most celebrated and innovative Greek edition of the *Poetics* published during the first half of the seventeenth century, at least in the Anglo-Dutch world—that being the work of Daniel Heinsius, Leiden scholar with strong and enduring connections to England.[6]

In his edition of Aristotle's *Poetics,* which features an emended and reorganized Greek text as well as facing-page Latin translation, Heinsius renders the definition of tragedy from Greek into Latin as such:

> Tragoedia ergo est, absolutae, & quae justam magnitudinem habeat, actionis imitatio; sermone constans ad voluptatem facto: ita ut singula genera in singulis parribus habeant locum: utque non errando, sed per misericordiam & metum, similium perturbationum expiationem inducat. Per sermonem autem factum ad voluptatem, eum intelligo, qui rythmo constat, harmonia, & metro.

> [Tragedy is the imitation of an action that is complete and that has proper dignity; with fit language to move desire; in such a way that distinct types of speech, in equal parts, each have a place; is not without direction or an end, but through pity and fear directs the expiation of similar perturbations. Moreover, I understand by "language to move desire" that form of language that works through rhythm, harmony, and meter.][7]

Heinsius supplemented his Latin translation with a detailed study of tragedy, *De tragoediae constitvtione liber* (published in 1611 and again in 1643), a work that bore considerable influence across northern Europe in the seventeenth century.[8] It was not only a crucial reference for continental poets, including Hugo Grotius (Hugo de Groot), Martin Opitz, and Jean Racine, but also for numerous English luminaries, from Ben Jonson to Dryden.[9] John Milton and his circle looked favorably upon Heinsius, a scholar of great renown who delved into poetry in addition to the study of classical languages. Milton's nephew and former student Edward Phillips names Heinsius "the most fam'd of Hollanders, and the most Celebrated by Learned Men for his egregious Wit, and deep proficiency in all kind of Literature."[10] Milton himself no doubt knew Daniel Heinsius's poetic and theological work just as he was familiar with the writing of his son Nicholaas Heinsius. All three men shared a formidable adversary in the Leiden scholar Claude Saumaise, or Salmasius.[11]

Stylistically, the preface to *Samson Agonistes*, "Of that sort of Dramatic Poem which is call'd Tragedy," bears close resemblance to Daniel Heinsius's commentary on the *Poetics*. His description of the utility of tragedy is particularly important:"Since this Muse is primarily engaged in arousing the passions [*affectibus*], Aristotle therefore thinks its end is to temper these very passions, and to put them back in order. The passions [*affectus*] proper to it are two: pity and horror. As it arouses them in the soul, so, as they gradually rise, it reduces them to the right measure and forces them into order. Accordingly, Aristotle called this the 'expiation' of the passions, or emotions [*affectuum . . . siue perturbationum*]" (*PT* 11; *CT* 10).[12] Milton, like Heinsius, attends to *misericordia, metus,* and *horror,* to the "power" of "raising pity and fear, or terror, to purge the mind of those and such like passions, that is to temper and reduce them to just measure with a kind of delight, stirr'd up by reading or seeing those passions well imitated" (*SA* 66). Fear (*metus*) and terror (*horror*) are, for both writers, equivalent. Milton's citation of Gregory Nazianzen's *Christ Suffering* strongly suggests a debt to Heinsius, who also cites Nazianzen in *De tragoediae constitutione liber;* Heinsius investigated christological tragedy in chapter 2 of his commentary, in terms of magnanimity and expiation, as well as in his own biblical poetry—particularly the *Lof-sanck van Jesus Christus* (1616), a Dutch work that, like *Paradise Lost,* echoes Guillaume de Salluste Du Bartas in scope and style (*PT* 130; *CT* 324).[13] Heinsius's studies in tragedy look forward to Milton's own.

But Heinsius is certainly not the only venerable classicist and antiquarian to comment extensively on Aristotle's *Poetics*. Gerardus Joannes Vossius published his own monumental *Poeticarum institutionum libri tres* in 1647, an ambitious work that outmatched Heinsius's in scope insofar as Vossius sought to show, among other things, "Hoc . . . commune habent poetæ, philosophi, & historici, quod doceant virtutem"— that is, "poets, philosophers, and historians have this in common, that they teach virtue."[14] Vossius wrote extensively on rhetoric as well as poetry and many varieties of history, including a history of philosophy published posthumously as *De philosophia et philosophorum sectis* (1657).[15] Vossius, like his contemporary Heinsius, drew heavily from the *Poetices libri septem* (1561), an exhaustive treatment of poetry by Julius Caesar Scaliger (Giulio Cesare della Scala) (1484–1558), itself a collation of classical and modern authorities (including Aristotle) wherein Scaliger affirmed "the true poet's call is to teach 'dispositions (*affectus*) with the help of actions.'"[16] Moreover, Vossius affirmed, after both Scaliger and Heinsius, the key difference between history and poetry—namely, that "Poetry attempts to express the universal, history the particular."[17]

The *Poeticarum institutionum* is not a work specifically on tragedy but rather on poetry in general. Vossius extends Heinsius's study to account for the nature and constitution of poetry rather than simply tragedy (a species of poetry). His is an expansive treatment of poetry, an investigation that seeks to discover if and how we "might comprehend the seed of every discipline" (videas omnium semina disciplinarum) in poetry.[18] It is in book 2 of the *Poeticarum institutionum* that Vossius attends to tragedy and to Aristotelian tragedy in particular. While tragedy is a species of poetry, here a topic treated under the larger aegis of the project, Vossius retains Heinsius's method and terminology, folding it into his much more encompassing approach. Vossius even retains the title of Heinsius's work as the heading to book 2, chapter 13: "De Tragoediae Constitutione." And here Vossius, citing Aristotle as well as more contemporary authorities, from Scaliger to the Italian Antonio Sebastiano Minturno, claims that "*Tragoedia est* poëma dramaticum, illustrem fortunam, sed infelicem, gravi & severâ oratione imitans...ad affectus ciendos, animumque ab iis purgandum" (2.11.2) (Tragedy is that dramatic poetry, imitating the fortune—or, rather, the misfortune—of men in a grave and serious language...[to this end:] the moving of the affects, and purging the mind of them).[19] Moreover, in book 2, chapter 13 of the *Poeticarm institutionum*, Vossius offers a particularly detailed anatomy of tragedy, rivaling Heinsius in his comparative treatment of ancient sources. Vossius illustrates, in a climactic moment in this chapter, precisely how and where the two most prominent philosophical authorities, Plato and Aristotle, differ with respect to tragedy, wherein

> The listener is shocked by the dreadfulness of the deed itself...[as the poet] wishes to shock the mind in order to cleanse it of its emotions

[*affectibus expurget*]. For just as a veteran soldier or a physician manage to be not more moved than is due by frequently seeing unhappy people, thus in tragedy, too, the mind, by watching such events, learns to put its emotions in order. Hence it is evident why Aristotle [in the *Poetics*, chapter 6], as has been said [in chapter 11, section 2, on application], establishes that the aim of tragedy is the purging of emotions. In this respect he differs from Plato. The latter thought that tragedies fan emotions. Aristotle, however, thinks tragedies remedy them. (*PILT* 510–11)

Vossius emphasizes the remedial and pathological function of tragedy, indicting Plato, however subtly, for his misunderstanding of tragedy (and, by extension, poetry); tragedy is useful to the body as well as to the commonwealth insofar as it enables an audience to reorder their affects accordingly. Vossius produces a set of "Institutes" after Quintilian detailing the qualities, types, and functions of poetry. It is in this sense distinct from Heinsius's commentary, a work meant to explicate the text, seldom straying from the letter of Aristotle's *Poetics*, in order to circumscribe the work of tragedy (rather than poetry at large). Nevertheless, though Vossius's project is markedly different from that of Heinsius, both scholars are at least in agreement concerning the purpose of tragedy as well as its scope.

This agreement sheds new light on the way Aristotle's seventeenth century annotators, in their treatments of tragedy, foreground the affective life of the auditor or participant. This is clear in Vossius's alternate Latinization of Aristotle's Greek definition of tragedy: "tragœdiæ finem statuat, esse affectuum [*purgationem*]"—that is, "Aristotle [in *Poetics* 6], as has been said, establishes that the aim of tragedy is the purging of emotions."[20] Recalling Heinsius's translation above, we notice only a few differences. First, Vossius uses the term *purgatio* instead of *expiatio*, to which I return below. Of more immediate significance is the substitution of *affectuum* for Heinsius's *perturbationum*, a difference that invites us to consider how these two terms may or may not work as synonyms. For tragedy to purge the auditor or participant of all its disturbances (*perturbationes*) is to accord art with a restorative, pathological function. To purge one of affects, however, affects that are not immediately identified as disturbances or perturbations, is something different.[21] Here tragedy affects the auditor or participant in more neutral terms, touching upon *affectus* rather than *perturbatio;* in this sense tragedy *transforms* or *changes* the basic affective composition of the listener and is not simply a means of purging the mind of those disturbances or disorders in an attempt to restore order. Tragedy certainly has the power to restore balance in the affective life of the audience, but it is not limited to this pathological function. It is thus not only useful for the reordering or calming of perturbations; the more neutral and basic term *affectus* extends its purchase beyond the restoration of order. In other words, tragedy affords these commentators an exacting philosophical language with which to examine the affective constitution of human life. Its work is much more general than the instrumental focus on fear and pity initially suggest.[22] This is evident where Vossius understands poetry (and thus tragedy) as integral to our understanding of the basic affective forces that comprise human life. Even the Greek formulation that Heinsius translates as "perturbationum expiationem" is rendered equivalent, proleptically, to Vossius's "affectuum [purgationem]."[23] Vossius nevertheless emphasizes in more detail the vital relationship between tragedy and affect (in the most general sense). Tragedy composes the affective lives of its auditors and participants.

Milton follows Heinsius and Vossius in their use of tragedy to investigate the affective fabric of human relations. Where Heinsius translates the *catharsis* element of Aristotle's Greek definition of tragedy as "perturbationum expiationem," Milton's translation is closer to Vossius's "affectuum [purgationem]" insofar as he renders Aristotle's Greek as "affectuum lustrationem."[24] Milton makes keen use of the affective register of tragedy, and *Samson Agonistes* probes the limits of our capacity to understand Samson's final act in terms of philosophical causality. Affects comprise the *constitutio* of the tragedy and, via *catharsis*, implicate the audience directly in the poetic project. For Milton this lends itself well to a study of divine inspiration—indeed, to as focused an investigation of faith and assurance as *Samson Agonistes*. Literary historians such as Nigel Smith and Jeffrey Shoulson have established the importance of affect to our understanding of religion in seventeenth century England.[25] When we read back through their treatments of religious radicalism, particularly enthusiasm and antinomianism, the extent to which seventeenth century believers imagined their most intimate spiritual engagements in affective terms is clear. Smith illustrates how "the expression of extremes of emotion as a supernatural encounter" became the "characteristic feature of mid-seventeenth-century radical religious prose"; moreover, with respect to antinomians, he shows how "contemporaries talked of enthusiasts as types of poet." Shoulson, in turn, reveals how early modern studies of enthusiasm focused on the humoral/pathological and performative origins of enthusiastic phenomena—phenomena that can easily be classified in terms of affect and affectation, respectively.[26]

Indeed, by the 1640s (as Vossius prepared his Latin studies of poetry and affect), a sizeable English vernacular literature already existed tying together such diverse phenomena as the impact of rhetoric and oratory; the "waies [we] are moved, by humors arising in our bodies"; various "internal senses" related to imagination, reason, and virtue; and the work of the Spirit in human life, from orthodox theologies of faith to the most heterodox forms of enthusiasm and antinomianism.[27] Even when enthusiasm is rendered as a passion, it is instructive to remember that passions are types of affects and that even John Calvin understood the faith of the Reformed in terms of a dynamic affective economy of activity and passivity, as a matter of affect and persuasion.[28] It is thus reasonable for Milton to bring issues of faith, divine inspiration, enthusiasm, and the work of the Spirit together with the Aristotelian discourse on tragedy: all of these seek to explain how human beings move and are moved in affective terms.

Constitutio in Tragedy: Arrangement and Causality

Affects, however, are only the stuff of tragedy; for Milton as well as for Heinsius and Vossius it is the way in which affects, together with actions, are arranged that constitutes the most important element of tragedy. Tragedy takes shape in affective terms, and affects are the grounds that unite poetry, rhetoric, and politics. But as a species of poetry, tragedy is cogent only insofar as it is defined by its constitution or structure.

Tragedy can only be partially understood in terms of affect—that is, with respect to fear and pity and its remedial, purgative function as well as its more broad and exacting attention to affective life. But this is merely the basis for a more complete definition. Both Heinsius and Vossius agree on the importance of *constitutio* in tragedy, on the proper structure of tragedy and the ways in which its very definition, for Aristotle, rests in the arrangement of action and its effects. Thus, the most important characteristic in a tragedy—really, what makes a tragedy a tragedy—is, foremost, the *rerum constitutionem*, the organization of things (for the Latin, see *CT* 138). This seems, at first, rather vague. But what is at stake here for Aristotle, Heinsius, and Vossius is the sense that tragedy is distinct from other forms or genres, such as history, based on the way tragedy foregrounds arrangements or structures instead of individual elements. Heinsius makes this clear in drawing the distinction between tragedy and history: "the task of the poet is much more serious than that of the historian because the one represents things that exist [the historian]; the other [the poet] represents not things that exist, but as they exist" (*PT* 20; *CT* 138). Tragedy, "unlike painting, is an imitation not of men but of actions and human life" (quod non ut pictura, hominum, sed actionum et humanae vitae imitatio est Traegoedia)—it does not render singular or individual men (nec personas modo singulas), "but men insofar as they act" (*PT* 20; *CT* 138).

Tragedy is not representative of individual elements or actions in the way a painting is; it is not merely mimetic, although this may in fact be a part of tragedy (and poetry in general). On the contrary, tragedy is defined by the way that it renders the general and universal conditions of actions, the terms in which an act or relationship takes shape. This structure or unity of actions is the most important facet of tragedy—hence, the emphasis on types or roles within a larger framework rather than individual actors. In retrieving this precise Aristotelian definition of tragedy, Heinsius and Vossius work to endow poetry with a more broad philosophical and ethical approach to human action than that afforded by contemporary poets and historians. Tragedy, as poetry but irreducible to verse, meter, or dramaturgical apparatus, attends to structural phenomena in a way that enables the reader, auditor, or participant to discern larger—even universal—patterns and truths.[29]

It is in this sense that a complete (absoluta, ut oportet) constitution or plot is the chief characteristic of tragedy (constitutio, haec quoque eius praecipua sit differentia) (*CT* 142). It is the *constitutio*, the overarching structure or unity, which takes precedence in the work. A proper tragedy does not immerse the viewer or participant in a world of disconnected or

random events. On the contrary, the attention is placed on the arrangement or arc of the action that in turn draws the auditor or participant
to a greater appreciation for the unity of events. Mere dramaturgy is not
enough; attention to character development, eloquent speech, or individual motivations may make a tragedy better, but they do not constitute
tragedy in any essential way. On this Heinsius is clear:

> Anyone who employs the kind of discourse in tragedy that both copies
> manners aright and decks itself in the finest words and thoughts...exqui-
> sitely fashioned according to the rule of art, will least attain to what is
> proper to the tragic poet. If, on the contrary, he takes no great account of
> either manners, diction, or thought, if he arranges the action carefully and
> with requisite artistry, if he structures the incidents, if he knits together
> and finishes the fable as he ought, he will accomplish the task of the tragic
> poet. (*PT* 21; *CT* 140)

Tragedy attends to the arrangements and unity of action; exemplary
tragedy does this while, at the same time, observing the rule of art (*prae-
scripto artis*) that prescribes eloquence, diction, and form. But the key
element is, unreservedly, the *constitutio* of tragedy, the attention to totality
that facilitates the study of species or types (*genera/species*) as opposed to
particulars [(*singulis/individuis*), the feature that makes the office of tragedian *magis philosophicum et operosum*—that is, "more philosophical and
exact"—than other poetic or intellectual offices.[30] It is hardly the meter
that makes a tragedy, but rather the "rationale underlying it and its
organization" (*PT* 29; *CT* 154). Vossius pushes this claim ever further
than Aristotle insofar as he is interested in the nature and constitution of
poetry rather than simply tragedy, which remains a species of poetry.

When we consider the philosophical purchase of tragedy in Heinsius's
account, or the elevation of tragedy (and poetry in general) in Vossius's
study, we see that the "nobility" of tragedy is not arbitrary but is, rather,
a principle derived from reason, with a philosophical history. Heinsius
works to clarify this point, the philosophical purchase of tragedy, in his
commentary on *De poetica*:

> To the degree that genus and species are nobler than particulars (one can
> have no knowledge of the latter, since they are infinite; precise knowledge
> of the former is impossible).... [Moreover,] when ancient philosophers
> saw that particulars are infinite and perpetually suffer either corruption

or generation, and when they felt that knowledge could properly handle lasting things that only and ever stay the same, they turned their attention from particulars to universals. And therefore a philosopher considers man generically, not individual men (e.g. some one individual from the multitude, an Alcibiades or a Socrates); not dogs, but *dog;* not horses, but *horse:* that is, the very species of man, of dog, of horse. The same must be said of the poet. (*PT* 31; *CT* 158, 160)

A proper tragedy, for Aristotle, thus emphasizes generic phenomena—in a more familiar dramaturgical vocabulary one might refer to these as "types" or "characters"—as well as the unity of action, where "An action does not become one from all kinds of disconnected actions, since an action becomes one only from actions so inter-related that if one of them is posited, another follows out of either necessity or verisimilitude" (*PT* 26; *CT* 150). We are drawn to consider the necessity as well as the universality of events in a philosophical way. Even if the tragedy is obviously contrived, a work of verisimilitude (as a dramatic performance, poem, or prose account certainly is), Heinsius reminds us that it "is said in the First Book of the *Rhetoric*, though in a slightly different connection, recognizing the true involves the same faculty as recognizing the verisimilar, just as dealing with the true seems to involve the same faculty as dealing with the verisimilar" (*PT* 32; *CT* 162). Thus, the distinction between, say, tragedy and history is not based on any modern notion of truth or verisimilitude. Tragedy foregrounds constitution; the "truth" of the events depicted is subordinate to the unity of action and thus to the apprehension of universal qualities. It matters less that a tragedy or history depicts "true" events but rather that the former depicts events in a way that draws our attention to generic or universal phenomena proper while the latter, history, attends particular phenomena. The philosophical stakes are high for the tragedian.[31]

Both Heinsius and Vossius do, of course, attend to the more familiar qualities of tragedy that Aristotle foregrounds in the *Poetics*, such as recognition (*anagnorisis*) and the sudden change of events (*peripeteia*) characteristic of Greek tragedy.[32] *Catharsis* in particular seems to take precedence in both commentaries, given the emphasis on purgation and expiation in the very definition of tragedy. It is in terms of *catharsis* that Aristotle and his early modern commentators sharpen the province of poetry within a larger arrangement of disciplines. Thus, "since both *peripeteia* and *anagnorisis* are intended to arouse the passions [*affectibus*], whatever forms of recognition are not agreeable to them are also necessarily alien to tragedy; as when a person recognizes something that is inanimate" (*PT* 39; *CT* 174). Recognition occurs between and among human beings. Borrowing a scholastic determination of recognition, Heinsius nevertheless notes that "any kind of recognition [*agnitionem*] is explained with respect to something else, like those things which are called 'relations' in the schools [quae Relata in scholis dicuntur]" (*PT* 39–40; *CT* 174); here he illustrates the philosophical purchase of tragedy at the same time as he attempts to explore different kinds of relations in terms of recognition in tragedy, where recognition may or may not be mutual between characters.

Where Aristotle understands the task of the poet as representing not things that exist, but as they exist, Heinsius follows him in investing *anagnorisis* with due philosophical significance. Moreover, Vossius follows Heinsius directly as he attends to the theological significance of *peripeteia* and *agnitione* with respect to plot, using the story of Joseph's betrayal and the eventual revelation of his identity to his brothers (Gen. 37–45) to illustrate how even "although peripetia can exist without recognition [*agnitione*], and there is sometimes recognition [*agnitio*] without peripetia, we are not dealing here with mere recognition [*agnitio simplex*], but one that contains a peripetia [which makes use of a conversion, or a sudden change in the opposite direction]. For the latter above all provokes emotions [*affectus...movet*]" (*PILT* 230–31). Tragedy does not merely enable us to talk about recognition. Rather, in both its constitution and the way in which it foregrounds pity and fear, tragedy enables us to recognize much more basic universal, structural, affective, and even spiritual elements of human life and to understand how these, in turn, inform our very capacity for recognition—indeed, our very capacity to experience revelation. This is Aristotle's innovation and the observation that sets Heinsius and Vossius to work.[33]

The purchase of Aristotle's discovery of recognition is seen in his distinction between tragedy and spectacle. Heinsius illustrates this where he repeats Aristotle's critique of Aeschylus, who relies too much on spectacle "to arouse prodigiously frightful stupor"—violating the dictum that the tragedy "must be so structured that without any artistry or assistance on the part of the actors, anyone should be sorely moved with pity and horror just upon reading it" (*PT* 46; *CT* 188.). Tragedy expresses a unity of actions and, in doing so, foregrounds a fabric of affective forces in relation to universal or generic concepts. Spectacle upsets this artful arrangement insofar as it merely moves the spectators without any attention or apprehension to the larger *constitutio* or the real affective relations that only tragedy makes clear. Where tragedy is a matter of poetry or art (literally, *arte*), the dramaturgical apparatus (*apparatu*) proper to spectacle is only able to "move portentious and prodigious wonder" (*PT* 46; *CT* 190).

Heinsius even addresses this distinction as a matter of the primary affects (*affectus*) of tragedy becoming obscured and thus taking shape as secondary affectations (*affectata*) (*PT* 45; *CT* 188)—this some 70 years before the posthumous publication of Baruch Spinoza's *Ethica*, a work famous for introducing, among many other things, a distinction between affects and affectations.[34] This is no mere artistic quibble. Rather, spectacle obscures the reality of the generic or universal concepts that structure the affective relations among humans, precisely the reality that tragedy foregrounds. It is in this sense that spectacle also obscures the basic claim concerning the function of tragedy, that it relies on natural affective relations between human beings in order to end in purgation: "man pities man as man. This the Philosopher [Aristotle] called the law of humanity" (hominem enim hommis miseret ut hominis. Hanc humanitatis legem Philosophus vocavit) (*PT* 53; *CT* 202). This does not pertain to the skill of the actors, to dramaturgy, or to the particular events, but rather to the very efficacy of tragedy to depict a unity of events in terms of the primary affective relations universal to mankind.

Aristotle's treatment of tragedy is celebrated as a depiction of a totality of relations that, in turn, enables human beings to understand the universal or generic qualities of reality. This understanding follows from the tragic emphasis on *constitutione* rather than particular details or qualities. Tragic characters are subordinate to the arrangement of actions and thus are more expressions of manners and affects than "individuals." Moreover, in its emphasis on the affective composition of the unity of events, tragedy moves its participants or spectators to reorder their own affective lives through purgation or expiation—the famed *catharsis* of tragic experience. It is not enough for participants or spectators to "identify" with particular characters depicted in the tragedy; it is, rather, the totality of events and the expression of common affective relations and generic experiences (such as *peripeteia* or *anagnorisis*) that enables one to achieve a healthy purgation. Tragedy, according to Heinsius and Vossius, is duly philosophical, exacting, and remedial in its arrangement of real affects and experiences. This is not to say that the stories trage- dians tell are true or false—this hardly matters, as the faculties proper to *catharsis* deal with true and verisimilar events in the same ways—but rather that the feelings depicted in the totality of events are real. In this way, tragedy foregrounds the reality of affective relations and subordi- nates questions of truth or falsity with respect to the plot or *fabula*. What matters is not whether the events depicted are true or not, but rather, what the totality or unity of relations enable participants and auditors to understand in exacting, almost philosophical terms. Tragedy makes visible a totality of relations, a plot, which in turn endows the audi- ence with an understanding of the conditions of things as they exist. It does not merely depict Oedipus but shows us how and why Oedipus is Oedipus and, duly, how and why the very species "man" exists and persists.

The *Constitutio* of *Samson Agonistes*

Milton, however, did not proceed to write a tragedy according to a set of Aristotelian rules. On the contrary, *Samson Agonistes* tests the tensile strength of Aristotelian tragedy insofar as Milton consistently challenges the ancient form's capacity to reduce divine inspiration to the *rerum constitutionem*. What is at stake is the extent to which one can ration- ally understand or depict the causality of divine inspiration. Hardly an endorsement of enthusiasm, Milton poses the causal and affective relations that comprise enthusiasm as a set of problems. An Aristotelian approach to tragedy makes these problems more apparent, particularly where Heinsius and Vossius draw our attention to the *loci* governing the introduction of *machinae* into the *constitutio* and the ways that such *machinae* complicate our understanding of causality as they contribute to the *solvendi* of the plot. For Heinsius, nothing in tragedy is as common or ordinary as a device involving a god (*machina cum Deo, nihil usitatius*)—

an observation that applies more to the staged entries of gods in the ancient dramas than to the "Secret refreshings" (665) and "divine disposal" (210) by inward persuasion of *Samson Agonistes*. Milton recognizes and exploits the extent to which this idea of inspiration complicates Aristotelian approaches to tragedy. One can see this as early as the Argument, where Samson is "at length perswaded inwardly that this was from God" and thus accompanies the "Publick Officer" to the feast of Dagon. In turn, after what Milton refers to in the Argument as "the Catastrophe," the Messenger reports what "Samson had done to the Philistins, and by accident to himself"; here *accident* is a philosophical term addressing causality, drawing our attention to the arch of the plot, the extent to which the *fabula* and *personae* from Judges are incorporated into the tragedy in such a way as to shed light on the generic conditions of divine inspiration with new philosophical precision.

Consider first how gods intervene in tragedy, according to Heinsius and Vossius. According to Heinsius, nothing is as common or ordinary as a device involving a god (machina cum Deo, nihil usitatius)—but this does not make such a move more excusable (*CT* 222). Tragedy, for Vossius as well as for Heinsius, is more philosophical than history precisely because attention to the unity or totality of affects, events, and actions enables the participant to understand how these things are connected and related, not merely individually but generically and universally. Tragedy, in its unity, affords the participant an adequate understanding of causality, where anything that takes shape in the tragedy can be explained by other elements in the same tragedy. A tragedy is an object lesson in immanent causality. The *machina cum Deo* violates this principle insofar as it introduces an element that is otherwise foreign to the unity or totality of action in the tragedy, and thus introduces a miraculous end (*finem miraculosum*) that does not follow necessarily from the totality of events and affects which would otherwise comprise the *constitutio* of the work.

Both writers give several examples. First, gods intervene in parts of tragedies that are nevertheless external to the drama of the work—in the prologue, for instance, where a *machina* "is both customary and held in great esteem," as is the case "with Minerva in Sophocles' *Ajax*, Juno in [Seneca's] *Hercules furens*, Mercury in Euripides' *Ion*, Venus in [Euripides's] *Hippolytus*"—all of whom "are found outside the drama [*extra Drama*], and in the episode [*in Episodio*]."[35] Gods also appear within the *drama* to explain things that have happened but which nevertheless cannot be known by the *personae* in the tragedy, within the scope of the *constitutio*. Heinsius's example here comes from the *solutio* or denouement of Sophocles's *Ajax*, where Athena reveals details of Ajax's behavior to Odysseus, details that he otherwise could not possibly know. In this example, the *machina* involving the god actually *maintains* the consistency or unity of the *constitutio*, where this is the only way to inform Odysseus of what the audience knows without resorting to an even less probable *machina* than a god. Such a *machina* is for Heinsius, as for Aristotle, a last resort; "when the poet cannot avoid this, it is plain that contrivance [*machina*] may be employed in the denouement [*Solutione*]" (*PT* 67; *CT* 230). Moreover, according to Vossius, Aristotle answers the question, "If the ancient poets have introduced an irrational element, should the modern ones retain it?" with the quip, "He allows indeed that such a plot, which contains an irrational element, should not be constructed in the first place" (*PILT* 490–91).

Lastly, gods appear in order to explain or unveil future events; this is much more rare and it is here that Heinsius summarizes Aristotle's comments on the placement of such contrivances within the tragic plot: "contrivance [*machina*] has to be employed in the complication [*connex-ione*] unless the subject demands it and this cannot be avoided" (*PT* 67; *CT* 230). A god should thus only appear when entirely necessary, and then only under certain circumstances. The entrance of a god, where the best tragedies are concerned, is very rare. Seneca's *Hercules Oetaeus* and Plautus's *Amphitryon* are precisely the kinds of tragedies referred to in the epigram above—where nothing is as common as a device involving a god—because, according to Heinsius, a god or gods intervene in order to express something that is not necessary for humans to know, which disrupts the consistency of the *constitutio* as well as the imminent causality in a superfluous way (see *PT* 68–70; *CT* 230–34). Here a god, as *machina*, becomes merely ornamental, what Milton may have seen as a sort of idolatry. Hence, Heinsius glosses Aristotle, particularly the section of the *Poetics* (1454b 1–5) that stipulates, "The artifice must be reserved for matters outside the play—for past events beyond human knowledge, or events yet to come, which require to be foretold or announced; since it is the privilege of the gods to know everything."[36]

Milton understands the importance of the *constitutio* or *dispositio,* after Heinsius and Vossius, in affirming the philosophical utility of tragedy. Where he asserts in the preface to *Samson Agonistes* that "It suffices if the whole Drama be found not produc't beyond the fift Act, of the style and uniformitie, and that commonly call'd the Plot, whether intricate or explicit, which is nothing indeed but such oeconomy, or disposition of the fable as may stand best with verisimilitude and decorum," he draws directly from contemporary commentaries on Aristotle's *Poetics* (*SA* 68). His treatment of tragedy in the epistle, "Of that sort of Dramatic Poem which is call'd Tragedy," is certainly indebted to Horace's *Ars poetica,* particularly to lines 179–201.[37] But Milton gives more attention to the "Plot," to the "oeconomy, or disposition of the fable" than Horace. Indeed, while Horace asserts that "A play that expects to be in demand and produced again should have no less and no more than five acts," he does not give any justification for this rule, as Aristotle does in the *Poetics.*[38] Moreover, Horace comments explicitly on the tragic *machina,* affirming, "no God should intervene unless the crux of the situation requires him to resolve it," yet nevertheless declining to offer any philosophical or aesthetic justification for this rule.[39] This is certainly no fault of the *Ars poetica,* but rather evidence that Milton's preoccupations in the epistle preceding *Samson Agonistes* exceed Horace's description of tragedy. This is clear in the extent to which he uses the preface to reflect on the shape of the entire published work[40] in relation to ancient models. Milton defends his preface, where "though antient Tragedy use no Prologue, yet using sometimes, in case of self defence, or explanation, that which *Martial* calls an Epistle" (*SA* 67).

This Milton makes clear: that the epistle, "Of that sort of Dramatic Poem which is call'd Tragedy," is outside of the "disposition" of the work, even as it helps us to understand the tragedy. Milton marks this separation with the invention of a new verb, "to epistle," where several observations on tragedy "may be Epistl'd" while nevertheless remaining outside the scope of the tragedy proper, "after the antient manner"; the "*Chorus* is here introduc'd after the Greek manner, not antient only but modern, and still in use among the *Italians*"; and the "Measure of Verse us'd in the Chorus...[is] not essential to the Poem, and therefore not material."[41] These observations follow directly from Heinsius's and

Vossius's treatments of tragedy, where tragedy is irreducible to meter and defined in terms of its composition, particularly in relation to the work of the Chorus. Milton, in a manner similar to Heinsius's treatment of episodes, reflects on how the prefatory epistle may or may not be integrated in order to mark the limits of the tragedy, thus drawing our attention to "the modelling…of this Poem," to "style and uniformitie," to the "Plot…which is nothing indeed but such œconomy, or disposition of the fable" (*SA* 67–68).

This emphasis on *constitutio* or *dispositio* shifts our attention from Samson, Manoa, and the other *personae* of the work to the arrangement of actions and affects. *Personae*, certainly a part of ancient tragedy, are ultimately subordinate to the totality of actions and affects that comprise the *constitutio* or plot. Milton, after Heinsius and Vossius, recognizes how *constitutio* in tragedy might foreground the necessity as well as the universality of events in a philosophically precise way; this is the purchase of Aristotelian tragedy, and the philosophical knowledge of causality it enables. Milton exploits these investigations of tragedy to pose formal-theological questions: where, if at all, does a god—that is, God—intervene in *Samson Agonistes*, in order to help either the *personae* or the audience understand the *constitutio* of the tragedy? Or, is knowledge of God at all necessary to understand the work? Can one really *understand* the work of the Spirit, whether according to the most orthodox determinations of faith or according to the wildest heterodox defenses of enthusiasm? Milton poses these questions artfully and, as I illustrate in what follows, declines to answer them with certainty. The ambiguity that Milton introduces, rather, between the formal consistency of Aristotelian tragedy, the Samson story in the book of Judges, and the work of the Spirit in Christian life challenges the reader, auditor, or participant in *Samson Agonistes* to reconsider their most hallowed assumptions concerning faith and action. This takes shape in his radical redefinition of *catharsis*.

If *Samson Agonistes* is an Aristotelian tragedy (according to Heinsius and Vossius), it yields crucial philosophical insight into generic or universal phenomena as well as adequate causality. Much of the text of the poem, however, is dedicated to complicating precisely this. In an exemplary study of *Samson Agonistes*, Mary Ann Radzinowicz argues that the poem works, in part, "by offering a representative figure of one kind of human being who discovers in the course of his life the inadequacy of his own conception of God, who by experience of his tragic existence learns a more adequate conception, and who, armed with the better understanding, modifies his nature in such a way as to perfect a relationship and thereby also give evidence of God's nature."[42] In this sense, Radzinowicz describes how one might understand Samson as a generic type—that is, if *Samson Agonistes* were in fact a proper tragedy that emphasized arrangements or structures instead of individual elements, as if Milton were a model Aristotelian tragedian according to Heinsius or Vossius. But this is not exactly the case. *Samson Agonistes* is, rather, a case study in "faintings, swounings of despair, / And sense of Heav'ns desertion" (631–32). These sad affects and desperate actions obscure the larger causal relationships that would otherwise comprise the *constitutio*. Instead, there is seldom an authoritative explanation of how events and affects follow from one another, to say nothing of a theological justification of this causality. It is the lack of both this knowledge and divine assurance that structures the poem.

In Samson's opening address (which would technically be the prologue), for instance, prior to the choral recitations or any of the episodic interactions between the characters and the Chorus, he asks, "Why was my breeding order'd and prescrib'd / As of a person separate to God, / Design'd for great exploits" (30–32), which remains a provocative question even after his own exhortation, "let me not rashly call in doubt / Divine Prediction" (43–44), and to the choral injunction, "Tax not divine disposal" (210) (*SA* 71–72, 77). Soon after, the Chorus offers a like rejoinder to its own affirmation, "Just are the ways of God, / And justifiable to Men" (293–94):

> Yet more there be who doubt his ways not just,
> As to his own edicts, found contradicting,
> Then give the rains to wandring thought,
> Regardless of his glories diminution;
> Till by thir own perplexities involv'd
> They ravel more, still less resolv'd,
> But never find self-satisfying solution.
> As if they would confine th' interminable,
> And tie him to his own prescript,

> Who made our Laws to bind us, not himself,
> And hath full right to exempt
> Whom so it pleases him by choice
> From National obstriction, without taint
> Of sin, or legal debt;
> For with his own Laws he can best dispence.　　(300–14; *SA* 79–80)

Thus the lines, "Just are the ways of God, / And justifiable to Men," take shape more as a provocation than an assertion. We are left to seek evidence of God's justice, evidence that Aristotelian tragedy, with its philosophical precision and singular concern for the unity or totality of affects and actions, is poised to reveal. With this said, however, whenever the poem affirms God's providence, it nevertheless gives little evidence of it. Where tragedy is defined by the way that it makes the general and universal conditions of actions and affects explicit, *Samson Agonistes* relegates these conditions to mystery and confusion. When the Hebrew Messenger probes the terms of providence, his testimony is confused:

> But providence or instinct of nature seems,
> Or reason though disturb'd, and scarce consulted
> To have guided me aright, I know not how,
> To thee first reverend Manoa, and to these
> My Countreymen, whom here I knew remaining,
> As at some distance from the place of horrour,
> So in the sad event too much concern'd.　　(1545–51; *SA* 113–14)

And when Manoa responds to the Messenger, it is explicitly in a language suited to formal investigations of tragedy. His response betrays a familiarity with the likes of Heinsius and Vossius. The Messenger's address "No Preface needs" (1554) in the sense that he is to eschew episode and adornment in his relation of the catastrophe; the importance of lines 1545–51 is thus reduced by Manoa, rendered unnecessary to his (and our) understanding of the truth of the catastrophe. Even here, the Messenger's indecision concerning the relevance of providence is relegated to the "Preface," understood as prefatory material that is superfluous, unnecessary.

To a certain degree, this is consistent with the scriptural account of Samson's life in the book of Judges. Judges famously concludes, "In those dayes there was no King in Israel: every man did that which was right in his owne eyes" (Judg. 21:25), a rejoinder that complicates the assumption that the narratives collected throughout the book are heroic tales of judges inspired by the Spirit.[43] There are, of course, clear indicators that God is at work throughout the book of Judges—Samson's birth is after all foretold by an angel—but Milton seizes upon ambiguous moments throughout the work in order to foreground the overwhelming illegibility of the Holy Spirit in human actions. As Joseph Wittreich explains, Milton's project is largely a reorganization of the Judges narrative based on recollection and repetition; moreover, "Through his scrambling of the Judges sequence, Milton produces unexpected and emphatic juxtapositions, attendant shifts of emphasis, and jarring dramatic ironies."[44] Milton does this to emphasize precisely how difficult it is to understand the stories in Judges. While the Chorus refers to events in Judges—to "The matchless Gideon" (280) and "Jephtha, who by argument, / Not worse then by his shield and spear / Defended Israel from the Ammonite" (283–85)—so does Dalila, who compares herself to scriptural heroine "Jael, who with inhospitable guile / Smote Sisera sleeping through the Temples nail'd" (989–90), a paradoxical citation that has attracted scholarly attention (*SA* 79, 98).[45] Ultimately this reorganization of Judges foregrounds the confusing and often illegible relationship between God's inspiration and actual events as well as the legitimacy of claims to divine inspiration.

Moreover, Milton disrupts the correspondence between providence and the *rerum constitutionem* of the tragedy, the arrangement of actions and affects throughout *Samson Agonistes*. When we hear about certain events, we are deprived of any adequate understanding of their causality. We, along with the Philistines, Manoa, and the Chorus, are barred from Samson's secret revelations by the Spirit, or at least his claims to such revelations:

> they knew not
> That what I motion'd was of God; I knew
> From intimate impulse, and therefore urg'd
> The Marriage on; that by occasion hence
> I might begin Israel's Deliverance,
> The work to which I was divinely call'd.   (221–26; *SA* 77)

Manoa, in turn, directly echoes these lines when he attempts to understand Samson's humiliation, his present state: "but thou didst plead /

Divine impulsion prompting how thou might'st / Find some occasion to infest our Foes" (421–23; *SA* 83). To make interpretive matters even more difficult, Samson, Manoa, and the Chorus are more than willing to offer alternative (or discursive) explanations for the affects and actions comprising the drama. Samson momentarily abandons his claims to "intimate impulse" when he defends God's providence. His is a seemingly contradictory exhortation, where the lines "Appoint not heavenly disposition, Father, / Nothing of all these evils hath befall'n me / But justly; I my self have brought them on, / Sole Author I, sole cause" (373–76) offer two conflicting sources for his present condition: "heavenly disposition," which we imagine to be distinct from God's providence and election in strict theological terms, and "Sole Author I" (*SA* 81).

In another attempt to understand Samson's disposition, Manoa attributes his despair to "suggestions which proceed / From anguish of the mind and humours black, / That mingle with thy fancy" (599–601; *SA* 88). The most sustained treatment of affect and causality in the poem, however, comes from the Chorus, which asserts,

> Many are the sayings of the wise
> In antient and in modern books enroll'd;
> Extolling Patience as the truest fortitude;
> And to the bearing well of all calamities,
> All chances incident to mans frail life
> Consolatories writ
> With studied argument, and much perswasion sought
> Lenient of grief and anxious thought,
> But with th' afflicted in his pangs thir sound
> Little prevails, or rather seems a tune,
> Harsh, and of dissonant mood from his complaint,
> Unless he feel within
> Some sourse of consolation from above;
> Secret refreshings, that repair his strength,
> And fainting spirits uphold.   (652–66; *SA* 89–90)

Though the Chorus asserts that there is respite from anxiety in "consolation from above," the connections between events, affects, and actions that one might initially attribute to providence are obscured, just as the conditions of "Patience" and "consolation" remain unexplained. We are left instead with "Secret refreshings."

But "Secret refreshings" are withheld from the audience by definition. This "sourse of consolation from above" does not exactly help one
to understand Samson's situation, a situation that comprises the bulk of
the *constitutio* of the poem. We encounter this difficulty as early as the
Argument, where Milton outlines the plot of the poem only to reveal
that Samson is "at length perswaded inwardly that this was from God"
and is thus led "offstage," where the *catastrophe* occurs. For an audience
seeking assurance, or an authoritative statement regarding Samson's
righteousness, or a definite explanation of the most intimate workings
of the Holy Spirit in human history, even the grammar of the phrase
"perswaded inwardly that this was from God" is troubling. In no sense is
it clear that God is the source of this persuasion. Nor is God the agent of
the persuasion. Samson, rather, is merely "perswaded inwardly that this
was from God"—an operation that might as easily refer to his human
capacity to convince himself or to his membership in an interpretive
community that includes Manoa and the Chorus, all of whom conclude
through deliberation that both the decision to accompany the Philistine
messenger peaceably as well as the catastrophe itself were inspired by
God. The poem thus traces this "inward persuasion" across a series of
encounters between Samson and his human interlocutors. This is not a
demonstration of "Rational Theology" or "Progressive Revelation," as
Mary Ann Radzinowicz argues.[46] There is no authority for revelation
to begin with.

Moreover, "Secret refreshings" are not themselves affects or actions and
are thus alien to the *constitutio* or arrangement of the plot in tragedy. The
invocation of "Secret refreshings" challenges both Heinsius and Vossius in
their investigations of the Aristotelian model of tragedy; these phenomena
are crucial to the plot but are nevertheless inaccessible (and unrepresent-
able). They are crucial to the unity of actions and affects but remain hidden. In turn, "Secret refreshings" complicates the necessity of causality in
tragedy because the terms of such phenomena are concealed. It is thus
impossible to understand the *constitutio* in any precise philosophical way
when crucial aspects are hidden from us. "Secret refreshings" introduce
an element of mystery. But this is hardly an endorsement of enthusiasm
on Milton's part, nor does he surrender philosophical precision to assurance and the illegibility of the Spirit. On the contrary, Milton tests the

limits of Aristotelian tragedy by keeping God's inspiration a secret, by forcing us to consider what it would mean if the "refreshings" were not secret but were, in fact, given by means of a more common poetic tactic, the introduction of a device involving a god.

For Heinsius and Vossius, as for Aristotle, a *machina cum Deo* introduces an element that is otherwise foreign to the unity or totality of action in the tragedy. Such a device interrupts the immanent causality of the tragedy and should thus be reserved for use only when necessary, and preferably in the complication of the *constitutio* rather than the *soluendi* or denouement. Upon closer inspection, it is unclear whether Milton introduces God via "Secret refreshings" out of necessity or whether he eschews any *machina* whatsoever. When Samson assures the Chorus, just prior to the *solutio,* to "Be of good courage, I begin to feel / Some rouzing motions in me which dispose / To something extraordinary my thoughts" (1381–83), his is an ambiguous statement that does not necessarily follow from the earlier choral description of "consolation from above." Moreover, Milton leaves it to the reader, auditor, or participant in the poem to discern whether and how Samson's late claim to "rouzing motions" follows from the Chorus's protracted description of God's inspiration in lines 1268–96, culminating in the celebration of patience, "more oft the exercise / Of Saints, the trial of thir fortitude, / Making them each his own Deliverer" (1287–89; *SA* 106–07). It is in this sense left to the reader to determine whether Milton introduces a *machina cum Deo* at all.

It is here that Milton exploits contemporary treatments of tragedy. Rather than make it explicit to the audience, he asks his readership to decide whether or not it is necessary to supplement the immanent causal relationships among the affects and actions depicted in *Samson Agonistes* with God's inspiration. Although the reference to "Secret refreshings" initially suggests a concealed reference or hidden source of inspiration, Milton compounds this with a subtle meditation on Heinsius's tenet, "Nothing is as common as a device involving a god." If God's special revelation, miracles, interruptions, and interventions via devices are best kept rare, and only used in necessity, Milton maintains a truly tragic vision of God (and consistency in the *constitutio* of *Samson Agonistes*) by absenting God from the play entirely. "Secret refreshings" need not be traced back to God at all. In fact, the term *secret,* so salient to the scriptural Samson story, refers specifically to human actions and affects—particularly to Samson's error in divulging the secret source of his strength—in every other iteration throughout the poem.[47] When the Chorus describes Dalila's effect on Samson, for instance, "secret" is used to make a causal relationship more clear, not to obscure the affective relations between former lovers:

> Yet beauty, though injurious, hath strange power,
> After offence returning, to regain
> Love once possest, nor can be easily
> Repuls't, without much inward passion felt
> And secret sting of amorous remorse.   (1003–07; *SA* 99)

For a reader versed in tragedy, whether or not God is necessary to understand the chain of events or the unity of actions and affects emerges as a problem rather than a given.

Moreover, the stakes are different for Milton than for Aristotle. If the *constitutio* of tragedy is indeed the province of necessity, and all unnecessary, superfluous, or unrelated causes and effects should be relegated to the status of adornment, save for in the most exceptional cases, it becomes quite difficult to locate God in the work without posing serious theological problems. If God is introduced via "Secret refreshings" as a device in the complication of the plot as given by the Chorus, then it is entirely necessary to render God in exceptional terms in order to understand the universal or generic situation depicted in Samson's plight. In a sense, this is proof of Heinsius's claim that nothing is as common as a device involving a god because, in effect, Milton asks us to consider how God treats each one of his elect exceptionally, steeling them against the traumas of human experience.[48] It is thus only in this sense that Samson is a generic "type," in his despair and experience of desertion that can only be alleviated by God—a situation that certainly complicates any easy typological relationship between Samson and Jesus. If *Samson Agonistes* is to remain an exemplary tragedy, if one is to accord the "Secret refreshings" to God's providence and justification, then such concealed phenomena *have* to be entirely necessary to the plot; they are spectacular phenomena in the truest sense insofar as they confound the audience and necessarily obscure the causal relationships between actions and affects.

God's providence, assurance, and the work of the Spirit cannot be merely ornamental. For Milton, to depict God ornamentally risks idolatry. Thus, if the "Secret refreshings" are not exceptional interventions by God on behalf of humanity, then they must be entirely consistent with the other relations, causes, and effects across the drama of the poem. In other words, if *Samson Agonistes* is to remain an Aristotelian tragedy on the model described by Heinsius and Vossius, and if the "Secret refreshings" are *not* accorded a special status as *machinae* or devices involving God's special grace and revelation, then Milton must change the meaning of Heinsius's statement entirely: nothing is as common as a device involving a god—not because of the lackluster skills of the majority of tragedians, but because devices involving God are immanent to the drama of the play and are thus not "special" or "exceptional" at all. It is as if Milton gives us several distinct ways to read *Samson Agonistes* as an Aristotelian tragedy, one of which is to affirm God's special and exceptional interest in his elect (which complicates our understanding of causality as well as the consistency of the *constitutio*), another of which is to affirm just how "common" God is, in the sense that it comprises all of the immanent actions and affects across the drama—a monist vision of God. The possibility still remains, of course, that *Samson Agonistes* is not an Aristotelian tragedy at all, despite the epistle and the Argument, and that Milton uses the apparatus of Aristotelian tragedy to draw attention to his deviations from the model. In this sense, it is as if he borrows the philosophical precision from the commentary tradition, including Heinsius and Vossius, only to produce a truly Christian tragedy where the consistency of the *constitutio* is much less important than God's special revelation and the terms of Samson's inspiration. This remains an option to the end of the work.

What Was *Catharsis?*

While I am inclined to believe that Milton uses existing theories of tragedy, and writing on tragedy, to pose more complex and ambiguous theological and poetic problems, there is certainly evidence that *Samson Agonistes* transforms—and perhaps *reforms*—Aristotelian tragedy entirely. Indeed, Milton uses the conventions and terms of Aristotelian tragedy to approach monism and to pose, in subtle terms, that most difficult question: what kind of a thing is God? This takes shape, in *Samson Agonistes,* in the translation of the Greek *catharsis.* In Milton's Latin translation of Aristotle's Greek, there is a remarkable break with preceding treatments of tragedy: his substitution of *lustratio* for Heinsius's *expiatio*[49] and Vossius's *purgatio.*[50] Thus, in place of *catharsis,* Milton offers *lustratio.* Not only is his translation markedly different from the language used by the most prominent classicists of the seventeenth century, it also points to his theological project in *Samson Agonistes,* to the retrieval of *lustratio,* the term at the heart of his definition of tragedy, as a concept central to human salvation. Lewis and Short define *lustratio* as "a purification by sacrifice, a lustration"; the editors of the *Oxford Latin Dictionary,* as both a "Ritual Cleansing, lustration" and the ceremonial "action of going round or traversing," related to the verb *lustrō,* "to purify ceremonially (with cathartic or apotropaic rites)" as well as "to move round," "traverse," "to surround," "to spread light over or around," and "to look around for, or seek."[51] In the *Oxford Classical Dictionary,* Jerzy Linderski provides an authoritative contextual definition of *lustratio* as "the performance (*lustrare*) of *lustrum* (*lustrum facere*), a ceremony of purification and of averting evil" where the "main ritual ingredient was a circular procession (*circumambulatio, circumagere,* often repeated three times)"—a ritual including an offering where, in many cases, the "victims were sacrificed at the end of the ceremony, and their entrails, *exta,* inspected."[52] Moreover, the ceremony "excluded evil, and kept the pure within the circle, but it also denoted a new beginning, especially for the Roman people at the census or for an army when a new commander arrived or when two armies were joined together."[53] For instance, *lustratio* is famously depicted on Trajan's Column—a work that Milton may have seen in Rome and which certainly figured prominently in the language of praise during the mid-seventeenth century.[54] To my knowledge, no other translator of Aristotle renders the Greek *catharsis* as the Latin *lustratio*—a word that recalls the Latin *lustricus,* a day when ritual purification is performed on a child, suggesting close proximity to Christian baptism across any number of orthodox and heterodox sects and confessions. Indeed, in his *De doctrina Christiana,* under the heading "Of the External Sealing of the Covenant of Grace," Milton uses *lustratio* to describe Christ's baptism by John: it "seems to have been a kind of initiation or purification [*lustratio*], rather than an absolute sealing [*absoluta obsignatio*] of the covenant [*foederis*]: for only the Spirit seals [*Spiritus enim solus obsignat*]" (YP 6:551–52).

At the beginning of *Samson Agonistes* Milton, deploying *lustratio*, deliberately complicates the *non errando* (not a wandering about) of Heinsius's Latin translation of Aristotle. For Milton, the perfecting (*perficiens*) through purification (*lustrationem*) is accomplished precisely through a sort of ambulatory ritual in such a way that rejects the strong and uncompromising sense of Heinsius's *induco:* a bringing forward, exhibiting, or introducing that nevertheless retains the imperious sense of *duco* (to lead, march, drag, carry off, or produce).[55] *Lustratio* is not an aimless wandering or erring, but it is also not the same as to be led, marched, or moved by force. Rather, it points to ritual and to sacrifice—but not in any way that ensures the participation or seal of the Spirit. None of Milton's changes seems to derive from Vossius's treatment of Aristotle's Greek; on the contrary, Vossius's is an argument with Heinsius regarding the terms of Scaliger's treatise on poetry. Milton's *lustratio* marks his departure from all three, to say nothing of the Italian commentary tradition. *Lustratio* is a purification experience, a sacrifice; it is not exactly a sacrament because it need not involve the Spirit. *Lustratio*, as *catharsis*, marks the importance of affective experience.

In this sense, *lustratio* helps us to understand the final lines of the work, spoken by the Chorus, and the extent to which it is here that we find Milton's most radical experiment with Aristotelian tragedy:

> All is best, though we oft doubt,
> What th' unsearchable dispose
> Of highest wisdom brings about,
> And ever best found in the close.
> Oft he seems to hide his face,
> But unexpectedly returns
> And to his faithful Champion hath in place
> Bore witness gloriously; whence Gaza mourns
> And all that band them to resist
> His uncontroulable intent,
> His servants he with new acquist
> Of true experience from this great event
> With peace and consolation hath dismist,
> And calm of mind all passion spent.   (1745–58; *SA* 119)

Here Milton recalls the Aristotelian tenets on tragedy, as well as the commentaries on Aristotelian tragedy, in order to mark the necessity not of plot but rather of *lustratio*—that is, the necessity of "true experience." Consider first how the final line, "calm of mind all passion spent," seems to mark the outcome of the classical Aristotelian *catharsis*, the purging or expiation of perturbations through fear and pity. We often assume that *catharsis* is subjective in the sense that the agent moved through pity and fear is the auditor or participant, that one experiences catharsis or purging at the level of one's emotions. To a certain degree this is true of Milton's treatment, but Milton seems to draw from Heinsius and Vossius insofar as tragedy is not merely about fear and pity but rather about the affective composition of human life. But it is not merely a subjective *catharsis;* if *lustratio* is something a subject—say, Samson—experiences, it also locates that subject in a larger dynamic economy of affects.

Milton makes this point suggestively and grammatically insofar as it is not necessarily the "faithful Champion" or Samson himself that is the subject of "all passion spent," but rather "th' unsearchable dispose / Of highest wisdom" personified. The agent of "spent" in the last line is not necessarily Samson, nor the heroic reader of the poem who is like Samson in faith, nor some "type" of Christ, even in an Antitrinitarian sense. It is, rather, the same agent of "dismist" in line 1757, the possessive subject "His" in lines 1754 and 1755, carried over from 1749—the God that "seems to hide his face" and who duly returns to "his faithful Champion." The grammar of the poem defies our expectations regarding who or what, precisely, "all passion spent." The 1671 poems are replete with such slips, the most famous example happening in book 4 of *Paradise Regained*, upon the "highest pinnacle" (549), where the "his" of "his uneasy station" (584) seems to refer to Satan but, in fact, refers to the Son. This action occurs immediately before *Samson Agonistes* and, in turn, establishes a precedent for how to read such slips with respect to possessive pronouns.

Considering this in light of the work of Heinsius and Vossius, we might read God here as the composition of affects that comprise the unity or totality of affects and actions proper to the tragedy. Milton seems to extend his storied monism from *De doctrina Christiana* to *Samson Agonistes* and, in a manner that looks forward to Spinoza's posthumous

Ethica, renders the *constitutio* of the drama, in all of its necessity, as the activity of an otherwise "unsearchable dispose / Of highest wisdom." God, here at the end of *Samson Agonistes,* is known in and through the active and affective constitution of human life. In a manner that takes shape through Aristotle's *Poetics,* a philosophical treatise in its own right, Milton considers God and *catharsis* together in a monist experiment. If Milton suggests that *catharsis* is indeed a sort of purging, a "passion spent" to achieve "calm of mind," then God is in this sense the subject of *catharsis* as expiation.

In order to make the philosophical import of this poetic innovation clear, we might revisit Heinsius's treatise, particularly insofar as Heinsius draws our attention to the first book of Aristotle's *Metaphysics.* Heinsius notes that it was Aristotle, the philosopher "who permitted nothing without reason and even made nature the measure of divine things," who criticized Anaxagoras for introducing a foreign element into the totality of forces, like the common poet, in a effort to make sense of the same totality (*PT* 64–65; *CT* 224). This is explicit in the *Metaphysics:* "Anaxagoras uses reason as a *deus ex machina* for the making of the world, and when he is at a loss to tell for what cause something necessarily is, then he drags reason in, but in all other cases ascribes events to anything rather than to reason."[56] In this example, Aristotle dismisses Anaxagoras based on his lack of consistency and on his confusion of causality. If nothing is as common as a device involving a god, Anaxagoras introduces such a device in his attempt to understand the world, obscuring the adequate causality of creation in the process. This follows the Aristotelian injunction against spectacle that Heinsius treats in chapter 8 of *De constitutione tragoediae,* where those poets who seek only to move spectators, "while they pursue pity and horror, they only move portentous and prodigious wonder. . . . Aristotle denies that this is the end of tragedy, especially since the passions spring from nature [e natura perturbationes nascantur]; and in fact anything either prodigious or portentous conflicts with this" (*PT* 46–47; *CT* 190). The introduction of a device, like recourse to spectacle, is to be avoided in tragedy as well as in philosophy. Milton invokes Aristotle here, in his monist experiment. Where the introduction of a god or device obscures the constitution of the elements in the tragedy, Milton, with Aristotle and Heinsius, pursues this to the opposite extreme: the slippery possessive pronouns invite us to consider that all is God here, at the end of *Samson Agonistes*, and this is precisely the object of expiation. God is the subject (or object) that has "all passion spent."

Lustratio, however, is something different, distinct. It enables Milton to pose complex questions concerning agency and the Spirit. While Milton reveals, in his translation of *catharsis* as *lustratio*, a generic comportment to a *constitutio* comprised by God, *lustratio* names the "true experience" of the tragedy, of "this great event," which Milton describes across *Samson Agonistes* as a patchwork of moments of assurance and desperation. *Lustratio* foregrounds the experience of tragedy; it is not merely a purging or an expiation, the usual translations of *catharsis*, but rather a more fundamental affective experience akin to a ritual, a rite, a purification by sacrifice that even perhaps approaches a Reformed sacrament. *Samson Agonistes* is certainly a meditation on the fundamental elements of tragedy, with *lustratio* as a categorical subjective position, for the elect and reprobate alike, given to wandering as well as to enlightenment. This is certainly a far cry from more conventional understandings of *catharsis* as expiation or purgation—truly, an unrecognized Miltonic innovation in the history of tragedy.

Princeton University

NOTES

Notes to McDowell, "How Laudian Was the Young Milton?"

This essay began as a plenary paper for the Canada Milton Seminar VI at the University of Toronto in May 2010. My great thanks to Paul Stevens for inviting me to speak and to the audience for their helpful comments and suggestions, particularly Edward Jones, Tom Keymer, Thomas Luxon, Lynne Magnusson, Annabel Patterson, David Quint, and Nigel Smith.

1. Barbara K. Lewalski, "How Radical Was the Young Milton?" in *Milton and Heresy*, ed. Stephen B. Dobranski and John P. Rumrich (Cambridge, 1998), 50.

2. David Norbrook, *Poetry and Politics in the English Renaissance* (1984; rev. ed., Oxford, 2002), 224–69.

3. Gordon Campbell and Thomas N. Corns, *John Milton: Life, Work, and Thought* (Oxford, 2008).

4. William Poole, "Laudian, Regicidal Milton?" *Times Literary Supplement*, March 11, 2009, responding to Jonathan Bate's review, "The Power of Milton," *Times Literary Supplement*, March 6, 2009, and quoting Campbell and Corns, *John Milton*, 84.

5. See Gordon Campbell, "The Life Records," in *A Companion to Milton*, ed. Thomas N. Corns (Oxford, 2001), 487. See also Edward Jones, "'Ere Half my Days': Milton's Life, 1608–1640," in *The Oxford Handbook of Milton*, ed. Nicholas McDowell and Nigel Smith (Oxford, 2009), who points out that the signature means Milton's father was either a justice of the peace or a churchwarden (14n31).

6. Campbell and Corns, *John Milton*, 68.

7. Ibid., 40.

8. Graham Parry, *Glory, Laud and Honour: The Arts of the Anglican Counter-Reformation* (Woodbridge, Suffolk, 2006), 154–55. See also Thomas N. Corns, "Milton Before 'Lycidas,'" in *Milton and the Terms of Liberty*, ed. Graham Parry and Joad Raymond (Cambridge, 2001), 23–36, which anticipates the arguments of the Campbell and Corns biography. Other notable essays to have questioned the extent to which we can or should ascribe radical and revolutionary positions to the early poems include Annabel Patterson, "'Forc'd Fingers':

Milton's Early Poems and Ideological Constraint," in *"The Muses Commonweale":
Poetry and Politics in the Seventeenth Century*, ed. Claude J. Summers and Ted-Larry
Pebworth (Columbia, Mo., 1988), 9–22; David Loewenstein, "'Fair offspring
nurs't in princely lore': On the Question of Milton's Early Radicalism," in
Milton Studies, vol. 28, ed. Albert C. Labriola (Pittsburgh, 1992), 37–48; Annabel
Patterson, "His Singing Robes," in *Milton Studies*, vol. 48, ed. Albert C. Labriola
(Pittsburgh, 2008), 178–94.

   9. Campbell and Corns, *John Milton*, 53.

   10. All references to Milton's poems are to John Milton, *Complete Shorter
Poems*, ed. Stella Revard (Oxford, 2009).

   11. Peter Lake, "The Laudian Style: Order, Uniformity and the Pursuit
of the Beauty of Holiness in the 1630s," in *The Early Stuart Church, 1603–42*,
ed. Kenneth Fincham (Basingstoke, 1993), 72–106.

   12. See Louis Martz, "The Rising Poet," in *The Lyric and Dramatic Milton*,
ed. J. H. Summers (New York, 1965), 3–33.

   13. Campbell and Corns, *John Milton*, 53. All references to Crashaw's poems
are to *Poems: English, Latin, and Greek*, ed. L. C. Martin, 2nd ed. (Oxford, 1957);
hereafter cited in the text by line number.

   14. Thomas N. Corns, "On the Morning of Christ's Nativity," "Upon the
Circumcision," and "The Passion," in Corns, *A Companion to Milton*, 219.

   15. For details see the excellent *Oxford Dictionary of National Biography* entry for
Crashaw by Thomas Healy. Cited hereafter as *ODNB*.

   16. John Carey, ed., *Complete Shorter Poems*, rev. ed. (Harlow, 1997), 123;
Campbell and Corns, *John Milton*, 53. All references to Milton's poems are to
this edition and are hereafter cited in the text by line number.

   17. Marshall Grossman, "'In pensive trance, and anguish, and ecstatic fit':
Milton on the Passion," in *A Fine Tuning: Studies of the Religious Poetry of Herbert
and Milton*, ed. Mary Maleski and Russell A. Peck (Binghamton, 1989), 206–
20; Barbara K. Lewalski, *The Life of John Milton* (Oxford, 2003), 424. For the
latest thinking about the mature Milton's Antitrinitarianism in relation to his
poetry, see John Rogers, "*Paradise Regained* and the Memory of *Paradise Lost*," in
McDowell and Smith, *Oxford Handbook of Milton*, 589–612.

   18. On this issue, see Nicholas Tyacke, "Puritanism, Arminianism and
Counter-Revolution," in *The Origins of the English Civil War*, ed. Conrad Russell
(London, 1973), 119–43.

   19. For a useful if polemical overview of reactions to Crashaw's style, see
Lorraine M. Roberts and John R. Roberts, "Crashavian Criticism: A Brief
Interpretative History," in *New Perspectives on the Life and Art of Richard Crashaw*,
ed. John R. Roberts (Columbia, Mo., 1990), 1–29. On the tendency to exclude
Crashaw from the English literary tradition because of his "foreign," that is,
Catholic, style, see also Alison Shell, *Catholicism, Controversy, and the English Literary
Imagination, 1558–1660* (Cambridge, 1999), 97–104.

20. See, for example, Austin Warren, *Richard Crashaw: A Study in Baroque Sensibility* (London, 1957); R. V. Young, *Richard Crashaw and the Spanish Golden Age* (New Haven, 1982).

21. Thomas Healy, *Richard Crashaw* (Leiden, 1986), 64.

22. British Library, Add. MSS 23146, fol. 33ᵛ.

23. Ann Hughes, "Thomas Dugard and His Circle in the 1630s: A 'Parliamentary-Puritan' Connexion?" *Historical Journal* 29 (1986): 784. See also Nicholas McDowell, *The English Radical Imagination: Culture, Religion, and Revolution* (Oxford, 2003), 92–95.

24. Samuel Rutherford, *Christ Dying and Drawing Sinners to Himself* (London, 1647), "To the Reader," sig. A3ʳ, A4ᵛ–B1ʳ.

25. See *Wonderfull predictions declared in a message, as from the Lord, to his Excellency Sr. Thomas Fairfax and the Councell of his Army. By John Saltmarsh preacher of the Gospell. His severall speeches, and the manner of his death. December 29. 1647* (London, 1647); *Englands Friend Raised from the Grave. Giving seasonable advice to the Lord Generall, Lieutenant-Generall, and the Councell of Warre. Being the true copies of three letters written by Mr John Saltmarsh, a little before his death* (London, 1649). See also Roger Pooley's entry for Saltmarsh in the *ODNB*.

26. John Saltmarsh, *Free-Grace; or, The Flowings of Christs Blood freely to Sinners* (London, 1645), 148. Hereafter cited by page number in the text.

27. L. F. Salt, "John Saltmarsh: New Model Army Chaplain," *Journal of Ecclesiastical History* 2 (1951): 69–80. A. L. Morton's extensive discussion of Saltmarsh in *The World of the Ranters* (London, 1970), 45–69, is misleading in this respect.

28. John Saltmarsh, *A Solemn Discourse upon the Grand Covenant* (London, 1643), 72.

29. John Saltmarsh, *Poemata sacra latine et anglice scripti* (Cambridge, 1636), 6.

30. Pooley, *ODNB*.

31. Saltmarsh, "Meditation IX," in *Poemata sacra*, vernacular book, 11.

32. The "Directions" are printed in *The Intellectual Development of John Milton*, 2 vols., ed. Harris Fletcher (Urbana, Ill., 1961), 2:623–64. See the illuminating discussion in relation to Crashaw in Healy, *Richard Crashaw*, 45–52.

33. Patrick Collinson, entry for Holdsworth in the *ODNB*.

34. Gerald M. Maclean, *Time's Witness: Historical Representation in English Poetry, 1603–1660* (Madison, 1990), 53–56; David Norbrook, *Writing the English Republic: Poetry, Rhetoric and Politics, 1627–1660* (Cambridge, 1999), 67; John Saltmarsh, "To his Ingenious Friend Master RUSSELL, upon his Heroick Poem," in John Russell, *The two famous pitcht battels of Lypsich, and Lutzen wherein the ever-renowned Prince Gustavus the Great lived and died a conquerour: with an elegie upon his untimely death, composed in heroick verse* (Cambridge, 1634), sig. 3ᵛ, lines 1–9.

35. Saltmarsh, "To his Ingenious Friend," 19–22.

36. John Saltmarsh, *Examinations; or, A Discovery of some dangerous positions delivered in a sermon of Reformation preached by Thomas Fuller* (London, 1643); Saltmarsh,

Peace but No Pacification (London, 1643); Sarah Barber, *A Revolutionary Rogue: Henry Marten and the English Republic* (Stroud, 2000), 9–10, 75.

37. Corns, *A Companion to Milton*, 231.

38. Burgess, "Radicalism and the English Revolution," in *English Radicalism, 1550–1850*, ed. Glenn Burgess and Matthew Fesenstein (Cambridge, 2007), 68. See also McDowell, *English Radical Imagination*, 1–21.

39. On the reluctance to engage with Arminian doctrine, as opposed to Laudian discipline, in the antiprelatical tracts, see Thomas N. Corns, "Milton's Antiprelatical Tracts and the Marginality of Doctrine," in Dobranski and Rumrich, *Milton and Heresy*, 39–48.

40. John Milton, *Doctrine and Discipline of Divorce*, in *The Complete Prose Works of John Milton*, 8 vols., ed. Don M. Wolfe et al. (New Haven, 1953–82), 2:223, 597.

41. On metaphors of insubstantiality in the divorce tracts, see Stephen M. Fallon, "The metaphysics of Milton's divorce tracts," in *Politics, Poetics, and Hermeneutics in Milton's Prose*, ed. David Loewenstein and James Grantham Turner (Cambridge, 1990), 69–84.

42. John Leonard, "'Trembling Ears': The Historical Moment of 'Lycidas,'" *Journal of Medieval and Early Modern Studies* 21 (1991): 59–81; Edward Jones, "'Church-Outed by the Prelates': Milton and the 1637 Inspection of the Horton Parish Church," *JEGP* 102 (2003): 42–58.

43. Cleveland, "On the Memory of Mr. Edward King, Drown'd in the Irish Seas," in *Justa Edouardo King Naufrago* (Cambridge, 1638), lines 1–8; repr. in Joseph Wittreich, *Visionary Poetics: Milton's Tradition and His Legacy* (San Marino, Calif., 1979), appendix.

44. Lewalski, *Life of John Milton*, 70–71.

45. See Carey, *Shorter Poems*, 251.

Notes to Walker, "Rhetoric, Passion, and Belief in *The Readie and Easie Way*"

1. See Blair Worden, "English Republicanism," in *The Cambridge History of Political Thought, 1450–1700*, ed. J. H. Burns with assistance of Mark Goldie (Cambridge, 1991), 456–57; Blair Worden, "Milton and Marchamont Nedham," 166, and Thomas Corns, "Milton and the Characteristics of a Free Commonwealth," 25–42, in *Milton and Republicanism*, ed. David Armitage, Armand Himy, and Quentin Skinner (Cambridge, 1995); Quentin Skinner, "John Milton and the Politics of Slavery," *Visions of Politics*, vol. 2 (Cambridge, 2002), 286–307.

2. Eric Nelson, "'Talmudical Commonwealthsmen' and the Rise of Republican Exclusivism," *Historical Journal* 50 (2007): 809, 823, 832, 825, 832.

3. For usages of *republicanism* in this sense, see J. G. A. Pocock, *The Machiavellian Moment* (Princeton, 1975); Worden, "English Republicanism";

Cary Nederman, "Rhetoric, Reason, and Republic: Republicanisms—Ancient, Medieval, and Modern," 247–69, and Paul Rahe, "Situating Machiavelli," 270–308, in *Renaissance Civic Humanism*, ed. James Hankins (Cambridge, 2000); Jonathan Scott, *Commonwealth Principles: Republican Writing of the English Revolution* (Cambridge, 2004); Paul Rahe, "The Classical Republicanism of John Milton," *History of Political Thought* 25 (2004): 243–75; Eric Nelson, *The Greek Tradition in Republican Thought* (Cambridge, 2004); William Walker, *"Paradise Lost" and Republican Tradition from Aristotle to Machiavelli* (Turnhout, Belgium, 2009).

4. *The readie and easie way to establish a free Commonwealth; and the excellence therof compar'd with the inconveniencies and dangers of readmitting Kingship in this Nation*, 2nd ed., in vol. 7, ed. Robert Ayers, of *The Complete Prose Works of John Milton*, 8 vols., ed. Don M. Wolfe et al. (New Haven, 1953–82), 7:409; hereafter cited as YP. All further references to the tract are to this edition and are cited in the text.

5. For discussions that highlight the Old Testament prophetic mode, see Stanley Stewart, "Milton Revises *The Readie and Easie Way*," in *Milton Studies*, vol. 20, ed. James D. Simmonds (Pittsburgh, 1984), 205–24; James Holstun, *A Rational Millennium: Puritan Utopias of Seventeenth-Century England and America* (Oxford, 1987), 246–65; Laura Lunger Knoppers, "Milton's *The Readie and Easie Way* and the English Jeremiad," in *Politics, Poetics, and Hermeneutics in Milton's Prose*, ed. David Loewenstein and James Grantham Turner (Cambridge, 1990), 213–25; Laura Lunger Knoppers, "Late Political Prose," in *A Companion to Milton*, ed. Thomas Corns (Oxford, 2001), 309–25. But whereas Stewart and Holstun argue that in assuming the prophetic stance Milton moves away from the attempt to persuade any contemporary audience, Knoppers argues, rightly in my view, that the prophetic mode supports this attempt, however desperate it may be.

6. See *The Present Means and Brief Delineation of a Free Commonwealth, Easy to be Put in Practice, and without Delay. In A Letter to General Monk*, in YP 7:389–95.

7. See Corns, *Uncloistered Virtue;* David Norbrook, *Writing the English Republic: Poetry, Rhetoric and Politics, 1627–1660* (Cambridge, 1999), 411–21; Derek Hirst, *England in Conflict, 1603–1660* (London, 1999), 327; Knoppers, "Late Political Prose"; Barbara Lewalski, *The Life of John Milton* (Oxford, 2000), 359.

8. For the identification and discussion of these various constituents of his imagined audience, see William Riley Parker, *Milton: A Biography*, 2nd ed., ed. Gordon Campbell (1968; repr., Oxford, 1996), 543–57; Austin Woolrych, "Introduction," in YP 7:101–218; Corns, *Uncloistered Virtue*, 275–93; Lewalski, *Life of John Milton*, 373–81, 389–97; Gordon Campbell and Thomas Corns, *John Milton: Life, Work, and Thought* (Oxford, 2008), 294–300.

9. Aristotle, *Rhetoric*, trans. Lane Cooper (Englewood Cliffs, N.J.: 1960), 1413a.

10. Longinus, *On Sublimity*, trans. D. A. Russell, in *Classical Literary Criticism*, ed. D. A. Russell and Michael Winterbottom (1989; Oxford, 1998), 38.1–6. Other discussions of hyperbole which Milton probably knew are in Cicero, *Ad*

Herennium, trans. Harry Caplan (Cambridge, Mass., 1981), 4.33; Quintilian, *Institutes of Oratory,* trans. H. E. Butler (Cambridge, Mass., 1986), 8.6.67–76.

11. *The Censure of the Rota Upon Mr Miltons Book, Entituled, The Ready and Easie way to Establish A Free Common-wealth"* (London, 1660). Wing (2nd ed.) H808; Thomason E.1019[5*],8; copy from Huntington Library. It was probably published in late March. For strong arguments in favor of attributing this tract to the poet Samuel Butler, see P. B. Anderson, "Anonymous Critic of Milton: Richard Leigh? or Samuel Butler?" *SP* 44 (1947): 504–18; Nicholas von Maltzahn, "Samuel Butler's Milton," *SP* 92 (1995): 482–95.

12. See William Walker, "Antiformalism, Antimonarchism, and Republicanism in the 'Regicide Tracts,'" *MP* 108 (2011): 507–37.

13. For further observations on how Milton's passions drive his prose, see Thomas Kranidas, *Milton and the Rhetoric of Zeal* (Pittsburgh, 2005); Paul Stevens, "Intolerance and the Virtues of Sacred Vehemence," in *Milton and Toleration,* ed. Sharon Achinstein and Elizabeth Sauer (Oxford, 2007), 243–67.

14. *Brief Notes upon a late Sermon, titl'd "The Fear of God and the King,"* in YP 7:469. A further problem for Nelson's account of the development of Milton's political thought is posed by Milton's *A Declaration, or Letters Patent* (1674), a work in which, as Nicholas von Maltzahn, "The Whig Milton, 1667–1700," in Armitage, Himy, and Skinner, *Milton and Republicanism,* 231, observes, Milton opposes the Catholic succession in England by "proposing the merits of elective kingship."

15. See Zera Fink, *The Classical Republicans* (1945; repr., Evanston, Ill., 1962), 90–122; Worden, "English Republicanism," 443–75; Martin Dzelzainis, "Milton's Classical Republicanism," in Armitage, Himy, and Skinner, *Milton and Republicanism,* 3–24; David Armitage, "John Milton: Poet against Empire," in Armitage, Himy, and Skinner, *Milton and Republicanism,* 206–25; Norbrook, *Writing the English Republic,* 192–212; Scott, *Commonwealth Principles;* Skinner, "Politics of Slavery"; Rahe, "Classical Republicanism"; Walker, *"Paradise Lost" and Republican Tradition.*

16. For the argument that Milton's reference to the Roman republic here recalls the Virgilian, republican, prophetic, but also cautionary registers of the *Second Defence,* see Andrew Barnaby, "'Another Rome in the West'? Milton and the Imperial Republic, 1654–1670," in *Milton Studies,* vol. 30, ed. Albert C. Labriola (Pittsburgh, 1993), 67–84.

17. Andrew Barnaby, "Machiavellian Hypotheses: Republican Settlement and the Question of Empire in Milton's *Readie and Easie Way,"* *Clio* 19 (1990): 251–70. But note that Barnaby ends up arguing—quite rightly as we will see—that "Milton, unlike Harrington, must reject the twin aspects of Machiavelli's ideal republic: popular ascendancy in matters of rule and an orientation toward imperial expansion" (267).

18. Nicholas von Maltzahn, "From Pillar to Post: Milton and the Attack on Republican Humanism at the Restoration," in *Soldiers, Writers and Statesmen of the*

English Revolution, ed. Ian Gentles, John Morrill, and Blair Worden (Cambridge, 1998), 273.

19. Aristotle, *Politics,* trans. Benjamin Jowett, in *The Basic Works of Aristotle,* ed. Richard McKeon (New York, 1941), 1279a–b; hereafter cited in the text.

20. See *A Defence of the People of England,* trans. Claire Gruzelier, in John Milton, *Political Writings,* ed. Martin Dzelzainis (Cambridge, 1991), 150–51, 162, 180, 199, 223.

21. John Milton, *Second Defence of the English People,* trans. Helen North, in YP 4:636, 672.

22. See Fink, *The Classical Republicans,* 119–22; Woolrych, "Introduction," in YP 7:215; Dzelzainis, "Milton's Classical Republicanism," 7–9; Dzelzainis, "Republicanism," in Corns, *A Companion to Milton,* 298–99.

23. See, for example, *Of Reformation,* in YP 1:599–600; *The Tenure of Kings and Magistrates,* in John Milton, *Political Writings,* 9–10; *Eikonoklastes,* in YP 1:412–13, 457, 462, 486; *A Defence,* in *Political Writings,* 84, 130, 166–67, 179–80, 187, 198, 205, 208, 210, 218–25.

24. For histories of the idea of the mixed constitution and accounts of how it is related to republican tradition, see J. G. A. Pocock, *The Machiavellian Moment* (Princeton, N.J., 1975); James Blythe, *Ideal Government and the Mixed Constitution in the Middle Ages* (Princeton, N.J., 1992); Scott, *Commonwealth Principles,* 19–40, 131–50.

25. Livy, *The Rise of Rome,* trans. T. J. Luce (Oxford, 1998), 2.1; Sallust, *The War with Catiline,* trans. J. C. Rolfe (1921; repr., Cambridge, Mass., 2000), 6.7; both hereafter cited in the text.

26. Niccolò Machiavelli, *The Discourses,* ed. Bernard Crick and trans. Leslie Walker, Bernard Crick, and Brian Richardson (1970; repr., New York, 1988), 198; hereafter cited in the text by page number.

27. There are, however, several different accounts of Harrington's relationship to the classical republicans and Machiavelli. For accounts that emphasize his commitments to them, see Pocock, *The Machiavellian Moment,* 383–400; Blair Worden, "James Harrington and *The Commonwealth of Oceana,* 1656," 82–110, and "Harrington's *Oceana:* Origins and Aftermath, 1651–1660," 111–38, both in *Republicanism, Liberty, and Commercial Society, 1649–1776,* ed. David Wootton (Stanford, Calif., 1994). For accounts that emphasize Harrington's departures from them, see J. C. Davis, *Utopia and the Ideal Society* (Cambridge, 1981), 205–40; Jonathan Scott, "The Rapture of Motion: James Harrington's Republicanism," in *Political Discourse in Early Modern Britain,* ed. Nicholas Phillipson and Quentin Skinner (Cambridge, 1993), 139–63; J. C. Davis, "Equality in an Unequal Commonwealth: James Harrington's Republicanism and the Meaning of Equality," in Gentles, Morrill, and Worden, *Soldiers, Writers and Statesmen,* 229–42; Alan Cromartie, "Harringtonian Virtue: Harrington, Machiavelli, and the Method of the *Moment,*" *Historical Journal* 41 (1998): 987–1009.

28. See Marchamont Nedham, *The Excellencie of a Free State; or, The Right Constitution of a Common-wealth* (London, 1656), Wing (2nd ed.) N388; Thomason E.1676 [1], esp. 23–80.

29. See *A Letter to a Friend*, in YP 7:330, and *Proposalls of certaine expedients for the preventing of a civill war now feard, and the settling of a firme government*, in YP 7:336–37. Note that as early as *A Letter to a Friend*, Milton is defending his proposal for a perpetual "senate or generall Councell of State" against the charge that it might be "an oligarchy of the faction of a few" (331).

30. For a brief account of Cicero's opposition to the Gracchi, see Nelson, *Greek Tradition*, 57–59. Nelson also observes that "the neo-Roman authors of the quattrocento in Italy" generally endorsed the Ciceronian position (68).

31. See the extensive discussion of property in book 2 of the *Politics;* the discussion of political societies with large middle classes in book 4 (1295b–1296b); the discussion of the means of preserving constitutions in book 5 (1307b–1309a); and the discussion of the best constitution in book 7 (1323a–b, 1330a).

32. Polybius, *The Histories*, 6 vols., trans. W. R. Paton (1923; repr., Cambridge, Mass., 2003), 6.45.3–4; hereafter cited in the text.

33. See the lives of all five figures in *The Lives of the Noble Grecians and Romans*, trans. John Dryden and Arthur Hugh Clough (1864; repr., New York, 1934).

34. See "Personal Letter 23, to the Very Distinguished Mr Henry de Brass," in *John Milton, Latin Writings*, ed. and trans. John K. Hale (Assen, Netherlands, 1998), 205–06.

35. See Sallust, *The War with Jugurtha*, trans. J. C. Rolfe (1921; repr., Cambridge, Mass., 2000), 31.1–2, 42.1–3.

36. See Machiavelli, *Discourses*, 120, 201–03, 246, 335, 452, 475; hereafter cited in the text.

37. See Philip Pettit, *Republicanism* (Oxford, 1997); Quentin Skinner, *Liberty before Liberalism* (Cambridge, 1998); Skinner, "Politics of Slavery"; Dzelzainis, "Republicanism," in Corns, *A Companion to Milton*, 301–08.

38. Cicero, *On the Republic*, trans. Niall Rudd, with introduction and notes by Jonathan Powell and Niall Rudd (Oxford, 1998), 2.3; hereafter cited in the text.

39. See *The Present Means*. For commentary that highlights the ways in which Milton turned to Monck, see also Laura Lunger Knoppers, "Late Political Prose."

40. Knoppers, "Late Political Prose," 321.

41. Machiavelli, *The Prince*, ed. Russell Price and Quentin Skinner and trans. Russell Price (Cambridge, 1988), 90.

42. Note that for the second edition of *The Readie and Easie Way*, Milton excised a passage from the first edition in which he emphasized that "civil States would do much better...if they would not meddle at all with Ecclesiastical matters." As Lewalski, *Life*, 391, observes, this excision is likely motivated by his concern to appease the Presbyterians.

43. Cicero, *On Laws*, trans. Niall Rudd, with introduction and notes by Jonathan Powell and Niall Rudd (Oxford, 1998), 2.16; hereafter cited in the text.

44. See *Journal of the History of Ideas* 60, no. 4 (1999): 579–682.

45. Livy, *The Rise of Rome*, 24–27; Plutarch, "Numa Pompilius," in Dryden and Clough, *Lives of the Noble*, 74–92.

46. For Harrington's defense of and proposals for a national church and an endowed ministry, see *The Commonwealth of Oceana*, ed. J. G. A. Pocock (Cambridge, 1992), 39–42, 81–83, 126–27, 198–203; Harrington, *Aphorisms Political* (London, [1659]), 2, Wing (2nd ed.) HG804, Thomason E. 995[8]; copy from British Library, 2–5, accessed through *Early English Books Online*.

47. Worden, "English Republicanism," 444.

Notes to Ng, "Pirating Paradise"

An early version of this paper was presented in 2008 at the Ninth International Milton Symposium in London. I would like to thank Sharon Achinstein for inviting me to participate in her panel on "International Milton"; my thanks also to the audience, in particular Martin Dzelzainis and Iain McClure. I would also like to thank the American Philosophical Society and British Academy for a Joint Fellowship for Research in London in 2007 and the National Humanities Center for a 2007–08 fellowship that supported this work as well as the anonymous readers for *Milton Studies*.

The epigraph is from Samuel Pecke, *A Perfect Diurnall of Some Passages in Parliament*, no. 288, Tuesday, January 30 (London, 1649), 2317.

1. David Quint, *Epic and Empire: Politics and Generic Form from Virgil to Milton* (Princeton, N.J., 1993), esp. 253–56.

2. The scholarship is ever growing; see, among others, Nabil Matar, *Turks, Moors, and Englishmen in the Age of Discovery* (New York, 1999); Richmond Barber, *Before Orientalism: London's Theatre of the East, 1576–1626* (Cambridge, 2003).

3. Gerald MacLean, "Milton, Islam and the Ottomans," in *Milton and Toleration*, ed. Sharon Achinstein and Elizabeth Sauer (New York, 2003), 284–98; Robert Markley, *The Far East and the English Imagination, 1600–1730* (Cambridge, 2006), 72–79; John Michael Archer, *Old Worlds: Egypt, Southwest Asia, India, and Russia in Early Modern English Writing* (Palo Alto, Calif., 2001), 99.

4. Blair Hoxby, *Mammon's Music: Literature and Economics in the Age of Milton* (New Haven, 2002), 155.

5. For an Empsonian reading, see Michael Bryson, *The Tyranny of Heaven: Milton's Rejection of God as King* (Newark, Del. 2004). Scholars distinguishing between good and bad kings in Milton include Robert Thomas Fallon, *Divided Empire: Milton's Political Imagery* (University Park, Pa., 1995); Stevie Davies, *Images of Kingship in "Paradise Lost": Milton's Politics and Christian Liberty* (Columbia, Mo., 1983); Joan S. Bennett, *Reviving Liberty: Radical Christian Humanism in Milton's Great Poems* (Cambridge, Mass., 1989).

6. David Norbrook, *Writing the English Republic: Poetry, Rhetoric and Politics, 1627–1660* (Cambridge, 1999), 477.

7. David Armitage, "John Milton: Poet against Empire," in *Milton and Republicanism,* ed. David Armitage, Armand Himy, and Quentin Skinner (Cambridge, 1995), 206–25; Blair Worden, "Milton's Republicanism and the Tyranny of Heaven," in *Machiavelli and Republicanism,* ed. Gisela Bock, Quentin Skinner, and Maurizio Viroli (Cambridge, 1990); and Andrew Barnaby, "'Another Rome in the West?': Milton and the Imperial Republic, 1654–1670," in *Milton Studies,* vol. 30, ed. Albert C. Labriola (Pittsburgh, 1993), 67–84. On Milton's criticism of empire, see Quint, *Epic and Empire,* 248–67.

8. J. Martin Evans, *Milton's Imperial Epic: "Paradise Lost" and the Discourse of Colonialism* (Ithaca, N.Y., 1996), 141–48; Paul Stevens, "*Paradise Lost* and the Colonial Imperative," in *Milton Studies,* vol. 34, ed. Albert C. Labriola (Pittsburgh, 1996), 3; Bruce McLeod, *The Geography of Empire in English Literature, 1580–1745* (Cambridge, 1999), 137. For arguments emphasizing Milton's colonialist bent, see Walter S. H. Lim, *The Arts of Empire: The Poetics of Colonialism from Raleigh to Milton* (Newark, Del., 1998); and Willy Maley, *Nation, State, and Empire in English Renaissance Literature: Shakespeare to Milton* (New York, 2003).

9. Quint, *Epic and Empire,* 265.

10. Robert Thomas Fallon, "Cromwell, Milton, and the Western Design," in *Milton and the Imperial Vision,* ed. Balachandra Rajan and Elizabeth Sauer (Pittsburgh, 1999), 154.

11. On trade empires in *Paradise Lost,* see Hoxby, *Mammon's Music,* 150–77.

12. Luís de Camões, *The Lusiad; or, Portugals Historicall Poem,* in Sir Richard Fanshawe, *The Poems and Translations of Sir Richard Fanshawe,* ed. Peter Davidson, vol. 2 (Oxford, 1999), 5.93.737–40, 10.156.6–8. Unless otherwise noted, all quotations of *The Lusiad* are from Fanshawe's 1655 translation, hereafter cited parenthetically in the text.

13. *Defensio prima,* in John Milton, *Political Writings,* ed. Martin Dzelzainis and trans. Claire Gruzelier (Cambridge, 1991), 80. Translations of this work are from this edition; hereafter cited parenthetically by page number in the text.

14. Jonathan I. Israel, *Dutch Primacy in World Trade, 1585–1740* (Oxford, 1989); Eli F. Heckscher, *Mercantilism,* 2 vols. (London, 1935), 1:351. For the growth of European maritime empires, diverging from centralized territorial empires, see Thomas A. Brady Jr., "The Rise of Merchant Empires, 1400–1700: A European Counterpoint," in *The Political Economy of Merchant Empires,* ed. James D. Tracy (Cambridge, 1991), 117–60. For Satan as conquistador, see Evans, *Milton's Imperial Epic,* 62–71; Robert Thomas Fallon, "Milton's Epics and the Spanish War: Toward a Poetics of Experience," in *Milton Studies,* vol. 15, ed. James D. Simmonds (Pittsburgh, 1981), 3–28; and Christopher Hodgkins, *Reforming Empire: Protestant Colonialism and Conscience in British Literature* (Columbia, Mo., 2002), 54–76.

15. My account in this paragraph depends on Israel, *Dutch Primacy in World Trade*, 197–213.

16. B. M., Harleian MS 6695, fols. 140–6; cited in Harland Taylor, "Trade, Neutrality and the 'English Road,' 1630–1648," *Economic History Review*, n.s. 25 (1972): 240.

17. Steven Pincus, *Protestantism and Patriotism: Ideologies and the Making of English Foreign Policy, 1650–1688* (Cambridge, 1996), 190, 260. For a critique of Pincus, see Jonathan Israel, "England, the Dutch Republic, and Europe in the Seventeenth Century," *Historical Journal* 40 (1997): 1117–21.

18. *Works of John Milton*, 18 vols. in 21, ed. Frank Allen Patterson et al., (New York, 1931–42), 13:133, 135; hereafter cited as CM in the text.

19. Leo Miller, *John Milton's Writings in the Anglo-Dutch Negotiations, 1651–1654* (Pittsburgh, 1992), 78.

20. Gordon Campbell and Thomas N. Corns, *John Milton: Life, Work, and Thought* (Oxford, 2008), 106–07. For Milton and Holland, see Tiemen de Vries, *Holland's Influence on English Language and Literature* (Chicago, 1916), 288–302. Another Dutch contemporary, Joost van den Vondel wrote a series of plays on similar themes: *Lucifer, Adam in Ballingschap* [*Adam in Exile*], and *Samson Agonistes*. But similarities likely arise from both poets' indebtedness to Grotius.

21. Campbell and Corns, *John Milton*, 236–38. For another connection to Leiden, see Paul Sellin, "Caesar Calandrini, the London Dutch, and Milton's Quarrels in Holland," *HLQ* 31 (1968): 239–49. Sellin suggests that Milton obtained Leiden information about Alexander More through Caesar Calandrini, but Blair Worden believes the letter to be Milton's own forgery (*Literature and Politics in Cromwellian England: John Milton, Andrew Marvell, Marchamont Nedham* [Oxford, 2007], 202–03).

22. John Kerrigan, *Archipelagic English: Literature, History, and Politics, 1603–1707* (Oxford, 2008), 223. For Anglo-Dutch cultural exchanges, see also Lisa Jardine, *Going Dutch: How England Plundered Holland's Glory* (New York, 2008).

23. Marvell, *An Account of the Growth of Popery, and Arbitrary Government in England* (London, 1677), 17–18; cited in Kerrigan, *Archipelagic English*, 225.

24. Kerrigan, *Archipelagic English*, 224.

25. Christopher A. Whatley and Derek J. Patrick, *The Scots and the Union* (Edinburgh, 2006), 72. For Scotland's connections with the Netherlands, see 72–80.

26. Kerrigan, *Archipelagic English*, 222–23.

27. G[eorge] S[tarkey], *The Dignity of Kingship Asserted: in Answer to Mr. Milton's Ready and Easie Way* (London, 1660), 106.

28. Worden, *Literature and Politics*, 202–03, 215.

29. Barbara K. Lewalski, *The Life of John Milton*, rev. ed. (Oxford, 2003), 238.

30. Pincus, *Protestantism and Patriotism*, 59–60.

31. [John Hall], *A True Relation of the Unjust, Cruel, and Barbarous Proceedings against the English at Amboyna in the East-Indies, by the Netherlandish Governour and Council There* (London, 1651), 4, 10.

32. Lewalski, *The Life of John Milton*, 244. See J. Milton French, ed., *The Life Records of John Milton*, 5 vols. (New Brunswick, 1948–58), 2:250.

33. Edward Phillips, *The Life of Mr. John Milton* (1694), in *The Riverside Milton*, ed. Roy Flannagan (Boston, 1998), 26.

34. Norbrook, *Writing the English Republic*, 433–35.

35. Martin Dzelzainis, "The Politics of *Paradise Lost*," in *The Oxford Handbook of Milton*, ed. Nicholas McDowell and Nigel Smith (Oxford, 2009), 549. My thanks to Martin Dzelzainis for showing me his paper while it was still in press.

36. Ibid., 564.

37. Milton, *The Readie and Easie Way*, in *The Complete Prose Works of John Milton*, 8 vols., ed. Don M. Wolfe et al. (New Haven, 1953–82), 7:357, 423, hereafter cited as YP; Kerrigan quotes this very passage in *Archipelagic English*, 242.

38. William Collinne, *The Spirit of the Phanatiques Dissected* (London, 1660), 7–8; S[tarkey], *The Dignity of Kingship Asserted*, 104; both replies are noted by Kerrigan, *Archipelagic English*, 242.

39. See Israel, *Dutch Primacy in World Trade*, 218–23.

40. Quint, *Epic and Empire*, 265.

41. Quotations from *Paradise Lost* are from Flannagan, *The Riverside Milton*; hereafter cited parenthetically in the text.

42. Markley, *The Far East*, 83; Timothy Morton, *The Poetics of Spice: Romantic Consumerism and the Exotic* (Cambridge, 2000), 71, 72; Hoxby, *Mammon's Music*, 155, 289n14.

43. Dzelzainis, "The Politics of *Paradise Lost*," 547–70.

44. "To Sir Henry Vane the Younger," in John Milton, *Complete Poems and Major Prose*, ed. Merritt Y. Hughes (Indianapolis, 2003), line 6.

45. Dzelzainis, "The Politics of *Paradise Lost*," 564–65.

46. For Dutch portrayals of the English as devils, see Elizabeth Staffell, "The Horrible Tail-Man and the Anglo-Dutch Wars," *Journal of the Warburg and Courtauld Institutes* 63 (2000): 169–86.

47. "The Character of Holland," in Andrew Marvell, *The Poems of Andrew Marvell*, ed. Nigel Smith, revised ed. (Harlow, 2007), 53–54.

48. Flannagan, *The Riverside Milton*, 399n164. It is doubtful that the word "Drugs" suggested evil; rather, spices were considered medicinal.

49. This atlas appeared in a two-volume edition in 1635, was expanded into four volumes in 1645, six in 1655, and finally twelve in 1662.

50. For European involvement in the Maluku, see Leonard Andaya, *The World of Maluku: Eastern Indonesia in the Early Modern Period* (Honolulu, 1993), 114–56.

51. Ibid., 139.

52. Peter Mundy, *The Travels of Peter Mundy, in Europe and Asia, 1608–1667*, 5 vols. (Cambridge, 1907), 2nd ser., no. 17, 1:16. See also Henry A. Ormerod, *Piracy in the Ancient World: An Essay in Mediterranean History* (Totowa, N.J., 1978), 37.

53. Philip Gosse, *The History of Piracy* (New York, 1932), 109–111; also cited in William Slights and Shelley Woloshyn, "English Bess, English Pirates, English Drama: Feminism and Imperialism on the High Seas," *Explorations in Renaissance Culture* 33 (2007): 261.

54. Anne Pérotin-Dumon, "The Pirate and the Emperor: Power and the Law on the Seas, 1450–1850," in *Political Economy*, ed. Tracy, 223–24; see Michael N. Pearson, "Corruption and Corsairs in Sixteenth-Century Western India: A Functional Analysis," in *The Age of Partnership: Europeans in Asia before Domination*, ed. Blair B. King and Michael Pearson (Honolulu, 1979); Pearson, *The Portuguese in India: New Cambridge History of India* (Cambridge, 1988), 44–51; and Denys Lombard, "Y a-t-il une continuité des réseaux marchands asiatiques?" in *Marchands et hommes d'affaires asiatiques dans l'Océan Indien et la Mer de Chine 13ᵉ–20ᵉ siècles*, ed. Denys Lombard and J. Aubin (Paris, 1988), 11–18.

55. Janice E. Thompson, *Mercenaries, Pirates, and Sovereigns: State-Building and Extraterritorial Violence in Early Modern Europe* (Princeton, N.J., 1994), 39, 32.

56. Ernst van Veen, *Decay or Defeat? An Inquiry into the Portuguese Decline in Asia, 1580–1645* (Leiden, 2000), 191n75. For VOC implementation of privateering against the Portuguese, see 173–207.

57. Sir Thomas Wilson, *The State of England, anno Dom. 1600*, ed. F. J. Fisher (London, 1936), 40.

58. For VOC methods, see Ernst van Veen, "VOC Strategies in the Far East (1605–1640)," *Bulletin of Portuguese/Japanese Studies* 3 (2001): 85–105. For the Chinese case, see Tonio Andrade, "The Company's Chinese Pirates: How the Dutch East India Company Tried to Lead a Coalition of Pirates to War against China, 1621–1662," *Journal of World History* 15 (2005): 415–44; outmaneuvered by the pirates, the VOC failed to prevail against state-sponsored privateering rivaling their own.

59. Quint, *Epic and Empire*, 254.

60. Luís de Camões, *Os Lusíadas*, ed. Frank Pierce (Oxford, 1973).

61. Staffell, "The Horrible Tail-Man," 175.

62. Stephen Gosson, *The Trumpet of Warre* (London, 1598), sig. F1v.

63. Thomas Watson, *A Body of Practical Divinity, Consisting of above One Hundred Seventy Six Sermons on the Lesser Catechism Composed by The Reverend Assembly of Divines at Westminster* (London, 1692), 835.

64. Cicero, *De officiis*, trans. Walter Miller, Loeb Classical Library (Cambridge, Mass., 1913), 3.29; translation, 385. Coke 2 *Institutes* 113 is cited in Sir William Blackstone, *Commentaries on the Laws of England*, 4 vols. (Philadelphia, 1902–15), 4:70–72. See also Mackenzie Dalzell Chalmers and Douglas Owen,

A Digest of the Law Relating to Marine Insurance, 2nd ed. (London, 1903), appendix 2, note E, 169.

65. Augustine, *City of God, II,* books 4–7, trans. W. M. Green (Cambridge, 1963), book 4.4, 2:16–17.

66. Hoxby, *Mammon's Music,* 155; Quint sees Satan wavering between the heroic and mercantile in *Epic and Empire,* 163–66.

67. David Loewenstein, *Milton and the Drama of History: Historical Vision, Iconoclasm, and the Literary Imagination* (Cambridge, 1990), 96, argues that Milton appropriates Augustine's sixfold scheme of history, while Regina Schwartz, *Remembering and Repeating: On Milton's Theology and Poetics* (1988, repr., Chicago, 1993), 51, notes, "All of the vices Augustine links to curiosity emerge in Satan's quest for knowledge." See also Peter A. Fiore, *Milton and Augustine: Patterns of Augustinian Thought in "Paradise Lost"* (University Park, 1981); and J. Christopher Warner, *The Augustinian Epic, Petrarch to Milton* (Ann Arbor, 2005).

68. Ormerod, *Piracy in the Ancient World,* 59.

69. Dzelzainis, "The Politics of *Paradise Lost,*" 565, suggests that when Satan considers, "Whether of open war or covert guile, / We now debate" (*PL* 2.41–42), he is "selectively quoting St. Augustine's dictum that if a war is just to begin with it does not matter whether you subsequently win it in open combat or by guile."

70. Augustine, *City of God,* book 4.15; Erasmus to Dukes Frederick and George of Saxony, June 5, 1517, in *Opus epistolarum Desiderii Erasmi,* 12 vols. (Oxford, 1906–58), 2:579–86, cited in David Armitage, "Literature and Empire," in *The Origins of Empire: British Overseas Enterprise to the Close of the Seventeenth Century,* ed. Nicholas Canny, vol. 1, *The Oxford History of the British Empire,* ed. William Roger Louis (Oxford, 1998), 109. Rosemary Masek, "Erasmus, Desiderius," in *A Milton Encyclopedia,* ed. William B. Hunter, John T. Shawcross, and John M. Steadman (Lewisburg, Pa., 1978–83), 3:66–67, suggests that several lines in *Paradise Lost* (2.496–505) are borrowed from Erasmus's commentary on war.

71. Samuel Pecke, *A Perfect Diurnall of Some Passages in Parliament,* no. 288, Tuesday, January 30 (London, 1649), 2317.

72. David Masson, *Life of John Milton: Narrated in Connexion with the Political, Ecclesiastical, and Literary History of His Time,* 7 vols. (London, 1859–94), 5:253, letter 75.

73. Marchamont Nedham, *Mercurius Politicus,* October 31, 1650, 346; Andrew Marvell, *The First Anniversary of the Government under... the Lord Protector,* l.384, in *The Poems of Andrew Marvell,* ed. Nigel Smith (Harrow, 2007).

74. James Harrington, *The Commonwealth of Oceana* and *A System of Politics,* ed. J. G. A. Pocock (Cambridge, 1992), 249.

75. Samuel R. Gardiner, *History of the Commonwealth and Protectorate, 1649–1656,* 4 vols. (London, 1903), 3:304–05. See also David Armitage, "The Cromwellian Protectorate and the Languages of Empire," *Historical Journal* 35 (1992): 531–55.

76. Worden, *Literature and Politics,* 114n124.

77. David Armitage, *The Ideological Origins of the British Empire* (Cambridge, 2000), 31.

78. Nicholas Canny, "The Origins of Empire: An Introduction," in *Origins of Empire*, 1; Armitage, *Ideological Origins*, 31.

79. Wilson, *The State of England*, 1.

80. Richard Koebner, *Empire* (Cambridge, 1961), 52–56.

81. James Henrisoun, *An Exhortacion to the Scottes to Conforme Themselves to the Honourable, Expedient, and Godly Union Betweene the Two Realmes of Englande and Scotland* (1547), in *The Complaynt of Scotlande with ane Exortatione to the Thre Estaits to be Vigilante in Deffens of Their Public Veil*, ed. James A. H. Murray (London, 1872), 218–19; cited in Armitage, *Ideological Origins*, 39.

82. *Journal of the House of Commons*, vol. 1:1547–1629 (1802), 182–83, from *British History Online*, 23 April 1604; available at http://www.british-history. ac.uk/report.aspx?compid=3772; accessed September 21, 2010.

83. Milton may be following the Augustinianism of Spenser, whom he admired. Book 1's Augustinian structure, with its House of Pride and House of Holiness corresponding to the cities of man and of God, has been noted by commentators: A. C. Hamilton, *The Structure of Allegory in the "Faerie Queene"* (Oxford, 1961), 67; John Erskine Hankins, *Source and Meaning in Spenser's Allegory* (Oxford, 1971), 114; Åke Bergvall, "The Theology of the Sign: St. Augustine and Spenser's Legend of Holiness," *SEL* 33 (1999): 21–42. Arguably, *The Faerie Queene*, book 1, similarly distinguishes between *rex* and *imperator:* true Una is the "daughter of a king" (*FQ* 1.1.48.5, 1.3.2.5, and 1.7.43.3), while the false Duessa is "sole daughter of an Emperour, / He that the wide West under his rule has, / And high hath set his throne, where *Tiberis* doth pas" (*FQ* 1.2.22.7–9). In his edition, Hamilton's gloss calls attention to "the distinction in the phrase 'Renowmed kings, and sacred Emperours' (III iii 23.1) and the contest at II x 51 between the Roman emperor and the British king." Associated with both the false Roman church and the Roman Empire, Duessa's descent from emperors is a hollow magnificence. All citations to *The Faerie Queene* are from Edmund Spenser, *The Faerie Queene*, ed. A. C. Hamilton (London, 1977).

84. On the difference between *imperium* and *regnum* in Augustine, see Robert Dodaro, "Pirates or Superpowers: Reading Augustine in a Hall of Mirrors," *New Blackfriars* 72.845 (1991): 9–19; and Michael Hanby, "Democracy and Its Demons," in *Augustine and Politics*, ed. John Doody, Kevin L. Hughes, and Kim Paffenroth (Lanham, 2005), 136n26.

85. Hugo Grotius, *The Free Sea*, trans. Richard Hakluyt, ed. David Armitage (Indianapolis, 2004), 13.

86. Grotius, *The Free Sea*, 15.

87. Pérotin-Dumon, "The Pirate and the Emperor," 197–98.

88. Donald F. Lach, *Asia in the Making of Europe*, 2 vols. (Chicago, 1970), 2:401–03; and R. J. Forbes, "The Sailing Chariot," in *The Principal Works of Simon Stevin*, ed. E. J. Dijksterhuis, 6 vols. (Amsterdam, 1955–66), 5:3–4. Abraham

Ortelius published his map of China in *Theatrum orbis terrarum* (Antwerp, 1584). The land yachts are clearly visible in the right bottom corner: see reproduction in Ashley and Miles Baynton-Williams, *New Worlds: Maps from the Age of Discovery* (London, 2006), 41.

89. My thanks to Iain McClure for pointing me to the engraving and suggesting the Orangist connection. The engraving is reproduced in Dijksterhuis, ed., *The Principal Works of Simon Stevin*, opposite 103.

90. Simon Schama, *The Embarrassment of Riches: An Interpretation of Dutch Culture in the Golden Age* (New York, 1987), 363–65. For other satirical prints featuring the *zeilwagen*, see Arthur Eijffinger, "Zin en beeld: Enige kanttekeningen bij twee historieprenten," *Oud Holland* 93 (1979): 251–69.

91. Sidney Gottlieb, "Milton's Land-Ships and John Wilkins," *MP* 84 (1986): 61. See also Frank Livingstone Huntley, "Vultures, Chinese Land-Ships, and Milton's 'Paradise of Fools,'" *Essays in Persuasion: On Seventeenth-Century Literature* (Chicago, 1981), 133–41.

92. See Pieter Geyl, *Orange and Stuart, 1641–1672* (New York, 1969).

93. Quint, *Epic and Empire*, 255.

94. Grotius, *The Free Sea*, 15.

95. Peter Borschberg, "Hugo Grotius, East India Trade and the King of Johor," *Journal of Southeast Asian Studies* 30 (1999): 225–48.

96. Karen Edwards, *Milton and the Natural World: Science and Poetry in "Paradise Lost"* (Cambridge, 1999), 153.

97. Benjamin Schmidt, *Innocence Abroad: The Dutch Imagination and the New World, 1570–1670* (Cambridge, 2001), 111–22.

Notes to Baker, " 'Greedily she ingorg'd' "

I thank Paul Harvey, Laura Lunger Knoppers, James Todesca, and an anonymous reader for *Milton Studies* for helpful comments on an earlier version of this essay, and especially the Reverend Dr. James Shumard, who first drew my attention to the language of John 6:54.

1. John Milton, *Paradise Lost*, 9.732, in *John Milton: Complete Poetry and Major Prose*, ed. Merritt Y. Hughes (New York, 1957). All citations of Milton's poetry are from this edition and are hereafter cited parenthetically in the text.

2. The rising intensity of the act of eating which I emphasize here (taste—eat—ingorge) complements Eve's related linguistic "descent [of] fair-fell-foul" identified by William G. Madsen, *From Shadowy Types to Truth: Studies in Milton's Symbolism* (New Haven, 1968), 150.

3. Christopher Ricks, *Milton's Grand Style* (Oxford, 1963), 63.

4. The *OED* states that a connection between *gorge* and the Latin *gurges* is "very doubtful," but the unabridged *Webster's Third New International Dictionary* (Springfield, Mo., 1981) lists no such qualification in describing it as an

alteration of the Latin. I thank Paul Harvey for privately pointing out the rather complicated Old French linkages between these words. For consistency, I have retained Milton's spelling.

5. See, for example, *The Hours of Catherine of Cleves,* intro. John Plummer (New York, [1966]), plates 47, 48, and 99.

6. Jamie Ferguson, "Satan's Supper: Language and Sacrament in *Paradise Lost,*" in *Uncircumscribed Mind: Reading Milton Deeply,* ed. Charles W. Durham and Kristin A. Pruitt (Selinsgrove, Pa., 2008), 134.

7. Contrast Eve's gluttonous eating of the apple with her frugality, moderation, and hospitality in the banquet with Raphael when, as Ann Torday Gulden, "Milton's Eve and Wisdom: The 'Dinner Party' Scene in *Paradise Lost,*" *MQ* 32 (1998): 140, notes, "she is aware of her role as Adam's helper and her association with the natural world, which indicates her 'regenerate reason.'"

8. See Michael Lieb, *The Dialectics of Creation: Patterns of Birth and Regeneration in "Paradise Lost"* (Amherst, Mass., 1970), 168–69; Glenda Jacobs, "John Milton: Division in Authority in *Paradise Lost,*" *English Studies in Africa* 27 (1984): 101; and Jun Harada, "Self and Language in the Fall," in *Milton Studies,* vol. 5, ed. James D. Simmonds (Pittsburgh, 1973), 217; Anne Cotterill, *Digressive Voices in Early Modern English Literature* (Oxford, 2004), 198; Mandy Green, *Milton's Ovidian Eve* (Farnham, UK, 2009), 173.

9. John N. King, *Milton and Religious Controversy: Satire and Polemic in "Paradise Lost"* (Cambridge, 2000), 156; Thomas Stroup, *Religious Rite and Ceremony in Milton's Poetry* (Lexington, Ky., 1968), 38; and Anne Barbeau Gardiner, "Milton's Parody of Catholic Hymns in Eve's Temptation and Fall: Original Sin as a Paradigm of 'Secret Idolatries,'" *SP* 91 (1994): 216–31. Stroup asserts that lines 14–44 of book 9 are intended by Milton "as an adumbration of the Lord's supper and that he expected his readers to recognize it as such" (43).

10. John C. Ulreich Jr., "Milton on the Eucharist: Some Second Thoughts about Sacramentalism," in *Milton and the Middle Ages,* ed. John C. Mulryan (Lewisburg, Pa., 1982), 32–56, argues that Milton's strict antisacramentalism as expressed in *De doctrina Christiana* is not as consistently maintained in *Paradise Lost;* he rejects William Madsen's contention that the sacramental nature of the physical world as expressed by Raphael in book 5 is characteristic only of the prelapsarian universe (cf. Madsen, *From Shadowy Types to Truth,* 87, 89). Ulreich finds it "difficult to accept the notion that Milton's vision is apparently sacramental in one place and radically secular in another" (40). However, it is not the nature of Milton's poetic vision itself but that which *is envisioned* which changes. Eve's action has severed the transubstantial bond joining matter and spirit as it existed before the Fall. As Susannah B. Mintz, *Threshold Poetics: Milton and Intersubjectivity* (Newark, Del., 2003), 107, points out, "Eve and Adam's greedy 'engorg[ing]' (9.791) of the forbidden fruit perverts the 'real hunger' (5.437) and intersubjective nourishing of the unfallen cosmos." Ulreich allows that, while Milton "emphatically rejects the Catholic dogma [of transubstantiation], he

embraces certain of its philosophical and imaginative implications" (44). One such artistic implication, I argue, is that Eve herself is parodically transubstantiated in a mockery of that doctrine.

11. Unless otherwise noted, citations from the Bible are to the King James (Authorized) Version.

12. Quotations from the Geneva translation of the Bible, cited in the text, are to *The Geneva Bible: A Facsimile of the 1560 Edition*, ed. Lloyd E. Berry (1969; repr., Peabody, Mass., 2007). As Luther explained in his sermon on John 6:35, "For to eat, to come to Christ, and to believe in Christ are all one and the same thing" (23:43). See *Luther's Works*, ed. Jaroslav Pelikan (St. Louis, 1959).

13. John 6:35 contains the first of the seven notable "I am" statements by Jesus in this Gospel, a pattern that Satan may be mocking in his own boasting, self-referential style in the temptation speech in *Paradise Lost*—for example, "look on mee, / Mee who have touch'd and tasted" (9.687–88), and also 9.680–81, 9.710–12, and 9.720. Satan's parody of these statements becomes explicit in *Paradise Regained* (4.518–20); see Stella Revard, "The Gospel of John and *Paradise Regained:* Jesus as 'True Light,'" in *Milton and Scriptural Tradition: The Bible into Poetry*, ed. James H. Sims and Leland Ryken (Columbia, Mo., 1984), 148–49. When Satan states, "Now I feel thy Power / Within me clear, not only to discern / Things in thir Causes, but to trace the ways / Of highest Agents deem'd however wise" (9.680–83), Milton may also be rendering a satanic version of Calvin's commentary on John 6:63: "But those who lift up their eyes to the virtue of the spirit diffused throughout the flesh will feel (*sentient*) from the effect itself and the experience of faith that it is not for nothing called 'life-giving'" (qtd. in Bruce A. Gerrish, *Grace and Gratitude: The Eucharistic Theology of John Calvin* [Minneapolis, 1993], 131). Compare also Adam and Eve, who "fancy that they feel / Divinity within them" (*PL* 9.1009–10) after they have eaten the fruit.

14. Henry Bettenson, ed., *Documents of the Christian Church*, 2nd ed. (London, 1963), 328.

15. Massey Hamilton Shepherd Jr., *The Oxford American Prayer Book Commentary* (New York, 1950), 608. An instance of Luther's rejection of the doctrine appears in article 2, section 5 of the Smalcald Articles; see *Martin Luther's Basic Theological Writings*, ed. Timothy F. Lull (Minneapolis, 1989), 529. The Protestant position is popularly expressed in a poem wrongly attributed to Elizabeth I in a 1688 broadside, "*Queen Elizabeth's Opinion concerning Transubstantiation, or the Real Presence of Christ in the Blessed Sacrament; with some Prayers and Thanksgivings composed by Her in Imminent Dangers.*" The broadside proclaims in part: "His real body was but in the Sign, / He gave his Flesh, and Blood in Bread and Wine: / For if his Body he did then divide / He must have eat himself before he dy'd." On the poem's erroneous attribution, see Steven W. May, *Queen Elizabeth I: Selected Works* (New York, 2004), 330.

16. Jeremy Taylor, *The real presence and spiritual of Christ in the blessed sacrament proved against the doctrine of transubstantiation* (London, 1653), 46, 50. Section 3 of this work is an extended discussion of John 6 as an argument against the Catholic position. In addition to the passage cited above, Taylor seems to parallel Milton's purpose concerning Eve's desire for the "Wisdom-giving Plant" (*PL* 9.679) when he cites Plato: "And *Socrates* in *Plato's* banquet said well; *Wisdome is not a thing that can be communicated by local or corporal contiguity*" (49).

17. Ibid., 61. In his commentary on John 6:52–59, C. K. Barrett, *Peake's Commentary on the Bible*, gen. ed. Matthew Black (Middlesex, 1962), 853, explains, "Through [Christ's] complete sacrifice of himself arises the possibility that men may feed upon him, that is, may enter into a relation with the Son analogous to the Son's relation with the Father."

18. Ira Clark, "*Paradise Regained* and the Gospel according to John," *MP* 71 (1973): 1–15, emphasizes that "John does not supply dogma alone; its foci provide the literary matrix for *Paradise Regained* as well," suggesting that Milton also used key theological terms peculiar to John's terminology. Louis Martz, "*Paradise Regained:* The Meditative Combat," *ELH* 27 (1960): 238, also notes the influence of John.

19. On Milton's use of Robert Estienne, see Harris Fletcher, *The Intellectual Development of John Milton*, 2 vols. (Urbana, Ill., 1961), 2:106–08. See also Henri Estienne (Stephanus), *He Kaine Diatheke Novum Testamentum: ad editionem H. Steph* (London, 1587), 143. The quality of Milton's three Greek poems is inferior to his accomplished knowledge of Greek literature in general and the Greek New Testament specifically; see Douglas Bush, *A Variorum Commentary on the Poems of John Milton: The Latin and Greek Poems* (New York, 1970), 255–56. W. R. Parker, *Milton: A Biography*, Vol. 1 (Oxford, 1968), notes that Milton had taught John and Edward Phillips a chapter of the Greek New Testament weekly (209, 293), that his memory of biblical texts in their original languages "was excellent" (481), and, significantly for Milton's understanding of John 6, that "he insists that knowledge of God's will is not for the literal-minded" (281). While Milton was certainly conversant with the Junius-Tremellius Latin Bible and the Authorized Version, David Norton, *A History of the English Bible as Literature* (Cambridge, 2000), 176, notes that "his fidelity was primarily to the originals" in Greek and Hebrew. In ascribing *De doctrina Christiana* to Milton, I follow the arguments advanced in *Milton and the Manuscript of "De Doctrina Christiana,"* ed. Gordon Campbell et al. (Oxford, 2007). Milton's use of Greek diction in his English work has also been discussed by John K. Hale, "Milton's Greek, 1644–1645: Two Notes," *MQ* 34 (March 2000): 13–16; Ann Keplinger, "Milton's *An Apology for Smectymnuus,*" *Explicator* 30 (Apr. 1972): item 66; and Carter Revard and Stella Revard, "Milton's Amerc't: The Lost Greek Connection," *MQ* 12 (1978): 105–06.

20. Henry George Liddell and Robert Scott, *A Greek-English Lexicon* (Oxford, 1968), s.v. τρώγω.

21. See the entry in Cleon L. Rogers Jr., and Cleon L. Rogers III, *The New Linguistic and Exegetical Key to the Greek New Testament* (Grand Rapids, Mich., 1998), 198. Leonhard Goppelt adds "to bite" and "(audibly) to chew" in his entry on τρώγω, in Gerhard Kittel et al., *Theological Dictionary of the New Testament* (Grand Rapids, Mich., 1972), 8:236. The Wakefield Master captures the mutual sense of *trōgo* and *ingorge* when his Satan instructs Eve (who then likewise instructs Adam) to "Bite on boldly." See the Wakefield play of *The Fall of Man* in *Medieval Drama*, ed. David Bevington (Boston, 1975), 270.

22. The other occurrences of *trōgo* appear in John 6:56–58. F. F. Bruce, *The Gospel and Epistles of John* (Grand Rapids, Mich., 1983), 159, doubts "if much significance can be read into the use of the one verb or the other in the present context; it may be a further instance of the Evangelist's predilection for ringing the changes on synonyms." However, the change in diction could be intentional. As Bruce notes in his comment on 6:34, Christ's audience "still understand[s] his words in a material sense; he therefore uses a new form of words to make his meaning plainer" (152). See also Luther's remark in note 28 below.

23. Ibid., 159. The German reformer Andreas Bodenstein von Karlstadt, in fact, made this distinction the subject of a humorous quip: "Wenn ein pfaff spricht. Das ist mein leyb, nemet esset das brodt, und wir essen, so fressen wir einen lausichten pfaffen" (When a priest says, This is my body, take, eat the bread, and we eat, we are gobbling up a lousy priest). Qtd. in Ronald J. Sider, *Andreas Bodenstein von Karlstadt: The Development of His Thought, 1517–1525* (Leiden, 1974), 293n355.

24. Rudolph Schnackenburg, *The Gospel according to St. John*, 2 vols. (New York, 1982), 2:62; and Rudolph Bultmann, *The Gospel of John: A Commentary* (Philadelphia, 1951), 236n3.

25. Rogers and Rogers, *New Linguistic and Exegetical Key*, 55.

26. Edward Leigh, *Critica Sacra in Two Parts* (London, 1662), 266.

27. Milton's linkage of gustatory and animal imagery in the antiprelatical tracts extends a pattern of imagery originating in his earlier works; see John A. Via, "Milton's Antiprelatical Tracts: The Poet Speaks in Prose," in *Milton Studies*, vol. 5, ed. James D. Simmonds (Pittsburgh, 1973), 87–127.

28. Docetism is addressed in the entry for τρώγω in Walter Bauer, *A Greek-English Lexicon of the New Testament and Other Early Christian Literature*, 2nd ed., revised and augmented by F. Wilbur Gingrich and Frederick W. Danker (Chicago, 1979), 829. A contemporary Roman Catholic commentator, Francis J. Moloney, S.J., *The Gospel of John* (Collegeville, Minn., 1998), 221, observes, "The shift from the more respectable verb 'to eat' (*phagein*) to another word that indicates the physical crunching with the teeth (*trōgein*) accentuates that Jesus refers to a real experience of eating." In his sermon on John 6:35, Luther

asserted that Christ chose his language carefully for its persuasive effect upon the Jews, whose devotion to their "bellies" recalls the prelates Milton targeted as well as Eve's gluttony: "In view of their coarse way of thinking, Christ adds a commentary. He puts the subject before them in puzzling words. Without such crude strange expressions it would be impossible to tear the thoughts of these coarse sows and bellies away from the idea of gluttony and carousing. Thus the Lord resorts to this manner of speech before these rude Jews that they might tell themselves…that he who believes in Him comes to Him and eats Him" (Pelikan, *Luther's Works*, 23:43).

29. Eve's sensuous perception of the fruit itself—especially its color and odor (*PL* 9.575–83)—only intensifies the physicality of her eating. For Augustine's influence on Calvin, see David J. Marshall's entry on Calvin in *Augustine through the Ages: An Encyclopedia*, gen. ed. Allan D. Fitzgerald, OSA (Grand Rapids, Mich., 1999), 116–20.

30. Gerrish, *Grace and Gratitude*, 106.

31. Ronald Wallace, *Calvin's Doctrine of the Word and Sacrament* (Edinburgh, 1953), 21.

32. William J. Bouwsma, *John Calvin: A Sixteenth Century Portrait* (New York, 1988), 217. Luther also criticized the practice of solitary communion as "uncertain and unnecessary" (Lull, *Basic Theological Writings*, 505).

33. For an overview of Milton's use of Augustine, see Peter A. Fiore, *Milton and Augustine: Patterns of Augustinian Thought in "Paradise Lost"* (University Park, Pa., 1981).

34. Compare also the Geneva gloss on John 6:52: "Flesh cannot make a difference between fleshly eating, which is done by the help of the teeth, and spiritual eating which consists in faith."

35. John Calvin, *Institutes of the Christian Religion*, trans. Henry Beveridge (Peabody, Mass., 2008), 921; hereafter cited parenthetically in the text.

36. Augustine's bluntest statement on his theology of the reception of the Eucharist is probably his frequently noted comment on John 6:27–29: "To what purpose dost thou make ready teeth also and stomach? Believe and thou hast eaten already"; see Philip Schaff, *A Select Library of the Nicene and Post-Nicene Fathers of the Christian Church. St. Augustin, Homilies on the Gospel of John* (1888; repr., Grand Rapids, Mich., 1986), vol. 7, tractate 25, 164. Luther repeats this statement (without mentioning Augustine) in his sermon on John 6:35 (Pelikan, *Luther's Works*, 23:43). On this point, however, as Ronald Wallace, *Calvin's Doctrine*, 211 notes, Calvin parts company with Augustine by rejecting the idea "that the life which we obtain from Him is obtained by simple knowledge (*simplici cognitione*)." On Augustine's understanding of the Communion as sacrament, see Pamela Jackson's entry on "Eucharist" in Fitzgerald, *Augustine through the Ages*, 330–34.

37. Pelikan, *Luther's Works*, 23:119. The words of administration for the Communion bread in the 1559 *Book of Common Prayer* (which were taken from the

1552 edition) employ English equivalents for both *phago* and *trōgo:* "Take and eat this in remembrance that Christ died for thee, and feed on him in thy heart by faith, with thanksgiving"; see *The Book of Common Prayer 1559*, ed. John E. Booty (Charlottesville, Va., 1976; reissued 2005), 264; see also 401. Thomas Cranmer, *Answer to a crafty and sophistical cavillation devised by Stephen Gardiner* (London, 1551), states that Christ "is effectually present, and effectually worketh not in the bread and wine, but in the godly receivers of them, to whome he giveth his own flesh spiritually to feed upon, and his own blood to quench their great inward thirst"; qtd. in Diarmaid MacCulloch, *Thomas Cranmer* (New Haven, 1996), 615.

38. *The New Testament of Our Lord Jesus Christ, Translated out of Greek by Theod. Beza* (London, 1577).

39. John Leonard, *Naming in Paradise: Milton and the Language of Adam and Eve* (Oxford, 1990), asserts, "The Latin phrase *mors edax* makes possible a third meaning: 'she did not know death, which devours'" (210). The Geneva gloss on John 6:53 may also contribute to the meaning of the passage: "If Christ is present, life is present, but when Christ is absent, then Death is present." Milton's line also recalls Death's desire to "stuff this Maw" (*PL* 10.601) and to "satisfy his Rav'nous Maw" (10.991).

40. Annabel Patterson, *Milton's Words* (Oxford, 2009), 105.

41. Kenneth Haynes, *English Literature and Ancient Languages* (Oxford, 2003), 79. Norton, *History of the English Bible*, 178, remarks, "The tension between classicism and Biblicism is fundamental to Milton as Christian artist, and the styles and methods of his great biblical works suggest that, in important ways, it remained unresolved.".

42. Timothy Rosendale, *Liturgy and Literature in the Making of Protestant England* (Cambridge, 2007), 187.

43. John Calvin, *Commentary on the Gospel according to John*, 2 vols., trans. William Pringle (Grand Rapids, Mich., 1949), 1:260. On Calvin's Eucharistic theology, see Wallace, *Calvin's Doctrine*, 197–233, and Gerrish, *Grace and Gratitude*, esp. 124–90. In his notable letter to Peter Martyr Vermigli of August 8, 1555, Calvin declared both his belief in the Real Presence of Communion and his inability to explain it: "Hence I adore the mystery rather than labor to understand it" (quoted in Gerrish, *Grace and Gratitude*, 128). Calvin's frank admission of his lack of wisdom concerning the nature of the sacrament contrasts ironically with Eve's confident expectation that she will possess complete wisdom. See also Gerrish, "Calvin's Eucharistic Piety," in *Calvin Studies Society Papers 1995, 1997*, ed. David Foxgrover (Grand Rapids, Mich., 1998), 52–65. For a general summary of major Protestant views on the nature of the Eucharist, see Hans J. Hillerbrand, *The Division of Christendom: Christianity in the Sixteenth Century* (Louisville, Ky., 2007), 389–93.

44. Cranmer's rejection of *ex opere operato* was explicit. Concerning the Communion elements, he said that, for those "as worthily receive the same, they

have a wholesome effect and operation; and yet not that of the work wrought, as some men speak. Which word, as it is strange, and unknown to Holy Scripture; so it engendereth no godly, but a very superstitious sense" (qtd. in Shepherd, *Oxford American Prayer*, 607). Milton is, like Calvin, critical of both Lutheran and Catholic theologies of Communion. As Gerrish, *Gratitude and Grace*, 160, notes, "No one who identifies sacramental mediation with the Roman Catholic doctrine of *ex opere operato* efficacy, or who accepts the Lutheran doctrine that there is no Real Presence without a *manducatio oralis* (orally consuming the body), will expect to find either doctrine in Calvin, who expressly rejected them both as mistaken."

45. According to Clark, *"Paradise Regained* and the Gospel," 12, "From the verse on the superiority of the spirit to the flesh, Zwingli formed the theory of signs and seals Milton followed when emphasizing the metaphorical and spiritual value of the bread to avoid the cannibalism he detected and detested in transubstantiation."

46. John Frith qtd. in Rosendale, *Liturgy and Literature*, 144.

47. When Luther describes the Jews' attitude toward Christ's command to eat, he captures Eve's eagerness for the fruit: "If Christ had gorged them with food and drink every day, then he would have been a welcome Christ" (Pelikan, *Luther's Works*, 23:30). Cranmer's views on the Eucharist changed over time, but MacCulloch, *Cranmer*, 392, contends that he held to "a 'spiritual presence' view of the Eucharist from at least 1548." I do not suggest that Milton's theology of Communion agreed with those of these reformers on every point (or that all of them presented a united front), but rather that, where the nature of the Eucharist is concerned, they saw the Roman doctrine of transubstantiation as fundamentally flawed. On the differences between Anglican and Puritan understandings of Communion, see John F. H. New, *Anglican and Puritan: The Basis of Their Opposition, 1558–1640* (Stanford, Calif., 1964), 67–72. Milton differed from Luther's opinion on consubstantiation, but as Georgia B. Christopher, *Milton and the Science of the Saints* (Princeton, N.J., 1982), 12, points out, he agreed with the text-centered position taken in the commentaries of Luther and Calvin "that one encountered the Real Presence in biblical promise."

48. Desiderius Erasmus, *The first tome or volume of the Paraphrase of Erasmus upon the newe testamente* (London, 1548).

49. Susannah B. Mintz, *Threshold Poetics: Milton and Intersubjectivity* (Newark, Del., 2003), 109.

50. The *OED* defines *mammock* as "to break, cut or tear into fragments or shreds" whether by hands or teeth, citing *Coriolanus* (1.3.71): "He did so set his teeth and tear it. Oh, I warrant how he mammocked it." One assumes this would also describe the eating habits of the "well-feasted Priest" in *Samson Agonistes* (line 1419).

51. Regina M. Schwartz, *Sacramental Poetics at the Dawn of Secularism: When God Left the World* (Stanford, Calif., 2008), 9.

52. R. A. Shoaf, *Milton, Poet of Duality: A Study of Semiosis in the Poetry and the Prose* (New Haven, 1985), 71, calls attention to Adam and Eve's replacement of an ideal human nature with a sinful one in their attempt to duplicate the divine knowledge of God: "But when man fell, he fell into impersonation, because the Fall itself, Christ makes clear, was impersonation, doubling, copying, substitution, reiteration." The mechanism by which this faulty doubling is attempted is, I suggest, their belief in what Milton sees as the flawed doctrine of transubstantiation.

53. Denise Gigante, "Milton's Aesthetics of Eating," *Diacritics* 30 (2000): 90. As Marshall Grossman, "Milton's 'Transubstantiate': Interpreting the Sacrament in *Paradise Lost*," *MQ* 16.2 (1982): 45, explains, "the value of the sacrament is not in eating the host but in following through the exercise of understanding that leads to a comprehension of God's grace and the prospect of salvation."

54. According to Wayne Shumaker, *Unpremeditated Verse: Feeling and Perception in "Paradise Lost"* (Princeton, N.J., 1967), 167–93, Eve's bodily awareness of her fall is an example of her "somatic perception."

55. The temptation of the bread is also alluded to by Christ in John 6:26, 31. Clark, "*Paradise Regained* and the Gospel," 13, notes that "Satan associates the bread imagery with prophecy, but what ought to be truthful, life-sustaining spirit is for him merely stuffing."

56. Christopher, *Milton and the Science of the Saints*, 16.

Notes Graves, "The Trinity in Milton's Hell"

1. Most famously this was proposed by Balachandra Rajan, *Paradise Lost and the Seventeenth Century Reader* (London, 1962), 46–47.

2. See for example, Stella Revard, "The Dramatic Function of the Son in *Paradise Lost*: A Commentary on Milton's Trinitarianism," *JEGP* 66 (1967): 45–58.

3. Compare Feisal G. Mohamed, "*Paradise Lost* and the Inversion of Catholic Angelology," *MQ* 36 (2002): 240–52, who argues that Milton attacks the traditional Catholic angelic hierarchies by inverting their order in his depiction of the angels in *Paradise Lost* while portraying them in an orthodox order in the devils of the epic.

4. Only twice have Miltonists suggested such a reading, and no critic has located explicit patristic references to validate it. Robert B. White, "Milton's Allegory of Sin and Death: A Comment on Backgrounds," *MP* 70 (1973): 337–41, asserts that Milton's satanic triad is essentially Trinitarian in composition, but argues that it functions merely as a diabolic imitation of Milton's Trinitarian heaven, and is not therefore satiric; it is simply "a grotesque parody in which all values have been inverted" (338). Gordon Campbell, "Popular

Traditions of God in the Renaissance," in *Reconsidering the Renaissance*, ed. Mario A. Di Cesare (Binghamton, N.Y., 1992), 501–20, proposes several aspects of Trinitarian dogma that Milton was thereby criticizing, asserting that "Milton's poem does not contain a heavenly Trinity, and that his Satanic Trinity is not a foil to the Godhead, but rather an attack on a theological doctrine which Milton regards as unsound" (509). Maureen Quilligan, *Milton's Spenser: The Politics of Reading* (London, 1983), 85–90, may have preceded Campbell by arguing that the satanic trinity is the only true representation of a nonappearing Trinity in *Paradise Lost.*

5. Michael Lieb, "Milton and 'Arianism,'" *Religion and Literature* 32 (2000): 197. Paradoxically, this contentious question has been reinvigorated by investigations into the provenance of Milton's only theological prose work, *De doctrina Christiana*. Recent important contributions from both sides of the debate include William B. Hunter, *Visitation Unimplor'd: Milton and the Authorship of "De Doctrina Christiana"* (Pittsburgh, 1998); and John P. Rumrich, "The Provenance of *De doctrina Christiana*: A View of the Present State of the Controversy," in *Milton and the Grounds of Contention*, ed. Mark R. Kelley, Michael Lieb, and John T. Shawcross (Pittsburgh, 2003), 214–33. Since Hunter's initial questioning of the treatise's provenance in 1992, Miltonists studying *Paradise Lost* have become increasingly wary of exegetical arguments based on the treatise due to the issues of authorship, attribution, collaboration, and genre that surround this document. See Stephen M. Fallon, "Milton's Arminianism and the Authorship of *De doctrina Christiana*," *TSLL* 41 (1999): 122; and Michael Lieb, "*De Doctrina Christiana* and the Question of Authorship," in *Milton Studies*, vol. 41, ed. Albert C. Labriola (Pittsburgh, 2002), 172–230. In light of this, I consider it to be prudent to investigate the thorny topic of Trinitarianism in Milton's epic poetry without a fundamental reliance on *De doctrina Christiana*. See, however, Gordon Campbell, Thomas N. Corns, John K. Hale, and Fiona J. Tweedie, *Milton and the Manuscript of "De Doctrina Christiana"* (Oxford, 2007), 161, which concludes that "*De Doctrina Christiana* rightfully belongs in the Milton canon."

6. The most comprehensive analysis of the precise nature of subordinationism in *Paradise Lost* and Milton's writings remains Michael Bauman's *Milton's Arianism* (Frankfurt am Main, 1987).

7. *John Milton: Paradise Lost*, 2nd ed., ed. Alastair Fowler (London, 1998), 2.745; references to Milton's poetry are from this Longman Annotated English Poets edition, hereafter cited in the text.

8. Athanasius, *Contra Arianos*, in *The Nicene and Post-Nicene Fathers*, 2nd ser., vol. 4, ed. Alexander Roberts, James Donaldson, Philip Schaff, and Henry Wace (Peabody, Mass., 1994), i.35. Scholars possess almost nothing thought to have been written by Arius himself, and it is important to be wary of gaining an understanding of Arius's doctrines from the writings of his avowed opponent Athanasius.

9. Athanasius, *Contra Arianos*, i.35, footnote 193. See also *A Patristic Greek Lexicon*, ed. G. W. H. Lampe (Oxford, 1961), 1402: "τρεπτός, B. moral; of rational beings, *mutable*, i.e. *liable to moral lapse*."

10. Alexander, *Epistles on the Arian Heresy*, in *The Ante-Nicene Fathers*, vol. 6, ed. Alexander Roberts, James Donaldson, Philip Schaff, Henry Wace, and A. Cleveland Coxe (Peabody, Mass., 2004), 2.2. For a brief summary of Arian beliefs at the time of Nicaea concerning the Son of God, see J. N. D. Kelly, *Early Christian Doctrines*, 5th ed. (London, 1985), 226–31. During his discussion of the Son's free-will decision to act as a savior in *Paradise Lost*, John Rumrich, *Matter of Glory: A New Preface to "Paradise Lost"* (Pittsburgh, 1987), makes the same argument for the ontological and therefore potential moral alterability of the Son: "The relegation of even the Son's existence to the realm of contingency means that his actions are voluntary…[he] could choose to forsake his father's moral will rather than be forsaken according to it" (164, 165).

11. See Maurice Kelley, "Milton and the Third Person of the Trinity," *SP* 32 (1935): 221–34; Kelley does, however, substantiate parts of his argument with a strong reliance on the epic's congruence with *De doctrina Christiana;* George W. Whiting, "The Father to the Son," *MLN* 65 (1950): 193; J. M. Evans, *"Paradise Lost" and the Genesis Tradition* (Oxford, 1968), 234; Campbell, "Popular Traditions," 508.

12. John Milton, *Of Reformation*, in *The Complete Prose Works of John Milton*, 8 vols., ed. Don M. Wolfe et al. (New Haven, 1953–82), 1:551–52; references to Milton's prose are to this edition, hereafter cited as YP.

13. See *The Letters of Saint Athanasius concerning the Holy Spirit*, trans. C. R. B. Shapland (London, 1951), 1.32.

14. David J. Melling, *"Filioque,"* in *The Blackwell Dictionary of Eastern Christianity*, ed. Ken Parry, David J. Melling, Dimitri Brady, Sidney H. Griffith, and John F. Healey (Oxford, 2001), 198–99.

15. For an exposition of these two triadologies, see Vladimir Lossky, "The Procession of the Holy Spirit in Orthodox Trinitarian Doctrine," in *In the Image and Likeness of God* (Oxford, 1975), 71–96.

16. For an account of the creation of pre-Nicene and Nicene Trinitarian doctrine, and the threats to this final orthodoxy, see Kelly, *Early Christian Doctrines*, 223–279.

17. Compare Joseph A. Galdon, *Typology and Seventeenth Century Literature* (The Hague, 1975), 15: "Steeped in this typological way of thinking and looking at Scripture, the Seventeenth Century reader would naturally have read the story of Isaac in terms of Christ's sacrifice on the cross."

18. Milton's known uncertainty about the precise identity of the brooding spirit in this biblical passage only supports an interpretation of the poem critical of Trinitarianism: in *De doctrina Christiana* Milton equivocates about how to "understand that passage in Gen. i. 2: *the spirit of God brooded*. It seems more likely, how-

ever, that we should here interpret the word as a reference to the Son, through whom, we are constantly told, the Father created all things" (YP 6:282).

19. Balachandra Rajan, *John Milton: Paradise Lost Books I and II* (London, 1964), xxix.

20. For clarification of Trinitarian doctrine, terminology, and formative argumentation, see G. L. Prestige, *God in Patristic Thought*, 2nd ed. (London, 1952); and Kelly, *Early Christian Doctrines*.

21. Adolphe Napoleon Didron, *Christian Iconography: The History of Christian Art in the Middle Ages*, vol. 2 (New York, 1965), 21.

22. Augustine, *De Trinitate*, in *The Nicene and Post-Nicene Fathers*, 1st ser., vol. 3, ed. Alexander Roberts, James Donaldson, Philip Schaff, and Henry Wace (Peabody, Mass., 1999), 6.10.12.

23. See Edgar Wind, "Appendix 2: Pagan Vestiges of the Trinity," in *Pagan Mysteries in the Renaissance*, rev. ed. (Oxford, 1980), 241–62. See also Didron, *Christian Iconography*, 1–173, for an exposition of Christian and satanic Trinitarian iconography, and Roland Mushat Frye, *Milton's Imagery and the Visual Arts: Iconographic Tradition in the Epic Poems* (Princeton, N.J., 1978), 111–24, for an examination of the iconography of Milton's infernal trinity.

24. J. McG. Bottkol, "The Holograph of Milton's Letter to Holstenius," *PMLA* 68.3 (1953): 619.

25. R. Pettazzoni, "The Pagan Origins of the Three-Headed Representation of the Christian Trinity," *Journal of the Warburg and Courtauld Institutes* 9 (1946): 151.

26. Fascinatingly, Milton in *Paradise Regained*, 4.572–76, makes a specific association between Oedipus and the Son of God; furthermore, this typological analogy also involves Satan.

27. Prestige, *God in Patristic Thought*, 254.

28. Augustine, *Homilies on the Gospel of John*, in *The Nicene and Post-Nicene Fathers*, 1st ser., vol. 7, ed. Alexander Roberts, James Donaldson, Philip Schaff, and Henry Wace (Peabody, Mass., 1999), 99.6; Athanasius, *De Trinitate et Spiritu Sancto*, n. 19, in J.-P. Migne, *Patrologiae Graecae,* 26.1212; Cyril, *Epistle xvii, Ad Nestorium, De excommunicatione*, in J.-P. Migne, *Patrologiae Graecae*, 77.117.

29. Origen, *Commentary on the Gospel of John*, in *The Ante-Nicene Fathers*, vol. 9, ed. Alexander Roberts, James Donaldson, Philip Schaff, Henry Wace, and A. Cleveland Coxe (Peabody, Mass., 2004), 2.6.

30. Shapland, *Letters of Saint Athanasius*, 1.15. Compare Gregory Nazianzen, *Oration XXXI*, in *The Nicene and Post-Nicene Fathers*, 2nd ser., vol. 7, ed. Alexander Roberts, James Donaldson, Philip Schaff, and Henry Wace (Peabody, Mass., 1994), 7.

31. Athanasius, *Contra Arianos*, 1.5.14, 1.16.

32. Tertullian, *Adversus Praxean*, in *The Ante-Nicene Fathers*, vol. 3, ed. Alexander Roberts, James Donaldson, Philip Schaff, Henry Wace, and A. Cleveland Coxe (Peabody, Mass., 2004), 10.

33. Augustine, *De Trinitate*, 15.47–48.

34. Ibid., 15.27.

35. Aquinas, *Summa Theologica*, Ia, q. 37, art. 1, ad 3um.

36. Augustine, *De Trinitate*, 8.14.

37. See, for instance, Joseph Summers, *The Muses' Method: An Introduction to "Paradise Lost"* (London, 1970), 53.

38. Justin Martyr, *First Apology*, in *The Ante-Nicene Fathers*, vol. 1, ed. Alexander Roberts, James Donaldson, Philip Schaff, Henry Wace, and A. Cleveland Coxe (Peabody, Mass., 2004), ch. lxiv.

39. Merritt Y. Hughes, "Devils to Adore for Deities," in *Studies in Honor of DeWitt T. Starnes*, ed. Thomas P. Harrison, Archibald A. Hill, Ernest C. Mossner, and James Sledd (Austin, 1967), 254.

40. Nathale Conti, *Mythologiae*, vol. 1, trans. and annotated John Mulryan and Steven Brown (Tempe, 2006), 4.5, p. 258.

41. Wind, *Pagan Mysteries*, 254; Didron, *Christian Iconography*, 160.

42. *The Poems of Abraham Cowley*, ed. A. R. Waller (Cambridge, 1905), 2.92.

43. Origen, *De Principiis*, in *The Ante-Nicene Fathers*, vol. 4, ed. Alexander Roberts, James Donaldson, Philip Schaff, Henry Wace, and A. Cleveland Coxe (Peabody, Mass., 2004), 1.2.2; Tertullian, *Adversus Praxean*, 6–7.

44. The name "Lucifer" occurs three times in *Paradise Lost* (5.760, 7.131, 10.425)—with the final instance making explicit reference to the early patristic identification "Of Lucifer, so by allusion called, / Of that bright star to Satan paragoned"; the sustained astrological metaphor of 5.700–14 equates the character Satan with "the morning star that guides / The starry flock" before his fall from heaven (5.708–09).

45. Tertullian, *Adversus Praxean*, 7.

46. James H. Sims, *The Bible in Milton's Epics* (Gainesville, Fla., 1962), 55, is typical, merely stating that the allusion is "the result of Milton's classical learning and great imaginative powers," but with no explanation of its suitability or meaning.

47. Richard Hooker, *Of the Laws of Ecclesiastical Polity*, in *Works*, 6th ed., ed. John Keble (Oxford, 1874), 1:214.

48. Theophilus, *To Autolycus*, in *The Ante-Nicene Fathers*, vol. 2, ed. Alexander Roberts, James Donaldson, Philip Schaff, Henry Wace, and A. Cleveland Coxe (Peabody, Mass., 2004), 2.22.

49. Aquinas, *Summa Theologica*, Ia, q. 27, art. 3.

50. Tertullian, *Adversus Praxean*, 5.

51. Prestige, *God in Patristic Thought*, 129.

52. Theophilus, *To Autolycus*, 2.x. See also 2.xxii.

53. Ibid., 2.x, fn. 19.

54. Tatian, *To the Greeks*, in *The Ante-Nicene Fathers*, vol. 2, ed. Alexander Roberts, James Donaldson, Philip Schaff, Henry Wace, and A. Cleveland Coxe (Peabody, Mass., 2004), ch. v.

55. This began with two seminal studies, Denis Saurat, *Milton: Man and Thinker* (London, 1925), and Harris Francis Fletcher, *Milton's Rabbinical Readings* (Urbana, Ill., 1930); some of these authors' claims for Milton's sources have subsequently been discredited.

56. Gershom Scholem, *Kabbalah* (Jerusalem, 1974), 320–26, 356–61, 385–88.

57. *The Zohar*, 5 vols., ed. Joshua Abelson, trans. Maurice Simon and Harry Sperling (1933; repr., London and New York, 1984), 2:170a.

58. Joseph Dan, "Samael, Lilith, and the Concept of Evil in Early Kabbalah," *Association of Jewish Studies Review* 5 (1980): 40.

59. Marshall Grossman, "The Genders of God and the Redemption of the Flesh in *Paradise Lost,*" in *Milton and Gender*, ed. Catherine Gimelli Martin (Cambridge, 2004), 109.

60. The fact that Milton was committed to *creatio ex Deo* cosmogony, and that Arianism adheres to orthodox *creatio ex nihilo* cosmogony, in no way fundamentally contradicts the Arian subordination of the Son of God in *Paradise Lost*.

61. Compare Frye, *Milton's Imagery and the Visual Arts*, 112: "Milton did not create the Infernal Trinity *ex nihilo*."

62. Basil, *Epistle 189*, in *The Nicene and Post-Nicene Fathers*, 2nd ser., vol. 8, ed. Alexander Roberts, James Donaldson, Philip Schaff, and Henry Wace (Peabody, Mass., 1994), 6.

63. Gregory of Nyssa, *Non Tres Dei*, in *The Nicene and Post-Nicene Fathers*, 2nd ser., vol. 5, ed. Alexander Roberts, James Donaldson, Philip Schaff, and Henry Wace (Peabody, Mass., 1994).

64. Milton's refutation in *De doctrina Christiana* of precisely this Trinitarian "proof" that explains the scriptural account of the emanation of the Holy Spirit in John 20:22 as pertaining specifically to the divine essence supports the portrayal of such a Trinitarian emanation in Milton's hell: "The terms 'emanation' and 'procession' are irrelevant to the question of the Holy Spirit's nature" (YP 6:281).

65. Basil, *De Spiritu Sancto*, in *The Nicene and Post-Nicene Fathers*, 2nd ser., vol. 8, ed. Alexander Roberts, James Donaldson, Philip Schaff, and Henry Wace (Peabody, Mass., 1994), 46.22.

66. Gregory Nazianzen, *Oration XXXII*, 8.

67. Stevie Davies and William B. Hunter, "Milton's Urania: 'The meaning, not the name I call,'" *SEL* 28 (1988): 103.

68. Origen, *Commentary on the Gospel of John*, 2.6; Irenaeus, *Adversus Haereses*, in *The Ante-Nicene Fathers*, vol. 1, ed. Alexander Roberts, James Donaldson, Philip Schaff, Henry Wace, and A. Cleveland Coxe (Peabody, Mass., 2004), 4.7.4.

69. Theophilus, *To Autolycus*, 2.15.

70. See Robert M. Grant, *The Early Christian Doctrine of God* (Charlottesville, Va., 1966), 92.

71. Origen, *De Principiis*, 1.2.6.

72. Gregory Nazianzen, *Oration XXXII*, 11. See also *Oration XXXIX*, 12.

73. John of Damascus, *An Exact Exposition of the Orthodox Faith*, in *The Nicene and Post-Nicene Fathers*, 2nd ser., vol. 9, ed. Alexander Roberts, James Donaldson, Philip Schaff, and Henry Wace (Peabody, Mass., 1994), 1.8.

74. John T. Shawcross, *John Milton: The Self and the World* (Lexington, Ky., 1993), 268.

75. See *Critical Essays from the Spectator by Joseph Addison*, ed. Donald F. Bond (Oxford, 1970), 68, 85; and *Johnson as Critic*, ed. John Wain (London, 1973), 293–94.

76. J. B. Broadbent, *Some Graver Subject: An Essay on "Paradise Lost"* (London, 1960), 131.

77. See John S. P. Tatlock, "Milton's *Sin* and *Death*," *MLN* 21 (1906): 239–40; John M. Steadman, "Milton and St. Basil: The Genesis of Sin and Death," *MLN* 73 (1958): 83–84.

78. For a good summation of sources for Milton's allegory, see John M. Steadman, "Tradition and Innovation in Milton's 'Sin': The Problem of Literary Indebtedness," *PQ* 39 (1960): 93–103.

79. For a summary of modern critical interpretations, see Samuel S. Stollman, "Satan, Sin, and Death: A Mosaic Trio in *Paradise Lost*," in *Milton Studies*, vol. 22, ed. James D. Simmonds (Pittsburgh, 1986), 101n2; see also Philip Gallagher, "'Real or Allegoric': The Ontology of Sin and Death in *Paradise Lost*," *ELR* 6 (1976): 317–35.

80. See Neil Forsyth, *The Satanic Epic* (Princeton, N.J., 2003); Michael Bryson, *The Tyranny of Heaven: Milton's Rejection of God as King* (Newark, Del., 2004); Neil D. Graves, "Typological Aporias in *Paradise Lost*," *MP* 104 (2006): 173–201.

81. John Wooten, "Satan, Satire, and Burlesque Fables in *Paradise Lost*," *MQ* 12 (1978): 52. Compare Kenneth Boris, "Allegory in *Paradise Lost*: Satan's Cosmic Journey," in *Milton Studies*, vol. 26, ed. James D. Simmonds (Pittsburgh, 1991), 101–33, who argues that the allegorical passages in *Paradise Lost*, and in particular the Odyssean wanderings of Milton's Satan, are not only understood thematically but "satirize human errors and confusions, especially false philosophical and religious beliefs.... The heroic poet could thus address considerations of doctrine in a full yet discreetly implicit way, while also attending to narrative needs; and the capacity of allegory to convey high matter in a conceitful, stimulating manner befits the heightened epic style" (116, 126).

82. See, for instance, Rajan, *John Milton*, xxix: "That Satan, Sin and Death should make up an Infernal Trinity is a natural consequence of the correspondences and contrasts that dominate the poem and establish its structural irony; and that Milton thought this particular contrast important enough to drive it virtually to the edge of blasphemy shows how vital a part of this 'structure' is intended to play in controlling and shaping our responses to the poem." For Rajan's illustrations, see 95–99.

83. See John P. Rumrich, "Milton's Arianism: Why It Matters," in *Milton and Heresy*, ed. Stephen B. Dobranski and John P. Rumrich (Cambridge, 1998),

75–92, who notes that denials of the Son's Trinitarian status "provoked authorities across seventeenth-century Europe as no other heresy could" (87).

Notes to Hequembourg, "Monism and Metaphor in *Paradise Lost*"

1. *John Milton: Complete Shorter Poems*, ed. Stella Revard (Malden, Mass., 2009).

2. Thomas Hobbes, *Leviathan*, ed. Richard Tuck (Cambridge, 1996), 20; hereafter cited in the text.

3. Thomas Hobbes, *A Short Tract on First Principles*, in *The Elements of Law Natural and Politic*, ed. Ferdinand Tönnies (London, 1969), 209.

4. Margaret Cavendish, *Philosophical and Physical Opinions* (London, 1655), 21.

5. Anne Conway, *The Principles of the Most Ancient and Modern Philosophy*, ed. Allison Coudert and Taylor Corse (Cambridge, 1996), 44, 70.

6. John Milton, *Paradise Lost: A Norton Critical Edition*, ed. Gordon Teskey (New York, 2005), 5.603–04, 3.3; hereafter cited in the text.

7. See, for example, Christopher Ricks, *Milton's Grand Style* (Oxford, 1963), 109–17; and Stanley Fish, *Surprised by Sin: The Reader in "Paradise Lost"* (Cambridge, Mass., 1967), 130–57.

8. David Masson, *The Poetical Works of John Milton* (London, 1890), 3:473; Herbert Grierson, *Milton and Wordsworth* (Cambridge, 1937), 99; and Denis Saurat, *Milton: Man and Thinker* (London, 1944), 174. For a summary and comparison of these positions, see also Maurice Kelley, *This Great Argument* (Princeton, N.J., 1941), 95–96.

9. Kelley, *This Great Argument*, 94; and Albert Cirillo, "'Hail Holy Light' and Divine Time in *Paradise Lost*," *JEGP* 68 (1969): 51.

10. Fish, *Surprised by Sin*, 130–57.

11. Nigel Smith, *Is Milton Better than Shakespeare?* (Cambridge, Mass., 2008), 36, claims that the reference to Hobbes would be "obvious to any informed contemporary reader."

12. Thomas Hobbes, "Answer to the Preface to Gondibert," in *The English Works*, ed. William Molesworth, vol. 4 (London, 1839), 441–58.

13. Fish, *Surprised by Sin*, 22–37.

14. Ibid., 26.

15. Jonathan Richardson, *Explanatory Notes and Remarks on Milton's "Paradise Lost"* (London, 1734), 275.

16. Stephen Fallon, *Milton among the Philosophers: Poetry and Materialism in Seventeenth-Century England* (Ithaca, 1991), 209.

17. Ricks, *Milton's Grand Style*, 76.

18. W. K. Wimsatt, *The Verbal Icon: Studies in the Meaning of Poetry* (Lexington, Ky., 1954), 128.

19. See A. J. A. Waldock, *"Paradise Lost" and Its Critics* (Cambridge, 1947), 139.

20. See William Empson, *Some Versions of Pastoral* (London, 1935), 172.

21. Ricks, *Milton's Grand Style*, 60.

22. Thomas Newton, ed., *Paradise Lost*, 2 vols. (London, 1749), 2:252.

23. Richardson, *Explanatory Notes*, clxvii.

24. John Guillory, *Poetic Authority: Spenser, Milton, and Literary History* (New York, 1983), 149.

25. Fish, *Surprised by Sin*, 147.

26. Gérard Genette, "Métonymie chez Proust," *Figures III* (Paris, 1972), 41–63.

27. John Milton, *Complete Prose Works of John Milton*, 8 vols., ed. Don M. Wolfe et al. (New Haven, 1953–82), 6:318; hereafter cited as YP.

28. Walter Clyde Curry, *Milton's Ontology, Cosmogony, and Physics* (Lexington, Ky., 1957), 170.

29. Isabel MacCaffrey, *"Paradise Lost" as "Myth"* (Cambridge, Mass., 1959), 109.

30. Fallon, *Milton among the Philosophers*, 105.

31. William Kerrigan, *The Sacred Complex: On the Psychogenesis of "Paradise Lost"* (Cambridge, Mass., 1983), 237.

32. Ibid., 238.

33. Teskey, ed., *Paradise Lost*, 122.

34. W. B. C. Watkins, *An Anatomy of Milton's Verse* (Baton Rouge, 1955), 15; and N. K. Sugimura, *"Matter of Glorious Trial": Spiritual and Material Substance in "Paradise Lost"* (New Haven, 2009), 215.

35. Kerrigan, *The Sacred Complex*, 241.

36. Ricks, *Milton's Grand Style*, 115.

37. Sugimura, *"Matter of Glorious Trial,"* 182, 46.

38. J. B. van Helmont, *Oriatrike* (London, 1648), 653–58. Also see John Rogers, *The Matter of Revolution: Science, Poetry, and Politics in the Age of Milton* (Ithaca, N.Y., 1996), 155–57, for a description of van Helmont and his possible influence on Milton.

39. J. W. N. Watkins, *Hobbes's System of Ideas: A Study in the Political Significance of Philosophical Theories* (London, 1965), 76.

40. Kerrigan, *The Sacred Complex*, 242.

41. Kenneth Burke, *A Grammar of Motives* (Berkeley and Los Angeles, 1969), 504.

Notes to Langer, " 'Pardon may be found in time besought' "

I would like to thank Sanford Budick of the Hebrew University of Jerusalem, under whose guidance the ideas in this essay first took shape. I would also like to thank Lilian Alweiss of Trinity College, Dublin, for her comments on the current version.

1. For the view that in *Paradise Lost* time is considered *sub specie aeternitatis*, see, for example, A. R. Cirillo, "'Hail Holy Light' and Divine Time in *Paradise Lost*," *JEGP* 68 (1969): 45–56, and R. L. Colie, "Time and Eternity: Paradox and Structure in *Paradise Lost*," *Journal of the Warburg and Courtauld Institutes* 23 (1960): 127–38.

2. In his groundbreaking work on the Miltonic concept of time, E. W. Tayler, *Milton's Poetry: Its Development in Time* (Pittsburgh, 1979), 123–47, considers time as an indispensable component for our understanding of the relationship between time and eternity. Tayler views time, *chronos*, as the domain within which eternity, *kairos*, is enclosed. Yet, for Tayler, "ordinary time" is still comprehended under the aspect of eternity.

3. Catherine Gimelli Martin, "The Enclosed Garden and the Apocalypse: Immanent versus Transcendent Time in Milton and Marvell," in *Milton and the Ends of Time*, ed. Juliet Cummins (Cambridge, 2003), 148 (emphasis mine). In a similar vein, Sherry Lutz Zivley, "The Thirty-Three Days of *Paradise Lost*," *MQ* 34 (2000): 117–27, assigns time to earth, "earthly time," which she then differentiates from "heavenly time" (119).

4. Anthony Welch, "Reconsidering Chronology in *Paradise Lost*," in *Milton Studies*, vol. 41, ed. Albert C. Labriola (Pittsburgh, 2002), 4. See also Elizabeth Jane Wood, "'Improv'd by Tract of Time': Metaphysics and Measurement in *Paradise Lost*," in *Milton Studies*, vol. 15, ed. James D. Simmonds (Pittsburgh, 1981), 49. Stasis is identified with hell also in Laurence Stapleton's reading of the poem, "Perspectives of Time in *Paradise Lost*," *PQ* 45 (1966): 734–48: "The building of Pandemonium and the Council in Hell takes place without any indication of time, nor is there reason to ponder their duration. More significant is the lack of any evidence of the length of Satan's voyage." This lack of time Stapleton dismisses as a poetic device chosen by Milton "when specific detail would detract from rather than add to the power of his narrative over the imagination" (738).

5. All quotations from *Paradise Lost* are from John Milton, *Paradise Lost*, 2nd ed., ed. Alastair Fowler (New York, 1998); hereafter cited in the text.

6. For a similar view regarding the moral stature that is reflected in one's perception and experiencing of time, see Valerie Carnes, "Time and Language in Milton's *Paradise Lost*," *ELH* 37 (1970): 518–19. Yet in contrast to my suggestion that time is a changeable form that reflects the structure of the unfallen mind, Carnes maintains that time is a mode of being that can be one of four fixed options: divine, diabolic, angelic, or human.

7. Gordon Teskey, "From Allegory to Dialectic: Imagining Error in Spenser and Milton," *PMLA* 101 (1986): 14.

8. John Ellis McTaggart, "The Unreality of Time," *Mind* 17 (1908): 458.

9. My understanding of McTaggart's theory of time is based on his *The Nature of Existence* (1921), vol. 2, ed. C. D. Broad (Cambridge, 1927), and his essay on the unreality of time in *Mind*, noted above. For the life and work of

McTaggart, see Peter Geach, "Cambridge Philosophers III: McTaggart," *Philosophy* 70 (1995): 567–79, and Gerald Rochelle, *The Life and Philosophy of J. M. E. McTaggart, 1866–1925* (Lewiston, N.Y., 1991). For a thorough exposition of McTaggart's philosophy, see C. D. Broad, *Examination of McTaggart's Philosophy* (Cambridge, 1933), and P. T. Geach, *Truth, Love, and Immortality: An Introduction to McTaggart's Philosophy* (London, 1979). See also Richard M. Gale, ed., *The Philosophy of Time: A Collection of Essays* (London, 1967), and Gerald Rochelle, *Behind Time: The Incoherence of Time and McTaggart's Atemporal Replacement* (Hants, U.K., 1998). For McTaggart's influence on the next generation of British philosophers, see Peter Hylton, *Russell, Idealism, and the Emergence of Analytic Philosophy* (Oxford, 1990).

10. McTaggart, "The Unreality of Time," 468–70. See also Rochelle, *Behind Time*, 31–74.

11. See Peter Geach, *Truth, Love, and Immortality: An Introduction to McTaggart's Philosophy* (London, 1979), 136.

12. McTaggart, *The Unreality of Time*, 461–62.

13. For an exposition of McTaggart's last term of the C-series, see Rochelle, *Behind Time*, 14–15.

14. McTaggart, "The Relation of Time to Eternity," in *Philosophical Studies*, ed. S. V. Keeling (London, 1934), 155.

15. That time is the means by which humankind can reach to eternity is also the opinion of Wood, "'Improv'd by Tract of Time.'" "Man," says Wood, "might be 'Improv'd by tract of time' by reading the works and learning the times exhibited in the visible, physical universe" (53). Yet in contrast to my interpretation of time in *Paradise Lost* as unreal, Wood maintains that "the elements required to form a concept of time and, perhaps, even to constitute the very existence of time, are presented in the universe of the poem" (46).

16. John Milton, *The Works of John Milton*, ed. Frank Allen Patterson et al. (New York, 1931), 11:93, 95.

17. See McTaggart, "The Unreality of Time," 458.

18. Permanent relations between events in time are expressed in *Paradise Lost* 1.271–82 (relevant lines: 1.274 and 1.279–81), 1.356–60 (relevant lines: 1.360–61), 1.607–608, and 2.748. See also 2.991, 1023.

19. Geoffrey Hartman, "Adam on the Grass with Balsamum," in *Beyond Formalism: Literary Essays, 1958–1970* (New Haven, 1970), 133.

Notes to Miller, "Reconstructing Milton's Lost *Index theologicus*"

I am very grateful to William Poole for generously sharing with me material from his forthcoming edition of Milton's Commonplace Book, part of Oxford University Press's ongoing *Complete Works of John Milton*. His work, and our conversations together, inspired this article and helped make it possible. I would also like to thank Gordon Campbell and Noel Malcolm, who each read this essay in draft and responded with kind enthusiasm and invaluable suggestions. This article began as a paper that I delivered as part of a panel on "Milton's Italian Influences" at the Fifty-Sixth Annual Renaissance Society of America Conference in Venice (April 2010), and I owe that opportunity to Rosanna Cox, Hannah Crawforth, and Sarah Van der Laan. Their invitation remains sincerely appreciated.

Throughout, I have regularized the use of *i/j* and *u/v* in titles and quotations. Abbreviations have been expanded in italics, and superscripts have been silently lowered, except where used for ordinals. All translations are my own unless otherwise noted.

1. For the manuscript of Milton's Commonplace Book (hereafter cited as CPB), see British Library (hereafter BL), Add. MS 36354; see also John Milton, *Commonplace Book*, ed. and trans. Ruth Mohl, in *Complete Prose Works of John Milton*, 8 vols, ed. Don M. Wolfe et al. (New Haven, 1953–83), 1:344–513. Except when referring to Milton's CPB, where I cite the page numbers of the original manuscript, all subsequent references to Milton's prose works are to this edition, hereafter cited as YP.

2. See appendix below for a full list of the 12 cross-references in the Commonplace Book to the *Index theologicus*. By convention, and for the sake of clarity, I will be referring to Milton's surviving commonplace book in moral philosophy as his Commonplace Book, and will be referring to the theological commonplace book cross-referenced therein as his *Index theologicus*.

3. CPB 12, 109, 112, 151, 183, 197, 221, 244, and 246. See also appendix below. That these were the names of headings is further confirmed by the fact that, in one instance, Milton specified that "de bonis Ecclesiasticis" was a *titulus* in the *Index* (CPB 109; appendix, no. 3). See also Gordon Campbell, "Milton's *Index Theologicus* and Bellarmine's *Disputationes de Controversiis Christianae Fidei Adversus Huius Temporis Haereticos,*" *MQ* 11 (1977): 12.

4. See CPB 221; appendix no. 9, where Milton directs himself to consult his *index alter*. For the possibility that Milton maintained even more "other" commonplace books, in addition to his *Index theologicus*, see William Poole, "The Genres of Milton's Commonplace Book," in *The Oxford Handbook of Milton*, ed. Nicholas McDowell and Nigel Smith (Oxford, 2009), 374. Certainly, in the prefatory epistle to *De doctrina*, Milton appears to refer to one such additional commonplace book: he says that in his youth he began gathering passages from Scripture under various *loci communes* (translated in YP as "general headings"), in accordance with certain "systems of theologians" ("Theologorum Systemata"); see YP 6:119. However, for reasons briefly elaborated elsewhere in this article, Milton's collection of scriptural passages arranged according to systematic headings cannot have been the same commonplace book as his so-called *Index theologicus*, a fact which Campbell definitively established. Furthermore,

as Campbell also noted, the fact that Milton referred to the *Index theologicus* as his *index alter* (*the* other index [of two]) and not as his *index alius* (*an* other index) might seem to argue against Milton's having kept a host of other commonplace books, as such (Campbell, "Milton's *Index Theologicus*," 12–13). At a minimum, it shows that Milton regarded the Commonplace Book and the *Index theologicus* as specially paired.

5. Campbell, "Milton's *Index Theologicus*," 12–16. For this essay, I have used the first complete folio edition of Bellarmine's *Disputationes*, which in fact comprises the second edition of volume 1 and 2 the first edition of volume 3; see Robert Bellarmine, *Disputationes de controversiis Christianae fidei, adversus huius temporis haereticos*, 2nd ed., 3 vols. (Ingolstadt, 1588–93), hereafter cited by volume, controversy, and column number.

6. A fine overview of Bellarmine's career is contained within Piet van Boxel's "Robert Bellarmine, Christian Hebraist, and Censor," in *The History of Scholarship: A Selection of Papers from the Seminar on the History of Scholarship Held Annually at the Warburg Institute*, ed. Christopher Ligota and Jean-Louis Quantin (Oxford, 2006), 251–75.

7. For a full bibliography of the many editions of Bellarmine's *Disputationes*, and of the many responses that it provoked, see Aloys de Backer, Augustin de Backer, and Carlos Sommervogel (eds.), *Bibliothèque de la Compagnie de Jésus*, new ed., 11 vols. (Brussels and Paris, 1890–1932), vol. 1, cols. 1156–80.

8. On the genre of systematic theology, see also Gordon Campbell, Thomas N. Corns, John K. Hale, and Fiona J. Tweedie, *Milton and the Manuscript of "De Doctrina Christiana"* (Oxford, 2007), 92–98, 159–61.

9. Compare William Ames, *Bellarminus enervatus, sive disputationes anti-Bellarminianae* (Oxford, 1629), with Ames, *Medulla ss.* [=*sacrosanctae*] *theologiae* (Amsterdam, 1627).

10. Campbell, "Milton's *Index Theologicus*," 14.

11. Poole, "Genres," 368.

12. The latter three—Willet, Downame, and Ames—had been fellows of Milton's own college, Christ's College, though none while Milton was a student there; see Campbell, "Milton's *Index Theologicus*," 13.

13. Poole, "Genres," 368n4.

14. Sidney Sussex College, Cambridge (hereafter SSC), Samuel Ward Papers, MSS D, I, J, K, M2, and M4. See also Margo Todd, "The Samuel Ward Papers at Sidney Sussex College, Cambridge," *Transactions of the Cambridge Bibliographical Society* 8 (1985): 582–92.

15. Margo Todd, "Samuel Ward," *Oxford Dictionary of National Biography*, ed. H. C. G. Matthew and Brian Harrison, 60 vols. (Oxford, 2004); hereafter cited as *ODNB*. For this and all subsequent references to the *ODNB*, I have consulted the online edition, available at www.oxforddnb.com. An excellent discussion of Ward also appears in Jean-Louis Quantin, *The Church of England and Christian*

Antiquity: The Construction of a Confessional Identity in the 17th Century (Oxford, 2009), 176–91.

16. On Mede, see Jeffrey K. Jue, *Heaven upon Earth: Joseph Mede (1586–1638) and the Legacy of Millenarianism* (Dordrecht, 2006). For an example of Mede paying Ward an apparently unscheduled and welcome visit at Sidney Sussex, see Ward's letter to James Ussher, undated but datable on the basis of internal evidence to sometime in 1638 between February (the death of Bishop Francis White) and October (the death of Mede), Bodleian Library (hereafter Bodl.), MS Cherry 23, 183.

17. The connection between Ward and Young has previously been unknown. See Gataker's letter to Ward, May 19, 1631, Bodl., MS Tanner 71, fol. 92r: "I have sent a copy of those considerations leaft with me by the Scottish minister [Thomas Young], who is returned againe. He told me *that* he heard *that* you had ben in town, & *that* he had repaired unto you, had he known it before *your* departure. The man seemeth to be much affected with the busienes, & desirous by any meanes or paines he can to promote it. But I feare there are so many difficulties in it, *that* we shal hardly be so happy as to see it donne in *our* days." The identity of *"the* Scottish minister" as Thomas Young seems beyond question. A minister from Scotland, Young worked for an unknown period of time between 1611 and 1620 as an assistant to Gataker, Surrey, before leaving in April of 1620 to take up residence in Hamburg as chaplain to the English Merchant Adventurers. Young made periodic trips back to England thereafter, but in 1628 he "returned againe," this time once and for all, to assume the living of a parish in Suffolk. Tellingly, Gataker further informs Ward elsewhere in the same letter that the said "Scottish minister" had also brought news of certain developments in Germany (specifically, in Brandenburg). For more on Young in general, see also Edward Jones, "Thomas Young," *ODNB*.

18. See Milton's surviving letters to Young in YP 1:310–12, 315–16. Young's letters to Milton, some number of which Milton is clearly responding to, are not known to survive.

19. See SSC, Samuel Ward Papers, MS K.

20. SSC, Samuel Ward Papers, MS J, fol. 69r; MS K, fol. 2r, 57r, 98r; MS M4, fol. 14r.

21. SSC, Samuel Ward Papers, MS K, fol. 66r.

22. See Samuel Ward, *Opera nonnulla*, ed. Seth Ward (London, 1658).

23. For the best account of the British presence at Dort, see Anthony Milton, ed., *The British Delegation and the Synod of Dort (1618–1619)* (Woodbridge, 2005).

24. See G. J. Toomer, *John Selden: A Life in Scholarship* (Oxford, 2009), 672, 726, noting references to Bellarmine in Selden's *Uxor Ebraica* (London, 1646) and his *De synedriis*, 3 vols. (London, 1650–55); In addition to those references noted by Toomer, one further reference on Selden's part to Bellarmine bears mentioning here: the reference to Bellarmine that appears specifically in book 2,

chapter 28 of *Uxor Ebraica*. Milton derived a Commonplace Book entry, placed under "Marriage," from that chapter—he cites "Seldenus Uxor Heb. l. 2. c. 28, toto"—and he cross-referenced the entry with the *Index theologicus*. See Selden, *Uxor Ebraica*, 299, and CPB 109; appendix no. 3. Toomer, *John Selden*, 690n489, regards the speculation that Milton might have had access to *Uxor Ebraica* in manuscript form as an "utterly implausible" one, "especially since there is no trace of intimacy between the two men." As such, Milton's cross-referencing of that entry concerning *Uxor Ebraica* augurs in itself Milton's extended use of the *Index theologicus*, which is a central concern of this essay.

25. Thomas Hobbes, *Leviathan* (London, 1651), 300. In what would seem to make this a classic example of confuting Bellarmine as a way of attacking one's "actual" opponents, Hobbes, *Leviathan*, 387, takes care to advise the reader subsequently that "it is not the Romane Clergy onely, that pretends the Kingdome of God to be of this World, and thereby to have a Power therein, distinct from that of the Civill State." He appears clearly to have had English Presbyterians in his sights: "But who knows that this Spirit of Rome, now gone out . . . may not return, or rather an Assembly of Spirits worse than he, enter, and inhabite this clean swept house," the "Assembly of Spirits" serving as a barely veiled reference to the Westminster Assembly.

26. SSC, Samuel Ward Papers, MS J, fol. 2v (reading retrograde).

27. Bellarmine, *Disputationes*, 1.3.584–1087; Ames, *Bellarminus enervatus*, 1:137–283. The fact that Milton's reference to the heading "Papa" included the further specification of a page number, alone among the Commonplace Book's cross-references to the *Index theologicus*, may also indicate that Milton had accumulated so much material in the *Index* on the topic of the pope that it necessitated the creation of more than one page therein with that heading. Within the Commonplace Book itself, Milton only ever included a page number in cross-referencing one part of the Commonplace Book with another when referring to a heading replicated atop multiple pages. Milton's "vide Papa 42," therefore, gives some reason to suspect that the heading "Papa" may have been especially prevalent as a heading in the *Index*—in the way that "Rex" is the most prevalent heading in the Commonplace Book—even though Milton only cross-referenced the heading "Papa" once in the Commonplace Book itself (compared, for example, to the heading "de bonis Ecclesiasticis," which he cross-referenced five times, but never with a page number).

28. See Poole, "Genres," 368.

29. The *OED* records this as the first and only instance of the word *Hecatontome* in English.

30. Campbell, "Milton's *Index Theologicus*," 14–15.

31. CPB 151; appendix no. 5. On the shift in Milton's minuscule *e*, see James Holly Hanford, "The Chronology of Milton's Private Studies," *PMLA* 36.2 (June 1921): 255–56.

32. See Poole, "Genres," 373, 377, 380–81. For another recent contribution to our understanding of how Milton used his surviving Commonplace Book, see also Thomas Fulton, *Historical Milton: Manuscript, Print, and Political Culture in Revolutionary England* (Amherst, Mass., 2010).

33. It should be conceded, in fact, that the cross-references may not even signal Milton's continued use of the *Index* as a reading notebook at all, though it seems hard to imagine Milton failing to continue adding fresh material to the *Index* if he were otherwise continuing to draw upon it.

34. As a notable exception to this customary diminution of the *Index*'s longevity and importance, John T. Shawcross, *Rethinking Milton Studies: Time Present and Time Past* (Newark, 2005), 109–14, 150, has also made a brief case for "the continued use and significance of the Theological Index through 1652." Unfortunately, however, Shawcross's vital claim loses its cogency through his conflation of the *Index* with another early (and also lost) manuscript of Milton's, one which Milton is known to have begun compiling in the 1640s and which consisted of passages extracted from various works of systematic theology. This was the manuscript out of which *De doctrina Christiana* emerged, as famously documented by Milton's nephew Edward Phillips in "The Life of John Milton," in John Milton, *Letters of State* (London, 1694), xviii–xix. Again, as Campbell established in his seminal article on the *Index*—an article Shawcross strangely neglects altogether—the collection of material out of which *De doctrina* emerged cannot have been the same collection of material cross-referenced in the Commonplace Book as the *Index theologicus*.

35. Joseph Hall, *The Peace of Rome. Proclaimed to All the World, by her Famous Cardinall Bellarmine* (London, 1609); see also Campbell, "Milton's *Index Theologicus*," 14–15.

36. Hall, *Peace of Rome*, sig. G1r.

37. As a relevant example, see ibid., 26, where Hall provides an essentially word for word translation of what was to Protestants one of Bellarmine's more noxious pronouncements regarding the supremacy of popes over church councils (taken from Bellarmine's fourth controversy in the *Disputationes*, "De Conciliis, & Ecclesia"): "The third is the more common opinion, That the Pope is so above the Councell, that he cannot subject himself unto the judgement thereof; if we speake of a coactive sentence; So al [*sic*] the old Schoolemen hold." Compare to Bellarmine, *Disputationes*, 1.4.125: "ULTIMA sententia est ferè communis, quòd videlicet Papa adeò sit supra Concilium, ut non possit etiam se subjicere eius sententiae, si propriè de sententia coactiva agatur. Haec sententia videtur esse omnium Scholasticorum veterum."

38. See, for example, Edward Jones, "'Ere Half My Days': Milton's Life, 1608–40," in McDowell and Smith, eds., *The Oxford Handbook of Milton*, 19, 25, which envisions Milton potentially reading Bellarmine's *Disputationes* in the Kedermister Library.

39. See Bodl., Vet. A2 f. 178, pp. 53, 55–56, 58, 64.

40. Early modern opponents of Bellarmine generally preferred to refer to the controversy "De Summo Pontifice" as Bellarmine's "De Romano Pontifice," for obvious polemical reasons, since referring to Bellarmine's work on "the Supreme Pontiff," as opposed to "the Roman Pontiff," might seem to concede the very point that one meant to reject.

41. Richard Stock, *A Sermon Preached at Paules Crosse* (London, 1609), 56.

42. See C. S. Knighton, "William Whitaker," *ODNB*. For early modern instances of this claim in circulation, see, among others, Henry Holland, *Herwologia Anglica* (Arnhem, 1620), 213; Jacob Verheiden, *The History of the Moderne Protestant Divines*, trans. Donald Lupton (London, 1637), 358–60; Anthony Wood, *Athenae Oxonienses*, 2 vols. (London, 1691–92), vol. 1, col. 303.

43. Samuel Clarke, ed., *A Martyrologie . . . with the Lives of Ten of our English Divines, Famous in their Generations for Learning, Piety, Parts, and for Their Sufferings in the Cause of Christ* (London, 1652), 2.141. On Whitaker's conjoined anti-Catholicism and moderate puritanism, and on his (and its) influence at St. John's, see Peter Lake, *Moderate Puritans and the Elizabethan Church* (Cambridge, 1982), 93–115, 169–200.

44. William Whitaker, *An Answere to the Ten Reasons of Edmund Campian*, trans. Richard Stock (London, 1606), a full translation of William Whitaker, *Ad rationes decem Edmundi Campiani . . . responsio*, 2nd ed. (London, 1581), with an abridged translation fitted into the margins of William Whitaker, *Responsionis ad decem illas rationes . . . defensio contra confutationem Joannis Duraei Scoti, Presbyteri, Iesuitae* (London, 1583).

45. Many of these sermons would seem to have formed the basis for most of Stock's (very) few publications, but a number of them survive as sermons only in a notebook kept by Gilbert Freville of Bishop Middleham, County Durham. See BL, MS Egerton 2877, fols. 46v–47r, 92r, and 159v–106v (written retrograde).

46. For the first complete collection of Whitaker's works against Bellarmine (and others), see William Whitaker, *Opera theologica*, 2 vols. (Geneva, 1610).

47. Poole, "Genres," 368n4.

48. See below, note 68, on the entries concerning Selden's *Historie of Tithes*.

49. Bodl., MS Rawlinson D 1425, p. 5. The anti-Bellarmine authors whom the commonplacer here references by surname only are William Barclay, William Ames, and Daniel Chamier.

50. John Dove, *Of Divorcement* (London, 1601), sig. A4r; quoted in Anthony Milton, *Catholic and Reformed: The Roman and Protestant Churches in English Protestant Thought, 1600–1640* (Cambridge, 1995), 425.

51. Ames, *Bellarminus enervatus*, vol. 1, book 3, chap. 7 ("De Coactiva Papae potestate"), 247–60.

52. John Rainolds, *De Romanae ecclesiae idololatria* (Oxford, 1596), sig. ¶2r.

53. Andrew Willett, *Synopsis Papismi* (London, 1592), with successively augmented editions published in 1594, 1600, and 1613. Willet's question "whether the visible church upon earth may fall away from God into Idolatrie and

apostasie" for example, targets Bellarmine's "Ecclesiam visibilem non posse deficere" (That it is not possible for the visible Church to fail), a chapter in the controversy "De Conciliis, & Ecclesia." Willet's "Of the Difference betweene Idols and Images" counters Bellarmine's "De nomine Imaginis & Idoli" (Of the designation "Image" and that of "Idol"), a chapter in the controversy "De Ecclesia Triumphante." And Willet's question "Of the ceremonies which they use in the idolatrous sacrifice of the Masse" targets Bellarmine's "*De Missa*," which occupies two books in the controversy "De Sacramento Eucharistiae"; specifically, that question of Willet's answers Bellarmine's three chapters "De caeremoniis Missae" in the second book of "*De Missa*." See, in its first edition, Willet, *Synopsis Papismi,* 49–55, 347–48, 488–90. And, for the corresponding sections in the *Disputationes,* see Bellarmine, *Disputationes,* 1.4.192–95, 1.7.943, 2.3.1101–1117.

54. Hieronymus Zanchius, *De primi hominis lapsu, de peccato & de Lege Dei,* in Zanchius, *Opera Theologica,* 8 vols. in 3 (Geneva, 1605), vol. 4, cols. 502–47. In three separate chapters in *De doctrina Christiana*—book 1, chaps 14, 27, and 33—Milton comments perceptively upon three different parts of Zanchius's *Opera:* respectively, Zanchius's *De tribus Elohim* (*Opera,* vol. 1), his *In Epistolam ad Ephesios commentarius* (vol. 6), and his *De fine seculi* (vol. 7). See YP 6:421–22, 527, 533–34, 615.

55. See Campbell, "Milton's *Index Theologicus,*" 14.

56. For Bellarmine's "De Matrimonii Sacramento," see Bellarmine, *Disputationes,* 2.5.1540–1731. The *Disputationes* does contain a very brief discussion of "*Bona Clericorum*" under the heading "An Clerici sint liberi à jugo potestatis secularis" (Whether the clergy are free from the bonds of the secular power), in the first book ("De Clericis") of the controversy "De Membris Ecclesiae Militantis." However, in the short two paragraphs that constitute the discussion, as Campbell notes, Bellarmine confines himself exclusively to the contention that the goods of the clergy are exempt from secular taxation. See Bellarmine, *Disputationes,* 1.5.409, 413; Campbell, "Milton's *Index Theologicus,*" 14. It is, I think, most unlikely that the *Index*'s "de bonis Ecclesiasticis" was related to this untitled sub-sub-section of the *Disputationes.* Based on the five cross-references in the Commonplace Book to "de bonis Ecclesiasticis," that section of the *Index* appears to have contained entries pertaining to different and much broader concerns, ones bearing upon different and more prominent parts of the *Disputationes.*

57. Wolfgang Musculus, *Loci communes theologiae sacrae,* final ed. (Basel, 1599), 216–17; Wolfgang Musculus, *Common Places of Christian Religion,* 2nd ed., trans. John Man (London, 1578), 440–41.

58. CPB 12: "Clericorum avaritiam apertè notat Dantes inferno. Cant: 7." In translation, in YP 1:366: "The avarice of the clergy Dante's *Inferno* openly censures. Cant: 7."

59. Giovanni Villani, *Croniche,* ed. Giacomo Fasolo (Venice, 1537), fols. 77r–87v.

60. Ibid., fol. 54r.

61. Phillips, "Life of John Milton," xviii.

62. Dante, *Purgatorio*, canto 24, ll. 20–24: "e quella faccia / di là da lui più che l'altre trapunta / ebbe la Santa Chiesa in le sue braccia: / dal Torso fu, e purga per digiuno / l'anguille di Bolsena e la vernaccia." The other pope noted by Dante in the *Purgatorio* is Pope Hadrian V, in canto 19, ll. 88–126.

63. I am, once more, grateful to William Poole for sharing with me part of an early draft of his forthcoming edition of the Commonplace Book, which nicely emphasizes this point.

64. This is again evidenced primarily by the divergence between the two references in the form of Milton's minuscule *e*.

65. See Villani, *Croniche*, fols. 85r, 87r.

66. See also James Holly Hanford, ed., *Milton's Commonplace Book*, trans. Nelson Glenn McCrea, in *The Works of John Milton*, 18 vols., ed. Frank Allen Patterson et al. (New York, 1931–38), 18:131.

67. Wyclif's position on tithes was first explicitly denounced by a formal church decree in 1382, when it took its place as one of the 24 specific "conclusions" of Wyclif condemned by the Blackfriars Council, which was presided over by Wyclif's great antagonist, Archbishop of Canterbury William Courtenay (1341/42–96). In the Blackfriars condemnation, Wyclif's position on tithes was recorded as follows: "Quod decimae sunt purae eleemosynae, et quod parochiani possunt, propter peccata suorum curatorum, eas detinere, et ad libitum aliis conferre" (That tithes are pure alms, and that parishioners have the power to withhold them, or to offer them, at their discretion, in response to the sins of their clergymen). See Thomas Walsingham, *Chronicon Angliae, 1328–1388*, ed. Edward Maunde Thompson (London, 1874), 344; see also Joseph H. Dahmus, *The Prosecution of John Wyclyf* [sic] (New Haven, 1952), 89–97.

68. Bellarmine, *Disputationes*, 1.5.396, 398. Perhaps surprisingly, while Bellarmine held tithes in general due "jure naturae & divino," he actually believed that the specific percentage of a tenth was not due *jure divino*, but was rather due "jure Ecclesiastico." In Bellarmine's view, this human, ecclesiastical law commanding that precisely a tenth be given to the clergy could thus be changed (*mutare*). As Bellarmine was quick to note, citing Thomas Aquinas, this meant that the percentage might lawfully be raised ("to an eighth") just as much as it meant that the percentage might lawfully be lowered ("to a twelfth"), but of course most English divines attacked Bellarmine for the scandal of the latter implication. See Bellarmine, 1.5.396–404. In seventeenth century England, the most notorious opponent of the divine right of the tenth, Protestant or papist, was not Bellarmine but John Selden, who was (rightly) regarded as having deliberately called the doctrine into question in his instantly controversial *The Historie of Tithes* (London, 1618). It is no surprise that *The Historie of Tithes* is *not* one of the works in which Selden mentions Bellarmine. Making it any clearer that one actually agreed with a controversial position advanced by the cardinal would not

have been wise. The correspondence between Bellarmine and Selden, however, did not go unnoticed, evidently not even within the compass of anti-Bellarmine commonplace books. Under the heading "Decimae debentur ministris jure divino" in the anonymous anti-Bellarmine commonplace book discussed above (Bodl., MS Rawlinson D 1425), the commonplacer placed Selden's name immediately after Bellarmine's in the enemy camp of those who did not believe the tenth due *jure divino*. Moreover, some of the principal men whom the commonplacer cited on that same page as in defiance of Bellarmine's position on tithes were in fact men who had engaged in confuting *Selden's* position on tithes: Sir James Sempill [in *Sacrilege Sacredly Handled* (London, 1619)], Richard Tillesley, [in *Animadversions upon M. Seldens History of Tithes* (London, 1619)], and Richard Montagu [in *Diatribae upon the First Part of the Late History of Tithes* (London, 1621)]. See Bodl., MS Rawlinson D 1425, p. 8. As noted by G. J. Toomer, "Selden's *Historie of Tithes:* Genesis, Publication, Aftermath," *HLQ* 65.3/4 (2002): 372, some part of Montagu's *Diatribae* appears to have been already in circulation in 1619—or, at the least, knowledge of Montagu's *Diatribae* was in circulation in 1619—and hence my circumspect claim, above, that at least part of this commonplace book must postdate 1618. These entries concerning Selden's *Historie of Tithes* provide a perfect example of an anti-Bellarmine commonplace book being bent to reflect an interest in a raging intra-*Protestant* controversy.

69. Walsingham, *Chronicon Angliae,* 173–83.

70. George Downame, *A Treatise concerning Antichrist, Divided into Two Bookes, the Former, Proving that the Pope Is Antichrist: The Latter, Maintaining the same assertion, against all the objections of Robert Bellarmine, Jesuit and Cardinall of the Church of Rome* (London, 1603), 98, 100.

71. [François Hotman], *Brutum fulmen Papae Sixti V* (s.l., 1585), 71: "Ecce nobis aliud ex libello, cui titulus est, Sylva locorum communium, sub exitum Concilii Basiliensis edito, ubi ratio confecta eius pecuniae, quae sub Papae Martini quinti Pontificatu ex sola Gallia Romam exportata est, excurrisse dicitur ad nonagies centena aureorum coronatorum millia." In the text, I have quoted the contemporary English translation of Hotman's work, which appeared almost immediately: [François Hotman], *The Brutish Thunderbolt; or, Rather Feeble Fier-Flash of Pope Sixtus the fift,* trans. Christopher Fetherstone (London, 1586), 100.

72. See Hotman, *Brutum fulmen,* 225–62.

73. John Foxe, *Actes and Monuments,* rev. 4th ed., 2 vols. (London, 1583), 1:723–24; hereafter cited as AM1583. This edition of *Acts and Monuments* was the last published in Foxe's lifetime; see Thomas S. Freeman, "John Foxe," *ODNB.*

74. The 45 articles of Wyclif condemned by the Council of Constance included all 24 of the articles that had been condemned by the Blackfriars Council; see Dahmus, *Prosecution of John Wyclyf,* 153.

75. Wyclif's bones had initially been condemned to the fire in 1415 at the Council of Constance, where Martin V was ultimately elected pope. However, the council's directive to burn Wyclif's bones, which preceded Martin's ascension

to the papacy, was not acted upon until 1427, when Martin V reissued the order and ensured that this time it was obeyed. See Dahmus, *Prosecution of John Wyclyf*, 153–54.

76. See AM1583, 1:766. The biblical citation is from the Authorized Version.

77. For the mistaken reference to "pope Martine the fourth" in this edition, see John Foxe, *Acts and Monuments*, 7th ed., 3 vols. (London, 1631–32), 1:887; hereafter cited as AM1631–32. For the two headers quoted above, see AM1631–32, 1:883–84. On Milton's potentially having used the 1631–32 edition, see YP 1:524n24.

78. By the time that Milton published *Considerations Touching the Likeliest Means to Remove Hirelings out of the Church* (London, 1659), his position on tithes had become appreciably more extreme than Wyclif's, and than the Wycliffite position that Milton himself insinuates in *Of Reformation*. In *The Likeliest Means*, Milton argued that the Old Testament practice of tithing had been typologically abolished with the coming of Christ. As a result, Milton did more than merely reject the belief that tithes were due by divine right. He himself now mounted a divine right argument *against* the payment of tithes: "As therefor *Abram* paid tithes to *Melchisedec* . . . so we ought to pay none." This was an intractable conclusion that did not follow from, and to a large degree was incompatible with, the Wycliffite belief that tithes were "alms." See Milton, *The Likeliest Means*, in YP 7:286, and see further Jeffrey Alan Miller, "Untypical Significance: Theological Typology, Milton, and the Aftermath of Writing," D.Phil. thesis (Oxford, 2011).

79. [Paolo Sarpi], *Historia del Concilio Tridentino* (London, 1619), 458. Ernest Sirluck tracks the close relation between the two passages in Sirluck, "Milton's Critical Use of Historical Sources: An Illustration," *MP* 50.4 (May 1953): 226–31.

80. For the passing reference to "Martino 4°," regarding the Council of Trent's judgment that it was not altogether forbidden to invoke the words of Scripture outside of strictly religious affairs (such as quoting the Gospels when begging pardon from an earthly authority), see Sarpi, *Historia del Concilio Tridentino*, 156.

81. For references to Sarpi, see CPB 109, 112, 179, 184, 189, 244; see also the list provided in YP 1:512.

82. See Sirluck, "Milton's Critical Use of Historical Sources," 228–29.

83. To be clear, I do not intend this as a claim that Milton never read Bellarmine's *Disputationes*. Rather, I simply mean to stress that Milton's having kept an anti-Bellarmine commonplace book does not constitute an indication in and of itself that Milton read Bellarmine's work, nor (obviously) does Milton's having referred to Bellarmine by name in *Animadversions*.

84. John Selden, *Titles of Honor* (London, 1614), sig. C4v.

85. Quoting, for example, Poole, "Genres," 376, where it is claimed that "Milton's CPB shows him turning over the pages—seemingly all the pages—of

some ninety-five authors." References to two widely separated pages from the same book need not signal that Milton had turned over all the pages of that book in between them. Indeed, in certain cases, intermediary sources would have made it *possible* for Milton to cite a book in this way without his ever even having held it.

86. See Milton's letter to Thomas Young, dated March 26, 162[7], in John Milton, *Epistolae familiares* (London, 1674), 9: "Biblia Hebraea, pergratum sane munus tuum, jampridem accepi." In translation, in YP 1:312: "The Hebrew Bible, your very welcome gift, I have long since received." If that Bible was the famous *Biblia rabbinica* edited by Johannes Buxtorf (the elder), 2 vols. (Basel, 1618–19), Milton would thus have had direct access to the glosses to which he alludes by "[David] *Kimchi* and the two other Rabbies [Levi Ben Gershom and Rashi]"; see YP 2:335–36n4.

87. Jason Rosenblatt, *Renaissance England's Chief Rabbi: John Selden*, rev. paperback ed. (Oxford, 2008), 5.

88. Edwin Rabbie, "Hugo Grotius and Judaism," in *Hugo Grotius, Theologian: Essays in Honour of G. H. M. Posthumus Meyjes*, ed. Henk J. M. Nellen and Edwin Rabbie (Leiden, 1994), 113.

89. Noel Malcolm, *Aspects of Hobbes* (Oxford, 2002), 459.

90. See AM1583, 1:723–24; Hotman, *Brutum fulmen*, 71. On Toke and the commonplace book attributed to him, see especially Heinrich Toke, *Der Wolfenbütteler "Rapularius,"* ed. Hildegund Hölzel-Ruggiu, a selected ed. (Hannover, 2002). This edition, however, does not contain the anecdote about Martin V's tithing. For a much sparser edition of entries from Toke's *Rapularius* that nonetheless does contain the entry regarding the "nine millions of gold" allegedly exacted out of France in Martin V's time, see Paul Lehmann, ed., "Aus dem Rapularius des Hinricus [*sic*] Token," in *Erforschung des Mittelalters: ausgewählte Abhandlungen und Aufsätze*, 5 vols. (Stuttgart, 1959–62), 4:187–205, with the said entry on page 191.

91. Matthias Flacius, *Catalogus testium veritatis* (Basel, 1556), 811. On Flacius and the *Catalogus*, consult further Irena Backus, *Historical Method and Confessional Identity in the Era of the Reformation, 1378–1615* (Leiden, 2003), 343–91.

92. Hotman, *Brutum fulmen*, 71.

93. Downame, *Treatise concerning Antichrist*, 100.

94. Of the authors listed here, Milton's extant writings only fail to mention Whitaker, Willet, and Stock. His exposure to the works of each, at least in some fashion, nonetheless remains something of a certainty. Milton, of course, spent his boyhood under Stock's pastoral instruction, and Stock, one of Whitaker's own favorite pupils, was a known propagator (and translator) of Whitaker's teachings, as discussed above. Willet's English prominence and influence endured for centuries, and he was, moreover, one of the most famous of the many English Calvinists of international repute who were alumni and

former fellows of Milton's own Cambridge college. Furthermore, irrespective of these personal, intermediary connections to Whitaker and Willet, it would have been most unusual for an educated English Protestant of Milton's background and ambitions to have neglected either man's works altogether. It also bears mentioning here, as a final aside, that in Milton's lifetime Stock's name would have seemed less out of place in the above list of anti-Catholic champions than it doubtless appears now.

Notes to "Milton's Aristotelian Experiments"

I would like to thank Luka Arsenjuk, Michelle Koerner, Jan van Ophuijsen, Britt Rusert, Nigel Smith, and the anonymous reviewer of *Milton Studies* for their invaluable comments on the present essay.

1. All quotations and references to *Samson Agonistes* are taken from the 1671 edition reproduced in *The Complete Works of John Milton*, vol. 2, *The 1671 Poems, "Paradise Regain'd," and "Samson Agonistes,"* ed. Laura Lunger Knoppers (Oxford, 2008); hereafter referred to as *SA*, cited by page number. For the ease of the reader, I give line numbers from the more standard emended edition in the text (with 1671 *Omissa* worked into the text).

2. See Jill Kraye, "Erasmus and the Canonization of Aristotle: The Letter to John More," in *England and the Continental Renaissance: Essays in Honour of J. B. Trapp*, ed. Edward Chaney and Peter Mack (Woodbridge, 1990), 37–52. See also F. Edward Cranz, *Bibliography, 1501–1600*, 2nd ed. (with addenda and revisions by Charles B. Schmitt) (Baden-Baden, 1984); and Omert J. Schrier, *The "Poetics" of Aristotle and the "Tractatus Coislinianus": A Bibliography from about 900 Till 1996* (Leiden, 1998).

3. See Cranz, *Bibliography of Aristotle*, 27, 53, 57, 103, 109, 216; and Schrier, *"Poetics" of Aristotle*, 30.

4. Cranz, *Bibliography of Aristotle*, xix, 215–16; Schrier, *"Poetics" of Aristotle*, 32.

5. Schrier, *"Poetics" of Aristotle*, 29–33. On Milton's tour of the Continent, see Barbara K. Lewalski, *The Life of John Milton: A Critical Biography*, rev. ed. (Malden, Mass., 2000), 87–119; and Gordon Campbell and Thomas N. Corns, *John Milton: Life, Work and Thought* (Oxford, 2008), 103–27.

6. Paul R. Sellin, *Daniel Heinsius and Stuart England, with a Short-Title Checklist of the Works of Daniel Heinsius* (Leiden, 1968), 71–119. The 1696 edition of Aristotle's *Poetics* is instructive, where Goulston's earlier Latin translation is supplemented by an edition of the Greek text as well as Heinsius's influential notes on the order and interpretation of the text; see *ΑΡΙΣΤΟΤΕΛΟΥΣ ΠΕΡΙ ΠΟΙΗΤΙΚΗΣ. Aristotelis De Poetica Liber. Ex Versione Theodori Goulstoni Perpetuis notis Analyticis illustrata. Accedunt Integrae Notr. Frid. Sylburgii, & Dan. Heinsii, Necnon Selectae aliorum* (Cambridge, 1696).

7. Daniel Heinsius, *Dan. Heinsii De Tragoediae Constitvtione Liber. In qvo inter caetera tota de hac Aristotelis sententia dilucide explicatur. Editio auctior multo. Cui &*

Aristotelis De Poëtica libellus, cum ejusdem Notis & Interpretatione, accedit (Amsterdam, 1643), 247. Although Heinsius first published a version of the work in 1611, I use the 1643 edition with revisions and additions by the author. This translation is my own. Unless otherwise noted, translations of Heinsius's work on tragedy are from Daniel Heinsius, *On Plot in Tragedy*, trans. Paul R. Sellin and John J. McManmon (Northridge, Calif., 1971), hereafter cited as *PT*.

8. Daniel Heinsius, *De constitutione tragoediae / La constitution de la tragédie dite La Poétique d'Heinsius*, ed. Anne Duprat (Geneva, 2001), 222; hereafter cited as *CT*.

9. See Paul R. Sellin, "Introduction," in *PT*, xi–xxiv; and Sellin, *Daniel Heinsius and Stuart England*, 123–99.

10. Edward Phillips, *Theatrum poetarum; or, A Compleat Collection of the Poets, Especially The most Eminent, of all Ages* (London, 1675), 29.

11. F. F. Blok, *Isaac Vossius and His Circle: His Life until His Farewell to Queen Christina of Sweden, 1618–1655* (Groningen, 2000), 27–43; and Lewalski, *Life of Milton*, 99, 236–64.

12. Note that Heinsius uses *perturbatio* and *affectus* interchangeably—something Milton does not do. See also Paul R. Sellin, "Sources of Milton's Catharsis: A Reconsideration," *JEGP* 60 (Oct. 1961): 712–S30. Sellin lays the groundwork for comparative treatments of Milton and Heinsius, although the ambit of the present study is to challenge his 1961 claim that *expiatio* "means about the same as *lustratio*." See Sellin, "Sources of Milton's Catharsis," 725. Nevertheless, Sellin's essay is invaluable insofar as it locates Milton's treatment of catharsis in conversation with Minturno, Heinsius, Antonio Scaino da Salo, Tarquino Galluzzi, and, most importantly, Giambattista Guarini.

13. See *Dan. Heinsii Lof-sanck van Iesus Christus* in *Bacchus en Christus: Twee Lofzangen van Daniel Heinsius*, ed. L. Ph. Rank, J. D. P. Warners, and F. L. Zwaan (Zwolle, 1965).

14. This text is actually from another 1647 work by Vossius, *De artis poeticæ natura, ac constitutione liber*, a companion piece to the *Poeticarum institutionum* that deliberately recalls Heinsius's *De tragoediae constitvtione liber* in the title and makes a case for the provenance of poetry among the arts and disciplines. Vossius dedicated the book to the poet Jacob Cats, then pensionary of the States of Holland. The proper definition of *virtutem*—particularly among these Dutch republican classicists—is, of course, another complex question, an issue that I ultimately eschew here. See Gerardus Joannes Vossius, *De artis poeticæ natura, ac constitutione liber* (Amsterdam, 1647), 38. See also Gerardus Joannes Vossius, "De artis poeticæ natura, ac constitutione liber / On the Nature and System of Poetics," *Poeticae institutiones libri tres / Institutes of Poetics in Three Books*, ed. and trans. Jan Bloemendal (with Edwin Rabbie), 2 vols. (Leiden, 2010), 1824–25; hereafter this edition cited in the text as *PILT*.

15. For an authoritative biography of Vossius, see C. S. M. Rademaker, *Life and Work of Gerardus Joannes Vossius (1577–1649)*, trans. H. P. Doezema (Assen, 1981).

16. See Luc Deitz, "'Aristoteles imperator noster...?': J. C. Scaliger and Aristotle on Poetic Theory," *International Journal of the Classical Tradition* 2 (Summer 1995): 60. Scholars argue over the character and fidelity of Scaliger's interest in Aristotle's *Poetics*, a critical debate that I eschew here. For a brief biography of Julius Caesar Scaliger, see Vernon Hall Jr., "Life of Julius Caesar Scaliger," *Transactions of the American Philosophical Society*, n.s. 40 (Oct. 1950): 85–170; and for the most authoritative and scholarly treatment of the Scaligers, both father Julius Caesar Scaliger and son Joseph Justus Scaliger, as well as their humanist milieu, see Anthony Grafton, *Joseph Scaliger: A Study in the History of Classical Scholarship*, 2 vols. (Oxford, 1983–93); and Anthony Grafton, *Defenders of the Text: The Traditions of Scholarship in an Age of Science, 1450–1800* (Cambridge, Mass., 1991).

17. My translation from the Dutch: "Poëzie tracht uitdrukking te geven aan het universele, geschiedenis aan het bijzondere"; quoted in Gerardus Vossius, *Geschiedenis als wetenschap*, ed. Cor Rademaker (Baarn, 1990), 25.

18. Vossius, *Poeticarum institutionum libri tres*, 1.6 (the pagination mistakenly skips from 1 to 6). See also *PILT* 106–07; and Paul R. Sellin, "The Last of the Renaissance Monsters: The *Poetical Institutions* of Gerardus Joannis Vossius, and Some Observations on English Criticism," in Paul R. Sellin and Stephen B. Baxter, eds., *Anglo-Dutch Cross Currents in the Seventeenth and Eighteenth Centuries: Papers Read at a Clark Library Seminar, May 10, 1975* (Los Angeles, 1976), 1–39.

19. My translation. Vossius relies heavily on Scaliger here, in his initial treatment of the importance of purgation in tragedy; for both the original Latin and another English translation, see *PILT* 456–61.

20. For the ease of the reader, I add the Latin *purgationem* in brackets in place of Aristotle's Greek term; here, in the *Poeticarum institutionum*, Vossius keeps the Greek term in the text and at the same time glosses it as *purgationem* in the margin to the right. *Purgatio* is his term, but consigned to the margin.

21. *Affectus* is, for Heinsius, Vossius, and Milton, more general than an emotion or passion. It is, rather, "A state of body, and especially of mind produced in one by some influence." Emotions, passions, and perturbations are *affectus*, but an *affectus* is irreducible to any of these. It is, rather, a more neutral term for a force in a more dynamic economy of activity and passivity—for instance, *affectus* might be used in the abstract to describe a possible effect of a rhetorical strategy before it is clear what the particular strategy, or even the content of the strategy, is. Much is revealed in the etymology of the term *affectus* (the verb *adficio/adficere*), where *ad* (here meaning, with regard to, in respect of, in relation to, as to, to, in), together with the root *facio/facere* (to make, to do, to bring to pass, to cause, to effect, to create), take shape together as a noun (*affectus*) or verb (*afficio*), meaning, respectively, "something done to, something caused or created to" and "to do something to" or "to cause to." In rhetorical terms, *affectus* is certainly used often to describe passion or emotion—hence Quintilian's use of the

noun in book 1 of the *Institutio oratoria*, where the arts of eloquence "ad movendos leniendosque adfectus plurimum valet" (are able to move and to moderate the emotions of many). Yet in other places it is more general than emotion, figuring instead a neutral state, disposition, mood, or expression, as in *Institutio oratoria* 2.13.9, where something "gives an impression of action and animation [*adfectum*]." With respect to subject formation, Laurie Shannon, "Likenings: Rhetorical Husbandries and Portia's 'True Conceit' of Friendship," *Renaissance Drama* 31 (2002): 4, understands affect "In its simplest grammars…from the past participle of *ad-facere*" as a means of being "made or fashioned toward or in respect of another. Most broadly construed, 'affect' thus names subject formation itself as a matter of comporting or comaking, since some other (person, thing) is always party to the process." See Charleton T. Lewis and Charles Short, *A Latin Dictionary* (Oxford, 1879), 66 (*affectus*), 716–18 (*facio*); Quintilian, *The Institutio Oratoria of Quintilian*, 4 vols., trans. H. E. Butler (London, 1920), 1:174, 292–93 (1.10.31, 2.13.9).

22. It is instructive to remember Michael Lieb's brilliant observations concerning fear and God as "our living Dread" in *Samson Agonistes*. Here fear, what Lieb calls "fear divinized," is really a constitutive element of the entire tragedy. See Michael Lieb, "'Our Living Dread': The God of *Samson Agonistes*," in *Milton Studies*, vol. 33, *The Miltonic Samson*, ed. Albert C. Labriola and Michael Lieb (Pittsburgh, 1997), 7; Michael Lieb, *Theological Milton: Deity, Discourse and Heresy in the Miltonic Canon* (Pittsburgh, 2006), 163–209.

23. Overall, Heinsius is less consistent than Vossius and does not seem to differentiate here between *perturbatione, passione,* and the more general *affectus*. Nevertheless, where Heinsius might initially seem to offer a more restrictive treatment of tragedy, limited to the purging of "perturbations" by fear and pity, he does seem to recognize *affectus* and *perturbatio* as equivalent terms, as is clear in both the 1611 and, subsequently, the 1643 editions of *De tragoediae liber*, or *De constitutione tragoediae* (*PT* 11; *CT* 124).

24. There is certainly a great deal at stake in the distinction between *perturbationem* and *affectuum*, and one could certainly argue that Vossius and Milton recognize and commit to Aristotle's alleged emphasis on the primacy of *affectus* in a way that Heinsius does not were it not for Heinsius's detailed-if-implicit commentary on this very matter.

25. Nigel Smith, *Perfection Proclaimed: Language and Literature in English Radical Religion, 1640–1660* (Oxford, 1989), 1, 14–19, 60–72, 73–78; Jeffrey S. Shoulson, "Milton and Enthusiasm: Radical Religion and the Poetics of *Paradise Regained*," in *Milton Studies*, vol. 47, ed. Albert C. Labriola (Pittsburgh, 2008), 219–57.

26. Smith, *Perfection Proclaimed*, 74, 229; Shoulson, "Milton and Enthusiasm," 221–27.

27. Given its popularity in histories of early modernity, I cite Thomas Wright's *The Passions of the Minde in Generall: A Reprint Based on the 1604 Edition,*

ed. Thomas O. Sloan (Urbana, Ill., 1971), 149, in an effort to show how various phenomena can be brought together under the auspices of a treatment on affect (and eschew for the moment the confessional and practical theological problems raised by assuming a declaredly Thomistic text to be exemplary).

28. This is evident, for instance, in book 3, chapter 2, of John Calvin, *Institutes of the Christian Religion* (1559), 2 vols., ed. John T. McNeill, trans. Ford Lewis Battles (Philadelphia, 1960), 542–92, on faith.

29. In a sense one might see this interest in tragedy as a means of staging a conversation between Heinsius, Vossius, Milton, Petrus Ramus, and William Ames (that is, the Ames of the *Technometria*) in their collective search for the common language or science under which all other disciplines take shape.

30. See *CT* 154, 158. It is worth pausing to consider the purchase (and even ascendancy) of philosophy here, where tragedy is celebrated precisely because it enables a more exacting philosophical treatment of phenomena. One would do well to trace the definition of philosophy at work in both Heinsius's and Vossius's studies of poetics and to put this definition directly in conversation with the allegedly anti-Aristotelian approaches to knowledge and philosophy advanced by such figures as Petrus Ramus and (in theology as well as dialectic) William Ames.

31. According to Vossius, the stakes are very different for poetry (in a general sense) than for history or natural science. This is most evident in chapter 3 of book 1 of his *Poeticarum institutionum libri tres*, where he treats the varieties of error across several disciplines in an effort to specify precisely what a poetic error is. See Vossius, "De Poetarum Erroribus," in *PILT* 159–201.

32. Heinsius notes how Aristotle uses the same term *peripeteia* to describe the reversal of fortune in tragedy and to describe, in his *De historia animalium*, "anything that happened unexpectedly" (praeter expectationem evenit). Again, this evinces an effort to align tragedy with philosophy in a way that is usually overlooked. See *PT* 36; *CT* 168.

33. Vossius's treatment of recognition and *peripeteia* with respect to tragedy is significantly slighter than Heinsius's. I eschew their substantial difference here in the interest of brevity, although there is certainly much at stake in their disagreement. Vossius attends to recognition and *peripeteia* in much more detail in book 1 of his *Poeticarum institutionum libri tres*, in a more general investigation of plot and poetry. These concepts and terms occupy relatively little, if any, space in his treatment of tragedy in book 2. In this sense Vossius retains the importance that Heinsius accords plot, but displaces the focus on plot from tragedy to poetry in general. See Vossius, *PILT* 202–41, 548–51.

34. For compelling evidence of Heinsius's contributions to modern philosophy, see Mark Somos, "Enter Secularisation: Heinsius's De tragoediae constitutione," *History of European Ideas* 36 (Mar. 2010): 19–38.

35. See *PT* 67; *CT* 228. I alter the Sellin and McManmon translation so that "quae sunt extra Drama, et in Episodio" reads "are found outside the drama,

and in the episode" rather than "exist external to the drama and episode," which directly contradicts Heinsius's writing on episodes. Vossius uses many of the same examples: "In a tragedy, too, gods speak, both in the complication and the dénouement.... Sometimes the gods speak on the scene, sometimes from a stage-artifice." See *PILT* 500–01.

36. Aristotle, *Poetics*, trans. Ingram Bywater, *The Complete Works of Aristotle: The Revised Oxford Translation*, ed. Jonathan Barnes, vol. 2 (Princeton, N.J., 1984), 2327.

37. Horace, *Quinti Horatii Flacci Opera Omnia (The Works of Horace)*, vol. 2 (The Satires, Epistles, and *De Arte Poetica*), ed. E. C. Wickham (Oxford, 1891), 405–08.

38. Ibid., 406–07, lines 189–90: "Neve minor neu sit quinto productior actu / Fabula, quae posci volt et spectata reponi." For an English translation, see Horace, *The Art of Poetry: A Verse Translation with an Introduction by Burton Raffel, with the Original Latin Text of Horace's "Ars Poetica," A Prose Translation and Biographical Note by James Hynd, Notes by David Armstrong, and an Afterword by W. R. Johnson* (Albany, N.Y., 1974), 51. See Horace, *De Arte Poetica*, 406–07.

39. Horace, *The Art of Poetry*, 51. (Nec deus intersit nisi dignus vindice nodus / Inciderit" [lines 191–92, *De Arte Poetica*, 407]).

40. That is, to *Samson Agonistes*, the second part of the 1671 publication. My hope is that this initial study of tragedy, form, and the scope of *constitutio* or *dispositio* may shed new light on how Milton might have intended *Paradise Regained* and *Samson Agonistes* to work together.

41. See the *Oxford English Dictionary*, "epistle, v." of which Milton's *Samson Agonistes* is the first example and the only example with specific reference to prefaces or prologues (*SA* 67).

42. Mary Ann Radzinowicz, *Toward "Samson Agonistes": The Growth of Milton's Mind* (Princeton, N.J., 1978), 290, 280. Radzinowicz's Milton is "Persistently a Biblicist," just as her approach to Milton's poetry foregrounds the influence of Scripture on style and content: "God's justice is simply asserted in a language recalling both Job and the Psalmist." This attention to Scripture—and to the Psalms in particular—proves Radzinowicz's work an invaluable resource toward understanding Milton's poetry and prose. Nevertheless, the priority she gives to Scripture in *Samson Agonistes* (a work modeled on classical tragedy) and *De doctrina Christiana* (a work of a particular genre, with a unique *ordo docendi* proceeding from Reformed Orthodox *disputatio* and tradition rather than emerging *sola scriptura*) risks obscuring Milton's experimental approaches to faith as well as his debts to heterodox and declaredly pagan sources. This is as true for *De doctrina Christiana* as it is for *Samson Agonistes*. Scripture, for instance, does not structure book 1 of *De doctrina Christiana;* on the contrary, Milton notes, "We may rightly insist that Christians should believe in the SCRIPTURES, from which [Christian] doctrine is drawn. Scriptural authority, however, will be discussed in its proper place" (Scripturis, unde haec hausimus, credi a Christianis haud inique postulamus; de earum vero auctoritate suo loco tractabimus). In book 1,

chapter 30, Milton introduces several mediations between God and Scripture, in the *ordo docendi* of the work as well as in his investigations of and commitments to an exegetical tradition, just as the prologue on classical tragedy mediates between Scripture and faith in *Samson Agonistes*. See ibid., 279, 31; Mary Ann Radzinowicz, *Milton's Epics and the Book of Psalms* (Princeton, N.J., 1989), 120; John Milton, *De doctrina Christiana*, ed. Maurice Kelley, trans. John Carey, in *Complete Prose Works of John Milton*, vol. 6, ed. Don M. Wolfe (New Haven, 1973), 126, hereafter cited as YP, followed by volume and page number; and John Milton, *De doctrina Christiana: Libri duo posthumi, quos ex schedis manuscriptis deprompsit, et typis mandari primus curavit Carolus Ricardus Sumner*, ed. Charles Richard Sumner (Cambridge, 1825), 7.

43. *The Holy Bible, conteyning the Old Testament, and the New* (London, 1611). In Annenberg Rare Book and Manuscript Library [BS185 1611.L65].

44. Joseph Wittreich, *Interpreting "Samson Agonistes"* (Princeton, N.J., 1986), 150.

45. See Norman T. Burns, "'Then Stood Up Phinehas': Milton's Antinomianism, and Samson's," in *Milton Studies*, vol. 33, *The Miltonic Samson*, ed. Albert C. Labriola and Michael Lieb (Pittsburgh, 1997), 27–46.

46. Radzinowicz, *Toward "Samson Agonistes,"* 269–312.

47. John Rogers, "The Secret of *Samson Agonistes*," in *Milton Studies*, vol. 33, *The Miltonic Samson*, ed. Albert C. Labriola and Michael Lieb (Pittsburgh, 1997), 111–32.

48. For a treatment of election and justification in Milton's oeuvre, see Stephen M. Fallon, *Milton's Peculiar Grace: Self-Representation and Authority* (Ithaca, N.Y., 2007), 182–263. For classic accounts of Milton's theology, see W. B. Hunter, C. A. Patrides, and J. H. Adamson, *Bright Essence: Studies in Milton's Theology* (Salt Lake City, 1971); and William Empson, *Milton's God*, rev. ed. (Cambridge, 1981).

49. Milton declines to use Heinsius's *expiatio*, a term on which he comments in the text of *Samson Agonistes*. A form of the English verb *expiate* is used three times in the poem. First, when Samson resigns himself to "pay on my punishment; / And expiate, if possible, my crime, / Shameful garrulity" (489–91); later, as Dalila seeks forgiveness from Samson, "if tears / May expiate…My penance hath not slack'n'd" (735–38); and, lastly, in Samson's retort to Dalila, where he reveals his "inexpiable hate" (839) for her (*SA* 84, 91, 94).

50. It is the only line of Latin in the entire 1671 volume; the titles, details of publication, and the subsequent text of *Samson Agonistes* itself (including the Argument and the note on tragedy) are all in English. The Latin paraphrase is conspicuous, almost out of place, especially given Milton's proficiency in Greek and the degree to which we might assume that a volume of poetry in English was intended for an Anglophone audience. Of course, the Latin might suggest distinction or sophistication to an audience interested in classical poetry but, if so, one wonders how effective a single line might have been in attracting would-be savants.

51. See Lewis and Short, *A Latin Dictionary*, 1087 (*lustratio*); and *The Oxford Latin Dictionary*, ed. P. G. W. Glare et al. (Oxford, 1968), 1052 (*lustrātiō, lustrō*).

52. Jerzy Linderski, "lustration," *The Oxford Classical Dictionary*, 3rd rev. ed., ed. Simon Hornblower and Antony Spawforth (Oxford, 2003), 893. Debora Shuger explores Hugo Grotius's use of *lustrum* and *lustrare* in his own path-making studies of the historicity of Scripture, studies which may have been familiar to Milton. See Debora Kuller Shuger, *The Renaissance Bible: Scholarship, Sacrifice, and Subjectivity* (Berkeley, 1994), 44, 73–76.

53. Linderski, "lustration," 893.

54. Ibid., 893. Andrew Marvell, in a letter dated June 2, 1654, famously referred to Milton's *Defensio secunda* as "a Trajan's column, on whose winding ascent we see embossed the several monuments of your learned victories." Marvell promised to "study it even to the getting it by heart." Quoted in Charles Symmons, *The Life of John Milton*, 3rd ed. (London, 1822), 336. See also David Masson, *The Life of John Milton: Narrated in Connexion with the Political, Ecclesiastical, and Literary History of His Time* (1649–54), vol. 4 (London, 1877), 624–26; and Nigel Smith, *Andrew Marvell: The Chameleon* (New Haven, 2010), 123–27.

55. See Lewis and Short, *A Latin Dictionary*, 615–16 (*duco*), 937 (*induco*).

56. Aristotle, *Metaphysics*, trans. W. D. Ross, *The Complete Works of Aristotle: The Revised Oxford Translation*, vol. 2, ed. Jonathan Barnes (Princeton, N.J., 1984), 1558 (985a 18–21). Heinsius, in his Latin translation of this section of the *Metaphysics*, gives the noun "Mens" where Ross translates the Greek term as "reason" (*PT* 71n10).

INDEX